National Developments in the Intersection of IPR and Competition Law

The Swedish Network for European Legal Studies is happy to announce the third volume in this series of annual publications which acts as a forum for the publication of studies on European law by Swedish scholars. This year's annual focuses on competition aspects of intellectual property law, and contains peer-reviewed articles aimed at spreading Swedish legal research on European law to a wide international audience. The editor of the yearbook is Hans Henrik Lidgard. The articles in the volume are concerned with European law, its development, impact and reform. They are original, analytical contributions to doctrinal debates and questions, by legal researchers mainly, but not exclusively, connected with the Swedish universities.

Swedish Studies in European Law

Swedish Studies in European Law **Volume 1**, 2006
Edited by Professor Nils Wahl and Professor Per Cramér.

Swedish Studies in European Law **Volume 2**, 2007
Edited by Per Cramér and Thomas Bull

National Developments in the Intersection of IPR and Competition Law: From Maglite to Pirate Bay **Volume 3**, 2008
Edited by Hans Henrik Lidgard

National Developments in the Intersection of IPR and Competition Law

From Maglite to Pirate Bay

Edited by

Hans Henrik Lidgard

·HART·
PUBLISHING

OXFORD AND PORTLAND, OREGON
2011

Hart Publishing, 16C Worcester Place, Oxford, OX1 2JW
Telephone: +44 (0)1865 517530 Fax: +44 (0)1865 510710
Email: mail@hartpub.co.uk
Website: http//:www.hartpub.co.uk

Published in North America (US and Canada) by
Hart Publishing
c/o International Specialized Book Services
920 NE 58th Avenue, Suite 300
Portland, OR 97213-3786
USA
Tel: +1 503 287 3093 or toll-free: (1) 800 944 6190
Fax: +1 503 280 8832
Email: orders@isbs.com
Website: www.isbs.com

British Library Cataloguing in Publication Data
Data Available

ISBN: 978-1-84113-944-9

Typeset by Criteria International
Printed and bound in Great Britain by
CPI Antony Rowe Ltd, Chippenham, Wiltshire

Introduction

HANS HENRIK LIDGARD

The Swedish Network for European Legal Studies is a national network comprised of several Swedish Universities focusing on highlighting recent legal developments within European Union Law. By joining forces the Universities have, for over a decade, supported legal research and education by organizing conferences, seminars, and generally supporting young researchers. The network also offers opportunities for publication at both national and international level. At national level the network is closely connected to the Swedish law journal, Europarättslig Tidskrift (ERT), and also has its own international series, *Swedish Studies in European Law*. Each volume in the series offers a wide range of peer-reviewed contributions by Swedish scholars analysing different aspects of European Union Law. The book series serves as a platform for Swedish researchers making their contributions available to the international audience to provide a Swedish perspective on current discussions on European Union Law. This is the third volume.

In this volume, Swedish researchers with specific interests in European Market law – IPR, competition and marketing law – join forces to review recent Swedish legislative enactments and case-law developments of particular European interest in national Swedish Courts or the Court of Justice of the European Union ('CJEU'). This volume also includes comments on general EU developments from a Swedish perspective.

I wish to thank Cecilia Cardner, coordinator of the Swedish Network for European Studies, for her helpful assistance in the production of this book. The Network is especially grateful to Robert M Schwartz Esq, who proofread the manuscript and contributed to the editorial work from his New York office.

In summary the different contributions to this edition address the following issues:

1. Swedish IP Case Law Development in a European Context: An Overview
by Marianne Levin, Stockholm University

Professor Levin begins the volume with an overview of IPR adjudication in Sweden since its accession to the EU and evaluates Sweden's progress towards harmonization by a comprehensive briefing of important Swedish cases involving copyright, design, Freedom of the Press, Patents, Trademarks and Trade Secrets. She comments on the effect of the paucity of IPR cases decided, compounded by their division among several courts with competence and few references to the CJEU. She concludes that this and the existing procedural system contribute significantly to harm delay, legal certainty and EU harmonisation. Levin notes that proposals for trying all IPR matters in one court have run into resistance due to the perceived lack of efficiency due to a small case-load and Nordic resistance to specialized courts with specialized judges. A commercial court would provide both speedy justice and judicial experience with IPR dispute resolution.

2. Dilemmas of Governance in a Multilevel European Patent System

by Antonina Bakardjieva Engelbrekt

Antonina Bakardjieva-Engelbrekt's contribution analyses the efforts to find an adequate institutional solution for the dysfunctional European patent system. The relations between the European Union and the European Patent Organisation are far from clear, something vividly demonstrated in the field of biotechnology. She traces the origins of the system and looks closer at the EPO process. She identifies problematic aspects from the point of view of governance and examines proposals for a Pan-European patent judiciary reform, including the latest initiative for a Patent Court with a decentralised first instance and a centralised appeal level. The author argues for enhancing the independence of the judicial bodies of the EPO, and ensuring greater degree of accountability and public involvement in the decision-making process.

3. The Swedish Doctrine of Equivalence

by Bengt Domeij, Uppsala University

Swedish case law, while moving away from the idea of a general inventive concept, has identified seven factors limiting the scope of patent protection from being extended past the literal wording of the patent's claims. This approach is designed as a means of determining the existence of patent infringement through a distinct and sophisticated interpretation of the patent's claims. These seven factors are identified, described and analysed. Bengt Domeij then examines whether or not there are any differences between the area covered by the seven exceptions and the practical application of patent law's doctrine of equivalence under the comparatively unique features of Swedish case law. The author concludes that a better practice would, in theory, be provided by a unified European approach to patent claim interpretation.

4. Distinctive Character in Compound Trademarks
by Per Jonas Nordell, Stockholm University

Jonas Nordell discusses compound trademarks against a background of recent linguistic research. This background, in combination with a review of the relatively extensive European case law, from the CJEU and the General Court, provides a platform for analysing the question of whether, and to what extent linguistics and jurisprudence should interrelate in interpreting compound trademarks. The author's conclusion, after referring to developments in the case law, is that the CJEU has been a bit too strict in interpreting compound trademarks. The author suggests that the CJEU take a position lying somewhere between the lenient position taken in its *Baby-dry* case and the stricter interpretations taken in some of the more recent cases.

5. Protection of Non-Registered Trademarks in Sweden and the EU
by Erika Lunell, Karlstad University

Erika Lunell deals with the protection of non-registered trademarks in Sweden and the EU. Is the protection of non-registered trademarks a purely national concern? How has Community law influenced the protection of non-registered trademarks in Sweden? Is there a continued need for non-registered trademark protection whether as it exists today or in a modified form? She addresses protection requirements, the scope of protection and the range of signs that can be protected through registration versus qualified use. A central question is the obstacle raised by the requirement of graphic representation, especially regarding unconventional trademarks, such as scents, sounds, etc. In a final section the role of bad faith provisions for the protection of non-registered trademarks is discussed.

6. Swedish Soda Club Dispute – Competition Law and IPR Intersection
by Ulf Maunsbach, Lund University

Ulf Maunsbach focuses his contribution on a recent dispute highlighting the intersection between trademark law and competition law. The dispute brings into play the relationship between abuse of a dominant position and IPRs in general. This case is the first example of the Swedish Competition Authority intervening in a civil infringement dispute under the Swedish equivalent of Regulation 1/2001. A final resolution of the case may well require a referral seeking a guiding opinion from the CJEU.

7. Copyright Contracts – EU solutions or National Concern? A Swedish Proposal to Amend the Copyright Act on Individual and Collective Contracts
by Jan Rosén, Stockholm University

Jan Rosén provides an account of the EU's difficulties to harmonize Copyright law and extended collective licensing in a digital age without an *acquis communautaire*. He summarizes his efforts under a government mandate to analyse Sweden's Copyright laws and his Inquiries' proposals for deep revisions to modernize them as well as to harmonize them with Community law and European Commission initiatives regarding individual and extended copyright licensing by licensing organizations. He examines the issues from the points of view of the interested parties, agencies and solutions from other Nordic countries. The author suggests that his proposed changes made using a Nordic model would be helpful in harmonizing these issues on an EU-wide basis.'

8. Swedish Copyright Evergreens Mini-Maglite?
by Hans Henrik Lidgard, Lund University

This article sheds light on the recent Swedish Supreme Court judgement which extended copyright protection to the shape of a flashlight. The Mini-Mag now enjoys far reaching protection in Sweden, beyond the term of its patent protection. The article contrasts the Swedish case with other European decisions concerning extending IPR protection for the Mini-Mag. It concludes that since IPRs are exceptions in a free market to unfettered competition they should be applied restrictively. This requires harmonization of copyright legislation on a European level.

9. Swedish Copyright Law Ends the Pirate Bay
by Jonas Ledendal, Lund University

Jonas Ledendal outlines the recent decision in the 'The Pirate Bay' case which has received so much attention in the media. There, four individuals were found guilty of secondary copyright infringement for having provided a haven where others could make protected material available for downloading over the internet. The case involves an analysis of primary, contrasted with secondary, liability for copyright infringement as well as a discussion of the offense of preparing to commit such a crime. The matter is presently under appeal.

10. Illicit File Sharing and Intermediary Services Within the Framework of the E-Commerce Directive

by Kristoffer Schollin, Gothenburg University

The 'Pirate Bay' case highlights some of the difficulties in legislating on copyright infringement. Kristoffer Schollin analyses liability issues and points out that the E-Commerce Directive which aims at enabling the provision of internet services creates some conflicts with the protection of intellectual property, specifically with the IPR Enforcement Directive. The article investigates whether this friction stems not from a lack of legal instruments to battle secondary infringers, but rather, from a discrepancy between the behavioural norms of internet users and entities protected by copyright law.

11. The Unfair Commercial Practices Directive and the Legislation Implementing it in Sweden: A Comparison

by Professor Ulf Bernitz, Stockholm University

The EU's 2005 Unfair Commercial Practices Directive was transposed into Swedish law by the Marketing act of 2008. Is the Swedish implementation correct as to its choice of legislative structure, its assessment of misleading advertising, its assessment of passing off and its mechanisms for supervision and enforcement? Ulf Bernitz concludes that the Swedish implementation has been fairly smooth. These results from the fact that the Directive finds common ground with Swedish legislation and legal tradition which both favour strong consumer protection and protection of competitors linked thereto. From a Swedish point of view Bernitz finds that the primary weaknesses of the Directive are the vague concept of 'the average consumer' and lack of strong enforcement mechanisms.

12. Two Novelties in Swedish Competition Law: Fine Order and Trading Prohibition – A Critical Review

by Lars Henriksson, Stockholm School of Economics

Procedural changes were made by the 2008 Swedish Competition Act. Most notable was the introduction of a fine order to permit swifter and more efficient resolution of competition infringements. However, according to Lars Henriksson, the fine order is a half measure and there are better alternatives. He advocates an organisational change, whereby the Swedish competition authority, in line with the powers of the EU Commission, becomes the decisional body of first instance for finding competition infringements. Henriksson also discusses the Act's introduction of a debatable 'disqualification order' against executives of infringing undertakings intended as a compromise alternative to penal sanctions.

13. Refusal to Supply in the EU Pharmaceutical Sector under the Rule of Reason

by Tu Thanh Nguyen, Xavier Groussot, and Timo Minssen, Lund University

A refusal to supply by a dominant undertaking on the pharmaceutical market does not *per se* violate Article 102 TFEU. In addition, dominant companies have the right to a reasonable and proportional degree of self-protection of their interests. The authors argue that the CJEU is now moving from a *per se* rule of liability to 'rule of reason' for such decisions. In cases of potential abuse of dominant position, the rule of reason promotes a more flexible approach where the factual and economic context of the specific case may be taken into account. They also analyse the role of national competition authorities in the procedure for preliminary rulings.

Hans Henrik Lidgard

Table of Contents

Abbreviations

AG	Attorney General
BoA	Board of Appeal of OHIM's Trademarks and Design Registration Office
BGH	Bundesgerichtshof (Federal Court of Justice Germany)
BTMO	Benelux-Merkenbureau
B2B	Business to business
B2C	Business to consumer relations
CA	The Swedish Competition Act (SFS 1993:20) as amended to (SFS 2008:579)
CDDA	UK Company Directors Disqualification Act of 1986 as amended
CJEU	Court of Justice of the European Union as of December 1, 2009
CMIR	Regulation (EC) No 2868/95 of 13 December 1995 implementing TMR as amended
CTM	Community Trademark
CTMR	Regulation (EC) No 207/2009 of 26 February 2009 on the Community trademark
DRM	Digital Rights Management
ECN	European Competition Network
ECR	European Community Reports
EFTA	European Free Trade Area
EHCR	European Convention for the Protection of Human Rights and Fundamental Freedoms
EPC	European Patent Convention
EPO	European Patent Office
EU	European Union
ITC	United States International Trade Commission

NCA	Swedish Competition Authority (Konkurrensverket)
NOU	Norwegian Government Official Report
OFT	UK Office of Fair Trading
OHIM	Office for Harmonization in the Internal Market
OJ	Official Journal of the European Union
PBR	Swedish Court of Patent Appeals
PIA69	Protocol on the Interpretation of Article 69 EPC
Prop	Proposed law
R&D	Research and Development
SOU	Swedish Government Official Report
TMR	Regulation 40/94/EC on the Community Trademark of 15
TRIPS	Agreement on Trade-Related Aspects of Intellectual Property Rights
WIPO	World Intellectual Property Organization

Explanations and Definitions

In all documents we will try to adhere to the nomenclature of the Lisbon Treaties – eg the EUFT rather than EC Treaty and EUCJ rather than ECJ - and use the Article numbers of EUFT (even in older quotations? Then with a # sign added after the number to indicate that in the original text a different article number has been used.)

BitTorrent (protocol)	A peer-to-peer (P2P) communications protocol for file sharing
CJEU	Before December 2009 the Court of Justice of the European Union (ECJ)
Directive 89/552/EEC	Directive 89/552/EEC of the European Parliament and of the Council of 3 October 1989 on the coordination of certain provisions laid down by law, regulation or administrative action in Member States concerning the provision of audio-visual media services
E-Commerce Directive	Directive 2000/31/EC of the European Parliament and of the Council of 8 June 2000 on certain legal aspects of information society services, in particular electronic commerce, in the Internal Market
EFTA Court	Court established under the Agreement on the European Economic Area of 2 May 1992
EHCR	European Convention for the Protection of Human Rights and Fundamental Freedoms
General Court	Before December 2009 the Court of First Instance of the European Communities
German Copyright Law	Gesetz vom 8.5.1998 zur Änderung der Urheberrechtsgesetzes und verwandte Schutzrechte (Urheberrechtsgesetz) vom 9.9.1965 zuletzt geändert durch Artikel 7 vom 22.7.1997

Högsta Domstolen	Swedish Supreme Court
Hovrätten	Swedish Court of Appeals
ITC	United States International Trade Commission
Konsumentombudsmannen	Consumer Ombudsman and Director General of the Consumer Protection Agency
Konsumentverket	Swedish Consumer Protection Agency
Market Court	Swedish Court with jurisdiction over violations of Swedish Marketing Act
MCAD	Directive 2006/114/EC, 2006 Directive on Misleading and Comparative Advertising
Mönsterskyddslag	Swedish Design Registration Law (SFS 1970:485) incorporating Directive 98/71/EC last amended (SFS 2009:112)
Paris Convention	Paris Convention for the Protection of Industrial Property of March 20, 1883, as revised
Paris Union	Member States acceding to the Paris Convention
Swedish Competition Act	Konkurrenslag (SFS 2008:579)
Swedish Copyright Act	Lag (1960:729) om upphovsrätt till litterära och konstnärliga verk Ändringar införda t.o.m. (SFS 1995:1274)
Swedish Design Act	1899 års lag om skydd för vissa mönster och modeller, (SFS 1899:59) as amended
Swedish Marketing Act	Marknadsföringslag (1995:450) Ändringar införda t.o.m. (SFS 1995:1472), (SFS 2008:486)
Swedish Trademarks Act	Varumärkeslag (SFS 1960:644) as amended
Tingsrätt	Swedish District Court
Trademark Directive	Directive 84/104/EEC, replaced by Directive 2008/95/EC December 1995 as amended
UCPD	Directive 2005/29/EC of the European Parliament and of the Council of 11 May 2005 concerning unfair business-to-consumer commercial practices in the internal market

UWG	German Unfair Competition Law Gesetz gegen den unlauteren Wettbewerb; (Änderung durch Art. 25 G v. 25.10.1994 I 3082)

Table of Cases

European Union

Court of First Instance (General Court)

Court of Justice

European Court of Human Rights

European Patent Office (EPO)

OHIM Board of Appeal

Court of Patent Appeals (PBR)

EFTA Court

Belgium

Brussels Court of First Instance (TGI)

Finland

Helsinki District Court

Germany

Federal Court (Bundesgerichtshof)

Cologne District Court (Landgericht)

Munich Provincial Court (Oberlandesgericht)

Munich District Court (Landgericht)

Norway

Supreme Court

Sweden

Supreme Court

Supreme Administrative Court

Svea Court of Appeal

Scania and Blekinge Court of Appeal (Malmö)

Market Court

Competition Authority (KKV)

United Kingdom

United States of America

Table of European Union, National and International Legislation

European Union

Primary legislation

Directives

Regulations

Denmark

Finland

France

Germany

Greece

Norway

Sweden

United Kingdom

United States of America

International

1

Swedish IP Case Law Development in a European Context: An Overview

PROFESSOR MARIANNE LEVIN

1. BACKGROUND

For many years, the Swedish Supreme Court (*'Högsta Domstolen'*, *HD*) and the Administrative Supreme Court (*'Regeringsrätten'*, *RR*) set a clear and important mark on the intellectual property (IP) field with their often-detailed decisions. Since 1 July 1986, when a special bar for appeals to the highest instances was introduced, *certiorari* however, has only been granted in cases where the decision may clarify a question of law or where there are serious grounds (eg serious omissions or gross errors). Thus, today rarely are appeals concerning infringements and registration of IP rights found admissible. In fact, these cases represent only a small percentage of those heard by the HD, and less than one per cent by the RR, corresponding to one to two cases and less than one case per year respectively.[1] Therefore, presently, the six judicial courts of appeal[2] (JCA) and the Patent Appeals Court[3] (PBR) are the last instance in the overwhelming number of IP cases.[4] Under Article 267 TFEU these second instance courts are not obliged to refer cases to the CJEU and in the past have rarely done so.[5] Thus, referrals from Sweden seeking an interpretation of EU law seldom occur although significant areas of IP legislation are objects of European efforts at harmonisation.

[1] It should however also be noted that the total number of IP cases in Sweden are not very great. In 2009 there were 27 patent cases decided at the first instance and approximately 160 other IP cases. The PBR entered decisions in 411 cases, of which 61 concerned patents.

[2] Collectively 'Hovrätter'.

[3] 'Patentbesvärsrätten'.

[4] For example, no design case has been tried by the RR since RÅ 1987 ref. 62, while the HD has tried only two such cases.

[5] Cf however Case C-371/02, *Björnekulla Fruktindustrier AB v Procordia Food AB*, [2004] ECR I-5791, which was referred by Svea JCA and Case C-16/03 *Peak Holding AB, v Axolin-Elinor AB* [2004] ECR I-11313, which was referred by the JCA for Skåne and Blekinge.

The following review in Parts 2 and 3 comprise IP cases from the highest instance,[6] in the HD from the time of Sweden's accession to the European Union on 1 January 1995 and in regard of the RR from 1990.[7] Cases from the HD are published in the *Nytt Juridiskt Arkiv I,* (New Judicial Archive I) and are referenced as **'*NJA*'**, while cases from the RR are published in *Regerigsrättens Årsbok* (Annual Report from the Administrative Supreme Court) and are referenced as **'*RÅ*'**. It is for the reader to form an opinion on how well the integration proceeds and whether a changed framework for the handling of IP cases would be more effective. That issue is treated in Part 3 of the article.

2. THE PRECEDENTS FROM THE HD

The following cases from the HD are just presented in alphabetical order depending on subject matter, starting with copyright, followed by freedom of speech and industrial property. Also within these main categories the cases are presented in a similar way. Thus, there is no other reason for their order of presentation.

2.1. Copyright[8]

2.1.1. Applied art

Two cases have concerned applied art, ***NJA 1995 p 164*** (Knitted tunic) and ***NJA 2009 p 159*** (Mini-Maglite).[9] Both confirm the principle laid down in ***NJA 1994 p 74*** (Wild strawberries), where the Court took the view that applied art works, in this case a naturalistic drapery design, should be granted protection to the extent that they are artistic, notwithstanding the fact that they are also useful and results of industrial production. However, in such cases the scope of protection was to be narrowly construed in order not to interfere with others' creative production in the same field. This attitude should be measured against the fact that the Swedish Design Act (in its then valid version), on the one hand, created new opportunities for maintaining relatively high standards for artistry on applied art through copyright protection, but, on the other,

[6] Petitions seeking *certiorari* for interlocutory injunctions are not included in the following cases: NJA 1995 p 631 (copyright), NJA 1995 p 635 (trademark), NJA 1997 p 109 (trademark), NJA 1998 p 179 (trade name), NJA 2002 p 660 (patent), NJA 2004 p 624 (trademark) and NJA 2006 p 380 (trademark).

[7] Sweden ratified its entry to the European Patent Convention (EPC) in 1978.

[8] Act on copyright in literary and artistic works (SFS 1960:729) as amended (Copyright Act).

[9] Because this case is extensively discussed by Hans Henrik Lidgard in chapter 8 of this publication it will not be described here.

contained formal requirements of, in principle, absolute novelty that in the end, turned out to be less suitable for the creative industries.[10]

In ***NJA 1995 p 164*** a design for a knitted tunic had been published in a women's magazine together with knitting instructions under authorization of the author. A tunic following this design later appeared in fashion shop marketed as made in Turkey. The questions were whether the tunic was protected under copyright law and whether the alleged infringer had negligently infringed the copyright by marketing it. The Stockholm City Court found that the degree of originality was not sufficient for protection; the JCA found that copyright had been established, especially under the argument that the registered design protection was not suited for fashion creations. The HD then found that the Swedish Design Act had not been able to provide adequate protection for products of applied art as was assumed when the legislation entered into force in 1970. This created a gap because it had become evident that there was a need for copyright protection for fashion products. Even though subject matter based solely on expertise, good taste and simple variations of well-known fashion ideas of a more routine nature, for obvious reasons, was held ineligible for copyright, it should be recognized that nowadays firms producing fashion products produce them on the basis of work created by artistically trained designers.[11] Counterfeiting activities in the fashion industry had long been extensive and has severely interfered with the technical progress of both manufacturing companies and independent designers. It was for these reasons that, the Court held that original and independently created garments with a unique and artistic design qualified for copyright protection.

In the case of the tunic, the HD found that the balance between its various knitting techniques and the combination between the head and the flared skirt-like lower section it comprised expressed such a degree of individual creativity as to represent a work of applied art.[12] The scope of protection, however, would normally be interpreted narrowly, to cover only the very closest of imitations, and when it came to fashion-embossed, or trend-driven products such as clothing, considerable similarities in overall appearance must be accepted as non-infringing. In the case before the court, the copying was obvious, and strong reasons existed to discourage too extensive copying activities and encourage competent and serious forms of creative efforts, even if seen just from a societal view point.

[10] History has shown that only such applied art should have copyright protection, which, in accordance with the generally prevailing perception should be assessed as a product of artistic creation notwithstanding that in respect of certain products and the limited possibilities for variation there is a reason to interpret them with a liberal spirit. See Prop. (Government Bill) 1969:168 pp 135 ff.

[11] The HD noticed an inappropriate reluctance to recognize fashion products as works of art, primarily because of their short lifetime and lack of expression of genuine innovation.

[12] The Court also noticed that the Swedish Design Board (a kind of honour court), in various opinions had considered articles of clothing to be copyright protected.

In regard to the issue of negligent infringement, the Court found that the alleged infringer had purchased garments by the Turkish manufacturer concerned several times in the past. Even if a professional entity were to be especially observant the Court saw no factors that could have given rise to suspicion that the producer was illegally selling copyrighted designs. Against this factual background, the alleged infringer could not have been negligent in failing to ascertain the origin of the tunic. Nor was it plausible that an inquiry to the manufacturer would have produced sufficient information to dissuade the company from selling the tunic.

2.1.2. Damages

NJA 2003 p 465 dealt with compensation under Article 47 for making available music in hotels. A hotel had been charged for the use of copyright music according to the rates charged by the collecting society in the field, SAMI.[13] The fee was roughly double the fees charged to members of the Swedish Hotel and Restaurant Association (SHR).[14] The HD held that since there was no contract between the hotel and SAMI, compensation should be determined according to what, under all the circumstances, would be considered reasonable. With regard to fairness in general, the Court stressed that there is normally a presumption that a representative professional association's negotiated tariff is reasonable. But since there was a framework agreement with discounts for members of SHR, the Court concluded that SAMI had to demonstrate, in the present case, that the higher compensation charged to a hotel unconnected to the SHR was reasonable. The SHR-agreement undoubtedly had advantages for SAMI, which might justify a slight discount. However, there had been no investigation to confirm that the benefits corresponded to a rebate of about half the price of what the hotel should have to pay. The HD therefore found the charged amount to be unfair in relation to the individual hotel, and then fixed the remuneration to the sum to the amount which the hotel had admitted to pay, SEK 1 (= around 10 euro cents) per room and night, which was slightly higher than the SHR tariff on SEK 0.85.

2.1.3. Databases

Databases can either be protected as a composite literary or artistic work because of its original structure under Article 1, or as '...a catalogue, a table or another similar product in which a large number of information items have been compiled or which is the result of a significant investment...' under Article 49.[15]

[13] *Svenska artisters och musikers intresseorganisation* is a non-profit organisation that is dedicated to the promotion of the interests of artists and musicians.

[14] Sveriges Hotell- och Restaurangföretagare.

[15] Cf Directive 96/9/EC of the European Parliament and of the Council of 11 March 1996 on the legal protection of databases [1996] OJ (L 77) 20.

The HD has considered one such case, ***NJA 2005 p 924***, which was first referred to the CJEU for a preliminary ruling. The final decision by the HD closely followed the CJEU's interpretation:[16] in the context of drawing up a fixture list for the purpose of organising football league fixtures the HD held that the data could not be protected as the result of any substantial investment. Therefore, the use of the data in this database was not considered to be a reproduction or a making available of the whole or substantial part of the database (the fixture).

2.1.4. Insolvency

NJA 2005 p 510 involved a so-called 'lift procedure', where the first instance, in this case the Stockholm City Court, may ask the HD for an interpretation of law. The factual background concerned an author of various decorative motifs who had concluded a contract with a publisher that subsequently went bankrupt. The agreement provided that the author transferred to the publisher the right to reproduce and sell products of her works in exchange for a royalty of 7 per cent of sales. The bankrupt estate sold its stock of the author's printed works and the author terminated the publishing contract by reason of an anticipated delay in payment. She then brought an action against the bankruptcy estate, contending eg that the estate should pay for the use of copyright works, as well as paying damages for copyright infringement and damages for losses due to the illegal sale of her works for a price below that stipulated in the contract.

The questions the City Court submitted to the HD were:

- Are the sales of copies a copyright infringement?
- Does the mass transfer arising from the bankruptcy estate sale eliminate the distribution right?
- Has an implicit acceptance of the publishing contract by the bankruptcy estate occurred due to the sale of a copy?
- What significance should be attributed to the publication, or other acts of making the works available regarding the possible rights of the bankruptcy estate to distribute copies?
- What is the effect of a cancellation of the publishing contract before the distribution date?

[16] Case C-338/02, *Fixtures Marketing Ltd v Svenska Spel AB* [2004] ECR I-10497, para 37: '… the expression 'investment in … the obtaining … of the contents' of a database in Art 7(1) of Directive 96/9/EC … must be understood to refer to the resources used to seek out existing independent materials and collect them in the database. It does not cover the resources used for the creation of materials which make up the contents of a database. In the context of drawing up a fixture list for the purpose of organising football league fixtures, therefore, it does not cover the resources used to establish the dates, times and the team pairings for the various matches in the league.' (Ellipsis in original). See also similar cases decided on the same day Case C-46/02, *Fixtures Marketing Ltd v Oy Veikkaus Ab*, [2004] ECR I-10365, Case C-444/02, *Fixtures Marketing Ltd v Organismos prognostikon agonon podosfairou AE (OPAP)* [2004] ECR I-10549, and Case C-203/02, *The British Horseracing Board Ltd and Others v William Hill Organization Ltd* [2004] ECR I-10415 as well as the later Case C-304/07 *Directmedia Publishing GmbH v Albert-Ludwigs-Universität Freiburg* [2008] ECR I-7565.

The HD found initially that the bankruptcy estate's transfers of the stock, in a copyright sense, represented a distribution of copies of the author's works to the public. As long as the publishing contract was valid, the estate's transfer did not infringe the copyright. Regarding whether the estate's disposal of the distribution right meant that a claim against the bankruptcy estate, must have priority over payment of other creditors' claims (mass claim) had arisen, the HD stated that the traditional principle – that a claim in the bankruptcy arises at the point in time when the material basis for the claim arises – might sometimes be difficult to apply to mutually binding agreements, where the principle of separation of bankruptcy claims and mass claims may lead to materially unsatisfactory results.

The HD was however not willing to deviate from established principles and concluded that the claims for royalties had been established under the publishing contract, and therefore prior to the declaration of bankruptcy. Thus, a mass claim had not been incurred prior to the estate's use of its acquired right to sell the author's works to a third party after the filing of the bankruptcy. Nor could it be inferred that the estate implicitly entered into the publishing contract. The author could not prevent exploitation of the distribution rights so long as the agreement was in force. The sales concerned works for which reproduction rights had been exhausted before the filing of the bankruptcy and for which the company had paid the production costs. The publishing right and the copies derived from it belonged to the bankrupt publisher's estate irrespective of the works in question having been published or made available to public, and the estate's mass responsibility was therefore unaffected by whether or not the current works, at the date of transfer had been published or issued. If however the author had terminated the contract before the filing of the bankruptcy, the estate would have had no distribution rights and the estate's non-consensual sale of copies of the author's works would have constituted copyright infringement and resulted in liability.

2.1.5. Internet-related Issues

NJA 1996 p 74 and *NJA 1996 p 79* both concerned system operators for a BBS (an electronic Bulletin Board System).

In the first case the operator was convicted of copyright infringement relating to computer programs. The infringement was obvious, and the JCA confiscated a computer containing a hard drive with software installed. The HD upheld the forfeiture of the software, while the forfeiture claim with respect to the computer was dismissed. The reason for this was that the computer, used for the BBS, could just as well be of use for lawful purposes and therefore, in isolation or in conjunction with the hard drive, could not constitute a 'criminal tool' as specifically required under Chapter 36 Article 3 of the Penal Code.

In *NJA 1996 p 79* computers connected to a BBS had transmitted copies of copyrighted software to the BBS without the authors' or his right-holders' consent. Other computer users in the BBS network then had the opportunity to copy the programmes to their computers. The operator of the BBS was prosecuted for making programmes available to copy. The allegations were dismissed, however, as there was no requisite auxiliary allegation of contributory infringement. This case gave rise to the new Act (SFS 1998:112) concerning the responsibility of bulletin boards. In addition by the implementation into Swedish law of the IPRED[17] an outcome in a similar case would be quite the opposite.

The holding in *NJA 2000 p 292* has also been superseded by subsequent legislation. There a man who had made links to music files available on the Internet was prosecuted and the question concerned whether his action constituted a copyright infringement. The (deep) links in question function in such a way that a visitor to his website, who clicked on a link, was immediately transferred to a music file and the file thus became available for transfer to the visitor‘s own computer. The making available of the music files was regarded as a 'public performance' in this case. Since at the time, Article 47 of the Swedish Copyright Act excluded public performance of an audio recording from the exclusive rights that performers and phonogram producers otherwise enjoyed under Articles 45 and 46 of the Act, and, although this was a possible infringement, the linking from the website was not punishable, and the indictment was dismissed.

The case *NJA 2010 p 135* concerned photographic images,[18] which with the photographer‘s consent had been published on a website. Two of these were later made available on another website during which time the web designer in question used a screenshot of a page that contained a number of thumbnail images for reference advertising purposes. The questions before the Court were eg if the photographs had been 'released to the public'[19] by the first website publication[20] and if the photographs on the web designer's site had constituted an insignificant part of an image within the meaning of Article 20 a of the Copyright Act,[21] which had been introduced by the Swedish implementation,

[17] European Directive 2004/48/EC of the European Parliament and of the Council of 29 April 2004 on the enforcement of intellectual property rights

[18] Today, in Sweden all photographs are protected under the Swedish Copyright Act, either as photographic pictures (Art 49 a) or as photographic work. The only difference is, in principle, the period of protection, ie 50 years after the making available or respectively 70 years after the year in which the author died.

[19] Art 8: 'A work is deemed to have been made public when it has lawfully been made available to the public. A work is deemed to have been published when copies thereof have, with the consent of the author, been placed on sale or otherwise been distributed to the public.'

[20] Many of the exceptions under Ch 2 of the Act, including Art 20 a, require a prior 'release to the public'.

[21] 'Anyone is entitled to prepare, by means of a film or a television program, and distribute copies of works of fine art, publicly perform works of fine art and communicate works of fine art to the public, if the exploitation made of the work is incidental in relation to the contents of the film or the television program. Corresponding acts of exploitation may also be carried out of works of fine art that appear in the background, or otherwise form an insignificant part, of a picture.

Exploitation as referred to in the first Paragraph may, however, take place only if the master copy for the copy made when the work of fine art is being included in the film, the television program or the picture is a copy that is covered by an act of publication or a copy that has been transferred by the author. If no making of a copy occurs, the same applies to the copy that is directly communicated to the public through the television program.'

on 1 July 2005, of the so-called Infosoc Directive.[22] Part of the unauthorized publication on the website occurred before this date and the Court was concerned with the transitional provisions; under the previous law petty cases had been excluded from infringement liability. The Court ultimately found that the photographs in question were small but could not be regarded as an insignificant part of the screenshot. The Court further reasoned that only works released to the public may be object of the exception under Article 20 a, including the requirement that such picture be in the background.[23] In this case the pictures had been made available on the Internet, but such publishing was not covered under the traditional concept of release to the public under Article 8, ie dissemination to the public of (a number of) tangible copies. The HD concluded by finding that the pictures had illegally been made available to the public both before and after 1 July 2005. However, as the photographs were small and minimized on the website, the damage caused by their use was set at SEK 400 each and the general moral damage, including the interest of the author in seeing that copyright infringements are not committed, set at another SEK 200, ie in total SEK 1,000 (around € 100).[24]

NJA 2004 p 363 should be mentioned in connection with this case. There the HD interpreted the scope of a client's rights when ordering photographs. A photographer argued that he should have obtained additional payment for his client's use of images which fell outside of the terms of his contract. The contract had had been renewed a number of times but had first been entered into at a time when the Act on Photographic Images was still in force.[25] This

[22] Directive 2001/29/EC of the European Parliament and of the Council of 22 May 2001 on the harmonisation of certain aspects of copyright and related rights in the information society. OJ (L 167) 10. Art 20 a of the Swedish Copyright Act was however for some time (5 months), mistakenly not extended to the photographic field; the amendment entered into force on 1 December of the same year.

[23] The JCA had found Art 20 a applicable, using a different interpretation of Art 8 than the HD applied.

[24] This case can be compared with *Kelly v Arriba Soft Corporation* (280 F.3d 934 (9th Cir 2002) withdrawn, re-filed, and superseded at 336 F.3d 811(9th Cir 2003)), which also concerned a commercial photographer and a search engine company, where thumbnail pictures were considered to fall within the fair use doctrine. But in this case the website inline links also gave access to the pictures in full size. On this point the 9th Circuit modified its initial decision by holding use of thumbnails to be 'fair use' and remanded the case to the District Court for trial on whether use of full sized images constituted copyright infringement. In this part Kelly obtained a decision to his favour on 18 March, 2004. However, at that point the owner of the Arriba search engine had gone out of business. This decision on remand is not reported. The 9th Circuit however reviewed and decided all of these issues later in *Perfect 10, Inc v Amazon.com, Inc* 508 F.3d 1146 (9th Cir 2007). There the 9th Cir held that it was holding, for the first time the issue of what constitutes 'making a copy' of an image on a computer. It held that the thumbnail images had been stored and displayed but that the ISP's computers merely used html code to 'link' the full scale images and therefore there was no copying. The Court also held that storing the thumbnail images on the computer was justified under the 'fair use' provisions of 17 U.S.C. § 107 codifying the common law and cited it's 2003 *Kelly* decision. *See* 508 F.3d at 1164.

[25] Act (SFS 1960:730) on the right to photographic images, which was integrated into the Copyright Act on 1 July 1994.

Act contained a special purchaser rule that was not made part of its later integration into the Swedish Copyright Act. The purchaser rule gave all rights to the purchaser, unless otherwise agreed. The renewal contracts were entered into when this rule had been repealed. From the investigation in the case the parties assumed that the same conditions would apply to the renewals as had existed under the first contract, where however the parties had diverging views on what had been agreed upon. Accordingly, the terms of the agreements were subject to the customary contractual interpretation. The substance of the agreements had been addressed at length and the scope of the user's right had not been addressed at all. The compensation was in the form of hourly rate and remuneration for expenses. The Court found that as the first contract did not contain any restriction of the user's right, subsequent contracts could not be deemed to include such the restriction claimed by the photographer.[26] In other words, there had been no infringement of the photographer's copyright by the client's additional uses of the images.

2.1.6. *Moral rights*

NJA 1996 p 354 confirmed the rather strictly-applied *right to be mentioned* as the author when a work is made available to the public under Article 3(1) of the Copyright Act,[27] as to which there are few exceptions. The circumstances of the case were as follows: The Swedish Television Company (SVT), in connection with a cultural TV programme, had illustrated a play based on well-known poems set to music by a composer, whose name was not credited during or after the programme. On this basis, the HD expressed the opinion that SVT, by failing to state the composer's name in connection with the broadcasting of his works had infringed the composer's copyright and breached his moral rights, which required giving him credit to the extent and in the manner required by normal usage. SVT could not have been unaware of such an obligation. Accordingly, the HD held that the company had acted negligently and ordered it to pay compensation for the infringement. The amount in question was not an issue in the case.

NJA 2005 p 905 concerned whether works had been made available in a manner that was prejudicial to their author. There, a radio program script utilizing several literary works about the fictional character Alfie Atkins had been compiled using lines from a Danish movie, 'The Pusher', in order to produce a comic effect. In this new context the kind character of Alfie Atkins was made to appear to deal with drugs and bargain over the price. The Court,

[26] The claimed restrictions of the client's use had been orally 'granted' by the photographer's fiancé, who at the time of the contracting of the photographer was employed by the client, but according to the client without legal competence to conclude such contracts as the one in question. Her competence or not was however not in the end regarded as decisive for the outcome of the case.

[27] 'When copies are made of a work, or when it is made available to the public, the name of the author shall be stated to the extent and in the manner required by proper usage.'

inter alia, stated that the alien and objectively denigrating context in which the lines were used in the film constituted a disparaging context for the literary character of Alfie Atkins, but hardly one to ridicule, offend, or otherwise prejudice the author's literary reputation or individuality. The HD concluded that the fact that an attack on a well-known fictional personality had been made by means of exploiting of the author's protected lines was not enough to violate her moral rights; the alterations made to Alfie Atkins' lines had been necessary to create the relevant part of the programme, and; the changes had not been more extensive than necessary to create the intended effect. The HD based upon these conclusions affirmed the decision made by the JCA of non-infringementA third case on moral rights is ***NJA 2008 p 308*** concerning interruptions of feature films by advertising, which were claimed to constitute violations of the author's individuality pursuant to Article 3(2) of the Act.[28] The Court stated that even when commercial breaks are inserted in between the films scenes, or inserted at a change of environment in the film, they break the director's intended sequencing of the various scenes by the sudden inclusion of the completely different environment and phenomena of an advertisement. Interruption by advertising also means that the film's actual length is extended, which is not an unimportant artistic feature of the work.

Under this assessment of the possibility of an infringement the HD held that account should be taken as to the type of work and its artistic importance, including the genre and intended use: a feature film – in the case in question a comedy and a drama – must be considered to be more sensitive to interference than a film consisting of short stories or one of an episodic nature with mutually independent finished parts; these do not necessarily have to be seen in an uninterrupted context. The same applies to a non-narrative movie, eg an instructional or educational film. Irrespective of a drama's artistic level, ambition and trend it is a fact that commercials normally break the continuity and drama of a film and the insertion of alien images are likely to prejudice the author's individuality. Finally, the purpose of the break must also be considered. Advertising breaks are of a commercial nature and designed to draw viewers' attention from the film to the commercials. As the JCA had found, the interests behind the commercials are not of such a nature as to outweigh the author's interest in his work not being reproduced in a way that violates his moral rights. In conclusion, these breaks for advertising changed the works' presentation and context in breach of law. The HD however, in agreement with the lower courts, did not find the commercial breaks to be prejudicial to the authors' artistic reputation.

The scope of the right to use quotations was object of the decision in ***NJA 1996 p 712***. The background concerned the fact that on 2 September 1993 the

[28] Art 3(2) 'A work may not be changed in a manner which is prejudicial to the author's literary or artistic reputation or to his individuality, nor may it be made available to the public in such a form or in such as context as is prejudicial in the manner stated.'

daily '*DN*' (the Daily News) published an article based on an interview with a lady who had witnessed and had herself been injured when a JAS aircraft crashed at a demonstration flight in Stockholm City on 8 August of that year. A different newspaper then published an abstract of the article. The main contents of the abstract were however the story of this victim largely reproduced as direct quotations taken from the DN interview.[29] The HD found that this reproduction constituted copyright infringement because it far exceeded the quotation permitted under Article 22 of the Act, which reads, 'Anyone may, in accordance with proper usage and to the extent necessary for the purpose, quote from works which have been made available to the public'. In this case the usage was deemed neither proper,[30] nor necessary.

2.1.7. Musical rights

NJA 2000 p 445 concerned identification of the appropriate organisation to collect artists' remuneration and to conclude agreements on the reduction of remuneration pursuant to the '*droit de suite*' (artists' resale royalty). The question was whether there can be more than one single organization 'representing a substantial number of Swedish authors and holders of neighbouring rights in the field concerned' to conclude such agreements. The background was that a well-known Swedish auction house had, in nine instances in 1996, paid a total amount of SEK 759 053 (around 75,000 euro) pursuant to the Act (SFS 1927:56) concerning the deposit of money by an authority, as their contributions to the artists' resale royalties under Article 26 j of the Copyright Act (now Article 26 m). The deposits had been made due to the uncertainty of whether the amounts should be distributed via the Visual Arts Copyright Society of Sweden (BUS) or the Artists' Interest Group for *droit de suite* in Sweden (DUR). The Court found that under the Act there was no formal requirement that such an organization was required to represent a majority of right owners.

In practice, this has led to the situation where the umbrella collecting society in the copyright field, Copyswede presently distributes such payments. An amendment to the provision has recently been proposed to make clear that the collecting organization in question must be one representing the majority of right owners.[31]

NJA 2002 p 178 concerned whether a melody in the popular music field, which contained a repeated and distinct element, was protected by copyright and whether an infringement had occurred when a later melody used in the same field contained more-or-less identical riffs. As had the lower courts, the HD also found the similarities to be so striking that the melodies might be considered to be the same work, and Melody 2 therefore, objectively interfered with the rights

[29] The copyright was regarded as jointly belonging to the journalist/the DN and the victim.

[30] That a usage may be common does not make it 'proper'.

[31] See SOU (Swedish State Government Reports) 2010:24 '*Avtalad upphovsrätt*' (Agreed copyright).

of the right holder of Melody 1. The question then arose as to whether this was an independent double creation. Melody 1 obviously was inspired by a Swedish folk song. The composer of Melody 2 claimed to have used the same inspiration. The Court however stated that with such a striking similarity between the melodies, a very high standard of evidence was required to demonstrate a true double creation. Since Melody 2 had been composed at a time when Melody 1 was already known on the market, it was less likely to have been independently created. Therefore, the HD concluded that Melody 2 should be regarded as an imitation of Melody 1 in violation of the right holder's exclusive right.

2.1.8.Technical Drawings

Among the 'literary' works that are subject to copyright under Article 1(2) of the Act are 'maps and other works of a descriptive nature executed as drawings, engravings, or in a three-dimensional form'. While the scope for independent design in these cases is usually considered to be less than in actual literary works, they are still required to be characterized by a degree of individuality and distinctiveness in relation to other similar works in order to be eligible for copyright protection.[32] It has also been suggested in the legal literature that the copyright protection accorded to such works is rather slim and mainly consists of protection against direct copying.[33] In cases concerning technical drawings the required 'level of originality' for copyright protection as a 'creative step' is the issue at stake.[34] The consensus for using this threshold criterion has gradually gained ground in preparatory works,[35] as well as in the case law. The HD, in a number of rulings has given a double-creation test certain significance in identifying this threshold.[36] In ***NJA 1994 p 74***, ***NJA 1995 p 256*** and ***NJA 1998 p 563*** as well as in the just mentioned ***NJA 2002 p 178*** the HD took account of the risk of double creation in order to assess the existence of protection.[37] One may nevertheless conclude, that the criterion of double creation has no independent function but rather, serves as a helpful rule of evidence assessment, as discussed below in ***NJA 2004 p 149*** regarding technical drawings.

[32] In the preparatory works it has been expressed that a certain distance from the earlier works of the same type is sufficient, or in other words that they have a certain independence from them. See Nytt Juridiskt Arkiv (New Judicial Archive) II, 1961, p 27 which contains a compilation of the Official Legislative Report 1956:25 and Prop 1960:17.

[33] See Henry Olsson, *Upphovsrättslagstiftningen* (The copyright law) (Norstedts juridik 2nd edn 2006) p 54.

[34] This can be compared with 'inventive step' in patent law and is the threshold of qualified originality that a work has to pass to be eligible for copyright but has later developed to be a general test for copyright qualification.

[35] See eg Prop 1988/89:85 p 27.

[36] This test was originally introduced as a way of assessing whether a work of applied art was eligible for copyright protection in Prop 1969:168 p 135.

[37] In *NJA 2002 p 178*, however, the Court had already taken a position on the existence of infringement and it may be assumed that the issue of double creation concerned only whether there had been such use of the work in regard to the question of reimbursement under Art 54(1) of the Act.

NJA 1998 p 563 dealt with the issue of drawings of building modules which were found to have copyright protection under Article 1(2) of the Act. In determining whether protection existed with regard to their personal characteristics the HD considered the risk of double creation. The three sets of drawings at issue in the case were analysed by the Court, namely, A-drawings by the plaintiff and B- and C-drawings by the alleged infringer. The B-drawings were found to exhibit such similarities to the A-drawings that they could not have come to existence without the A-drawings serving as models. Although there were many differences in regard to details, the B-drawings were still characterized by containing most of the individual characteristics of the A's. The B-drawings were viewed by the HD as comprising – sometimes very intimate – copies of the A-drawings modified and adapted in various respects but still not in such a comprehensive way as to lose their character as copies. The C-drawings, on the other hand, were different. According to the evidence given during the trial, contrary to the A-drawings the C-drawings did not have the primary purpose of being prototypes for production of modules, but were rather, intended to serve as the basis for supplier procurement. These drawings were less detailed than the A-drawings and many of them were not much more than free-hand sketches. Even if they resembled the A-drawings, they could not be seen to be the result of duplication or as close imitations. Because of the relatively slim copyright protection of the A-drawings, the C- drawings were not considered to fall within that scope of protection.

Finally, *NJA 2004 p 149* concerned whether two quite simple and standard drawings of a flooring panel were protected works under Article 1(2). The appellant argued for of copyright on the basis that these technical drawings were not copies of somebody else's work. The Court stated *inter alia*, that it was hardly a controversial principle that a work which has been independently created is not, solely on that basis, eligible for copyright protection. Therefore, the criterion of possible double creation cannot be the sole criterion for assessing the existence of protection. That a drawing is independently created did not suffice for copyright protection under Swedish law. The HD held that it was obvious that the 'creative level' in this case did not meet the comparatively low threshold requirements under Article 1(2) and dismissed the appeal.

2.1.9. Video Games

NJA 2000 p 580 dealt with the possible violation of software and film copyright. There, a person, who had been trading in the exchange, purchase and sale of video games, was prosecuted for infringement on the bases of the video games being cinematographic works and/or to be regarded as computer programmes.[38] It was clear that his activities were not renting, and that issue was not brought up,

[38] As of the trial, copies of film were never exhausted. This is why the attribution of the videogames as films would have been advantageous to the infringement claims.

but the question in relation to computer programmes was whether his activities included acts that were comparable to their rental.[39] The HD dismissed the case and confirmed the JCA's judgment, partly because the video games in question were deemed not to be 'films',[40] and partly because dealing with the video games as software was deemed not include acts comparable to rentals under the Act.

2.2. Freedom of Speech/Freedom of the Press[41]

NJA 1998 p 838 is a very special case involving the publication of 'Mein Kampf' in 1992 by a Swedish publishing house on the claimed interest in the freedom of expression. The State of Bavaria brought suit against the publisher claiming infringement of the copyright that Bavaria allegedly had acquired by the seizure of Adolf Hitler's estate. The HD found that the German confiscation order of the work was not recognized under Swedish copyright law. The HD also considered its previous ruling in ***NJA 1985 p 893***, where Court had stated, that as a principle, the Copyright Act balances opposing interests and that questions with respect to limiting criminal liability for copyright infringement in favour of an opposing interest in freedom of expression should be reserved for the legislature, even though situations might be present where the freedom of expression interests asserted were so strong that the courts were required to enter an acquittal on charges of copyright infringement. Such a situation was however not present in this case, and the fact that it might be difficult to obtain copies of this work of historical interest was not sufficient to require dismissal of the claims. Although it was not proven that the State of Bavaria was the copyright holder of Mein Kampf in Sweden, the HD nonetheless found infringement. The Court concluded that it was not necessary to establish the rightful owner in order to support a case for infringement; it sufficed to establish that an infringement has been made.

[39] Another purpose of banning such acts is that renter's rights should not be circumvented by acts which do not constitute 'rental' in the formal sense but which have similar meaning or effect. Cf (now) Art 19 of the Copyright Act: 'When a copy of a work has been has been transferred, with the consent of its author, within the European Economic Area, that copy may be further distributed.

The provisions of the first Paragraph do not confer a right to make available to the public

1. copies of works, with the exception of buildings and works of applied art, through rental or similar legal acts…'

[40] In this context the HD reasoned that the video games in question contained moving pictures and sound operated by a computer programme. Initially these movements and sounds have no independent meaning. It is thus the player who directs how the series of moving images will appear, albeit in a pre-frame, and this varies from game to game. But without playing it, the game seems pointless; it is to be played and not to be watched. It should however be noted that the case is 10 years old, and the games in question hardly had any resemblance to the sophisticated video games presently on the market.

[41] These rights are part of the Swedish Constitution and enshrined in the Act on Freedom of the Press (SFS 1949:105), the Constitution Act (SFS 194:152) and the Act on Freedom of Expression (SFS 1991:1469).

NJA 2003 p 25 concerned claims that the name of a TV series and pictures of actors in this series had been used in a youth magazine with an attached calendar. Compensation for the use of the pictures was demanded. However, as the pictures were used in part of a magazine they were subject to the protection of the Freedom of the Press Act. Under such circumstances Swedish law provides that there are no rights to compensation for use.[42] However claims regarding the marketing of the calendar under the TV series' title, 'Tre kronor' (Three Crowns) in a radio channel were not insulated under the Freedom of Speech Act.

2.3. Industrial Property

2.3.1. Choice of Law and Jurisdiction[43]

In *NJA 2007 p 287* infringement claims by a company owning exclusive rights to a trademark in Sweden and some other EU countries were dismissed under Article 5(3) of the Brussels I Regulation against a company located in Germany for infringement of exclusive rights in these countries, apart from claims of infringement of the Swedish trademark. The company's request for a preliminary ruling from the CJEU was refused.

In *NJA 2000 p 273* the HD stated that the special forum provision in Article 5(3) of the Lugano Convention[44] is not applicable to consideration of a request for a negative declaration. Here, a Swedish company applied for a declaration that certain technologies did not fall within the scope protection of another's patent rights. The HD held that although there were good reasons for allowing the appellant's claim in Sweden one of several arguments against allowing negative declarations under Article 5(3) was that such an option to enjoy the advantages of process at one's own residence could lead to a situation in which, a producer of goods that caused injury in another country to any resident of that country, might bring an action in a country of production where there is no liability. The result of such a measure would be to deprive an aggrieved party of the opportunity, in accordance with Article 5(3), to bring an action where the damage actually occurred. Since here, there was no question of an action for damages being raised in the state in which the injury occurred, it followed that the appellant's action did not fall within the scope of Article 5(3).

[42] The special Act (SFS 1978:800) on name and picture gives a right to an injunction and compensation, but only in cases of commercial marketing of another's name or picture.

[43] Council Regulation (EC) No 44/2001 of 22 December 2000 on jurisdiction and the recognition and enforcement of judgments in civil and commercial matters. OJ (L12) 1. (Brussels I Regulation).

[44] Art 5(3) of the Lugano convention on Jurisdiction and the Enforcement of Judgments in Civil and Commercial Matters, concluded in Lugano on 16 September 1988, corresponds to Art 5(3) in the Brussels I Regulation.

2.3.2. Designs[45]

The importance of ***NJA 2005 p 180*** lies primarily in the HD's discussion on the principles for computation of damages. This has relevance not only to design cases but to the whole field of IP. The case concerned a company's claims of approximately SEK 40,000 plus 95,000 (in total roughly 13,500 euros) as damages for infringements to their protected cookware design. The infringements had occurred on a limited scale in terms of marketing of representations of design protected products and the import of samples into Sweden.

The HD held that, since the infringements in the case had been made with intent, the company was, in principle, entitled to reasonable compensation for the exploitation of the protected designs with respect to all of the infringing actions. The Court stressed the principle of full compensation and that compensation should not be so low to make it more economically profitable to infringe another's exclusive right than to acquire a legitimate right, ie damages should satisfy both their compensatory and the preventive functions. In this case, the claims had not been supported by evidence of any losses, and without a detailed inquiry into the extent of the damage by reason of the products incorporating the design having been offered on the market, including any additional damage, the Court could not apply the estimation rule of Chapter 35 Article 5 of the Procedural Act.[46] Nevertheless, the HD reasoned that under the provisions on damages in the Design Act (Article 36), when determining the amount of compensation, account should also be taken of the right owner's interest in design infringements not being committed and to factors other than those of purely economic importance in order to fully calculate the economic damage.

Finally, the HD stated that since, from the facts of the case it was evident that the plaintiff suffered some sort of compensable injury, without evidence as to its extent and value, the consideration rule in Article 36 of the Design Act should be applied. But this rule is not intended to permit compensation in excess of the full economic harm and the damages must therefore be determined with caution.[47] For that reason and having regard to the infringements admittedly being intentional, even if not of a particularly serious nature, the reasonable amount of damages was determined to be SEK 10,000 (around 1,000 euros).

NJA 2009 p 695 dealt with what is required to obtain a transfer of a better right to a design. In this case materials cited by the parties were: a prototype

[45] Design Protection Act (SFS 1970:485) as amended.

[46] 'In the case of appreciation of a past injury and full proof of the damage are not or only with difficulty can be brought, the court may estimate the damage at a reasonable amount. That may also happen if the evidence is likely to cost or inconvenience is not proportionate to the amount of the damage and the damages claimed relate to a smaller amount.' This rule provides no relief from the need for presenting evidence that damage has occurred but rather only as to calculating the amount of the damages.

[47] The victim must be fully compensated for his loss, but no more; moreover, it does not seem possible when calculating the damages to include some form of moral damage, the court said.

of the so-called WWW-walker (the original), a walker-RollX (the alleged same design), drawings and photographs of these and the artwork which were the bases for the recorded designs.[48] The HD ruled that to be entitled to a transfer of registration of a design due to a better right to the design requires more-or-less total identity between the designs in question. When comparing the WWW-walker and the walker RollX designs no such match was found between their appearances. The action requesting transfer of the design was therefore rejected.

2.3.3. *Patents*[49]

NJA 2000 p 497 concerned interpretation of patent claims of a so-called twin-card for telephones and whether there was an infringement by defendant Europolitan of Comviq's rights under the patent doctrine of equivalence.[50] As to this the HD stated that: Comviq's patent claim, when compared with the claims of Europolitan's application, which occur in a GSM environment, must be interpreted in relation to the GSM standard, regardless of what the reference to the GSM meant for the application of the invention in other systems. According to the GSM standard the so-called SIM (Scientific Instrument Module) consisted of only a single physical unit. Such an interpretation was also consistent with the inventive idea which, as embodied in the patent document, refers to the technical problem of the manner in which various categories of calls made using the same physical control unit may be distinguished; the solution proposed in the claim is that the subscriber identity module is given at least two identities, which are selectively usable and activated by the user. The patent document at issue did not contain anything else that could give rise to a different interpretation. Since both the problem that the twin card aims at solving and the solution to the problem differed from Comviq's inventive idea, the Twin Card could not be subsumed into the scope of Comviq's patent protection under the doctrine of equivalence.

NJA 2005 p 66 concerned a default litigation where the viability of the action was based on an invention being patentable. The claim was dismissed since the plaintiff had let the patent lapse. The plaintiff applied for a new trial, arguing that the patent had been granted after a renewed application. He was not regarded to have a valid excuse under the rather strict procedural rules.

In ***NJA 2008 p 1192*** a pharmaceutical company had requested that the relevant authority determine the price of a generic drug, which was covered by a patent. The question was whether this request was equivalent to offering the article for sale under patent law. The HD found that the measure taken did not mean that

[48] The designs at issue had been made by the same designers and bought by the respective companies; the question of double sales was not in issue.

[49] Patent Act (SFS 1967:837) as amended.

[50] As to the Equivalence Doctrine, *See* Bengt Domeij's separate article in Ch 3 of this work.

the company had offered the medicine to the market within the meaning of Article 3 of the Patent Act.[51]

NJA 2006 p 354 dealt with a US based company which held a European patent which had been validated in eg Sweden. This patent was found to be subject to Swedish jurisdiction in a case concerning a request for negative declaration on the patent‘s scope of protection. The fact that the defendant had also brought an action concerning patent infringement with a claim of injunction and compensatory damages was not considered to provide grounds to dismiss the declaratory action for lack of interest.[52]

2.3.4. Trademarks[53]

In ***NJA 1998 p 474*** a workshop, which provided service, maintenance and repair of cars but was not accredited by the Volvo Company, was precluded against penalty to use the VOLVO sign for their services in the combination 'Volvo Service'. This decision was rendered only about a month before the CJEU delivered its judgement in the BMW case with a more or less identical conflict.[54] The CJEU's solution was however somewhat different.

NJA 2003 p 163 concerned whether the mark 'Jägarbrännvin' (hunters' brandy) was confusingly similar to the registered, well-established brands 'Jäger' and 'Jägermeister' for alcoholic beverages. The HD reasoned in the following manner: Market surveys showed that the marks 'Jäger' and 'Jägermeister' were well established as symbols for alcoholic drinks. In addition to a distinctive character, both marks seemed to possess a significant acquired distinctiveness and were thus eligible to enjoy the special extended protection provided under Article 6(2) of the Trademark Act, implementing Article 5(2) of the Trademark Directive.[55] The goods were similar. As for the similarity between the marks 'Jägarbrännvin' and 'Jägermeister'/ 'Jäger' the dominant prefix 'Jägar' in 'Jägarbrännvin' had both linguistic and conceptual similarities and also audio and visual similarities were present, not least regarding the prefixes 'Jägar' and 'Jäger'. The Court concluded that there was a risk of confusion between 'Jägarbrännvin' and 'Jägermeister'/ 'Jäger' in such a way that the public might believe the spirits coming from companies with at least common economic

[51] 'The exclusive right conferred by a patent implies, with the exceptions stated below, that no one, without the proprietor's consent, may use the invention by (1) making, offering, putting on the market or using a product protected by the patent or importing or possessing such product for these purposes...'.

[52] See NJA 2000 p 273 above.

[53] Trademark Act (SFS 1960:644) as amended.

[54] Case C-63/97, *Bayerische Motorenwerke AG (BMW) and BMW Nederland BV v Ronald Karel Deenik*. [1999] ECR I-905.

[55] First Council Directive 89/104/EEC of 21 December 1988 to approximate the laws of the Member States relating to trademarks. OJ (L 40) 1 Repealed and replaced by: Directive 2008/95/ EC of the European Parliament and the Council of 22 October 2008 to approximate the laws of the Member States relating to trademarks OJ (L 299) 25.

links and that the use of the sign 'Jägarbrännvin' therefore infringed upon the trademarks 'Jägermeister' and 'Jäger'.[56]

The question in ***NJA 2003 p 555*** was whether one company's use of the mark CHECK•POINT for stock market information services interfered with another company's registered right to the mark Check Point registered in the whole of class 35 and 41 and for legal consulting/trademark services in class 42. Check Point was found to have a weak original distinctiveness for the services covered by the registration. As the mark had barely, if at all, been used by the trademark holder before the infringement proceedings were instituted, it had acquired no additional distinctive character. In this light, and the HD, finding support in the CJEU decision in case C-39/97 (Canon),[57] the scope of protection was considered to be limited. By its overall assessment of the likelihood of confusion between the registered mark Check Point and the use of the sign CHECK•POINT the HD found that, although there was more or less identity between the marks, the low degree of similarity between the services supplied by the other company and the services in class 35, in addition to the registered mark's weak distinctiveness, CHECK•POINT was not confusingly similar to Check Point.

Three cases have concerned the use requirement in Article 10 of the Trademark Directive, found in Article 25 (a and b) of the Swedish Act, namely ***NJA 2001 p 265, 2005 p 643*** and ***2006 p 7***.

NJA 2001 p 265 concerned a registered figurative trademark 'Spotlightserien', which during the prior five years was not used in its entire registered form, but only in the form of 'SPOTLIGHT', written in capital letters and uniform in sequence. The form used was deemed to have deviated so much from the form in which the mark was registered that its distinctive character had changed. Therefore, the HD ruled that registration should be cancelled.

NJA 2005 p 643 dealt with what constitutes genuine use sufficient to satisfy the use requirement. The word and figurative trademarks ENTELCARD were registered for telecommunication services. The registration was challenged by Intel Corporation. Two cases from the CJEU C-40/01 (Ansul) and C-259/02 (La Mer Technology)[58] were cited by the HD, where the CJEU applied a liberal view of the scope of the use requirement. In this case the HD nevertheless found in favour of Intel; the use shown to have been made, in the absence of other evidence, was regarded to be too little to be accepted as genuine use of the marks.

NJA 2006 p 7 concerned the interpretation of the beginning of the five-year period of the required use of a trademark. Article 25 a of the Swedish Trademark Act contains the same language as Article 10 of the Trademark Directive: '...following the date of the completion of the registration

[56] This result corresponds to the decision of the PBR on 3 September 1999 in case 97-088 between the same parties.

[57] Case C-39/97, *Canon Kabushiki Kaisha v Metro-Goldwyn-Mayer Inc, formerly Pathe Communications Corporation* [1998] ECR 1998 p I-5507).

[58] Case C-40/01 *Ansul BV v Ajax Brandbeveiliging BV*, [2003] ECR I-02439 and Case C-259/02 *La Mer Technology Inc v Laboratoires Goemar SA*, [2004] ECR I-1159, respectively.

procedure.' The Court upheld the decision of the JCA, reasoning that the Directive does not specify what is meant by the term 'registration procedure'. However, it was clear that Member States had the freedom to establish procedural rules for registration of trademarks. While the language of the Directive does not have an independent effect relative to national laws, the HD reasoned that it cannot be an EU-autonomous concept. On this ground the HD dismissed the request by one of the parties to make a referral to the CJEU and held that the period does not begin to run until the (Swedish) opposition period has expired or the opposition proceedings are completed.[59]

It should also be noted that, following ***NJA 2008 p 1033***, when a trader brings an action under Article 25 a for cancellation of a trademark registration due to lack of use, the requirement of injury in the first sentence of Article 26(1) of the Trademark Act[60] should be applied in such a way that the action will be barred only where the circumstances allow the court to conclude that the trader is wrong in his claim that registration is detrimental to him.

In ***NJA 2005 p 214*** the HD examined the customs authority's decision to postpone the release of goods because of an alleged infringement of the VOLVO trademark. Some goods were then ordered to be detained, while a packaging of spare parts was released. The HD based its decision on the following facts: The packaging consisted of a plastic sleeve with the importer's logo printed several times throughout the package. The packaging was provided with a glued label containing a number, a logo with the words 'Volvo Rod' and 'Stabilizer Link Volvo'. These words were reproduced with a uniform font and format, and the word 'Volvo' was not particularly emphasized. The current use of Volvo's trademark on the packaging might thus be deemed necessary for preventing errors in a simple way in respect of spare parts users. The imported parts were not intended for the importer's own use, but for resale to workshops. There was nothing that suggested there being an association between Volvo and the importer, or to give the impression that the contents were original spare parts. Against this background there was no reason to believe that the packages infringed Volvo's exclusive right.

In ***NJA 2007 p 431*** a person had imported mobile phone accessories marked 'Nokia', which was registered both as a national mark in Sweden and as a Community trademark. The imported items were therefore considered to infringe those marks. Since a preliminary ruling on Article 98 of the Trademark Regulation[61] had been previously obtained from the CJEU,[62] an injunction under penalty

[59] See however Case C-246/05, *Armin Häupl v Lidl Stiftung & Co KG*, [2007] ECR I-4673, which suggests a similar outcome as in the Swedish decision.

[60] 'Anyone who suffers injury from a registration is entitled to bring an action in Court for the invalidation of the registration'.

[61] Council Regulation (EC) No 40/94 of 20 December 1993 on Community trademarks [1994] OJ (L 11) 1. (Repealed and replaced by Council Regulation (EC) No 207/2009 of 26 February 2009 on the Community trademark [2009] OJ (L 78) 1, effective 13 April 2009).

[62] Case C-316/05, *Nokia Corp. v Joacim Wärdell*, [2006] ECR I-12083.

was issued in regard of the use of the EU trademark against this import of mobile phone accessories. The HD, however, also stated that there was no reason to make a different decision in regard of the infringement of Nokia's Swedish trademark.

NJA 2008 p 1082 also dealt with an injunction with a penalty based on infringement of a Community trademark (The North Face, TNF). The circumstances of this case were special and concerned whether a man had infringed TNF's trademark rights by importing goods from China. His dealings with the goods were not in connection with his own business, but he had been helping his daughter by paying for the goods on a business visit to China and later clearing them at customs. The daughter had ordered the goods, some of which were intended to be family presents and others to be gratuities to employees at her riding school. The latter became identified as use in trade. The HD cited the CJEU Case C-405/03 (Class International)[63] and found that import in the sense of the Trademark Regulation should be deemed to occur as soon as goods intended to be used in trade are brought into the country and customs formalities are cleared. Trademark use in interference with TNF's exclusive trademark rights had therefore been made as part of the father's business. It was the father who had taken all the measure constituting import. He also knew about the content of the parcels, as his daughter had first seen the jackets in question when one of his Chinese business contacts on a visit wore this type of garment, which the daughter later ordered.

In conclusion, apart from the injunction under penalty to refrain from dealing with the trademarks, the father was also required to pay a reasonable licence fee as compensation for the damages,[64] and was ordered to pay compensation to TNF for the storage costs of the seized goods prior to their destruction.

2.3.5. *Trade names*[65]

NJA 1999 p 3 dealt with the expression 'Vacuum plast' (plastic vacuum) as part of a registered trade name (*Vakuum Plast Industri Aktiebolag*). Since it was regarded to be such a descriptive name it was held to enjoy fairly weak protection against the use of the word by another trader in a not quite identical trade name (*HS Vacuumplast Aktiebolag*). Accordingly, there was no infringement.

2.3.6. *Trade Secrets*[66]

Trade secret law is not harmonised in Europe, apart from what is prescribed under Article 39 of the TRIPS Agreement.[67] It can also be disputed whether

[63] Case C-405/03 *Class International BV v Colgate-Palmolive Company and Others* [2005] ECR I-8735.

[64] These however had been moderately set by the JCA to SEK 10,000 (around 1,000 euros).

[65] Trade Names Act (SFS1974:156) as amended.

[66] Act (SFS 1990:409) on the Protection of Trade Secrets. It should be noted that the Swedish Labour Court is a final instance court with respect to on trade secrets between employers and employees.

[67] The Agreement on Trade-Related Aspects of Intellectual Property Rights, Annex 1C of the Marrakesh Agreement Establishing the World Trade Organization, signed in Marrakesh, Morocco on 15 April 1994.

trade secrets belong to the family of IP rights. From the viewpoint of exclusive ownership to a work, they are of course not IP. On the other hand, from a protection point of view, when information has a commercial value and is kept secret, it bears a great resemblance to IP, including the type of sanctions for violations. A further reason to include trade secrets in the present context is that as a special feature of Swedish law their regulation is covered by a special Act and does not just form part of unfair competition law, which however normally is also included under the overarching IP umbrella.

NJA 1995 p 347 and ***NJA 1999 p 469*** both concerned a bank's instruction relating to bank officials' obligation to verify identification documents during cash withdrawals. These have been considered a trade secret under Article 1 of the Act.[68] Claims in a production order for the banks instructions were therefore rejected in both cases. A party is required to produce a document whose content constitutes a trade secret only on a showing that there is extreme need for it.

In ***NJA 1998 p 633*** the Court determined that market research information, marketing plans, prices and advertising campaigns and any other information related to the business and operation of the company fell under the definition of trade secret in Article 1 of the Act. Accordingly, unauthorized disclosure and use of trade secrets disclosed in confidence and in connection with a business transaction will give rise to the right to claim and be compensated for damages under Article 6 of the Act. Here, SEK 2 million (around 200,000 euros) were awarded.

A unique feature of the Swedish trade secrets Act is that employees normally do not have penal liability in situations where they use or disclose an employer's trade secrets. This was decided in by ***NJA 2001 p 362***, which held that an employee's copying of a customer database which constituted a trade secret, but as to which the employee had lawful access in his work, was not to be seen as business espionage under the Act nor as unlawful disposal. As the description of the offense is formulated, such act could not be understood as unlawful use under Chapter 10 Article 7 of the Penal Code. No unauthorized disposal under the Penal Code had occurred here, and the indictment was dismissed in its entirety.

2.4. Some Concluding Remarks on the HD Cases

It is striking that only one patent case has been tried by the Court in regard of subject matter.[69] At the same time the dominance of copyright law issues in the

[68] Even though Swedish case law points out the need to make clear that the information is to be treated in a confidential way, how that is to be done is up to the entity which wants to keep the information secret. Moreover, information will remain secret if disclosed only to employees who need to know this information in order to perform their duties.

[69] The other three patent cases concerned formalities.

HD is as striking; around half of the IP cases granted *certiorari* has concerned this area. To these some interesting results have been achieved in cases regarding the scope of protected technical drawings, the interpretation of the exception for quotations and the balancing of moral rights, as well as the very strong freedom of the press under the Constitution. [70] How well the principles laid down on advertising breaks in television broadcasts will be upheld in a European perspective may however be doubted.[71] Among the more important decisions is also the discussion on damages in IP matters in ***NJA 2005 p 180***. These remain decisive also after the implementation of the IPRED in 2009, not least as the considerations for computing damages in the Directive have been added with the already existing consideration under Swedish law concerning the right owner's interest in infringements not being committed.[72]

In view of the formulation of the provisions on the protection of databases in the Swedish Copyright Act,[73] it seemed very wise that the HD in ***NJA 2005 p 924*** initially referred the case to the CJEU. It may be such an action in regard of ***NJA 2000 p 273*** on the interpretation of the Lugano Convention might have shed light on some other perspectives.[74]

The HD has – for better and for worse – applied a generous applied art protection, which at the time in 1994–95 was well meaning. In ***NJA 1995 p 164*** (Knitted tunic) obvious copying and practically no alternative means of protection can be seen as having been decisive to the outcome, not least as they were informed by the heated discussions on increased problems of counterfeiting and piracy coinciding with the signing of the TRIPS Agreement. As the scope of applied art protection should be narrow, the reasons for the decision are however quite acceptable – that is if the garment or fashion products have those 'unique' qualities, which partly is a subjective assessment. The decision ***NJA 2009 p 159*** on the protect ability of the Mini Maglite design is very much the result of the same reasoning: a direct copy and lack of realistic protective possibilities at the time of introduction on the Swedish

[70] The very strong press freedom protection stands in conflict with claims of right to one's own picture, and in this regard Swedish law does not seem in line with the European principles, cf the European Court of Human Rights on 24 June 2004 the in the case of *von Hannover v Germany*, ECHR 294.

[71] Cf Directive 2007/65/EC of the European Parliament and of the Council of 11 December 2007 amending Council Directive 89/552/EC on the coordination of certain provisions laid down by law, regulation or administrative action in Member States concerning the pursuit of television broadcasting activities. [2007] OJ (L 332) 27.

[72] The Directive is a minimum directive, under which Member States should remain free to adopt or maintain stricter sanctions and measures.

[73] The scope of Art 49 is obviously broader than that of Database Directive 96/9/EC and its compliance with the EU legislation may be doubted. The original part of this rule stems from Sweden's copyright legislation of 1960, and has the similar (broad) wording of all the Nordic countries' statutes. Nordic legislators do not seem keen on abolishing their old catalogue rule.

[74] For a critical discussion of this case see Lydia Lundstedt, 'Jurisdiction and the Principle of Territoriality in Intellectual Property Law: Has the Pendulum Swung Too Far in the Other Direction?' 32 *IIC* (2001) pp 124 ff.

market. The remaining problem in regard of the limited number of cases from the HD is primarily its signal to the lower courts on the availability of applied art protection to protect anything individual that is not a copy, at least from the garment industry.[75] Easily forgotten is that the artistic element is also a requirement under copyright law.

However, today the lack of suitable design protection has long since become history. With the enactment of European design legislation[76] with a three year unregistered design protection and a 12 months grace period almost all of the fundamental reasoning of the HD has become obsolete. Therefore, only design classics are in need of copyright protection, ie those works that after 25 years still are attractive on the market due to their maybe sometimes indefinable artistic (attractive) qualities. In this respect, I personally find the Mini Maglite worthy of protection.[77]

Amongst the trademark cases the decision in ***NJA 2003 p 555*** on the Check Point registration was the first instance where the HD seriously considered CJEU case law, which probably was decisive to the material outcome of this case. If the Court had done a similar investigation into the underlying EU law in a 1995 case[78] concerning the interpretation of Article 6(2) of the Trademark Act, which implements Article 5(2) of the Trademark Directive, the final result would most probably have been the reverse. But in this case the HD – as such correctly – emphasized that there was no obligation to refer questions on preliminary measures as interlocutory injunctions to the CJEU.

In conclusion, apart from the changed wording of a number of provisions in the Swedish IP legislation, the imprint of European harmonisation is not very apparent in the decisions of the HD. One possible explanation could be that the HD focuses more on procedural matters and principles than on material rights.

3. THE PRECEDENTS OF THE RR

In the following section precedents from the RR over the last decades are discussed with respect to overarching principles of Europeanization, the hierarchy of legal sources (and the possibility of such conflicts), and the length of time from application to decision.

[75] Cf Stockholm City Court's decision of 2 December 2009, case No T 16022-06 (Leather coat).

[76] Directive 98/71/EC of the European Parliament and of the Council of 13 October 1998 on the legal protection of designs and the Council Regulation (EC) No 6/2002 of 12 December 2001 on Community designs.

[77] Cf For another opinion Hans Henrik in Chapter 8 of this work.

[78] NJA 1995 p 635.

3.1. Europeanization

3.1.1. Europeanization of Patent Law

RÅ 1990 ref. 84 (Speech signal) on the patentability of a computer programme, where the RR in a plenary proceeding stated: 'Sweden's accession to the European Patent Convention makes it necessary for us in our domestic law in the context of what is compatible with Swedish law to take into account the case law as it is expressed by the European Patent Office'. In fact, there was nothing in the EPC that at the time required Swedish case law to follow the European Patent Office (EPO).[79] But the RR found reason to give progress at the EPO great importance in view of the close similarity between the wordings on the exclusions from patentability of Article 1(2) of the Swedish Patents Act and Article 52 of the EPC. This ruling broke with a long and restrictive practice in Sweden in regard of the patenting of computer-implemented inventions.[80] It also gave rise to an extensive discussion in the legal literature.[81]

RR subsequently partly relied on this decision and developed what was established there in two rulings from 1998. Particularly notable is the general statement in ***RÅ 1998 ref. 55*** (Agricultural roller) that 'great importance should be given to the development of practices at the EPO ... and how the methods of assessment including inventive step as been developed there'. In ***RÅ 1998 ref. 4*** (Marking strip), the Court held that EPO practice supported placing a certain weight on the mere discovery of a problem in the assessment of an inventive step.

A similar approach towards conformity with the EPO's practice was demonstrated in connection with the complaint resulting in the PBR's plenary decision of June 13, 1986,[82] which held that the so-called second medical indication should be accepted in a formulation of so-called Swiss Claims. [83] This decision was appealed against, ***RÅ 1991 note 483*** (Appeal of Bioinvest). But the RR supported the views of the Swedish Patent and Registration Office (PRV) and the PBR that the provisions of the Patent Act, which conform to the

[79] See Marianne Levin, 'EPC och nationell patenträtt, särskilt vad gäller datorprogram' (EPC and National Patent Law, Especially Concerning Computer Programs) (1991) *Nordiskt immateriellt rättsskydd* (Nordic Intellectual Property Rights, NIR) pp 197 ff, 200.

[80] See RÅ 1974:11, RÅ 1983 2:25 and RÅ 1984 Ab 283.

[81] See Ulf Bernitz, *Juridisk tidskrift vid Stockholms universitet* (Legal Journal at Stockholm University), JT 1990-91 pp 476 ff; Levin, *Nordiskt immateriellt rättsskydd* (1991) pp 197 ff.; and Berndt Godenhielm, *Patentskyddets omfattning i europeisk and nordisk rätt* (The scope of patent protection in European and Nordic law) (Helsingfors, Juristförbundets förlag 1994) pp 41 ff and 54 ff. See also Lennart Törnroth, 'Datorprogram och patentskydd – utvecklingen av svensk rättspraxis i belysning av främst EPO-praxis' (Computer programs and patent protection - Swedish case law developments foremost in the light of EPO-decisions) (1999) *Nordiskt immateriellt rättsskydd* pp 87, 92 ff (On the Swedish developments of computer-related inventions); Claes Sandgren, JT 2000–01 pp 941 ff.

[82] Reported in *Nordiskt immateriellt rättsskydd* 1987 p 248; accordingly, this case followed the decision of the EPO Enlarged Board of Appeal in the case G 5/83.

EPC, did not rule out such claims.[84] The interpretation of the EPC made by EPO's Enlarged Board of Appeal was regarded to be in accordance with Swedish law. Applying the approach of ***RÅ 1990 ref. 84*** would thus mean that the patent claims were valid.[85]

3.1.2. Europeanization of trademark law

In ***RÅ 2000 ref. 62*** **I** and **II**, the registrability of the shape of goods in the form of striped toothpaste and of a set of coloured plugs, respectively, were considered, both with a negative result for the applicant, as had been the case in the PBR. It is questionable why the *certiorari* was granted at all, especially in the Thorsman plug case, where the RR did not even give any additional guidance merely confirming the PBR decision, which held that admittedly the colour code could, as a whole, probably function as an identifier of the Thorsman plugs but there was not enough proof that the public perceived each of the current colours as an indication of some specific length Thorsman plug.In the toothpaste case, the appellant referred to an earlier similar mark that had been registered after appeal as well as to its own earlier, foreign registrations for the same get up.[86] However, in the present case this did not help the applicant. In its refusal the RR stressed that there was no clear practice regarding the distinctiveness of product get ups of its type. However, it distinguished refusals of registration in similar cases by the OHIM; [87] where washing and dishwashing tablets with different-coloured layers had been considered devoid of distinctive character. [88]

In both cases, the applicants failed to demonstrate that the shapes applied for as trademarks were perceived as signs of origin by the public. These precedents were confirmed later in principles adopted by the CJEU in a number of cases.[89] A three-dimensional sign must be perceived as a mark by the public in order to be registerable.[90] It is indeed difficult to imagine that the shape of a good, which has not achieved a secondary meaning or repute, can justify registration as a trademark. This does not mean that get-ups are assessed more strictly; trademark distinctiveness is assessed in the same way for all types of signs. But when it comes to the shape of goods as trademarks,

[83] Cf EPO's Enlarged Board of Appeal, case G 5/83.

[84] This is the principle of several medical indications nowadays found in EPC 2000, namely Art 54(4) compared to Art 53(c).

[85] Cf however the dismissal in case RÅ 1992 not 2001, where the applicant applied for a retrial of his earlier rejected patent on a computer programme after the RÅ 1990 ref. 84. But the Court obviously found that its decisions could not be given a 'retroactive effect'.

[86] Cf however RÅ 2003 ref. 74 below.

[87] The Office of Harmonization for the Internal Market (trademarks and design).

[88] See eg cases R 510/1999-1 and R 707/1999-1.

[89] See eg the Joint Cases C-468–472/01 P and 473-474/01 P *Procter & Gamble Company v OHIM*, [2004] ECR I-5141 resp. I-5173, and the Joint Cases C-456-57/01 P *Henkel KGaA v OHIM*, [2004] ECR I-5089.

[90] Cf eg Case C-136/02 P *Mag Instrument Inc v OHIM*, [2004] ECR 2004 I-9165 paras 30 ff, 61 ff: Case C-144/06 P *Henkel KGaA v OHIM*, [2007] ECR I-8109 para 36.

however unique or artistic it may be, the basic prerequisite of this type of sign being inherently capable of distinguishing goods fails. Consumers are simply not accustomed to perceive the shape of goods as a trademark.[91] This must therefore be clearly demonstrated.[92]

RÅ 2001 ref. 14 **I** (SAF) and **II** (Champis) concerned well-known trademarks as obstacles to registration, cf Article 6(2) and Article 14(1) No 6 of the Trademark Act that correspond to Article 5(2) of the Trademark Directive.

I: In the SAF case the RR found that the Swedish Employers' Association used SAF as a well-known and accepted abbreviation, thus barring a German company's trademark application for vehicle axles and parts thereof. The PBR found no ground for refusal of the application. However, the RR pronounced, referring for support to CJEU Case C-375/97[93] that the use of the mark applied to vehicle parts would be detrimental to the distinctiveness of the SAF brand.

II: In the Champis case the RR found that the figure mark CHAMPIS in a specific design registered for soft drinks precluded a clothing company's application for Champis as a word mark for clothing. Neither the PRV nor the PBR had considered the existence of the soft drink brand as a ground for denial. However, according to the RR, there was a risk of prejudice to the mark and a risk that a use in connection with clothing would take unfair advantage of the CHAMPIS mark's distinctive character and reputation.

In ***RÅ 2003 ref. 74*** the Court found that the international trademark R for filter cigarettes was also registerable in Sweden. [94] The PBR and the PRV had refused the application because of the mark's lack of distinctiveness. The RR referred to its earlier holding in, ***RÅ 1999 ref. 20***, in support of the proposition that the national legal developments should, as far as possible, correspond to similar developments in other EU/EEA countries, with special focus on the OHIM and its Boards of Appeal. In ***RÅ 1999 ref. 20*** the RR found that European trademark law had evolved, and that the signs L 10, L 11 and L 12 could serve as distinguishing features. There were no other obstacles to the registration, and the Court held that the mark R1 had been found to be registrable in the vast majority of EU/EEA countries. OHIM's practice showed that a mark consisting of two characters must be evaluated in the same way as other trademarks,[95] ie the only assessment to be made is if the mark can be considered inherently distinctive. Since R 1 could not be considered descriptive

[91] Ibid.

[92] The Thorsman Company had supported its claim of the colour code being able to be distinguished using a 20 years old opinion by the Trademark Board of Stockholm Chamber of Commerce. But this concerned the colour code as such and not the distinguishability of each coloured plug.

[93] Case C-375/97 *General Motors Corporation v Yplon SA*, [1999] ECR I-5421 para 30.

[94] Cf The Protocol of 27 June 1989 to the Madrid Agreement for the international registration of marks (1891) and Arts 50 ff of the Trademark Act.

[95] Especially OHIM's decisions on the trademarks IX (R 4/1998-2), DS (R 294/2000-3) and HD (R 345/2000-3).

and there was not otherwise any need for availability of this combination, the RR found no obstacle to its registration.[96]

The question in ***RÅ 2003 ref. 26*** was whether 'Parmigiano Reggiano' could be registered as a collective mark. The PRV and the PBR had rejected the application due to a lack of distinctiveness; the sign indicated the nature and origin of the goods. The RR noted that under the Collective Marks Act[97] an association of professionals may acquire exclusive rights to guarantee marks or other trademarks on condition of showing distinctiveness. The Court further stated that Article 64(2) of the EC Trademark Regulation provides for collective marks also as designations of geographical origin, while national provisions on the positive legal protection of geographical indications were absent, even though the (then) Council Regulation (EEC) No 2081/92 of 14 July 1992 on the protection of geographical indications and designations of origin for agricultural products and foodstuffs[98] was valid in Sweden. The RR argued that a geographical indication protected under this Regulation does not as such mean that the sign already has the distinctiveness required for a trademark registration under Article 13 of the Trademark Act. It is basically still descriptive. However, since it was assumed that only a very limited part of the Swedish public would perceive the consortium's mark (in Italian) as an indication of the product type and its geographical origin, this fact was not considered to exclude its registration as a collective mark in Sweden.[99]

In ***RÅ 2006 ref. 75*** the RR took a position on confusion between a trademark and a trade name. The application (for a figurative mark) concerned PIZZA PAPA JOHN'S. In a not unanimous decision the PBR found that the applicant's Community (figure) mark No 000025262 PIZZA PAPA JOHN'S had a prior validity than the alleged obstacle to the registration, the auxiliary trade name PAPA JOHN'S PIZZA and, although the trade name was likely to be invalidated before a judicial court, it should remain and the trademark applicant was denied registration. The RR eventually annulled the PBR's judgement, because the obstacles to registration at the time of application no longer existed. The RR stated in its decision though, that the PBR's refusal at the time had been proper.

[96] With support of RÅ 2003 ref. 74 the PBR on 2 July 2003 the PBR decided to admit registration of the figurative mark J! (Case No 00-244).

[97] (SFS 1960:645). It should be noted that a new Trademark Act has been proposed, Prop 2009/10:225, which will incorporate collective marks into the law and which also, addresses geographical indications.

[98] Repealed and replaced by Council Regulation (EEC) No 510/2006 of 20 March 2006 on protected geographical indications and protected designations of origin. [2006] OJ (L 93) 12. (Art 8(2), with effect from 1 May 2009).

[99] Cf also RÅ 1997 not 17 (PEAUDOUCE), where it was 'supposed that only a small part of the relevant Swedish public has such knowledge of French to render this descriptive character any importance'.

3.2. Hierarchy of Legal Sources and Legal Conflicts

As already indicated, RR judgments are usually detailed when they are issued. This Court has had a commendable tendency to articulate the manner in which it takes account of Sweden's international commitments, for example under the Madrid Protocol. In ***RÅ 2003 ref. 74*** the Court signalled a willingness to consider the *telle-quelle*-rule in Article 6*quinquies* of Paris Convention for the Protection of Industrial Property. There are also good reasons, as this Court has recognized, for attaching great importance to the developments of practice at the EPO and before the OHIM's Boards of Appeal. In the field of patents, this is a very convenient position, as national special solutions are often difficult to justify.[100] The same applies to OHIM's case law. It would not be particularly appropriate if Sweden unilaterally tried to restrict the criteria for protection. This must be done jointly, either within the framework of EPO-cooperation or under EU law. Even if it is sometimes unavoidable, it is usually unsatisfactory if the assessments differ in substance among parallel national and European patent and trademark applications.[101]

In other words, Europeanization in all its glory should receive proper attention. But there must also be room for national development, especially in areas where there is no European consensus. One such example is on certain biotechnological inventions related to genes or stem cells.[102] It would be unfortunate if Sweden, without further consideration aligned itself to the rationale of the Warf-Patent, decided by the EPO's Enlarged Board of Appeal[103] with a result that seems to go against the dominant Swedish approach.[104] In any case, the extent of the exemptions under the EU Biotech Directive[105] has to be interpreted by the CJEU, which is now likely to happen.[106] But such important developments of the law, in turn, require that the highest instances such as the RR also refer questions of EU-related law to the CJEU and not merely refer to its own or EPO or OHIM case law.

As pointed out in relation to ***RÅ 1998 ref. 55***, it is not meaningful when the RR in supporting its reasons for assessments refers only to the EPO

[100] See Levin, NIR 1991 p 202.

[101] Cf divergent resolutions of identical applications for patent limitations in EPO, DG2 Opposition, appl No 92 920 319.8, EP 0615642 B and Svea JCA 28 October 2007 in Case T 4019-03 (*SPORT Ident International AB v LE*).

[102] Cf Case C-377/98, *The Netherlands v The European Parliament* [2001] ECRI-7079 (Pays-Bas v The European Parliament and the Council), and Case C-456/03, *Commission v Italy*, [2005] ECR I-5335.

[103] Case G 2/06.

[104] Cf SOU 2008:20 *'Patentskydd för biotekniska uppfinningar'* (Patent protection for biotechnological inventions).

[105] Directive 98/44/EC of the European Parliament and of the Council of 6 July 1998 on the legal protection of biotechnological inventions.

[106] See Case C-34/10 *Brüstle v Greenpeace eV*, which has been referred to the CJEU from the German Federal Patent Court and remains pending.

Guidelines[107] or for that matter the Guidelines of the OHIM. Such rules of thumb have been designed to facilitate the offices' daily work, but are less suitable for the few complex cases which are subject to appeal in the highest instance. The OHIM's Boards of Appeal already explicitly make their own solutions which differ from the Guidelines. Adherence to the EPO or OHIM's case law and the hierarchy of the offices' different sources of law should therefore be respected. Both the EPO and OHIM's Boards of Appeal also take account of national decisions, and of course of the binding case law of the CJEU.[108] It is particularly relevant to raise this point on the ranking of legal sources because in recent years also the Swedish (judicial) courts have tended to quote the EPO Guidelines in their decision making as if they were included in Swedish statutory law.[109]

It is often wise to consider the EPO's or OHIM's case law in the administrative process. The same attitude is however not as evident when it comes to the judicial process – of course for as long as there is no European or national superior court to follow for assessing validity and/or infringement. But in the absence of such decisions all Swedish courts should give careful consideration to the fact that developments in European law take place not only in the EPO and the OHIM, but also through court decisions in the other EPC and EU member states, and especially by their highest instances; a fact which is also acknowledged by these international bodies in their reasoning and opinions.

In this context, the scope of protection for prestigious brands granted in ***RÅ 2001 ref. 14*** may be discussed. The rule under Article 5(2) of the Trademark Directive and thus under Article 6(2) of the Trademark Act is that the later sign 'without due cause takes unfair advantage of or is detrimental to the distinctive character or repute' of the reputed mark. The question of whether such (risk of) adverse passing off/blurring exists is a matter of opinion. But the outcome of this case is likely to be deemed to comply with today's increasingly strong 'property protection' given to well-known trademarks.

While most of the trademark cases discussed above, may be said to have support in EU law, the compliance of ***RÅ 2003 ref. 26*** with EU law is, however, questionable, and ***RÅ 2006 ref. 75*** raises a number of questions. For Parmigiano Reggiano it is true, as the RR pointed out, that by the consortium's registered geographical indication the mark is not 'to be regarded as distinctive within the meaning of Article 13 of the Trademark Act'. However, by its acceptance of the registration (because of little knowledge of Italian in Sweden) the RR disregarded the fact that a conflict of laws had been inferred under Arts. 13–14 of Regulation (EEC) No 2081/92 from which it may be understood that, while it is possible to convert a trademark or a collective mark to a designation of origin,

[107] Cf Tomas Randes, NIR 1998 p 749 and Rolf Nöteberg, NIR 1999 p 535.

[108] Cf Nöteberg above.

[109] Complaint by Peter Sande, attorney at law, at a conference on '*Skärpta krav på uppfinningshöjd?*' (Raising the bar?) Arranged by the Swedish Association for the Protection of Industrial Property Rights on 3 December 2008.

the reverse is not possible![110] In other words, under EU law, a later national registration as a trademark of what is already a geographical indication, such as Parmigiano Reggiano, should not have been possible. On the other hand, the geographical indication must be seen as a strong enough protection.[111]

That the applicant in PIZZA PAPA JOHN'S would have to initiate a cancellation process in a judicial court to have the obstacle to its trademark registration removed, ie a confusingly similar trade name of a later date than the applicant's identical, registered Community trademark, because the registration authority had manifestly disregarded the priority of the EU system, cannot be considered fair or reasonable or in compliance with EU law. Nor did RR's decision offer any solution for a possible future conflict concerning an improperly registered trade name. It seems strange that such a supreme body is unable to find a way to correct a wrong decision within the legal system, especially in comparison with the analysis made in ***RÅ 2003 ref. 26*** on Parmigiano Reggiano. The decision further emphasizes the somewhat cryptic relationship between trademarks and trade names with full parallel IP protection, and in consequence with parallel barring effects to registration of confusingly similar signs.[112]

3.2.1. Aspects of Time

Apart from the precedent value of the patent cases that have been decided in recent years, the length of the RR's – and the PBR's – case administration raises questions regarding the effectiveness of the Swedish registration procedure and the societal benefits of national designs, patents, or trademarks.

In ***RÅ 1998 ref. 4*** and ***RÅ 1998 ref. 55*** the final decisions took 11 and 9 years respectively from their dates of application.[113] While these patent applicants' thrift and patience was eventually crowned with success, one must ask what use was the wait from a market competitive point of view. Such extensive handling periods thus must be seriously questioned. This applies particularly with regard to small and medium-sized enterprises, which could be destroyed if a (groundless) application for *certiorari* drags on.

The trademark cases have not been quite so blatantly lengthy. Yet it did take eight years from the publication of the marks until final decision in ***RÅ 2001***

[110] The relation between geographical indications and Community trademarks is today made clearer by Art 7(1)(k) of the Trademark Regulation and Art 14 of Council Regulation (EC) No 510/2006.

[111] See regarding the indicator 'parmesan' Case C-132/05 *Commission v Germany* [2008] ECR I-957 .

[112] Cf for a more flexible approach Case C-17/06, *Céline SARL v Céline SA* [2007] ECR I-7041 and Case C-245/02, *Anheuser-Busch Inc v Budějovický Budvar, národní podnik*, [2004] ECR I-10989.

[113] The patent application for the Marking strip had reached the PRV on 11 February 1983; it was denied protection by the Office on 22 July 1987. The patent for the Agricultural roller was applied for on 5 December 1986 and the PRV granted the patent on 22 September 1989. The judgements by the PBR were delivered in September 1992 and January 1995, respectively.

ref. 14 (SAF and CHAMPIS). The SAF decision is thus from the same year as the merger between SAF and the Federation of Swedish Industries to form the Confederation of Swedish Enterprise, and the SAF organization as such no longer existed when the decision was rendered. The question of time is also pertinent to the situation in PIZZA PAPA JOHN'S. Is it really reasonable that a trader should be required to wait for six years and six months to obtain information concerning a trademark application?[114] In ***RÅ 2006 ref. 75*** the obstacles to registration had finally been removed by the intervention of a bankruptcy at the time the RR finally decided this case. But the RR's ruling came a full year later, after the opposing company had been deleted from the Company registry.

4. CONCLUSIONS

Because of the low IP case volume and the natural lack of special IP expertise in the highest instances,[115] the precedents in the IP area seem to have focused on rather specific and sometimes odd issues. It is a matter of subjective assessment as to whether the cases granted *certiorari* have been the most central, and whether the highest courts always have correctly identified the core issues of the IP system where a decision could provide guidance for future decision making. In addition, in a considerable number of cases the precedents have merely confirmed the material outcome of the JCA's and the PBR's decisions. There has also been a noticeable reluctance in referring cases to the CJEU. It is easy to demonstrate that Swedish courts have been comparatively shy about making requests for preliminary rulings from the CJEU. In fact, IP-related matters emanating from Sweden have so far only been decided by this Court six times since 1995.[116] No

[114] The PRV decided on 5 April 2000, the PBR on 13 January 2004 and the RR on 18 October 2006.

[115] It should however be noticed that the HD traditionally has included one judge with such expertise or special interest.

[116] The cases in question are Case C-223/98, *Adidas AG* [1999] ECR 1999 I-7081, which was referred by the '*Kammarrätten*' (Administrative Appeals Court in Stockholm) concerning prohibition of release for free circulation, export, re-export or entry for a suspensive procedure of counterfeit and pirated goods – Provision of national law requiring the names of consignees of consignments detained by the customs authorities pursuant to the regulation to be kept confidential – Compatibility of the provision with Regulation (EC) No 3295/94); Case C-338/02 (Fixtures Marketing), above in note 16 concerning Directive 96/9/EC on the Legal protection of databases – Definition of investment in the obtaining, verification or presentation of the contents of a database; Case C-371/02, [2004] ECR p I-5791 (Björnekulla Fruktindustrier): Art 12(2) (a) of Directive 89/104/EEC) on revocation of rights conferred by the trademark, which as sad in note 5 above was referred by the Svea JCA; Case C-16/03 (Peak Holdings): Art 7(1) – Exhaustion of the rights conferred by a trademark, which as said in note 5 above was referred by the JCA for Skåne and Blekinge; Case C-316/05 (Nokia), above in note 62: Art 98(1) of Regulation (EC) No 40/94 and obligation of a Community trademark court to issue an order prohibiting a third party from proceeding with such acts; and Case C-52/07, *Kanal 5 Ltd, TV 4 AB v Föreningen Svenska Tonsättares Internationella Musikbyrå (STIM) upa* [2008] ECR I-9275: Copyright management organisation enjoying a de facto monopoly and method of calculating royalties relating to the broadcast of musical works. The STIM case was referred by the Market Court.

case has ever been referred by the RR. The HD did, however, on 24 August 2010 refer another set of questions to the CJEU on the interpretation of the IPRED.[117]

Despite the comparatively few rulings on IP matters by the HD and the RR, and the time consuming process – not less than five years – access to justice in these courts has played a certain role. Even though that primarily applies to individual cases, there are also some important rulings where the Court has ploughed some new ground. For instance, in the 1990's the RR appears to have speeded up Sweden's adaptation to the EPC and to EU trademark law. As a proposition though, both courts are very formalistic and unwilling to develop new principles to arrive at materially reasonable outcomes. This is especially obvious in HD's decision in ***NJA 2005 p 510*** concerning copyrighted items owned by a bankrupt company, which has been heavily criticized by legal scholars for its formalistic approach and is viewed as an obstacle to the development of new activities, products, services and markets based on IP resources.[118] RR's decision ***RÅ 2006 ref. 75*** in the PIZZA PAPA JOHN'S case is a similar, telling example.

In view of the case-law it is not unreasonable to argue that IP decision making processes, in the best of all possible worlds, should be different and directed into a 'commercial court' with expert judges familiar not only with law but also with technology, arts, economics and marketing conditions. In recent years it has also been proposed that administrative review of IP cases should be transferred to the judicial courts to concentrate the best possible specialization into one forum.[119]

Legal decision making in the areas of competition, IP and market law must be rapid, competent and reliable in order to correspond to the requirements of modern business. To achieve this, in addition to specialization, specific technical and financial skills and a large sample of well-reasoned precedents are needed.[120] As the pace of change in the economy quickens, legal decision must be made and made final while a market still exists. Otherwise they cannot provide the basis for

[117] The questions concern IPRED's compliance with other EU legislation, namely Directive 2006/24/EC of the European Parliament and the Council of 15 March 2006 on the retention of data generated or processed in connection with the provision of publicly available electronic communications services or of public communications networks and amending Directive 2002/58/EC, OJ (l 105 54, case No Ö 4817-09. It should be noted that on 4 February 2010 the CJEU in Case C-185/09 *Commission v Sweden* found that Sweden had failed to fulfil obligations on time in regard of this Directive.

[118] See eg SOU 2010:2 '*Ett samlat insolvensförfarande – förslag till ny lag*' (A single insolvency procedure with proposals for a new Act) pp 375 ff, 380, Jens Andreasson in SvJT No 5-6 2006 pp 437 ff and Annina H Persson in JT 2006/07 pp 175 ff who at p 184 states that after this decision there is an even greater need for a new law. See also SOU 2001:80 '*Gäldenärens avtal vid insolvensförfaranden*' (Debtor contracts in insolvency proceedings) p230 ff where a proposed rule states that if an estate in bankruptcy disposes over an asset so that it can not be returned essentially unchanged and undiminished, or the asset is such that it can not be returned, the estate shall be deemed to have entered into the contract in regard of that asset The HD rejected such reasoning because it had not (yet) been implemented as a legal rule.

[119] Since Sweden's adherence to the EPC in 1978 the low number of cases on appeal does not require a specialized court such as the PBR.

[120] Similar suggestions were set out in directives, (Dir 2008:49) the so-called 'Objectives inquiry' which has now been presented as SOU 2010:44.

future business actions and decisions. Therefore, it would be preferable that such cases are not heard in more than two instances and even in some cases access to an optional single instance.[121] That would also correspond to the more stringent requirements for justice of the JCA which are part of changes introduced in 2008 to promote a more efficient judicial process. The prototype for a two-instance system already exists in the area of market law, where the Market Court is either the first (and last) instance, in cases where only an injunction is claimed, or second (and final) instance if more than an injunction, eg damages, is claimed; albeit there is still a possibility to have a case appealed to the HD if serious omissions or gross errors have been committed by the Market Court.[122]

The need for a system with a special 'commercial court' for competition law, IP matters and marketing practices, and possibly other related fields, has been discussed for years and is on interested circles' wish list.[123] A further argument for implementation of such a solution is that European developments have given rise to a greater element of competition law influenced considerations, which suggests a broader perspective on IP.[124] That such an overarching judicial solution for IP and related matters to date continues to elude resolution has many explanations, traditional, technical and procedural. Regardless of the cause specialised courts would, no doubt, create greater legal certainty and speed up proceedings, especially if these 'commercial' cases were to be decided in only two instances; and then specialist skills could be built up, developed and preserved.[125]

There are two main obstacles to such a solution. The first one is the diminishing number of IP-related cases in the Swedish court system, so that it might be questioned whether a special Court is economically efficient. The second is the traditional Swedish antipathy towards special courts including the view that all courts and judges should be able to deal with all types of legal matters, and the concern that a judge's training and orientation might be forgotten if a court were too specialized.[126]

[121] Cf the Swedish Market Court, which can decide as the first and last instance if only an injunction is claimed. Questions of damages may later be based on that decision and proceed through the normal channels of the judicial system.

[122] See eg NJA 2001 p 319 where the Market Court's judgement was held clearly contrary to law and *certiorari* was granted. HD's decision was announced May 14, 2001.

[123] See eg Responses by SFIR to SOU 2001:33, '*Patentprocessutredningen*' (The patent process investigation), comments of the Confederation of Swedish industry of 4 April 2007 to several ministries, including the ministry of Justice, and cf Örjan Grundén at the XXVIII Nordic Industrial Property meeting in 2006, NIR 2006 pp 605 ff.

[124] As noted by the Confederation of Swedish industry to the Swedish government ibid.

[125] A starting point is that regarding technology the Stockholm City Court is the exclusive forum in patent cases, and technical experts already sit in as judges. The same applies to Svea JCA in patent cases. In addition, the Market Court that decides cases involving competition and marketing practices matters includes economic specialists on the panel.

[126] Cf SOU 2010:44 '*Mål och medel – särskilda åtgärder för vissa måltyper i domstol*' (Objectives and means – Specific measures for certain procedural settings in court). Among the general conclusions of this investigation are that, basically no requirements of special urgency or special

However, a positive sign in the right direction may be seen in the recently published SOU 2010:44 where it is admitted that IP, competition and marketing practices proceedings are generally amongst the most complex and comprehensive of all cases handled by the court system. This, together with the limited number of cases, points to a great need for concentration. The report concludes that the complexity and scope of these cases makes it appropriate to consolidate them into a special unit to ensure that judges handling the cases over a prolonged period may obtain experience with the substance and type of case in question.[127] In other words, the future may be quite promising and offer some of the since long-wished-for specializations, including at least a 'commercial court' department. When this becomes a reality, *certiorari* in IP cases will become an even less common element of Swedish law than it is today while benefiting legal certainty.

skills require establishing special courts, and that a coherent judicial system without special courts, or in any event, with as few special courts as possible, is more likely to be cost-effective.

[127] SOU 2010:2 pp 413 ff.

2

Dilemmas of Governance in a Multilevel European Patent System

ANTONINA BAKARDJIEVA ENGELBREKT

1. INTRODUCTION

One of the most important achievements of the Swedish Presidency of the European Union in 2009 was the progress that could be reported on a unified patent system in Europe. This issue was announced as a clear priority during the Presidency by the Swedish Minister of Economy, Ewa Björling and was set high on the agenda of the Competitiveness Council held on 4 December 2009.[1] Indeed it is widely acknowledged that the present institutional landscape of patenting in Europe is fragmented and dysfunctional. Under the current legal regime patenting involves many institutions at national, supranational and intergovernmental level and the coordination between these different bodies and procedures is highly imperfect. As is well known, the European Patent Office (EPO) is a key institution which grants, through a single procedure, so-called European patents for most EU and non-EU states in Europe on the basis of the European Patent Convention (EPC).[2] Whereas the granting procedure of the EPO is uniform, once a patent is granted it is refracted into as many national patents as there are designated countries in the application (bundle of patents). National patent offices and (patent) courts are still the

[1] See conclusions on an enhanced patent system in Europe, 2982nd Competitiveness (Internal market, Industry and Research) Council meeting, Brussels, 4 December 2009, http://www.se2009.eu/polopoly_fs/1.26592!menu/standard/file/CC%20patent.pdf.

[2] The Convention on the Grant of European Patents of 5 October 1973 as amended by the act revising Article 63 EPC of 17 December 1991 and by decisions of the Administrative Council of the European Patent Organisation of 21 December 1978, 13 December 1994, 20 October 1995, 5 December 1996, 10 December 1998 and 27 October 2005 and its Implementing Regulations as last amended by the Administrative Council on 9 December 2004. EPC 1973 was amended by Act revising the Convention on the Grant of European Patents (European Patent Convention) of 5 October 1973, last revised on 17 December 1991, of 29 November 2000, effective as of 13 December 2007 (EPC 2000).There are presently 38 Member States acceding to the European Patent Organisation, the last accessions being those of Albania (May 2010) and of Serbia (October 2010).

chief institutions granting and enforcing national patents, but also seized with supervising the post-grant life of European patents.

The European Union's (EU) attempts at introducing a unified title of protection modelled on the European Trademark and the European Design regimes, have thus far, been notorious failures.[3] Instead the Union has been forced to intervene in a piecemeal fashion only in areas where disparities in national approaches and interpretations of national and European patent law have led to intolerable fissures in the Internal Market. The Directive on Biotechnological Inventions (hereinafter the Biotech Directive)[4] represents one such intervention seeking an approximation of patenting standards in the volatile and sensitive field of life sciences. Another, less successful attempt, was the failed Draft Directive on Software Patents.[5]

Stakeholders and politicians agree that the current system is fraught with deficiencies, something becoming all the more evident in the age of globalisation and knowledge economy.[6] The increased transaction costs for business, and especially for SMEs, even if in a common grant procedure, from having to apply separately for each state of the European Union are obvious. Similarly, the split of legal regime in the post-grant phase of a European patent creates not insignificant complications in terms of forum shopping and fragmented infringement proceedings, and also regarding uncertainty as to the still lingering risk of divergent interpretation of the European Patent Convention by national courts.[7]

A vivid illustration of the dysfunctionality of the present system is provided by the jurisdictional conundrum in the area of biotechnology where the European Union intervened legislatively with the Biotech Directive.[8] As is well known, the Directive sought to harmonise national patent laws in respect to the patentability of biotechnological inventions with the objective of eliminating divergences

[3] See H Ullrich, 'Harmony and Unity of European Intellectual Property Protection' in D Vaver and L Bently, *Intellectual Property in the New Millenium* (Cambridge: Cambridge University Press, 2004); O Bossung, 'A Union Patent Instead of the Community Patent – Developing the European Patent Into an EU Patent' (2003) 34(1) *International Review of Intellectual Property and Competition Law* pp 1–30, 34.

[4] Directive (EC) 98/44 of the European Parliament and of the Council on the legal protection of biotechnological inventions, OJ [1998] (L 213)13.

[5] See AWS Williams, 'European Commission: Proposed Directive for Patents for Software Related Inventions' (2004) 26 *European Intellectual Property Review* pp 368–72; R Bray, 'The European Union 'Software Patents' Directive: What Is It? Why Is It? Where Are We Now?' (2005) 11 *Duke Law & Technology Review*.

[6] See G Artelsmair, 'A Comprehensive Patent System Needed For Europe' in A Kur, S Luginbühl and E Waage (Eds) '*...und sie bewegt sich doch!' - Patent Law on the Move, Festschrift für Gert Kolle und Dieter Stauder zum 65. Geburtstag* (Köln Berlin, München: Carl Heymanns Verlag, 2005).

[7] See Altersmair (2005).

[8] For a detailed analysis of the institutional and jurisdictional implications in the area of embryonic stem cell patenting see A Bakardjieva Engelbrekt, 'Institutional and Jurisdictional Aspects of Stem Cell Patenting in Europe (EC and EPO): Tensions and Prospects' in A Plomer and P Torremans, *Embryonic Stem Cell Patents: European Patent Law and Ethics* (Oxford: Oxford University Press, 2010) pp 227–69.

in national law and practices and improving the smooth functioning of the Internal Market. In its turn the European Patent Organisation, with the best of intentions, voluntarily incorporated the rules of the Biotech Directive into the Implementing Regulations of the EPC. This move was supposed to ensure harmony between the pre-grant and post-grant phase in the life of European patents. However, whereas as a legislative act of the European Union, the Directive is ultimately to be interpreted by the CJEU, when 'transplanted' into the Implementing Regulations of the EPC it falls within the jurisdiction of the competent bodies within the EPO, *ie* the Examination Divisions, the Opposition Division (OD) and finally the EPO Boards of Appeal with the Enlarged Board of Appeal (EBA). Consequently this creates ample risk of incongruent judicial interpretations between the CJEU and the EPO while at the same time, there is today no direct link between the two institutions.[9]

The problem is by no means hypothetical. In the much debated *Edinburgh patent* case the Opposition Division of the EPO was asked to decide on the patentability of human embryonic stem cells (hESC) and thus to interpret the morality exception in Biotech Directive Article 6(2)(c), as transposed in Rule 23d (c) (now Rule 28 (c)) of the Implementing Regulations. The very extensive interpretation delivered by the OD, largely denying patentability[10] aroused a heated controversy, but was later on confirmed by the EBA in its decision of 25 November 2008 in the *WARF* case.[11] The request by the appellant that the case be referred to the CJEU was, not surprisingly, categorically rejected by the EBA stressing the absence of formal institutional hierarchy between the EPO and the EU.

Quite independently, the CJEU has also been invited to take a stand on certain controversial provisions of the Directive.[12] More recently in the case C-94/10 the German Federal Supreme Court has referred to the CJEU a request for a preliminary ruling in a dispute between Greenpeace and the German biotechnology scholar Oliver Brüstle concerning, once again, the patentability of hESC and the interpretation of the morality provisions of the Directive. It is unclear what effect a possible divergent interpretation by the CJEU might have on EPO decision-making bodies.[13]

[9] On the stem cell patenting controversy see the comprehensive analysis in *Embryonic Stem Cell Patents: European Patent Law and Ethics* note 8 above.

[10] European Patent No EP 0 695 351. See Decision of the Opposition Division of 21.07.03. The decision was appealed both in respect of the interpretation of the sufficiency of disclosure requirement (Art 83) as well as on grounds of the morality exception (appeal procedure T 1079/03). The Board of Appeal decided to discuss only the objections under Art 83 and await the decision of the EBA in the *WARF* case (see below) regarding the morality exception. Meanwhile, given the preliminary conclusion of the Board that the patent did not fulfil the disclosure requirements under Art 83, the proprietor withdrew his appeal. The patent is thus valid in the version as amended by the Opposition Division.

[11] EP 0 770 125, T 1374/04 (OJ EPO 2007, 313), EBA, Case G 0002/06, decision of 25 November 2008.

[12] Case C-377/98 *Netherlands v European Parliament and Council* [2001] ECR I-07079; Case C-456/03 *Commission v Italy* [2005] ECR I-5335.

[13] This delicate situation was predicted by Bossung: 'There is a strong probability that parties to proceedings before the EPO (patent applicants or opponents) will apply to the ECJ for a preliminary

Obviously, the multi-polar institutional structure of the European patent system is becoming increasingly untenable. It is therefore not surprising that the goal of a unitary system of patenting in Europe has emerged as a matter of political priority. The proposal supported at the December 2009 Competitiveness Council builds on three essential elements: (i) accession of the EU to the EPC; (ii) an EU patent with unitary effects for the whole territory of the Union granted and administered by the EPO and (iii) a uniform European Patent Judiciary for tackling post-grant disputes for both EU and European patents. By envisaging a patent judiciary outside the confines of the EU, the proposal makes a substantial concession and commitment to continued close cooperation with the European Patent Organisation. Judging from the political support for the proposal the European institutions have probably never before been as close to finding a solution to the institutional fragmentation as they are today.

The question, however, is in what ways the interlocking of the two systems will affect the governance of the multilevel patenting system in Europe? Obviously the European Patent Organisation and the European Union work within a complex web of institutional and jurisdictional rules and practices defining, in different ways, the competence of their internal decision-making bodies and the relations of the respective international organisations with their constituent Member States and the public at large.[14] What kind of adjustment will be necessary in order to ensure a satisfactory level of democratic accountability, transparency, and legitimacy in the evolving integrated European Patent system?

In the following I will briefly trace the origins of the present bifurcated system. I will then take a closer look at some distinctive institutional features of the legislative, rule-making and decision-making process under the auspices of the European Patent Organisation. I will identify certain aspects that may be problematic from the point of view of governance and will explore in what way through the envisaged merger these governance problems may have viral effects for the European Union. In a next step I will examine the most recent proposals for a Pan-European Patent Judiciary in order to evaluate the prospects of improving the governance design of European patenting through the proposed reform. In the final section I offer some concluding reflections on the institutional architecture of the future patent system.

Following the governance literature, the notion of governance is understood as extending beyond government to encompass any form of steering conduct in order to achieve certain goals and solve societal problems. It involves

ruling under Art 234 (ex 177) ECT on the legal questions arising from the implementation of the Biotechnology Directive under the EPC. Problems are likely to be encountered, first by the EPO's Enlarged Board of Appeal and then by the ECJ.' See Bossung n 3.

[14] Or, as Ullrich put it, annexing the Union to the EPO or the EPO to the Community. See H Ullrich, 'Patent Protection in Europe: Integrating Europe into the Community or the Community into Europe?' (2002) 8 *European Law Journal* 433.

legislative governance and classical top-down forms of command and control by governmental agencies as well as judicial governance and various 'soft' forms of governance involving both private and public actors and institutions. Implied in the concept of multilevel governance is, in turn, that the powers and the resources for political action are shared by a multitude of public as well as private actors, operating at different mutually interconnected levels, not necessarily in a hierarchical relationship to each other.[15] In the European patent law context, the question of governance thus refers not only to the relationship between governments, patent agencies, patent judiciaries and private actors at the horizontal level, but also between member states and supranational and international institutions at the vertical level. As we shall see below, the multitude of actors and levels involved creates governance dilemmas that are distinct for Europe and that require creative and unconventional institutional design.

2. BACKGROUND

The complex relationship, if not tension, between the European Community/ Union and the European Patent Organisation has a long history that can be traced back to the two competing visions of cooperation and integration in post-war Europe. As is well known, an intergovernmentalist approach based on classical intergovernmental agreements and on greater reticence for national sovereignty was preferred and supported by a number of countries in Europe, notably the UK and the Scandinavian countries. This vision culminated in the setting up of the Council of Europe with the European Convention on the Protection of Human Rights as a major statutory instrument, and the European Court of Human Rights as a chief institutional achievement. On the other hand, a functionalist approach of gradually interlocking of the economies of the European states as a first step to an ever closer economic and political union was the path taken by the six founding members of the European Communities (the Benelux countries, France, Italy and Germany).[16]

These alternative visions produced institutional structures which proved to be markedly tenacious and the consequences of which are still felt today. In the domain of human rights we are at present witnessing the constitutional efforts of overcoming the bifurcated institutional legacies of post-war Europe through

[15] F Scharpf, *Regieren im europäischen Mehrebenensystem – Ansätze zu eine Theorie*, Leviatan, 65 (2002); C Joerges and E-U Petersmann (Eds), *Constitutionalism, Multilevel Trade Governance and Social Regulation* (Oxford and Portland, Hart Publishing, 2006). See also C Scott, 'The Governance of the European Union: The Potential for Multi-Level Control' (2002) 8(1) *European Law Journal* pp 59–79; J Scott and DM Trubek, 'Mind the Gap: Law and New Approaches to Governance in the European Union' (2002) 8(1) *European Law Journal* p 1. For patent law *see* Interview with Ingrid Schneider, at http://documents.epo.org/projects/babylon/eponet.nsf/0/f172de5bb2b9b15bc12572dc0031a3cb/$file/interview_schneider.pdf, p 581, 18 May 2008.

[16] See P Craig and G de Búrca, *EU Law: Text, Cases, and Materials* (Oxford, Oxford University Press, 4th Ed, 2008).

accession of the European Union to the European Convention of Human Rights. In a not quite dissimilar manner, this dual-track legacy still troubles the institutional development of the European Patent system.

Certainly the European Patent Organisation is not part of the Council of Europe. However, the European Patent Convention is a successor of the so called Strasbourg Convention, first conceived within the Committee on Economic Affairs of the Consultative Assembly (now Parliamentary Assembly) of the Council of Europe. At its very first session of 8 September 1949, the Consultative Assembly of the Council adopted Recommendation 22, advancing the idea of a unified European patent system.[17] The Recommendation was followed by intense work by experts within a specially set Expert Committee on Patents. A decade and a half later, in 1963, the Council of Europe adopted the Strasbourg Patent Convention.[18] The Convention entered into force in 1980, but proved largely obsolete after the patenting system based on the European Patent Convention became operational. Its substantive provisions, however, have been almost literally incorporated in the EPC and have provided a blueprint for the harmonisation of patentability requirements in Europe and internationally.

As noted by Christopher Wadlow in an illuminating review of the history of the Strasbourg Convention, the fact that work on a statutory instrument in the field of patent law started under the auspices of the Council of Europe (and not in the European Community) was a matter of historical accident rather than logical necessity.[19] The expert committee on patent law was set up in the absence of better ideas for common projects in the sphere of the economy. The progress achieved within a relatively short time can probably be explained by the involvement of the heads of the national patent agencies in the drafting process. This tightly-knit epistemic community guaranteed expertise, a high degree of institutional commitment and a common language stemming from widely accepted international instruments such as the Paris Convention.

The ambition of the drafters of the Strasbourg Convention was no less than that of achieving European unity. However, there was also awareness that political acceptance of the Convention was conditional on finding a point of balance between a common European patenting system and preserving the integrity of the national patenting systems. As the author of one influential proposal in the drafting process put it:

[17] See Recommendation 23 of the First Session of the Council of Europe, September 8, 1949, Doc 110. Arguments in support of the proposal were contained in the Report presented by MH Longchambon on Behalf of the Committee for Economic Questions, COE Document No 75, September 3, 1949. See also Christopher Wadlow, 'Strasbourg, the Forgotten Patent Convention, and the Origins of the European Patents Jurisdiction' (2010) 41 *International Review of Industrial Property and Copyright Law (IIC)* pp 123–149.

[18] Convention on the Unification of Certain Points of Substantive Law on Patents for Invention, opened for signature by the Member States of the Council of Europe on 27 November 1963, entered into force on 1 August 1980 (ETS No 047, 27/11/1963).

[19] Wadlow (2010); see O Mills, *Biotechnological Inventions. Moral Restraints and Patent Law* (Aldershot Burlington: Ashgate, 2005) p 22.

> The system proposed here affords the possibility of coming gradually to European unity in the matter of patents without imposing for this as a prime necessity important changes in the law of the contracting countries or any measures leading to the abandonment of national sovereignty....[20]

Interestingly, whereas in its final version the Strasbourg Convention focused exclusively on substantive law, during the course of drafting much thought was devoted to matters of procedure and institutional design. Two competing proposals were discussed. The first one, submitted by the German Prof. Reimer envisaged a model based on mutual recognition of national patents supervised by a special judicial body, a so-called European Court of Justice.[21] The alternative proposal of De Haan acknowledged the advantages of a common judiciary, however, assessed the political difficulties of building up a supranational judicial body as considerable. It therefore, more modestly, advanced a model of a European Patent Council, a supranational administrative organisation that was to grant European patents. This proposal may be seen to have materialised in the form of the present European Patent Office. By contrast, the idea of a European patent court was never brought to fruition. Yet, as noted by Wadlow, the absence of such a court is still felt as an important missing link ('the keystone of the arch') in the multi-level governance system of patenting in Europe and constitutes one important reason for continuing reform endeavours (see below).[22]

The European Union (then the European Economic Community) also initiated its own efforts on approximation and unification of patent law at a very early stage. For an organisation built on the idea of a common market, this was an indispensable development, since a territorially limited patent law strikes a dissonant note against the fundamental principles of free movement and elimination of trade barriers. A Working Party of experts of the six member states of the EEC was already established in 1958, soon after the founding of the Communities, under the chairmanship of the President of the German Patent Office Haertel, as part of a comprehensive work package on harmonisation and unification of intellectual property regimes in the Community.[23]

Still, given the membership of all EEC countries in the Council of Europe and the rapid progress of the work with the Strasbourg Convention, the Community was bound to take these developments into account. Thus, an original draft of a European Patent Convention establishing a Community patent with unitary effects for the territory of the Common Market was abandoned, chiefly over uncertainty as to the treatment of non-member countries.[24] After a period

[20] De Haan, as quoted by Wadlow (2010) at p 139.

[21] It may come as a surprise to many that the first mention of the notion of a European Court of Justice appears exactly in these early institutional plans for a common patent system for Europe. See Wadlow (2010).

[22] Ibid.

[23] S P Ladas, *Patents, Trade Marks and Related Rights: National and International Protection* (Cambridge, Mass, Harvard University Press, 1975) vol 3, p 632.

[24] See Ladas (1975) at p 63.

of stalemate, a breakthrough was initiated by the French Government which proposed to work on a system with broad European membership beyond the EC and a parallel Community Convention. It was this diplomatic turn that opened the way to the present system with a European Patent Organisation and to the grant of a European patent through a common procedure. The Community was instrumental in the successful establishment of the European Patent Organisation on 7 October 1973.[25]

Ironically, however, the success of the EPO to a great extent predetermined the failure, or at least the slowing down, of the Community patent project, where the questions of institutional design became exceedingly complicated. In 1975 the Community Patent Convention (the Luxembourg Convention) was adopted, subsequently amended by the Agreement relating to Community Patents.[26] However, these intergovernmental instruments never garnered the necessary number of ratifications and never entered into force, chiefly due to the excessive costs of the envisaged Community patent and highly complex judicial arrangement.

So the historical accident of the Council of Europe being first with a European patent initiative predestined the approach of the European Community/Union to patent law as one of adaptation and building on the achievements of the European Patent Organisation.[27] The model of integration shaped by the Council of Europe and followed by the EPO with its more cautious approach to transfer of national sovereignty, attracted a greater number of countries, outside the complex and demanding EU project, which additionally boosted the independent European patent system.

3. SOME ASPECTS OF GOVERNANCE OF THE EUROPEAN PATENT ORGANISATION

Given the authority gained by the European Patent Organisation, there is obviously no way toward a joint European Patent System without heavy reliance upon the substantive standards of the European Patent Convention and on the expertise of the European Patent Office as a granting authority. This is also the case of the proposal that is now on the negotiating table of the European Union Member States. Before coming to the details of this and other proposals

[25] The chief reason for this expediency is, by many, seen to lie in the advancement of the Patent Cooperation Treaty and the desire of Europeans to protect the position of their industry. See Ladas (1975).

[26] On the early developments which led to the split between the EPC and the Community Patent Convention see Otto Bossung n 3 above. Cf Convention for the European Patent for the Common Market (Community Patent Convention), OJ [1976] (L 17) 1; Agreement Relating to Community Patents, Dec 15 1989, 89/695/EEC [hereinafter, Community Patent Convention]. The Convention has been ratified only by seven out of twelve signatory states and is consequently not in force.

[27] Ullrich refers to this as a system 'in the shadow' of the European Patent Organisation. See Ullrich n 14.

currently into the pipeline, a few words are in order on the institutional features and governance design of the European Patent Organisation and the EPO.

The European Patent Organisation (hereinafter: the Organisation) has the structure of a classical intergovernmental organisation. It is based on an international treaty, the EPC, which must be interpreted in compliance with the Vienna Convention on International Treaties.[28] In accordance with the intergovernmental nature of the cooperation it establishes, the EPC may only be amended by a full diplomatic conference and in accordance with a complex procedure laid down in Article 172 EPC. Following this provision, the Convention may be revised by a Conference of the Contracting States at which three-quarters of the Contracting States are represented. For the adoption of a revised text there must be a majority of three-quarters of the represented and voting Contracting States, whereby abstentions are not considered a vote. A State that has not ratified or acceded to a revised text of the Convention ceases to be party to the EPC. Given the increasing number of Contracting States, Advocate General Jacobs' qualification of the revision procedure as 'very cumbersome' appears justified.[29] Revision of the articles of the EPC has so far been successfully accomplished only twice.[30]

3.1. Relationship with the Contracting States and with National Law: Harmonisation through Emulation

Being a traditional international law instrument, the relationship between the EPC and the national law of the Contracting States is determined under the constitutional law and doctrine of the respective State. Thus, in states following the dualist approach (eg UK and Sweden), international law becomes part of national law only after an express act of transposition, typically an act of Parliament. In terms of hierarchy, international law is in some states placed on equal level with domestic law. In contrast, in monist countries (eg Netherlands), international law becomes integral part of the law of the state by the very act of

[28] G Paterson, *The European Patent System, The Law and Practice of the European Patent Convention* (London, Sweet & Maxwell, 1992) pp 24 ff. On supranational elements in the structure of the Organisation and its financial autonomy see Martijn van Empel, *The Granting of European Patents* (Leyden, AW Sijthoff, 1975) p 27.

[29] See Opinion of AG Jacobs, delivered 14 June 2001 in C-377/98 *Netherlands v European Parliament and Council*, [2002] ECR I-7079, para 53.

[30] The second revision took place in 2000, when among others the rules for rule-making by the Administrative Council were amended. The planned revision by integrating the rules of the Biotech Convention into the text of the Convention notoriously failed. Ullrich, Patent Protection in Europe, n 14 above; see U Joos, 'Revisionen des Europäischen Patentubereinkommens' in Kur et al (eds), *Und sie bewegt sich doch!' – Patent Law on the Move, Festschrift für Gert Kolle und Dieter Stauder zum 65. Geburtstag,* n 6 above at p 429. The 2000 EPC entered into force on 13 December 2007 in all states that were members of the Organisation at that date. See X Buffet-Delmas, L Morelli, '*Modifications to the European Patent System*' (August 2008) 20(8) *Intellectual Property & Technology Law Journal* p 18.

ratification. Typically international law also takes precedence over conflicting national law. In between these two approaches there are a number of variations of and combinations between the two. In the light of these general principles, it becomes clear that the status of the EPC under national law differs depending on the member countries' constitutional traditions.

In contrast to the European Community/Union, the Organisation only has powers in a specific and well defined field of activity. Judging from the Preamble, the main objective of the EPC is to strengthen co-operation between the States of Europe in respect of the protection of inventions. Its more specific objective is to ensure that protection may be obtained in the Contracting States by a single procedure for the grant of patents and by the establishment of certain standard rules governing patents so granted. Needless to say these objectives are much more limited and specific than those of the European Union/Community. Moreover they indicate clearly that the intent of the founders has been to achieve uniformity (single procedure) only in the pre-grant phase of European patents, whereas to limit the influence of the EPC in the post-grant phase solely to 'certain standard rules', leaving the rest to the national patent law of the Contracting States.[31] Membership in the Organisation does not involve formal harmonisation of laws. The EPC established 'a system of law, common to the Contracting States, for the grant of patents for invention' (Article 1 EPC). Contacting States are only committed to accept a European patent issued by the EPO when it is granted for their territory and to treat it as a national patent.[32]

While ratification of the EPC does not bind the Contracting States to bring their national patent laws in conformity with the EPC, most of the States have actually amended their laws to achieve such conformity. This has, however, taken place chiefly by way of emulation and voluntary harmonisation.[33] An important impetus for harmonisation has been provided by Article 138 EPC, establishing common and binding grounds for revocation of European patents. Further vehicles for harmonisation may be seen in the proclivity of national courts to follow the decisions of the Boards of Appeal, probably due to the perceived high professional expertise and quality of the decisions of this body. More generally, the explanation for this much celebrated emulation effect lies partly in the desire of national law-makers to reduce transaction costs for local industry and local administration and judiciary that would otherwise ensue from the necessity of following two different sets of rules of national and European procedure.

[31] Paterson (1992), n 28 at p 25.

[32] Article 2 EPC 1973 'The European patent shall, in each of the Contracting States for which it is granted, have the effect of and be subject to the same conditions as a national patent granted by that State, unless otherwise provided in this Convention'. [EPC 2000 changed the language slightly.]

3.2. Internal Structure and Distribution of Competences

The European Patent Organisation has two main organs: the European Patent Office (EPO), which exercises executive functions and the Administrative Council, which according to its self-description on the Organisation's website 'exercises legislative powers on behalf of the Organisation, is responsible for policy issues relating to the Organisation and supervises the Office's activities.'[34] The Administrative Council of the EPO is composed by representatives of the contracting states. With only few exceptions, these are the Directors of the National Patent Offices, alternated by the Deputy-Directors or other high-ranking national officials at the National Patent Offices. In other words, the composition is highly specialised and confined to those most initiated in the patent profession.

3.3. Legislative and Rule-making Process

The European Patent Organisation has no formal legislative powers in the proper sense of the word, recognised as such in the text of the EPC.[35] However, probably because amendments to the articles of the Convention are so difficult, considerable powers have been vested in the Administrative Council. The Council can amend the Implementing Regulations of the Convention (Article 33(1) (b) EPC).[36] It is moreover competent to authorize the President of the EPO to negotiate and, with its approval, to conclude agreements on behalf of the Organisation, with States and with intergovernmental organisations (Article 33(4) EPC). With the latest revision of the EPC[37] the concentration of powers in the Administrative Council has been enhanced. This has been achieved following two main routes: first, the Council has been squarely declared competent to amend the text of the Convention, namely Parts II to VIII and Part X of the Convention, in order to bring them into line with an international treaty or EU legislation relating to patents. The second tool of empowerment has been the transfer of a number of provisions, in particular on procedure, from the text of the Convention into its Implementing Regulations[38], thus increasing the number

[33] See E Waage, 'Beyond the Harmonisation of Statute Law: Adapting the National Court's Exercise of Discretion to the Practice of the EPO' in Kur et al (Eds) *Festschrift für Gert Kolle und Dieter Stauder zum 65*, n 6 above at pp 487 ff.

[34] See http://www.epo.org/about-us/epo/legal-foundations.html.

[35] See however, in the decision of the EBA in the WARF case where the Administrative Council is called the EPO's legislator. *Wisconsin Alumni Research Foundation*, EPO, No G002/06 (Enlarged Board of Appeal of the European Patent Office 25 November 2008) at 14.

[36] Decision on such amendment can be taken with qualified majority of three-quarters of the votes of the Contracting States represented and voting, *cf* Art 35(2) EPC.

[37] EPC 2000, applicable from 13 December 2007.

[38] See Implementing Regulations to the Convention on the Grant of European Patents of 5 October

of issues within the legislative competence of the Council and simplifying the procedure for changing such rules.

The rule-making and legislative powers vested in the European Patent Organisation have not been the subject of much scholarly or political attention, but are indeed remarkable since they give the Organisation broad freedom in setting patent philosophy and economic policy in both the national and the European context, and since both governments and the EU have little control over the functioning of the EPO.[39] Only recently has certain criticism been voiced, chiefly in respect to the above-described additional delegation of legislative powers to the Administrative Council with the 2000 EPC revision, and in the context of the on-going debate over the future of the patent system in Europe.[40] It has rightly been pointed out that the decisions of the Administrative Council easily escape public scrutiny and democratic accountability given the prevailingly technocratic nature of the national representation in the Council through Heads of National Patent Agencies.[41]

This is well illustrated by the developments surrounding the much discussed take- over of the Biotech Directive of the EU by the EPO in the form of amendments to the Implementing Regulations of October 5, 1973. This transformation was carried out by way of a decision of the Administrative Council of June 16, 1999.[42] According to Rule 23 b (1) (now Rule 26(1)) Implementing Regulations to the EPC:

> For European patent applications and patents concerning biotechnological inventions, the relevant provisions of the Convention shall be applied and interpreted in accordance with the provisions of this chapter. Directive 98/44/EC of 6 July 1998 on the legal protection of biotechnological inventions shall be used as a *supplementary means of interpretation* (Emphasis added).

The legitimacy of this type of rule-making has rightly been questioned in the literature. Bossung wonders whether the executive was not 'overstepping its competence by assuming a legislative role or anticipating decisions which are the prerogative of the judiciary...'[43] Ullrich notes with regret the failure of the 2000 revision conference of the EPC to deal with the biotechnology issues since he also sees a

1973 as adopted by decision of the Administrative Council of the European Patent Organisation of 7 December 2006.

[39] P Leith, 'Harmonising European patent laws: Why so Little Call for a European Appellate System?' in P Craig and C Harlow (Eds) *Lawmaking in the European Union* (London/Cambridge: Kluwer, 1998) pp 511 ff, at 526. For the more detailed study, see P Leith, *Harmonisation of Intellectual Property in Europe: A Case Study of Patent Law* (London: Sweet & Maxwell, 1998).

[40] Ullrich n 14 above; See also interview with Dr Ingrid Schneider, n 15 above.

[41] Schneider, ibid.

[42] See Decision of the Administrative Council of 16 June 1999 amending the Implementing Regulations to the European Patent Convention OJ EPO 1999, p 437; cf Notice dated 1 July 1999 concerning the amendment of the Implementing Regulations to the European Patent Convention, The new provisions relating to biotechnological inventions OJ EPO 1999, p 573 for official commentaries.

[43] Bossung, n 3 above at p 14.

decision of the executive as democratically deficient.[44] Indeed, given that the implementing regulations of Article 164 EPC are characterised as being an integral part of the Convention, an amendment leading to substantial concretisation of major concepts of the Convention appears to represent 'legislation in disguise'.

The EPC has not been drafted with a view to substitute nor even to directly harmonise national patent laws of its member States. Quite to the contrary, differences in national law are acknowledged and accepted. In terms of international law, States parties to an international convention are only bound by the document they have ratified. Certainly further international treaties and agreements between the same parties can be used as means of interpretation of an earlier international treaty as pointed by Straus with reference to the Vienna Convention on the Law of International Treaties.[45] This should, however, rationally require the participation of all Contracting States to the original agreement in subsequent agreements.

Cumbersome procedures for amending the Convention have often been officially recognised as a decisive reason to make changes by way of amended Implementing Regulations. While acknowledging the practicality of the latter approach as a sort of a short-cut around lengthy processes of intergovernmental law-making, this does not compensate for its major deficiencies in terms of democratic legitimacy. Again, looking at the example of the Biotech Directive, the legitimacy of the legislative process should be questioned not least due to the divergent circle of states, participating in the elaboration of the Directive as part of EU law and those accepting the Directive as a source of interpretation of the EPC through a decision of the Administrative Council. At the time of drafting the Biotech Directive divergence may not have been perceived as a problem because of the overall overlap in membership of the two organisations. Yet, with the current thirty eight EPC Member States and a few more extension states and accession candidates, the EPC system comprises a number of countries, whose future membership in the EU is uncertain, to say the least.

Interestingly, while the Biotech Directive aroused heated debate in the EU and provoked controversies not only at the negotiating stage and drafting but also later on, at the stage of transposing the already-adopted text into national law, this decision of the Administrative Council does not seem to have attracted similar attention. The governmental representatives of countries such as the Netherlands and Italy, which challenged the Directive before the CJEU, and Germany, which delayed in implementing the Directive due to public opposition, had apparently no problem in voting for the incorporation of the Directive rules into the body text of the EPC.[46]

[44] See Ullrich, Patent Protection in Europe n 14 above at pp 433, 451, n 88.

[45] See J Straus, *Völkerrechtliche Verträge und Gemeinschaftsrecht als Auslegungsfaktoren des Europäischen Patentübereinkommens – Dargestellt am Patentierungsausschluss von Pflanzensorten in Artikel 53 (b)*, (1998) GRUR [Int], 1-15, p 2 on the applicability of the Vienna Convention on International Treaties to the EPC and the implications for the latter's interpretation.

[46] See ER Gold and A Gallochat, 'The European Biotech Directive: Past as Prologue' (September 2001) 7 *European Law Journal* p 331, about the eventuality of state parties to the EPO receiving

This may only underscore the difference in the nature of the EU and the European Patent Organisation as international organisations and the particular characteristics of decision-making in their institutions. Decision-making in the EU, despite the stark critique of democratic deficit, and partly as a result of this critique, is nowadays exposed to broad public debate and can in general be said to be reasonably transparent. Institutions like the European Parliament are part of the decision-making process and interest groups have access to the debate which goes through stages of Commission green papers, follow-up papers and political deliberations. By contrast, the work of the Administrative Council of the Organisation is much more insulated from public scrutiny. There are no institutionalised forms for involving the public in deliberations and no channel for effective communication with Member States legislatures.[47]

In a similar vein, if we look again at the example of the Biotech Directive, where the rules of the Directive were incorporated in the Implementing Rules of the Convention by a decision of the Administrative Council and applicable to non-EU countries that could not have possibly been involved in the negotiations surrounding the Directive, this legislation by the executive becomes all the more troublesome. Some of these countries are now indirectly bound by the provisions of the Biotech Directive, as interpreted by the EPO bodies, without ever offering their constituencies the possibility of participating in democratic deliberations on the controversial issues addressed in the Directive.

3.4. Administrative and Quasi-judicial Process

The grant of a European patent is a complex process which may go through several stages and involves numerous administrative and quasi-judicial bodies of the EPO.[48] Whereas all the departments are technically speaking part of the Office, the institutional and procedural rules show an attempt at securing the independence of the Boards of Appeal in view of their essentially judicial functions. In particular, in their decisions members of the Boards 'shall not be bound by any instructions and shall comply only with the provisions of this Convention' (Article 23).[49] Thus in many respects the Boards of Appeal meet

biotechnology patents issued by the EPO on the basis of the transposed rules of the Biotech Directive, even before the Directive was been implemented into national law.

[47] For a discussion on the need to ensure a greater degree of political, as opposed to technocratic (expert), representation of Member States on the Administrative Council see Schneider n 15 above at p 605.

[48] The departments charged with the procedure are the following: (a) a Receiving Section; (b) Search Divisions; (c) Examining Divisions; (d) Opposition Divisions; (e) a Legal Division; (f) Boards of Appeal; (g) an Enlarged Board of Appeal (Art 15 EPC).

[49] Cf Report from the Commission to the European Parliament and the Council, Development and implications of patent law in the field of biotechnology and genetic engineering, COM(2002) 545 final, [Not published in the OJ] p 7. Available at http://eur-lex.europa.eu/smartapi/cgi/sga_doc?smartapi!celexplus!prodDocNumber&lg=en&type_doc=COMfinal&an_doc=2002&nu_doc=545.

the requirements for an 'impartial tribunal' within the meaning of Article 6 ECHR.[50]

Nevertheless, there are a number of features in the present institutional design of the Boards that appear problematic from the point of view of independence. The position of the President of the EPO, who is administratively responsible for the management of the Boards but also with a right to nominate members of the Boards, is one example of an arrangement which undermines the confidence in the fairness of the system. [51] Another, in my view questionable, channel of influence of the President is provided by Article 11a of the Rules of Procedure of the Enlarged Board of Appeal[52], granting the EPO President a right to comment on questions of general interest which arise in the course of proceedings pending before the EBA. This can follow either upon the invitation of the Board or at the written, reasoned request of the President. This right was used by the President for instance in the hotly *contested* WARF case.[53]

Other points of criticism concern the poor transparency of the distribution plan for assigning cases to members of the Boards and the practice of appointing the Vice President of the EPO as Chairman of the EBA.[54] Interestingly, in contrast to other international courts such as the ECJ and the European Court of Human Rights (ECtHR) there are no rules on representation of Member States within the Boards of Appeal.[55] This probably reveals the wide-spread perception of the Boards as dealing with non-political technocratic work.[56]

The impasse on the question of independence is well-understood by the Organisation. A separate legislative initiative which is directed at securing greater autonomy for the Boards of Appeal is well under way. Following the current proposals dating from 2004 the goal is to secure an institutional separation of the Boards of Appeal from the Office, in order to bolster their judicial status and enhance the public confidence in their impartiality.[57] Whereas

[50] See Art 24 EPC on exclusion and objections. See also Peter Messerli, 'Die organisatorische Verselbständigung der Beschwerdekammern des Europäischen Patentamts' in Kur et al, *Festschrift für Gert Kolle und Dieter Stauder zum 65,* n 6 above at p 441.

[51] See Art 11(3) EPC. 'The members, including the Chairmen, of the Boards of Appeal and of the Enlarged Board of Appeal shall be appointed by the Administrative Council on a proposal from the President of the European Patent Office. They may be re-appointed by the Administrative Council after the President of the European Patent Office has been consulted'. *See* Messerli, n 50 *above*, at p 442. For a very thorough critical analysis of the institutional structure and procedure of the EPO in the light of due process requirements of Art 6 ECHR see C Holtz, *Due Process for Industrial Property: European Patenting under Human Rights Control* (Unpublished PhD dissertation, Stockholm University Handelshögsk, 2003).

[52] Version consolidating the amendments published in OJ EPO 1989, 362; OJ EPO 1994, 443, and in OJ EPO 2003, 58.

[53] See G 2/06 n 35 above, Comments by the President of the EPO.

[54] According to Holtz this practice creates a basic problem with regard to upholding the integrity of the BAs and to the protection of their independence. Holtz n 51 above at p 263.

[55] Ibid at p 253.

[56] For criticism of this perception see Schneider (2008) n 15 above.

[57] See Draft basic proposal for a revision of the EPC implementing the organisational autonomy of the Boards of Appeal of the European Patent Office within the European Patent Organisation.

nowadays the Boards of Appeal are integrated into the structure of the Office, forming Directorate General Three, the proposal envisages reforming the Boards of Appeal into a European Patent Appeals Court, largely autonomous from the Office.[58] According to the summary of this reform proposal found on the website of the Organisation, '[t]he Organisation would then have the three-way separation of powers typical of a state bound by the rule of law, into legislature, executive and judiciary, the latter being the new judicial body.'[59] It should be noted, however, that while the reform would certainly be a step in the right direction, it still leaves important questions of governance unaddressed. Importantly, for this reform to materialize it has to pass through the lengthy and cumbersome legislative machinery of the Organisation.

Finally, it deserves mentioning that the procedure governing the grant of individual patents includes the possibility of opposition and appeal. Any person may give notice of opposition to the European patent granted on the grounds laid down in the Convention[60] or submit third party observations according to Article 115 EPC without having to demonstrate an interest in the case. Oral proceedings can be held either at the instance of the EPO, or at the request of any party (Article 116 EPC). Proceedings before the Opposition Division and the Boards of Appeal are as a rule public.[61]

These procedural rules have provided rather generous access to the patent granting procedure, which has been intensely used by various political groups and NGOs in particular following the expansion of patent law in the sensitive sphere of biotechnology and life sciences. It is well known that already in the *Onco mouse* case the opposition was filed not by competitors but by political, religious and other non-governmental organisations such as the group of the Greens in the European Parliament, other ecological parties, associations for animal protection etc.[62] Likewise in the *Edinburgh* case opposition was filed by numerous religious and political NGOs.[63] In the *WARF* proceedings, in the words of the EBA 'numerous submissions were made by third parties, of which

Document CA/46/04, Munich, 28.05.2004. Available at http://documents.epo.org/projects/babylon/eponet.nsf/0/d962420980837159c125730d002c6579 $file/financial_statements_2007_en.pdf.

[58] Ibid at p 73 (Proposed Amendment to Article 21 (d) (1) Presidium shall function as an autonomous authority of the Court of Appeals).

[59] *Autonomy of the boards of appeal*. Available at http://www.epo.org/patents/law/legislative-initiatives/autonomy.html.

[60] See Art 99 EPC.

[61] Arts 116(4) and 128(4) EPC.

[62] See Ökologische Demokratische Partei, Fraktion Bündnis 90, Grüner Klub im Parlament, Fraktion Die Grünen im Bayrischen Landtag, Bundesverband der Tierversuchsgegner et al, British union for the abolition of vivisection, Evangelischer Stadtkirchenverband Köln, association 'No Patents on Life' etc.

[63] See Opposition in the Edinburgh patent EP 069531 proceedings by Greenpeace Deutschland, PDS-Budestagsfraktion, Ökomenischer Rad der Kirchen Österreich, Bundesrepublik Deutschland, Bundesministerium der Justiz, Alliance pour les droits de la vie, Bündnis 90, die Grünen, the Italian government. *See* Legal Status of EP0695351 (A1) 1996-02-07; EP0695351 (B1) 1999-12-08; EP0695351 (B2) 2008-10-29. Available at http://v3.espacenet.com/publicationDetails/inpadoc?CC=EP&NR=0695351A1&KC=A1&FT=D&date=19960207&DB=&locale=.

some were made in identical form by hundreds of individuals.'[64] This openness has been largely hailed as an important channel for influx of public interest and ethical considerations in the decision-making practice of the EPO.[65] Certainly, the active engagement of NGOs in the proceedings before the EPO has the important function of raising public awareness and sensitising decision-makers of the broad public policy and ethical implications of the patent system.[66]

At the same time, while participation and access have an undeniably positive impact, one should also be cautious about possible drawbacks in the context of quasi-judicial proceedings at the supranational level. Importantly, opening for political participation may have the effect of depriving the decision-making process within the EPO of one of the typical institutional advantages of judicial bodies, namely isolation from political and popular pressure.[67] At present there is no advisory body to the EPO to provide guidance on ethical or other non-patent issues possibly invoked in the granting procedure.[68] If one adds the already mentioned technocratic composition of the patent quasi-judiciary and the absence of mechanisms securing the balanced representation of Member States in it, the precarious position of the EPO can be easily appreciated. It may be surmised that in the absence of such expert guidance the numerous and lengthy considerations of third parties in the form of *amicus curia* briefs may have a non-negligible impact on the decision-making of the Boards on sensitive ethical issues. The participation in proceedings is however, only imperfectly representative and may create a distorted perception of the public opinion. The well studied dynamic of collective action suggests that vocal catalyst groups within broad and passive majorities may not always represent the real interests of the majority and may manipulate decision making to their own advantage.

To some extent, it appears that the accessibility of the opposition and appeal procedure under the EPC aggregates to compensate for some of the deficiencies in the institutional design of the Organisation, eg the poor democratic legitimacy and accountability of the rule-making process. Yet, participation in the judicial process follows a different logic and can hardly substitute democratic participation in legislative processes.

[64] EBA, G002/06, 10. A public hearing was also held on 24 June 2006 in the same proceedings.

[65] Schneider, n 15 above at p 595.

[66] One example is the embarrassing admission of the EPO of not having realized that the notion 'animal' in the Edinburgh patent, initially granted for among others method of preparing a transgenic animal, would in scientific English also encompass humans. See Schneider, n 15 above at p 593.

[67] See M Olson, *The Logic of Collective Action* (Cambridge, Mass.: Harvard University Press, 1965). N K Komesar (1994) *Imperfect Alternatives: Choosing Institutions in Law Economics and Public Policy* (Chicago: University of Chicago Press, 1994).

[68] Recommendation in this respect have been extended by the EGE Opinion No 16 as well as by scholars, see Schneider n 15 above, and G Van Overwalle, *Study on the Patenting of Inventions Related to Human Stem Cell Research,* European Group on Ethics in Science and New Technologies (Luxembourg, Office for Official Publications of the European Communities, 2002), 74. Available at http://ec.europa.eu/european_group_ethics/publications/index_en.htm.

All in all, despite the very significant role of the EPO in awarding private property rights with serious public policy implications, there are remarkably few procedural rules in the EPC governing the work of the relevant decision-making bodies.[69] The fact that the latest revision of the EPC moves some of the provisions on procedural matters from the Convention text to the Implementing Regulations seems to further indicate that the importance of such rules for securing the quality and democratic legitimacy of the work of the EPO is not fully appreciated.[70]

4. THE PROPOSED MERGER

Attempts to overcome the fragmented state of the European patent system predictably have been undertaken by both the EU and the European Patent Organisation. In 1999 the Organization set off a process of elaborating optional protocols to the EPC with the ultimate objective of putting in place a full-fledged intergovernmental patent judicial system. This reform catered mainly to the interests of industry in establishing a more effective, uniform and predictable judicial control of the post-grant phase of European patents and coping with notorious problems of forum shopping, torpedo litigations and similar anomalies. This process has so far resulted in two protocols: the London Agreement on languages signed in October 2000 and the European Patent Litigation Agreement (EPLA).[71] The EPLA ambitiously envisages the setting up of a new international organisation – the European Patent Judiciary (EPJ), comprised of a European Patent Court and an Administrative Committee. The Court would in turn consist of a starkly decentralised first instance (Regional Divisions and a Central Division) and a Court of Appeal. Regional Divisions would be set up upon request of individual Contracting States or groups of States, whereas the Central Division would be set up at the seat of the EPJ. The Appeal Court would be a central institution with guarantees of independence and impartiality sufficient to meet the requirements of a true judicial body.[72] Notably, the Draft Statute of the European Patent Court seeks to achieve balanced representation of Member States in the EPJ. Following Article 39 (2) of the Draft Statute of the European Patent Court, at least one legally qualified

[69] See Holtz n 51 above.

[70] Ullrich notes that the details conditioning submission of observations by third parties in the proceedings are now moved to the Implementing Regulations and could be changed only by a decision of the Administrative Council. See Ullrich n 14 above.

[71] The EPLA builds on two draft instruments: a Draft Agreement on the Establishment of a European Patent Litigation System (last draft of December 2005) and a Draft Statute on the European Patent Court. The draft instruments are available at http://www.epo.org/patents/law/legislative-initiatives/epla/latestdrafts.html last visited on 20 September 2010.

[72] G Artelsmair, 'A Comprehensive Patent System Needed for Europe' in Kur et al (Eds) *Festschrift für Gert Kolle und Dieter Stauder zum 65*, n 6 above at pp 5 ff, 25.

judge or assessor and one technically qualified judge or assessor from each Contracting State would initially be appointed to the Court of First Instance and the Court of Appeal.

Following the EPLA the jurisdiction of the European Patent Court would encompass infringement proceedings and revocation proceedings with the possibility of selective revocation. The competence of the Court is not planned to extend to opposition proceedings, the latter remaining within the ambit of the EPO's Boards of Appeal.[73] Interestingly, the Draft EPLA provides for the possibility of a preliminary reference to the CJEU in patent proceedings affecting patents for Member States of the European Union (Article 40 Draft Agreement). There seem to be no limitations on the issues which such reference may concern, but it should logically be confined to issues of interpretation of Community/EU law. This would possibly open an avenue of consulting the CJEU as to the interpretation of patent-related EU instruments (like the Biotech Directive), but again only in the post-grant phase. Despite relatively broad support among Member States for the EPLA, developments ground to a halt mainly because of EU concerns regarding the place of Community/EU patents in the system and the position of EU law.

In its turn the EU also kept pursuing the idea of an EU patent of a unitary nature valid in all the Member States of the European Union and a corresponding institutional structure to deal with the enforcement of such patent. After the failure of the Luxembourg Convention of 1975 renewed attempts to find a compromise solution were next undertaken in 2000, when the Commission submitted a proposal for a Regulation on the Community patent.[74] The proposal tried to achieve a 'symbiosis' between the European patent system of the EPC and a Community patent with unitary effect for the whole of the Community. It built on a two-tier approach. On the one hand a Regulation on the Community Patent was advanced, referring on most issues of substantive law basically to the EPC, and entrusting the EPO with the competence of granting the Community Patent.[75] An obvious prerequisite for this part of the proposal was the accession of the European Community to the EPC given the exclusive competence of the Community on certain issues.[76]

The second and more controversial tier envisaged channelling control over the post-grant phase of Community/EU Patents into a specialised Community Patent Court within the EU judicial system in order to ensure conformity with EU law

[73] The distribution of jurisdictional competences between the Regional Division is envisaged to follow the rules of the Brussels and Lugano Conventions and Community Regulation 44/2001, whereas direct revocation proceedings will be placed with the Central Division (Art 41(2) and (3) Draft Agreement).

[74] COM(2000) 412 final, 1.8.2000.

[75] Council Doc 10786/00 PI 49; 7119/04 PI 28; 9399/04 PI 42 containing a compromise solution proposed by the President of the Council on the Regulation and doc 7120/04 PI 29 – on a proposal for amendment of the EPC.

[76] Commission Staff working paper, A Community policy for the realization of the Community patent in the context of a revision of the European Patent Convention, Brussels, 7.5.2001, SEC(2001) 744.

and adequate judicial oversight.[77] This proposal was constitutionally prepared by amendments introduced by the Treaty of Nice, whereby Article 257 TFEU envisages the setting up of specialised judicial panels attached to the General Court with right of appeal on matters of fact to the General Court and right of appeal on matters of law to the CJEU. The proposal was criticized chiefly for its excessively centralistic character, the ensuing costs for SMEs and the threat it was seen to pose to national patent systems. The reform package was subject to several modifications by the Council[78] but was finally rejected at the Brussels Competitiveness Council on 17 and 18 May 2004 due to lacking consensus over a number of questions, including the soaring question of languages.[79]

The proposal that now lies on the negotiating table was initiated in 2009 when DG Internal Market with Commissioner McCreevy embarked on a 'last ditch' attempt to rationalise and restructure the highly disjointed patent system in Europe. After wide consultations with stake holders[80] in March 2009 the Commission issued a Recommendation urging the Council to authorise it to open negotiations for the adoption of a mixed Agreement setting up a Unified Patent Litigation System (UPLSA).[81] This time the proposal takes an integrated approach seeking a compromise between the institutional design advanced in the EPLA, on the one hand, and preserving the EU patent as a key objective, on the other.

The proposed patent litigation system builds on two instruments: (i) Draft Agreement on the European and Community Patents Court and (ii) Draft Statute of the Court.[82] The structure of the unified European patents court incorporates many of the features in the EPLA, notably the decentralised approach and ensuing proximity to users of the system, with local and regional divisions set up in Member States willing to host such divisions. Coherence

[77] Proposal for a Council Decision conferring jurisdiction on the Court of Justice in disputes relating to the Community patent, COM(2003)827 final; Proposal for a Council Decision establishing the Community Patent Court and concerning appeals before the Court of First Instance – COM(2003)828 final. Available at http://europa.eu/legislation_summaries/internal_market/businesses/intellectual_property/l26056a_en.htm.

[78] Proposed Community Patent Regulation as modified by the Council, 4 September 2003, Doc. 12219/03; 14130/03.

[79] See Council Doc 9586/04 of 15.06.2004. The delegations of Germany, France, Spain and Portugal voted against the proposal and the Italian delegation abstained.

[80] Enhancing the patent system in Europe, Communication from the Commission to the European Parliament and Council, 3.4.2007, COM(2007) 165 final. Available at http://eur-lex.europa.eu/LexUriServ/LexUriServ.do?uri=CELEX:52007DC0165:EN:NOT.

[81] Recommendation from the Commission to the Council, SEC (2009) 330 final, 20.3.2009. Available at http://ec.europa.eu/internal_market/indprop/patent/index_en.htm#system. See also Dietmar Harhoff, *Economic Cost-Benefit Analysis of a Unified and Integrated European Patent Litigation System*, 26.02.2009. Available at http://ec.europa.eu/internal_market/indprop/patent/index_en.htm#docs.

[82] See Council Doc 5072/09 Draft Agreement on the European and Community Patents Court and Draft Statute 8 January 2009 Available at http://register.consilium.europa.eu/pdf/en/09/st05/st05072.en09.pdf; cf Council Doc 7928/09 revised draft of the Presidency 23 March 2009. Available at http://register.consilium.europa.eu/pdf/en/09/st07/st07928.en09.pdf. Following the entry into force of the Lisbon Treaty, the title of the Court should be European and EU Patents Court. See

of interpretation is to be ensured by a central division, and a single appeal court, which however, in contrast to the 2004 proposal, is independent from the CJEU. The new unified patent judiciary is to assume jurisdiction over post-grant proceedings concerning both European patents under the EPC as well as the new EU patent, conceived as an IP title with unitary effect for the whole of the Union and granted and administered by the EPO. The proposal presupposes accession of the EU to the EPC and corresponding amendments to the Convention to enable the accession.

The European and Community Court Draft Agreement and Draft Statute set out a sophisticated procedure for nomination and appointment of judges involving an Advisory Committee with predominantly expert professional composition and a Mixed Committee with representatives of each Contracting Party.[83] The appointment of judges is, according to the proposal, to be based upon principles seeking to ensure competence, impartiality and integrity, but also balanced representation of the Contracting Parties. The principle of balanced geographical representation is explicitly stated as guiding the work of the Mixed Committee.[84] It is reiterated in the provisions on appointment of both the Court of First Instance (Article 6(1) Draft Agreement) and the Court of Appeal (Article 7(1) Draft Agreement). As noted by others, in particular the requirement of multinational composition of local divisions can contribute to 'invigorate the debate between legal traditions and to softly align differing traditions.'[85] Moreover, it indirectly acknowledges that patent litigation is not a purely technical matter, but involves sensitive law and policy making issues, where diversity of views across European states shall be taken seriously.

One of the challenges the European institutions are facing is obviously framing the relationship between the new specialised judiciary and the CJEU and, more generally ensuring a link between the EPC and EU law.[86] In the Commission recommendation of March 2009 and the most recent drafts of the Agreement on the Unified Patent Litigation System, the competence of the CJEU on issues of interpretation of EU law is safeguarded chiefly through a

Conclusions from the Competitiveness Council. See Council Doc 7928/09 at Annex Part I General and Institutional Provisions.

[83] See Arts 9, 57, 57b Draft Agreement, Council Doc 7928/09.

[84] See Art 3(3) Draft Statute of the European and Community Patent Court: '[w]hen [...] appointing judges, the [...] Mixed Committee shall ensure a balanced composition of the Court on as broad geographical basis as possible among nationals of the Contracting States.'

[85] See Art 6 (1) Any panel of the Court of First Instance shall have a multinational composition. ...', Draft Agreement on the European and Community Patents Court and Draft Statute, Council Doc 7928/09. For a positive assessment see T Jaeger, R Hilty, J Drexl, H Ullrich, 'Comments of the Max Planck Institute for Intellectual Property, Competition and Tax Law on the 2009 Commission Proposal for the Establishment of a Unified European Patent Judiciary' (2009) 40 *IIC* pp 817–838.

[86] The Community patent is governed by the EPC (see Recital 4a Draft Regulation on Community Patent), but given the planned accession of the Community to the EPC the latter essentially becomes part of the Community *acquis* and can be interpreted by the CJEU (see Recital 4a).

preliminary reference procedure.[87] It is noteworthy that according to an earlier draft of November 2008, a more far-reaching possibility for cassation procedure before the CJEU (petition on further appeal on points of law) was proposed.[88] Such procedural avenue is now only included in the procedural issues still to be discussed. Nevertheless, relying on a preliminary reference procedure can be considered a good point of balance between requirements of ensuring the primacy and uniform interpretation of EU law, on the one side, and efficiency on the other.[89]

5. CRITICAL ASSESSMENT

The new proposal seems to enjoy wide-spread political support.[90] In many respects it represents a significant step forward, advancing a flexible institutional design, trying to build on existing synergies and combining the advantages of the two institutional entities. Yet there are a number of unresolved issues that may require further consideration from the point of view of governance.

In terms of *legislative process*, as mentioned above it is agreed that the EU patent will build extensively on the European Patent Convention. In this the European Union can certainly rely on an instrument approved in conventional procedure for international agreements and tested through a long lasting implementation and adjustment. Nevertheless, despite its seeming technocratic nature and political neutrality, patent law is an important element in innovation policy which requires not infrequent adjustments to both technological and political realities. This was vividly illustrated by the debate on patenting biotechnology where the patentability of gene sequences and of embryonic stem cells, to take just a few examples, wrecked substantial political havoc in certain Member States and political constituencies in the EU. It may be questioned to what extent the European Patent Convention with its heavy ratification

[87] 'The Court of Justice of the European Communities would rule on preliminary questions asked by the court structure established in the framework of the Unified Patent Litigation System on the interpretation of EC law and on the validity and interpretation of acts of the institutions of the Community', see Recommendation, SEC (2009) 330 final, 10. See Council Doc 5072/09 Draft Agreement on the European and Community Patents Court and Draft Statute; cf Council Doc 7928/09 revised draft of the Presidency. See in particular Art 48 Draft Agreement and Art 37 Draft Statute.

[88] See Council Document 14970/08, 8.11.2008 on Draft Agreement on the European Union Patent Court and Draft Statute, Art 48 Draft Agreement, Ch IV Procedural Provisions, Draft Statute.

[89] See in this sense Jaeger et al n 85 above ; For a comprehensive analysis of the Draft Agreement and Draft Statute in light of European Union Law see Thomas Jaeger, 'The European Patent: Qui Bono et Quo Vadit?' (2010) 47 *Common Market Law Review* pp 63–115.

[90] See Council Competitiveness Meeting of 5–6 March 2009, Press release 7216/09. In this contributions I deliberately do not address the question of languages, which remains a major stumbling block. See more recently steps to break the stalemate by using the 'enhanced cooperation procedure', European Parliament, legislative resolution of 15 February 2011, P7_TA-PROV(2011)0054.

machinery will be able to keep pace with such developments? Conversely, if the European Union through its more dynamic decision-making process introduces changes in carved-out areas of patent law, there may be a growing risk of 'back-door' legislation by administrative decisions of the Administrative Council, incorporating EU law in the texture of the EPC. This, in turn, may raise concerns about legality and legitimacy for those states parties to the Convention which are not members of the Union.[91]

In terms of *administrative and judicial process*, both the EPLA and the newly proposed Unified European Patent Judiciary are directed at the post-grant phase of European and Community patents. The objective is to put an end to multiple-forum litigation on infringement and invalidity and on diverging national interpretations of the EPC. This limitation implies that both proposals leave untouched the granting phase of European patents and the institutional modalities framing the work of the EPO bodies. Moreover, following the Proposal for a Council Regulation on the Community patent,[92] the EPO will be entrusted with the administration of the unitary EU patent. Given the shortcomings in the procedural and institutional rules framing the work of the EPO bodies outlined above, including insufficient guarantees of independence and adequate representation, these deficiencies in the governance of the EPO may affect the EU patent as well. There may therefore be an urgent need to press forward the reform toward autonomy of the Boards of Appeal. Additional review of the institutional design of the examining and opposition bodies of the Office may also be in order.

Importantly, none of the proposals opens an avenue for control by the ECJ of the decisions of the EPO on granting or refusing to grant European or EU patent. In an early Commission Staff Working Paper, the Commission opined:

> The Convention already contains a judicial system which provides legal certainty for the parties. By acceding to the Convention, the Community accepts its system of appeals, as the Member States have already done. It is neither necessary nor appropriate to lodge subsequent appeals against decisions of the Office. Moreover, direct appeals against decisions by the Office would lead to a proliferation of appeal bodies and an unnecessary increase in the workload of the Community court. Nor is it clear whether it would be possible to introduce a system of appeals before the Community court without further amending the EC Treaty.[93]

Apparently building on this assessment, the jurisdiction of the proposed European and EU Patent Court is limited solely to infringement and revocation

[91] See also Draft Art 14a (3) requiring non-EU Member States to bring their legislation in line with the EU acquis in the area of Patent Law. This provision is one indication that the reform will result in a considerable shift of power toward the EU.

[92] See Council Doc 16113/09 of 27 November 2009. Available at http://register.consilium.europa.eu/pdf/en/09/st16/st16113-ad01.en09.pdf

[93] Commission Staff Working Paper, A Community policy for the realisation of the Community patent in the context of a revision of the European patent convention, Brussels, 7.5.2001, SEC(2001) 744, at 5.

proceedings, leaving the decisions of the EPO outside the scope of jurisdiction of the Court. While all proposals recognize the need for consistent interpretation of EU law, somewhat paradoxically, no procedural and institutional channel for achieving the desired consistency between the EPO and EU is ensured. Thus, an earlier draft proposal for revision of the EPC to accommodate the new EU initiatives instructs the EPC bodies to take due account of Community law and in particular of Community provisions of identical content as the EPC.[94] The CJEU is, however, not given the possibility to be the final arbiter as to the interpretation of EU law, nor even to answer questions of interpretation of EU law in a preliminary fashion.

Particularly problematic under this institutional arrangement appear to be situations, as in the case of embryonic stem cell patents, in which the Office rejects patent applications based upon grounds of interpretation from what was originally an EU legislative instrument. Clearly, if no patent is granted, invalidity or infringement proceedings are foreclosed and there is no avenue left for the disgruntled party. This may be against well-established general principles of EU law such as rule of law and right of judicial review. A recent analysis of the CJEU case law on EU external relations demonstrates convincingly that the principles of rule of law and effective judicial review of administrative acts are seen by the CJEU as important preconditions for accepting a transfer of administrative power from a EU to a non-EU body.[95] In this light, there may be serious legal obstacles to proceeding with the proposal.

The benevolent opinion of the Commission about the EPO 'judicial system' cited above appears *prima facie* to be based on efficiency considerations. Yet at a closer look it reveals a more fundamental problem. Since the EU patent will be granted by the bodies of the EPO and on the basis of the EPC, opening for such control by the CJEU would essentially mean bringing the EPO under the jurisdiction of the Community court. This institutional subjugation is certainly a source of controversy and of constitutional conundrums. This notwithstanding, it is submitted that if one wants to achieve a fully satisfactory institutional solution for the European patent system, a link to the CJEU should be established at the granting and opposition stages.[96]

[94] See Art 24a Consistent interpretation: With regard to the interpretation and application of this Convention, the European Patent Office shall take due account of the principles deriving from any judgement of the Court of Justice of the European Communities concerning the interpretation of this Convention or of such provisions of Community law which are identical in substance to the provisions of this Convention. See also proposed Article 149a which stipulates that the Administration Division for the Community Patent of the EPO and the Select Committee of the Administrative Council shall pay particular attention to the established body of Community law in relation to patents, notably the Biotech Directive. Council Doc. 10958/03, 27.6.2003 Presidency Proposal, Revision of the European Patent Convention. The latest proposal by the Council for amendment of the EPC is from 21.11.2003 but is not publicly available, see Council Doc 15088/03.

[95] See Jaeger n 85 at p 110.

[96] See Bakardjieva Engelbrekt n 8 *above*. Holtz notes critically the lack of co-ordination between the two stages of patent procedure, patenting and patent litigation, Holtz, n 51 at pp 523 ff. For

In May 2009 a request was filed with the ECJ for an Opinion under Article 218 TFEU on the compatibility of the draft Agreement with the EC Treaty (now TFEU).[97] Whereas the final word of the ECJ is not said yet, in July 2010 the Advocates General came with their Joint Opinion in the Case.[98] The Opinion is still not officially published, but its text in French and the summary of conclusions in English can be found on the Internet. From the text of the Opinion it is evident that at least some of the considerations put forward in this article have also been a matter of concern for the Advocates General.

According to the Opinion the guarantees contained in the draft Agreement for ensuring full application and respect of the primacy of the European Union law by the European and Community Patents Court are insufficient. The AGs also find insufficient, the remedies available in case of breach of the European Union law by the European and Community Patents Court and in case of failure to comply with its obligation of reference for a preliminary ruling pursuant to Article 48, paragraph 1, of the draft Agreement. (Paragraphs 104 to 115 of the Opinion).

Finally, the Opinion confirms that the lack of recourse to the CJEU for parties to administrative litigation proceedings of the EPO is incompatible with EU law, and more specifically with the need to ensure an effective court control and a correct and uniform application of European Union law. The Opinion notes as particularly problematic the blocking effect in the case of rejecting patentability with express reference to the *WARF* case.[99] All in all, the Advocates General conclude that the Draft Agreement, read in the light of all measures contemplated in the matter of patents, does not meet the need to ensure effective judicial control and a correct and uniform application of European Union law in administrative litigation relating to the grant of Community patents (see paragraphs 68 to 75 of the Opinion).

interesting proposals for improvement of the European Patent system see G Van Overwalle and J Schovsbo, 'Policy options for the improvement of the European Patent System' (2007) 38 *International Review of Intellectual Property and Competition Law* p 834.

[97] See Council Doc 9549/09 PI 38; cf Doc 9076/09 Request for an opinion by the European Court of Justice on the compatibility with the EC Treaty of the envisaged Agreement creating a unified patent litigation system. Partially Accessible version available at http://register.consilium.europa.eu/pdf/en/09/st09/st09076.en09.pdf

[98] See Opinion 1/09 of 2 July 2010. Available at http://www.eplawpatentblog.com/2010/August/2010-07-02_Opinion_AG_FR%5B1%5D.pdf

[99] See Opinion 1/09, para 68: 'Il convient de vérifier, en second lieu, s'il n'aurait pas nécessaire d'inclure dans les compétences de la future JB un volet sur le contentieux administratif. Ce contentieux concerne notamment les recours contre l'OEB introduits par des enterprises ayant demandé sans succès, qu'un brevet leur soit délivré, ainsi que les recours des tiers ayant fait sans succès opposition contre la délivrance d'un brevet'.

6. CONCLUDING REFLECTIONS

The two visions of Europe still plague European institutional architecture, not only in the field of human and fundamental rights, but also in the field of innovation and technology governance. The advantages of an intergovernmental approach within narrowly-defined spheres of cooperation were unquestioned in post-war Europe. At that juncture many states were reluctant to transfer more of their sovereignty to supranational bodies and institutions. Certainly, in the area of patenting the intergovernmental approach represented by the European Patent Organisation and the EPC has been an overwhelming success. Its attraction still holds, given the inconclusive state of European integration. Yet a closer look at the governance of the European Patent Organisation suggests that despite the intergovernmental character of the cooperation taking place within the auspices of the Organisation, a substantial transfer of sovereignty from the Contracting States to the Organisation is in fact taking place in the area of innovation policy and technology governance. More importantly, buried in the seeming technicalities of patenting rules and procedures, this transfer of sovereignty has remained largely outside public scrutiny and has not always been backed by institutional mechanisms required to ensure democratic control and public oversight of the work of the Organisation.

The path to integration taken by the Member States of the European Union is considerably more complex and demanding and its evolution has been far from unproblematic. However, in the gradual process of interlocking national economies and polities, the Union institutions, notably the CJEU, have elaborated sophisticated principles governing the relations of the Union with its constituent Member States (eg enumerated powers, subsidiarity and proportionality), as well as elaborate rules on participation in the legislative process. These principles ensure that Member States shall not surrender more of their sovereign legislative powers than needed for the achievement of the objectives of the Union. The CJEU, operating as guardian of the Treaty is carefully designed to ensure competence, independence and fair representation of the Member States of the Union. It is in constant dialogue with national courts thus adjusting the division of decision-making competences to changing political and social conditions.

The patent reform that is currently underway in Europe aims to bridge the gap between the two forms of European cooperation and to establish closer institutional ties between the EU and the EPO. The proposal for a Unified European Patent Judiciary launched at the Competitiveness Council in December 2009 is characterized by pragmatism and flexibility. It seeks, through inventive institutional design, to achieve interlinking between the two organisations, while preserving their institutional integrity and actively involving national patenting institutions. This pragmatism is generally to be acclaimed. Institutional trajectories and lock-ins are tenacious but they can, and should, be broken if evidence of inefficiency is overwhelming. At the same time, for Contracting States, accession of the Union to the European Patent Organisation and a uniform patent judiciary may imply further loss of regulatory powers in the sphere of innovation and technology policy. For this step to be accepted, the institutional architecture of the reformed patent system needs to be carefully scrutinized, and guarantees for access, representation and due process must be available at all levels. The momentum for reform should be used to look more broadly at issues of governance and to improve the level of accountability, openness and public involvement in the multilevel patenting system in Europe.

3
The Swedish Doctrine of Equivalence

PROFESSOR BENGT DOMEIJ

1. INTRODUCTION

Patent claims are single sentences found at the end of the patent document statutorily charged with the task of defining the patented invention (Article 69 European Patent Convention[1] (EPC) and Section 39 Swedish Patent Act). During the prosecution of an application the claims are refined in communications between the examiner and the applicant. That is only one part of the determination of the scope of protection accorded by the claims. The patent's worth also depends on the possibility of an alternative to a stated feature in a patent claim. Such an alternative may allow competitors to avoid the literal wording of the patent by substituting a feature in the claim. This will usually result in a rapid diminution of the value of the patent. However, one exception to the rule that a patent can be avoided by a departure from the 'semantic' meaning of the claim exists under Swedish law on claim interpretation. If an alternative is deemed equivalent to the feature in the claim it constitutes an infringement under the doctrine of equivalence. Needless to say, the doctrine is of considerable practical importance to patent law practitioners and technology-based firms.

Theoretically there should be a unified European approach to patent claim interpretation. Article 69 of the EPC provides that the claims determine the scope of patent protection and that the patent description may be used as an aid in interpreting the claims. The Protocol on the Interpretation of Article 69 EPC adds that the claims shall neither be interpreted literally nor treated as mere guidelines for the scope of protection. Additional efforts were made to harmonize European claim interpretation in the revision that goes by the name

[1] Convention on the Grant of European Patents (European Patent Convention) of 5 October 1973 as revised by the Act revising Art 63 EPC of 17 December 1991 and the Act revising the EPC of 29 November 2001.

of EPC 2000[2] and came into force on 13 December 2007. A new second article was added to the Protocol with the heading 'Equivalents'. It reads:

> For the purpose of determining the extent of protection conferred by a European patent, due account shall be taken of any element which is equivalent to an element specified in the claims.

The reference to 'any element which is equivalent to an element specified in the claims' echoes the doctrine of equivalents with its long history in patent law. This is not a complete solution to the problem. The new provision only prescribes that 'due account' is to be taken of equivalent elements.

No unified doctrine of equivalence exists, but there are similarities, of course, in all formulations of claim interpretation.[3] Some countries, notably the UK, do without a doctrine of equivalence separate from the skilled person's construction of the meaning of the claim.[4] This is not the case in Sweden, where it is considered that there is a meaningful distinction to be made, even in the context of interpreting the patent as a whole, between a skilled person's normal literal/technical understanding of a claim feature, and the additional protection sometimes available to a patentee under the doctrine of equivalence. My purpose in this article is to set out the development of the Swedish approach to the doctrine of equivalence. These developments are found almost exclusively in case law and accordingly, the most important Swedish cases by the Stockholm District Court, the Svea Court of Appeal and the Swedish Supreme Court will be discussed and analysed. These courts have exclusive jurisdiction in Sweden over cases on patent infringement, and the centralization has resulted in the accumulation of experience in this specialist field of law and, more importantly for this article, the development of a distinct Swedish approach to the doctrine of equivalence.

2. STARTING-POINT – REJECTION OF THE GENERAL INVENTIVE CONCEPT

The second sentence of the first article in the Protocol to Article 69 EPC bars a claim interpretation restricted to a perception of what the patent proprietor contemplated. The Protocol states that Article 69 EPC 'should [not] be taken

[2] See Art 3(2) of the 2001 Revisions of EPC.2000. Administrative Council of the European Patent Organisation decision of 28 June 2001 OJ EPO 2001, Special edition No 4, p 55.

[3] See Pumfrey et al, 'The Doctrine of Equivalents in Various Patent Regimes – Does Anybody Have It Right?' (2009) 11 *Yale Journal of Law & Technology* p 261.

[4] 'Equivalence as a guide to construction. Although article 69 prevents equivalence from extending protection outside the claims, there is no reason why it cannot be an important part of the background of facts known to the skilled man which would affect what he understood the claims to mean. That is no more than common sense. It is also expressly provided by the new article 2 added to the Protocol by the Munich Act revising the EPC, dated 29 November 2000'. Lord Hoffman in *Kirin-Amgen Inc v Transkaryotic Therapies Inc No 2*, [2004] UKHL 46.

to mean that the claims serve only as a guideline and that the actual protection conferred may extend to what, from a consideration of the description and drawings by a person skilled in the art, the patent proprietor has contemplated.' Some believe this to be a repudiation of an old German approach to claim interpretation based on the notion of a general inventive concept. However, that would probably be a caricature of the former German approach.[5]

The rejection of a claim interpretation based on an amorphous general inventive idea also forms the starting-point for the post-EPC Swedish approach. The claim interpretations of today can be derived from case-law developments starting with *Lännen Tehtaat Oy v Svedbro Smide Aktiebolag* which saw the debut of a critical view towards a doctrine of equivalence based on the notion of a general inventive idea devised by the inventor.

Stockholm District Court held that the defendant infringed a patent on a mechanical tool under the doctrine of equivalence.[6] The chief reason put forward was that the general inventive idea of the patent (how a pedal was used in operating a planting tool) had been used in the accused object. This similarity trumped the fact that there were three differences between the patent claims and the accused device held to be infringing. The Court held that the skilled person could have substituted the unfulfilled claim features by the features in the accused device. Svea Court of Appeal, however, held that there was no infringement.[7] The Court referred to the Swedish provision on scope of protection being identical to Article 69 EPC and stated that an infringement analysis must assume that patent protection is limited to the claims. Svea Court of Appeal agreed with the District Court that the operation of the pedal was the novel and inventive aspect in the invention (the same general inventive idea was used) and that a skilled person could by applying her skills have overcome the differences between the claims and the accused product. Nevertheless, the applicant had set out a certain design in the claims, even though it must have been apparent that the inventive idea could have been used in alternative ways. Svea Court of Appeal emphasized the notice function of the claims and the importance of legal certainty for third parties. A patent was not to be interpreted on the basis of a general inventive idea, largely unrestricted by the wording of the claim. Such an interpretation would unduly burden competitors moving into the technical field of the patent who sought a new solution to the problem solved by the patentee (in one way).

Swedish case law was thus set in motion, in common with many other European countries, most notably Germany, into a gradual departure from assuming a

[5] Lord Hoffman described the 'claims as guidelines' approach as a caricature of the former German approach to scope of protection. See *Kirin-Amgen Inc v Transkaryotic Therapies Inc No 2*, [2004] UKHL 46.

[6] Stockholm District Court, *Lännen Tehtaat Oy v Svedbro Smide Aktiebolag*, case No T 7-92-85, 11 March 1987.

[7] Svea Court of Appeal, *Lännen Tehtaat Oy v Svedbro Smide Aktiebolag*, case No T 356/87, 7 October 1988.

general inventive idea.[8] That approach seems to stretch the forbidden field too far and endangers legal certainty. Svea Court of Appeal firmly established that claim limitations cannot easily be disregarded, even if a person skilled in the art realizes that the usefulness of the invention is not delimited according to the claims.

3. FACTORS LIMITING EQUIVALENCE – THE SWEDISH MODEL

The departure from an interpretive doctrine based upon a general inventive concept for determining the scope of protection under the doctrine of equivalence immediately leads to a new difficulty. Inevitably some feasible alternatives to the patent claims that the skilled person can identify are equivalents, while others are not. The question is how to separate one from the other. Swedish courts have dealt with this dilemma by identifying a number of criteria that rein in the scope of protection that would otherwise arise from an unencumbered doctrine of equivalence. Certain factors or circumstances in a dispute prevent the scope of protection from being stretched beyond the literal/technical wording of the claims. The Swedish model is to restrain use of a general inventive idea by identifying circumstances binding the patentee to the precise claim wording. An example of this reasoning can be found in *Aventis Pharma v Bristol Myers Squibb*, decided by Stockholm District Court:

> An issue that the parties in this case have presented their views on is the possibility of awarding a patent a scope of protection beyond its immediate wording, an issue often addressed under the heading equivalence. European legal systems have approached this question from different angels. At the moment there seems to be unity in so far as that there is a scope for including equivalents, however the reach and also the methods for applying the doctrine of equivalence remain unclear. ... Some factors should under all circumstances be considered. The state of the art at the application day limits the reach of the scope of protection. The capacity of the person skilled in the art is a factor in the application of the doctrine of equivalence. And in the same vein, a departure from the patent claims, which in itself constitutes a patentable invention, will not be included in the scope of protection under the doctrine of equivalence.[9]

[8] German case law moving away from the use of a general inventive idea has been described by von Drathen: '[I]n the three judgments of the 'quintet', the Federal Supreme Court relates the third Schneidmesser question to the 'responsibility of the patentee' explicitly [citation omitted]. The passage makes clear that the patent specification is an expression of intent by the patentee concerning the protection he wants, and that it is interpreted from the (objectifying) position of a competing inventor who is entitled to rely on the meaning communicated to him. Thus, if the patentee does not formulate the patent claim wide enough to reflect the entire technical content of the invention, a later clarification by him will not permit the courts to grant this protection to him. Article 69 prevents the courts from using a wording-detached 'general inventive idea' [citation omitted] to help the patentee. This reflects the balance of fairness to the patentee and legal certainty for third parties as required by PIA69 [Protocol on the Interpretation of Article 69 EPC]' (footnotes to cases from the Bundesgerichtshof have been excluded from the quote). See C von Drathen, 'Patent Scope in English and German Law Under the European Patent Convention 1973 and 2000' (2008) 39 *IIC* p 384 (409).

[9] *Aventis Pharma v Bristol Myers Squibb*, Stockholm District Court, case T 5761-99 of 31 May 2002.

Case law reveals that Swedish courts have identified seven limiting factors that bar the scope of protection from extending past the literal wording: 1. the invention was a simple adaptation of a known technology; 2. the feature not present in the accused device has been labelled as an important element of the invention in the patent; 3. the invention and the accused product serve different purposes (solve different technical problems); 4. the accused product leads to an improvement over the patented invention; 5. the capacity of the skilled person would not have been sufficient to allow him to substitute the feature in the patent claim with the corresponding feature in the accused product; 6. stretching the scope of protection under the doctrine of equivalence would overlap with the state of the art on the application day of the patent; and, 7. a deliberate limitation of the feature has taken place during the patent examination process. The technique of identifying situations where there is no recourse to the doctrine of equivalence is believed to allow Swedish courts to substitute a middle ground between use of a general inventive concept and a strict literal interpretation of the claims. The above-listed enumeration of circumstances is similar to claim interpretations used in other European countries based upon questions such as whether or not the same technical problem is solved by the patented invention and the accused embodiment. I call these 'limits' or 'circumstances' because they have not been framed as questions in Swedish case law. Nevertheless, their function under the enumerated circumstances is the same as the questions.

An important issue though, is what scope this Swedish practice leaves for the doctrine of equivalence? Do the seven reasons for not applying the doctrine of equivalence arise frequently in infringement situations? If that is the case, then there can rarely be any protection beyond the wording of the claims. On the other hand, if the seven circumstances do not occur frequently there would normally be a scope of protection stretching beyond the claims. I shall attempt to answer the question at the conclusion of this article.

4. THE LEADING SWEDISH CASE – DELAVAL V LELY

A patent on a robot for milking free-ranging cows led, on 10 March 2008 to a ruling of infringement by the Svea Court of Appeal, in *DeLaval v Lely*, clarifying and confirming the previous case law on the doctrine of equivalence. *DeLaval* can be seen as a culmination of many years of practice starting with *Lännen Tehtaat Oy v Svedbro Smide Aktiebolag*. The claim in suit read, in relevant part, '... if a pre-determined time has passed since the cow in question was milked ... a milking operation would be initiated by the robot'. The purpose of the feature was to determine that the robot would not initiate a milking operation on a cow approaching the robot, unless a certain span of time had passed since milking the same cow last.

This was the second infringement case between the same parties concerning the robot patent. The first litigation resulted in a ruling on 8 March 2002 by

Svea Court of Appeal and forms a necessary background for the later case. The accused product in the first litigation was a milking robot in which the time span during which the robot was prevented from milking the cow was determined by an algorithm where the time period was calculated in hours and minutes but also with regard to how much the cow had been eating. If the algorithm indicated that a cow would yield more than a certain number of litres of milk it permitted the robot to milk the cow. Svea Court of Appeal ruled that this solution fell within the terms of the claim. 'Pre-determined time' did not have to be interpreted as fixed exclusively in hours and minutes. A pre-determined time could be dependent on inputs other than clock time. In such a case the Svea Court of Appeal ruled that it was still pre-determined by the algorithm. The court specifically mentioned that a broad claim interpretation was justified in this case, taking into account the considerable technical progress made by the inventor in designing the milking robot.

After being deemed an infringer, the defendant, Lely introduced a new version of the robot which initiated further litigation. The new product had a setting that allowed a cow to be milked if a certain percentage of the other cows in the herd had been milked, since the same cow had been milked the last time. Lely held its own patent on this milking criterion. Under the new Lely patent the farmer would decide on the percentage of the herd that had to be milked before one cow could be milked a second time. This solution was also primarily aimed at preventing too frequent milking operations, but the difference was that Lely's criterion was now dependent on the entire herd of animals while the prior criterion was determined individually for each cow. Both Stockholm District Court and Svea Appeal Court found a difference between the literal/technical meaning of the claim feature 'pre-determined time' and the solution employed in the accused product, ie 'counting cows until a certain percentage had been milked'. The redesigned robot used no pre-determined time in the sense that the skilled person would interpret this claim feature after having read the content of the patent specification.

DeLaval, however, argued that the new robot infringed its patent under the doctrine of equivalence. Stockholm District Court ruled:

> The Court of Appeal held in the previous case between the parties that there were grounds for a broad determination of the scope of protection because the patent in suit represents a considerable technical advance. ... As far as [the doctrine of equivalence and] the claim feature 'a pre-determined time', the Court finds ... that it is clear to a skilled person that the aim of the feature is to prevent milking operations occurring too frequently. The accused embodiment must be seen as having the same purpose. The solution to this problem in Lely's product entails a decision when a cow enters the milking boot on whether it should be permitted to be milked by a calculation based on the number of milking operations performed in the herd since the cow in question was last milked. Even if the length of the interval may vary depending on how often or seldom the cows have been milked during the last 24 hours and how long each milking operation has taken, the effect achieved by the Lely design is that a minimum duration passes between the milking of one and the same cow. With this background it is, in the

> opinion of the District court, obvious that the purpose of the Lely design is the same as that of the invention.
>
> Lely has also argued that their milking criterion entails advantages in comparison to the solution in the patent. Lely did in this regard emphasis that their criterion adapts to the behaviour of the herd which may vary depending on eg the weather conditions. Another advantage put forward by Lely is that its method of determining if a cow is to be milked entails that the cows will always be milked in the 'correct' order, which will be important in case of a technical break-down. The possible advantages gained by Lely's design over the solution according to the patent cannot be considered to be of a magnitude that would lead to the conclusion that the Lely milking criterion achieves a different functional result than with the solution in the patent in suit. The result, irrespective of the solution, is that the cow will be milked at a time when the cow has sufficient milk in the udder. Lely's design must therefore been seen as equally suitable as the invention according to the patent.
>
> According to the determination by the District Court the feature 'a pre-determined time' in patent claim 1 cannot, on the basis of the purpose of the invention being to prevent too frequent milking operations, have such decisive significance for the patentability of the invention that the scope for an application of the doctrine of equivalence should be limited for this reason. Nor has it been concluded that DeLaval introduced the feature 'a pre-determined time' in order to delineate the invention against the state of the art or in any other way intentionally limit the scope of protection. Lely's milking equipment must on these grounds be concluded to fall within the scope of the patent. The motion brought by DeLaval shall therefore be granted.

The Stockholm District Court held that the accused milking robot infringed under the doctrine of equivalence. The judgment was appealed to Svea Court of Appeal, which essentially agreed with the lower court. Lely argued that an important difference was that in the operation of their product it was unknown at the time of one milking operation when the cow could be milked the next time. However, this argument did not sway the Court of Appeal which held that:

> The arguments presented before the Court of Appeal do not lead to a different assessment than the one made by the District court. To what has been said by the District court the following can be added. When determining if Lely's milking criterion falls literally within the feature 'if a pre-determined time has elapsed' in DeLaval's patent it is in the view of the Court of Appeal not decisive if the time that shall elapse between the milking according to DeLaval's milking criterion is calculated – or can be calculated – already at the time a certain cow is milked, or if the calculation is only performed at the time a cow returns for a possible new milking. For interpreting the literal meaning of the claim and the accused milking criterion it is, however, not insignificant that DeLaval's feature (irrespective of the time when the calculation occurs) is related to whether a sufficient time has elapsed, while the decisive factor in Lely's milking criterion is whether a sufficient number of milking operations have been performed.
>
> With regard to the algorithm used in Lely's milking criterion [a witness for Lely] stated in the Court of Appeal inter alia that animal owners themselves chose a value so that the calculation should fit the number of times a day that the cow is to be

> milked: if the animal owner eg wishes the cow to be milked three times a day it is calculated how many other cows that need to be milked in between. On the basis of this information the District Court's analysis of equivalence seems even more robust, in particular since the purpose of the Lely design and its usefulness, are the same as in the DeLaval invention. Thus, the Court of Appeal shares the District Court's determination that the use of Lely's disputed milking criterion does not literally infringe DeLaval's patent claim, but that an infringement has occurred under the doctrine of equivalence. The judgment by the District Court is upheld.

The Swedish Supreme Court did not grant leave to appeal.

To summarize, in the two *DeLaval v Lely* rulings, the courts held that 'a pre-determined time' literally encompasses a milking criterion made up of other components than hours and minutes. When, however, the algorithm did not use any temporal measurement, the feature was not literally infringing. The alternative method of counting cows, which ascertained that a certain portion of the herd had been milked before the same cow could again be milked, was not deemed to be a use of a 'pre-determined time'. No overlap existed between the skilled technician's understanding of the claim and the modified robot. However, the method of counting cows was held to be an equivalent, and therefore an infringement.

The two courts applied criteria for determining equivalence referred to in earlier Swedish patent infringement cases, but the criteria had not previously been applied sequentially, to a finding of infringement under the doctrine of equivalence. The *DeLaval v Lely* case therefore confirms an approach for evaluating possible protection outside the literal/technical meaning of the claims. The same criteria have been used in Swedish cases on equivalence since at least 1988 in the case of *Lännen Tehtaat Oy v Svedbro Smide Aktiebolag*. However, in previous cases only one circumstance was evaluated at a time which led to the rejection of an extended scope of protection under the doctrine of equivalence. If, for example, the accused product was designed differently than a feature that had been emphasized and presented as essential during prosecution, it led to the conclusion that the accused product was non-infringing. In the next section of the article the seven factors will be exemplified analysing cases where the factors have been presented.

5. CONSIDERABLE TECHNICAL ADVANCE OR A SIMPLE ADAPTATION

In *DeLaval v Lely* the invention was deemed a considerable technical advance over the prior art on the priority date. This was perceived as a prerequisite for application of the doctrine of equivalence. A factor barring application of the doctrine in earlier cases had been that the invention was characterized as a simple adaptation of the technology known on the priority day. Svea Court of Appeal expressed this view in the decision *Lännen Tehtaat Oy v Svedbro Smide Aktiebolag*. The invention was, as mentioned above, a design for a handheld tool used for planting. Later, the same approach was applied in *Kvistberga Produkter*

AB v Guldmann Sverige AB.[10] The invention in that case was a telescopic ramp. Stockholm District Court held that: 'The invention according to the patent constitutes a simple adaptation. The court will therefore take as its starting point that the patent has a narrow scope of protection'. In *Hattos Patent AB v vau De Svenska AB*, Stockholm District Court explained that: 'A simple adaptation of this nature has a narrow scope of protection that regularly coincides with the wording of the independent claims'.[11] The invention at hand was a certain use of an elastic string in the design of a rucksack. The inventive step was small. In *Molok Oy v BISSY Försäljnings AB*, Stockholm District Court held that: 'A patent on an invention which only forms a combination of individually known and simple elements warrants a restricted scope of protection. The interpretation of the patent claims cannot be allowed to significantly depart from the literal wording.'[12] The invention in that case concerned equipment for waste disposal.

A principle that seems to characterize simple adaptations of known technology is that these are of modest inventive step and lack important industrial consequences, ie, they are incrementally innovative. No surprising result is achieved. The courts have not excluded outright the application of the doctrine of equivalence in these cases, but no invention deemed a 'simple adaptation' has been granted a range of equivalents. It is worth noting that this criterion requires consideration in an infringement case to the degree of technical advance made by the patentee. I will revert to this in the conclusion.

6. AN ESSENTIAL ELEMENT FOR PATENTABILITY

In *DeLaval v Lely* the courts held that the feature 'a pre-determined time' did not contribute to the patentability of the robot. A reason to deny protection beyond the claims in earlier cases had been that the feature lacking in the accused product was essential for the patentability of the invention, ie related to novelty/inventive step or in some other way contributed to the grant decision. This approach can be exemplified by the following statement made in *Hattos Patent AB v Peak Performance Production AB*: 'The Court of Appeal shares the view of the District Court that the word 'free-sliding' in patent claim 1 is not due to a mistake. On the contrary, the Court of Appeal has from the state of the art on the application day, been able to conclude that this feature constituted a central element for the patented invention. The scope for application of the doctrine of equivalence is thus limited.'[13]

[10] *Kvistberga Produkter AB v Guldmann Sverige AB*, Stockholm District Court case T 2367-01, 19 March 2002.

[11] *Hattos Patent AB v vau De Svenska AB,* Stockholm District Court case no T 13826-99, 8 February 2001.

[12] *Molok Oy v BISSY Försäljnings AB*, Stockholm District Court case T 18214-98, 4 April 2000.

[13] *Hattos Patent AB v Peak Performance Production AB*, Svea Court of Appeal case T 8915-01, 18 October 2002.

The Swedish Supreme Court held in *Eli Lilly v ratiopharm* that the importance, which was ascribed in the patent description to the feature, precluded an equivalent infringement.[14] The invention was a pharmaceutical formulation. The claims recited the use of three disintegrants (sodium starch glycolate, polymeric derivatives of acrylic acid and crospovidone). The product accused of trespassing on the patent did not utilize any of these chemical entities, but instead croscarmellose sodium. Croscarmellose sodium was not mentioned in the patent, but technical literature available on the application day indicated that a person skilled in the art would have considered croscarmellose sodium a functional substitute to the disintegrants in the claim. The Supreme Court held that:

> Even if a patent clearly states which components to use equivalence is not excluded if one of the components can be substituted by another of similar technical characteristics. However, in the present case the patent indicates that it is the combination of the components in the claim for producing the tablet, which forms the basis of patentability. Claim 1 defines which disintegrants to use and in the patent description it is said that the choice of disintegrant is one of the most important steps. This entails ... that the scope of protection of this patent is limited to pharmaceutical compositions with one of the disintegrants mentioned in the claim.

The patent description claimed that the choice of disintegrant was an important part of the invention and accordingly the Supreme Court believed that it was important for patentability, denying application of the doctrine of equivalence. Only features tangential to the patentability of the invention have a range of equivalents.

7. A DIFFERENT PURPOSE

In *DeLaval v Lely* the courts found that the purpose of the pre-determined claim feature was to prevent milking operations from occurring too frequently. The accused embodiment achieved the same purpose by means of counting cows. It was held to be obvious that the purpose of the Lely criterion was the same as that of the claim criterion in the invention. In previous cases, Swedish courts denied infringement under the doctrine of equivalence if there was a difference between the purpose stated in the patent claim for the feature at issue and the purpose for using the corresponding part in the accused product. If the technical problem being solved is different, there is no room for stretching the scope of protection to encompass the attacked product.[15]

In *Kvaerner Masa-Yards v Götaverken Arendal Aktiebolag* Svea Court of Appeal held that: 'The shape of the bow on the ship Oden does not rely on

[14] *Eli Lilly v ratiopharm,* Swedish Supreme Court case Ö 2667-02, 20 December 2002.

[15] A Stenvik, *Patenters beskyttelsesomfang* p 690 (Oslo 2001); M Nyberg, *Patenträttsliga bedömningsgrunder* p 312 (Stockholm Jure 2000).

solutions to problems that are addressed in the patent in suit. As the Odengroup has maintained, this precludes an application of the doctrine of equivalence.'[16] The defendant's ship design did not possess the technical advantages that were associated in the patent description with the shape of the patented bow. In a similar vein, the Supreme Court held in *Comviq GSM AB v Europolitan AB* that: 'Since both the problem that the Twincard is made for and the solution it proposes, is different from Comviq's patented invention, the Twincard cannot be comprised under the scope of protection by an application of the doctrine of equivalence'.[17] Comviq's patent description stated that the main purpose of the invention was to enable differentiation between costs for phone calls of different categories (private, work related, etc). The Twincard did not seek such a categorization. The latter phone card was aimed at enabling the use of one phone subscription in mobile phones having different card formats.

8. IMPROVED RESULT IN ACCUSED PRODUCT

As the above-mentioned cases demonstrate, if the design of the accused product has a purpose different from those claimed in the patent there is no room for the doctrine of equivalence. Claims for equivalence may also be denied if the accused product fulfils the same purpose as the patented invention, but represents an important advance compared to the patent claims. Here, the same technical problem is addressed, but the quality of the solution in the accused product is superior. In such a case there is hardly any room for stretching the scope of protection to the accused product. In the second *DeLaval v Lely* case considerable efforts were invested in analysing the possible advantages of 'counting cows' compared to the use of a minimum time measure. The finding that possible advantages to 'counting cows' were insignificant permitted application of the doctrine of equivalence.

Stockholm District Court held in *FMT v Safegate* that lasers were not equivalent to microwaves (radar) in a system for measuring distances at airports.[18] The Court held: 'For the skilled person, who is aware of the difference between radar and laser, it appears as if the patent scope was deliberately restricted. Irrespective thereof, there is no room for the doctrine of equivalence in this case because Safedock's solution provides advantages compared to the patented invention, which the inventor must not be allowed to take advantage of them. Thus, Safedock does not infringe claim 1'.

Technical advantages in the accused device compared to the product according to the patent claims, are thus valuable for a defendant accused of infringement

[16] *Kvaerner Masa-Yards v Götaverken Arendal Aktiebolag*, Svea Court of Appeal, case T 644/96, 15 April 1998.

[17] *Comviq GSM AB v Europolitan AB*, Swedish Supreme Court, Nytt Juridiskt Arkiv 2000 at 497.

[18] *FMT International Trade Aktiebolag v Safegate International Aktiebolag*, Stockholm District Court cases No T 7-552-95 and T 7-824-95, 20 October 1997.

under the doctrine of equivalence. A patent holder can hardly, by recourse to the doctrine of equivalence, prevent the marketing of significant improvements over the patent holder's solution. Further innovation, inspired by and based upon the original invention, in the zone surrounding the granted claims is thus not unduly stifled. Protection extended under the doctrine of equivalence, due to the pioneering nature of the invention, is balanced against any significant technical advance by the defendant which overrides the former and prevents an infringement.

9. THE DIFFERENCE WAS BEYOND THE CAPACITY OF THE SKILLED PERSON

A fifth reason to deny protection beyond the metes and bounds of the claims may be that the accused product is sufficiently technically advanced for a person skilled in the art to be unable to devise it commencing with the claims for the product.[19] Stockholm District Court applied this reasoning in *Aventis Pharma v Bristol Myers Squibb*.[20] The invention was a new process for manufacturing a medicinal product. The Court made the following statement, based on whether the skilled person would have been able to use the technical teaching in the accused process:

> To use β-lactam [the compound in the accused process which was not mentioned in the claim] … with the purpose of manufacturing paclitaxol was in the view of the District Court in no way apparent to a skilled person if he took the patent as his point of departure. On the contrary, the success being achieved by the use of β-lactam in the production of paclitaxol must be considered highly surprising and cannot have appeared to the skilled person as an obvious alternative method in achieving the necessary esterification, but the result of inventive activity. Due to these circumstances the District Court concludes that the method used by Bristol does not infringe under the doctrine of equivalence.

The District Court rejected the application of the doctrine of equivalence, because a person skilled in the art would not have realized that β-lactam in the accused method was a viable alternative to the process according to the patent claim. Equivalents must according to this ruling be within the reach of the skilled person.

However, after the *DeLaval v Lely* case it is much more difficult to argue that a patent on the accused alternative is relevant. It does not seem to prevent an application of the doctrine of equivalence if the variation is patentable in its own right. Lely's milking criterion 'counting cows' had been patented in the EPO with DeLaval's solution being the closest prior article. The lawyer

[19] M Nyberg, n 15 p 303.

[20] *Aventis Pharma v Bristol Myers Squibb*, Stockholm District Court case No T 5761-99, 31 May 2002.

representing Lely in the Swedish infringement case argued that the patentability of Lely's solution over DeLaval's solution prevented application of the doctrine of equivalence. Non-obvious adaptations of a claim were not equivalent, according to Lely. Unfortunately, the two courts did not comment on the relevance of Lely's 'counting cows-patent'. What can be made of this silence? It is obviously incorrect to now hold that all inventive modifications of a patent are non-infringing in Swedish patent law. Dependent patents exist even if they do not literally infringe. But it is unclear how to distinguish between, on the one hand, inventive developments that are dependent and, on the other, inventive developments that are independent of the basic patent. No other means than the ordinary rules for claim interpretation appear to carry this burden. If so, patentability of the accused inventive product has no role to play in deciding whether it infringes. An inventive modification is judged according to the same rules as a non-inventive modification. *DeLaval v Lely* leads to the conclusion that the patentability of the accused product is in itself practically irrelevant under the Swedish doctrine of equivalence.

10. AN OVERLAP WITH THE STATE OF THE ART

Not mentioned in the *DeLaval v Lely* cases, but held in previous Swedish case law is the point that the doctrine of equivalence may not lead to a scope of protection encompassing solutions forming part of the state of the art on the priority date (the so-called Formstein or Gillette defences).[21] This issue was not relevant to *DeLaval v Lely* due to the pioneering nature of the invention, but the principle that the doctrine of equivalence may not encroach upon technology known or available to a skilled person on the priority date is obviously still valid. Svea Court of Appeal held in *Comviq GSM AB v Europolitan AB* that: 'Due to the state of the art on the application date, the doctrine of equivalence cannot produce the scope of protection argued by Comviq.'[22] It is only natural that the state of the art bounds the reach of the doctrine of equivalence. What has been in the public domain should not be monopolized later on.

The same line of reasoning can probably be taken one step further. Everything obvious for a skilled person over the state of the art on the application day is not protected by the doctrine of equivalence. No Swedish court seems as of yet to have expressed this view, but it can hardly be in doubt. Not only what is known on the application day, but also that which is obvious over the known, shall be at the free disposal of everyone.[23]

[21] *Formstein* (*Moulded Kerbstone*) BGHZ 98, 12 = GRUR 1986, 803, 6 IIC p 795 (1987) is the source of a defence in German law called the Formstein objection, which is to the effect that the patent cannot be extended to cover equivalent embodiments if such embodiments were either known or were obvious in the light of the state of the art. The UK Gillette defence is similar.

[22] *Comviq GSM AB v Europolitan AB*, Svea Court of Appeal case No T 1512-96, 23 October 1998.

[23] A Stenvik above note 15 p 673.

11. AMENDMENTS OR STATEMENTS MADE DURING GRANT PROCEEDINGS

Finally, the courts in *DeLaval v Lely* held that DeLaval did not, during prosecution of the patent introduce the feature 'a pre-determined time' in order to delineate the invention against the state of the art, or in any other way expressed a particular intent to limit the scope of protection to the literal claim wording. In other cases, Swedish courts have denied application of the doctrine of equivalence if, during grant proceedings, the feature was added in response to the state of the article. This entails scope discrepancies between a first filing with a claim to 'a chair with three legs and a leaning back' and a claim to 'a chair with three legs' which was amended by the addition of the feature 'a leaning back', in response to an action from the examiner. It is unlikely that the added feature 'a leaning back' can be stretched to eg a functionally equivalent vertical back in an infringement case. If a feature is added or redrafted in prosecution it seems that the applicant thereby relinquishes possible equivalents.

In *Eli Lilly v ratiopharm* the Swedish Supreme Court held with respect to documents from the prosecution history that they could be 'used to interpret unclear patent claims and statements made in the description, as long as it leads to a narrowing of the scope of protection'.[24] The prosecution history must not result in a stretching of the protection but can be used to block an application of the doctrine of equivalence. When Svea Court of Appeal tried the same case it held that:

> In deciding whether the product of ratiopharm infringes under the doctrine of equivalence there are ... reasons to note that the patent claims state '... *are* the disintegrants for the formulations in this invention' ... while in the patent application it was stated that '... *are suitable* disintegrants for the formulations in this invention ...' The discarding from the application of the word 'suitable' supports the holding that the encompassed disintegrates have been intentionally limited. The scope for the doctrine of equivalence at this claim juncture is therefore limited. In these circumstances ... the Court of Appeal concludes ... that the claimant has not made a patent infringement sufficiently probable.[25]

The applicant may interpret a feature in the claim in its contacts with the patent office, without actually amending the claim. The interpretation will be recorded in the patent office file. The rule barring equivalents applies equally to an interpretation which did not result in an amendment of the wording. All actions on the part of the applicant during the grant proceedings, whether the introduction of a new claims limitation or the narrow interpretation of an existing feature, seem to affect equivalents. An example can be seen in *Sandströms Transportprodukter v SCHMITZ Cargobull* where Stockholm District Court held that:

[24] *Eli Lilly v ratiopharma*, Swedish Supreme Court case No Ö 2667-02, 20 December 2002.
[25] *Eli Lilly v ratiopharma*, Svea Court of Appeal case No Ö 4949-02, 17 June 2002.

> In the determination of the scope of protection guidance can be had from the prosecution history. In a document … containing a drawing and text submitted together with the patent application it was stated that … In a document sent to the Patent Office the applicant maintained … In a brief appealing the rejection of the application by the Patent Office the applicant stated … According to a protocol from the hearing in the Patents Appeal Court the applicant asserted that … In a document submitted to the Patent Office … the feature … was given its final wording … In the previous claim this feature was lacking and it was only stated that … What has occurred in the granting proceedings entails that the patent cannot be given a broader interpretation than that it is directed to a distinct design, with the consequences that this will have for the scope of protection.[26]

Third parties can assume that under Swedish law limitations a patentee has put forth in the grant proceedings remain in force many years later in an infringement case. A patentee may not go back on anything he has said or represented to either the Swedish or the European Patent Office. This is important because the vast majority of granted patents have amended or interpreted claims features. Prosecution history estoppel, or file wrapper estoppel, of this kind appears not to be available in some important EPC countries.[27] The estoppel in Swedish law is believed to be valuable, eg because the file history often provides pertinent interpretations from the relevant time and is readily accessible by electronic means. Equivalents of course still remain available for features in an amended claim that has been unaffected by an amendment or interpretation.

12. CONCLUDING REMARKS ON THE SWEDISH DOCTRINE OF EQUIVALENTS

The Swedish case law discussed in this article limits the scope for applying the doctrine of equivalents considerably. Ever since the *Lännen Tehtaat Oy v Svedbro Smide Aktiebolag* case, patentees have consistently been denied the benefit of stretching the scope of protection. *DeLaval v Lely* was an exception – the first case since *Lännen* – in which none of the factors barring the doctrine were present. Anyone basing an infringement accusation on the doctrine of equivalents will therefore face an uphill battle. She will have to prove that the circumstances discussed above are not present in the case. The doctrine of equivalence is repeatedly referred to by Swedish courts as an opportunity

[26] *Sandströms Transportprodukter v SCHMITZ Cargobull*, Stockholm District Court case No T 7-664-96, 5 November 1999.

[27] Lord Hoffman in the House of Lords (UK Supreme Court) held in *Kirin-Amgen Inc v Transkaryotic Therapies Inc No 2*, [2004] UKHL 46, that: 'The courts of the United Kingdom, the Netherlands and Germany certainly discourage, if they do not actually prohibit, use of the patent office file in aid of construction. There are good reasons: the meaning of the patent should not change according to whether or not the person skilled in the art has access to the file and in any case life is too short for the limited assistance which it can provide'.

available to patent holders, but it does not in practice appear to come into play on many occasions.

The doctrine of equivalence is framed in Sweden as an enumeration of situations in which no extended protection is granted. The question of what characterizes an equivalent is not really part of the analysis. Equivalence is what remains when all reasons for not extending protection have been exhausted. Other countries have questions left to be answered and these function more or less the same as the factual circumstances utilized in Swedish law, although I am not sure any other country has as many as seven circumstances that prevent protection going beyond the technical meaning of the claims. The factors barring the doctrine of equivalence in Swedish law appear to entail a relatively restrictive claim interpretation, out of a number of possible ways to reach what in European patent law is the much sought-after middle position between purely literal claim interpretation and a nebulous general inventive concept.[28]

The most interesting and unusual aspect of Swedish case law though, is, that scope of protection is largely assessed in a balancing of the technical achievements of the patentee and the accused infringer. Equivalents are relevant in cases pertaining to inventions of superior technical and commercial significance, a group sometimes described as pioneering inventions. In the first *Lely v DeLaval* case Svea Court of Appeal held that: 'An interpretation of the wording of the claim is not enough to ascertain the scope of protection. In addition a weighing together of all facts pertaining to the case must be done. From the facts of this case it can be seen that the invention in its entirety at the priority date meant a considerable technical progress. … Taking this into consideration, opportunities for a broad interpretation of the patent are opened up …'[29] The doctrine of equivalence was applied subsequently on this basis in the second *DeLaval v Lely* case. For the infringement to be found it was also necessary that any advantages to the method of counting cows were insignificant.

I believe that it is not common practice in Europe to, in this manner, openly compare the patentee's and defendant's respective technical progress in an infringement case. It might even appear as an inappropriate blending of infringement and invalidity issues. This may have a legal foundation, though, in the Protocol to Article 69 EPC which provides that claim interpretation should afford: 'a fair protection for the patentee'. Fairness can be judged from the relative importance of the technical advance made by the applicant and by the defendant. Patent law is about technical progress and little else. Thus, all claims do not receive equal treatment in Sweden. Fair protection for the patentee balanced with legal certainty for third parties, is believed to demand literal claim interpretation except for the most important inventions which may qualify for a grant of extra reach. Technical progress in the accused product may bar

[28] H Bleken, 'Ekvivalens i norsk patentrett' (2010) 2 *Nordiskt immateriellt rättsskydd* p 108 (130).

[29] *Lely Industries v DeLaval International,* Svea Court of Appeal case No T 7924-00, 8 March 2002.

the doctrine of equivalents, though, even in cases of important inventions. The courts in *DeLaval v Lely* were prepared to disregard minor advantages in Lely's product. The possible improvements were deemed insignificant compared to the technical advance made by the patent holder.

This balancing of technical achievements seems to be quite different in nature from a skilled person's understanding of what the claims were intended to protect, the latter being a crude summary of what the author perceives as the principal mode of claim interpretation today in Germany and England.[30] From a policy perspective, the Swedish balancing approach may facilitate valuable innovations, inspired by and based upon the original invention, in the zone surrounding granted claims. Incentives will be maintained in the claim penumbra if competitors are told that added-value in their solution will propel them outside the scope of protection.[31]

To summarize, this article has tried to present recent Swedish experiences with the doctrine of equivalence. Primarily it has tried to show the restrictions applying to an argument based on an alleged general inventive concept that disregards the literal meaning. These restrictions have repeatedly been upheld and have developed into a well-established body of law under the heading of the doctrine of equivalence, but without defining what constitutes 'equivalence'. It has also been argued that these limitations, as a practical matter, are frequent in patent infringement cases and therefore that the technical meaning of the

[30] '[There] is only one compulsory question, namely that set by article 69 and its Protocol: what would a person skilled in the art have understood the patentee to have used the language of the claim to mean?' per Lord Hoffman in *Kirin-Amgen v Transkaryotic Therapies Inc No 2* [2004] UKHL 46. In Germany the Bundesgerichtshof held in *Cutting Blade I* (case X ZR 168/00, 33 IIC p 874 (2002)) that: '[I]f an embodiment departing from the essential meaning of the patent claim is to be included within the extent of protection, it is not sufficient that (1.) it solves the problem underlying the invention with modified but objectively equivalent means and (2.) that the person skilled in the art is able to use his specialist knowledge to identify the modified means as having the same effect. Just as the same effect cannot be found without focusing on the patent claim, (3.) the considerations that the person skilled in the art must apply must in addition be focused on the essential meaning of the technical teaching protected in the patent claim in such a way that the person skilled in the art regards the different embodiment with its modified means as being equivalent to the solution in question.'

'[I]t is not decisive for the scope of protection whether the variant has a material effect upon the way the invention works. The point is whether the essential considerations required by a person skilled in the art to find the variant are sufficiently close to the patent claim to constitute an equivalent alternative. Both approaches require a value judgment in the end'. See P Meier-Beck, 'Scope of Patent Protection and Equivalence' (2005) 36 *IIC* p 339 (344). 'Overall, both the third Protocol question [in England] and Schneidmesser questions have one purpose in common, which is to emphasise the patentee's responsibility. In the sense of the third sentence of PIA69 this helps to provide a 'a reasonable degree of certainty for third parties' and to counterbalance the questions which, in favour of a 'fair protection for the patentee', call for the technical equivalence of effect and means of a patent and embodiment (Protocol question one and Schneidmesser questions one and three).' See C von Drathen, 'Patent Scope in English and German Law Under the European Patent Convention 1973 and 2000' (2008) 39 *International Review of Intellectual Property and Competition Law* p 384 (409).

[31] For an extended argument to this effect see B Domeij, 'Patent Claim Scope: Initial and Follow-on Pharmaceutical Inventions' (2001) 23 *European Intellectual Property Review* p 326.

claim wording regularly exhausts the scope of patent protection in Swedish law. *DeLaval v Lely* is an exception illustrating and confirming a strong bias for a literal/technical claim interpretation. Finally, it has been argued that the Swedish doctrine of equivalence entails an open balancing of the parties respective technical achievements and that this appears to be a hallmark of Swedish claim interpretation.

In much the same way that animals on the Galapagos Islands have developed unique features in isolation and managed to maintain their characteristics after contacts with other parts of the world, the Swedish approach to claim interpretation has been affected by Article 69 EPC and European case law – foremost by abandoning the general inventive idea – however many unique traits survive the encounter. Article 69 EPC and the Protocol thus seem to be able to accommodate a wide variety of species. European harmonization is obviously desirable, but I believe most practising Swedish lawyers are comfortable with the developments that have taken place in case law. It provides a well-defined template for legal arguments and in most infringement disputes it is relatively easy to determine that no protection beyond a technical and dictionary-like understanding of the claim is available. This furthers legal certainty. It seems likely that the present Swedish law on claim interpretation will survive for quite some time yet, maybe until the ever elusive EU-patent comes in to existence. It is, however, perhaps too much to expect that the Swedish approach will find new habitats.

4
Distinctive Character in Compound Trademarks

PROFESSOR PER JONAS NORDELL

A trademark may be expressed in many different ways. However, *word marks* are the most common kind of trademark today. In this respect it may be of some interest that the Court of Justice of the European Union ('CJEU') has extensively assessed the issue of *distinctive character* in *compound trademarks*, ie word marks consisting of two (or more) *constituents* or *morphemes*. Its case law can be seen as a mental journey from the very first so-called *Baby-dry* decision[1] to the so-called *Postkantoor* decision.[2]

The aim of this article is to describe and analyse the EU case law development of distinctive character in compound trademarks and to demonstrate how principles for the protection of word marks can, or have to, interrelate with other disciplines, such as linguistics and semantics. The question here is whether and to what extent linguistics and jurisprudence should go hand in hand, interrelate, or follow different regimes. I begin with a brief description of the framework of research on compound words in linguistic theory. Indeed, this can only be a sketch, the aim of which is to give perspective to the analysis of distinctive character in trademark law. This article goes on to describe the development of distinctive character in EU case law and ends up with an analysis of distinctive character in compound trademarks viewed in light of linguistic theories' description of compound words.

1. A LINGUISTIC STARTING POINT

As compound marks in one way or another consist of two or more words or word parts, it is natural to draw a parallel between the legal prerequisites for obtaining protection of such marks and the more general linguistic phenomenon

[1] Case C-383/99 P *Procter & Gamble Company v OHIM*, [2002] ECR I-6251 (Baby-dry).

[2] Case C-363/99 *Koninklijke KPN Nederland NV v Benelux-Merkenbureau*, [2002] ECR I-1619 (Postkantoor).

of compound words. Such words consist of more than one stem. Compounding occurs when two or more *morphemes* are attached together to make them operate as one new word. The meanings of the word parts interrelate in such a way that a new meaning arises, which is different from the meanings of the individual words in isolation. The status of compound words has been widely debated within linguistic theory and remains controversial. The debate includes questions such as what constitutes a compound word, how are such words composed in the language and how are they stored and processed in the human mind? In the anthology *The Representation and Processing of Compound Words*[3] influential scholars in the linguistic field present the discourse from different angles and attempt to describe what is going on in the human mind in the process of storing, structuring and processing compound words.

Cognitive science and linguistics assumes that words are stored in a *mental lexicon*, which is the backbone of human language processing. It encompasses the manner in which words are represented and processed in the mind.[4] The *lexicon* refers to the user's knowledge of language and words, the vocabulary and the representation of knowledge about words in the mind. The fact that the word *boat*, for example, refers to a water vehicle must be stored in this lexicon. Its meaning cannot be divined from the meaning of the letters *b*, *o*, *a*, and *t* because its phonological components are not meaningful.[5]

Even if the term *lexicon* in this context should be understood as a metaphor, the human mind has been assumed to operate in the same way as a *dictionary*. Until quite recently this view of the mental lexicon had not been questioned. Linguistic and neuro-linguistic research on compound representation and processing has seen great advances in recent decades.[6] Even though the concept of mental lexicon remains as a means to describe how words are stored in the human mind, alternative views have been postulated, pointing to a more interactive base where storage of empirical knowledge is put together with processing of information. Rather than putting word knowledge into a passive storage, word processing should be seen as a system that seeks to maximise the opportunities for activation at all levels.[7] Thus, a compound word involves the activation of its constituents as well as the whole word.[8]

Compounding is a common word formation process in all languages.[9] It represents perhaps the easiest way to form a new cognitive representation from two or more existing ones. However, the system of compounding may differ

[3] Libben and Jarema (Eds), *The Representation and Processing of Compound Words, Oxford Linguistics* (Oxford University Press, 2007).

[4] *The Representation and Processing of Compound Words* p vi; see Dressler at p 23.

[5] Ibid Libben at p 4.

[6] Ibid at p vi.

[7] See Elman, *An alternative view of the mental lexicon. Trends in Cognitive Sciences, 2004* p 301, available at http://crl.ucsd.edu/~elman/Papers/elman_tics_opinion_2004.pdf.

[8] See Jarema in *The Representation and Processing of Compound Words* at p 45.

[9] Ibid Gagné and Spalding at p 145.

from one language to another.[10] In some cases it may be difficult to determine whether a word should be seen as a compound, or as a single word. In some languages compound words are not simple concatenations of elements, but rather structures that are analogous to phrases. Examples of such structures are compounds containing prepositional phrases (eg Italian *mulino a vento*, ie *windmill*). Such structures originated as phrases have been lexicalised over time. This is also reflected in the changing, and sometimes varying, orthography of compounds (eg *trademark—trade-mark—trade mark*).[11] In some languages constituents can be connected by an intervening interfix, linking morpheme, or element, and the question therefore arises as to whether these elements play a determining role in compound processing, or whether they merely serve as a sort of *glue* that binds constituents and signals boundaries.[12]

Although compound words can take many forms in most languages there is a general preference for combinations of two nouns. Significant for most compound words is that they also denote contrasts between subcategories and distinguish among members of single categories. In the word *motor boat* the modifier *motor* (cf *sailing boat*) indicates its propelling force and in the word *plastic boat* (cf *wooden boat*) the material constitutes the subcategory.[13] The word is built upon constituents, which are fixed expressions in the language. As novel combinations of the constituents are easily comprehended by native speakers of the language, the words *boat motor*, *house boat* and *boat house* can be available for the compounding word formation process.[14] *Prima facie* their morphemes seem to give clear meanings to the words. However, it is not *a priori* obvious why other types of boats, such as *cargo* or *cruise ships*, are not called *motor boats* or *house boats*. This indicates that lexical processing systems do not represent compound words solely in terms of their constituents. It also indicates that they are not semantically transparent in the sense that the meanings of the compounds are fully inferable from the meanings of their constituent parts.[15] Whereas some scholars have argued an analysis from *decomposition*, ie that compound words are separated into its morphemic constituents, others have found evidence for *whole-word processing*.[16] This is typically more common for known compound words.[17] According to *Libben*, a *maximisation of opportunity* system would allow for whole-word processing and morphological processing to occur simultaneously. Thus, a word such as *motor boat* would be simultaneously

[10] Ibid Dressler at p 23.
[11] Ibid Jarema at pp 57–58.
[12] Ibid at p 62.
[13] Ibid Gagné at pp 145–46.
[14] See ibid Dressler at p 23.
[15] See ibid Libben at p 11.
[16] Ibid Gagné and Spalding at p 147.
[17] Caramazza, Laudanna, and Romani, 'Lexical Access and Inflectional Morphology' (1988) 28 *Cognition* No 3 pp 297–332; see Fiorentino and Poeppel, 'Compound Words and Structure in the Lexicon' 22 *Language and Cognitive Processes* No 7 953-100 1t p 962.

processed as a whole as well as in terms of its constituents *motor* and *boat*. It would result in bi-directional activation, such that the constituents of *motor boat* received activation from the process of morphological parsing, as well as from the structured representation of the compound in the mental lexicon.[18] If a compound word is presented often enough so that it can be lexicalised, it is probably stored as a representation that can be retrieved as a single representation. This, however, does not shut down the process of *morphological decomposition* for that word and its constituent morphemes.[19]

A recent discourse focuses on so called *conceptual combination*. The conceptual representation of the word *motor boat* is formed from the concepts *motor* and *boat*. An assumption within the field of conceptual combination is that understanding a combined concept involves creating a new concept because a combined concept is more than a hybrid of its parts. Theories of conceptual combination have focused on understanding how the new concept is formed, eg how the concept of the head noun (*boat*) is modified in some way by the addition of the modifier (*motor*). The interpretation of combined concepts involves an interaction between the two constituents, rather than an additive process. *Motor* cannot be adding the same feature to eg *boat* and *man*.[20] This strikes a difference between lexicalised and novel compound words. Lexicalised compound words refer to compounds that are familiar and have a common usage. The meaning of lexicalised compounds can therefore be retrieved directly from the lexicon. In contrast, the meanings of novel or less familiar combinations must be processed or computed, because they are not yet established.[21] To interpret a novel compound, one must therefore access the concepts denoted by the words and select a relation which links them together.[22]

The understanding of a compound word also depends on the *transparency* or *opacity* of its constituents. Transparency refers to the extent to which the meaning of a compound word may be predicted from its constituents. Examples given within linguistics are compositions of the morpheme *berry*. While both constituents in the word *blueberry* are fully transparent, the constituents *straw* and *huckle* are – at least partially – opaque in the words *strawberry* and *huckleberry*, because of the absent link between the two levels of representation. This explains the interoperability of compounds mediated by interplay of facilitatory and inhibitory links between the lexical and the conceptual levels of interpretation and processing, as well as for constituent activation in opaque compounds.[23] It has been suggested that

[18] Libben in *The Representation and Processing of Compound Words* at p 9.

[19] Ibid at p 6.

[20] Ibid Gagné and Spalding at p 149.

[21] See Gagné and Spalding, 'Using Conceptual Combination Research to Better Understand Novel Compound Words' available at http://www.pulib.sk/skase/Volumes/JTL06/2.pdf.

[22] C Gagné, 'Lexical and Relational Influences on the Processing of Novel Compounds' (April 2002) 81 *Brain and Language* Issue 1-3 pp 723–35, available at http://www.idealibrary.com.

[23] Jarema, *The Representation and Processing of Compound Words* pp 48 ff.

> the meaning of the constituents of opaque compounds might not be available during the processing of compound words, even though the lexical forms are retrieved. In contrast, the constituents of transparent compounds are represented (and available) at both the lexical and conceptual level. This highlights the need to distinguish between lexical and conceptual information in compound word processing.[24]

A problem related to compound words is how to determine the *morphological head* of the word, ie how it is immediately clear that the word *boat house* is a type of *house* and that *house boat* is a type of *boat*. One suggestion is that the concept of the head is not represented in the word at all, but might be derived from what is known about the properties of the language in general, because all English compounds have their heads as the last constituent.[25] As so many *berry* compounds are semantically opaque, native speakers also have a higher tolerance for opacity in compounds with *berry* as their morphological and semantic head, as compared to words that have a morpheme such as *stick* as the final constituent (cf *walking stick*, *candle stick* and *joystick*).[26]

Combinations of nouns are probably also the most common type of compound word mark. A famous example is *Coca-Cola*. Some further examples taken from case-law are: *Company-line, Post-kantoor (post office)*, *Cell-tech*, *Car-card* and *Rock-bass*. Closely connected to a combination of two ordinary nouns stand their combination of or with proper names, such as *Rolls-Royce*, or *Sony Ericsson*. Because they often originate from mergers of two distinctive trade names their distinctive character would not be questioned. The second most common type of compound word mark is probably the combination of noun and adjective or adverb, the aim of which, in most cases, is to indicate capacity or quality to the goods or services. This can be illustrated with some examples from case law such as *Baby-dry*, *Double-mint*, *Euro-hypo*, *Euro-health*, *Bio(metric)-ID(entification)* and *Best-buy*. A compound trademark may also consist of any other combination of word classes. It can consist of a noun and a verb. If so, the mark is usually composed so as to indicate either what to do with the labelled goods or services (cf *Stream-serve* for a technique to stream digital data from a server), or to indicate something that characterises a certain service (cf *Rent a Car*). The mark can also consist of a verb and adjective or adverb, of two verbs (cf. *Twist & pour*), or a combination of two adjectives or adverbs (cf *Bio(logical)-mild*). Finally, compound trademarks may consist of other word classes, such as pronouns or numerals (cf. *SAT.1*) or of several word classes, such as *The Laughing Cow* (*La vache qui rit*). This final situation will usually occur for slogans (cf *Das Prinzip der Bequemlichkeit*[27], *Live Richly*[28] or *Real people real solutions*).[29]

[24] See Gagné and Spalding, above note 21.

[25] Libben, *The Representation and Processing of Compound Words* at p 17.

[26] See ibid Libben at p 15; and Jarema at p 45.

[27] Case C-64/02 P, [2002] ECR I-10031 (Das Prinzip der Bequemlichkeit).

[28] Case T-320/03, *Citicorp v OHIM*, [2005] ECR II-3411 (Live Richly).

[29] Case T-130/01, *Sykes Enterprises, Incorp v OHIM*, [2002] ECR II-5179 (Real people real solutions).

2. A LEGAL STARTING POINT

To acquire trademark protection a mark must possess a *distinctive character* or *distinctiveness*. The requirement of distinctive character follows from Article 6*quinquies* B ii in the Paris Convention for the Protection of Industrial Property, and Article 15(1) of the so-called TRIPS Agreement.[30] It is harmonised via Article 3(1)(b)–(d) of the European Trademarks Directive[31] (cf Article 7(1)(b)–(c) of the Trademarks Regulation[32]), according to which trademarks which are devoid of any distinctive character (Article 3(1) (b)) or consist exclusively of signs or indications which may serve to designate the kind, quality, quantity, intended purpose, value, geographical origin, or the time of production of the goods or of rendering of the service, or other characteristics of the goods, shall not be registered – or if registered – shall be liable to be declared invalid (Article 3(1)(c)). Article 3(1) (d) mentions trademarks which consist exclusively of signs or indications which have become customary in the current language or in the *bona fide* and established practices of the trade, ie *degeneration*. The relationship between the provisions of Article 3(1) (b)–(d) was stressed by the CJEU in the so-called *Postkantoor* decision,[33] in which the Court identified a clear overlap between the scope of subparagraphs (b), (c), and (d) of Article 3(l):

> In particular, a word mark which is descriptive of characteristics of goods or services for the purposes of Article 3(1)(c) of the Directive is, on that account, necessarily devoid of any distinctive character with regard to the same goods or services within the meaning of Article 3(1)(b) of the Directive. A mark may none the less be devoid of any distinctive character in relation to goods or services for reasons other than the fact that it may be descriptive.[34]

The requirement of distinctive character is based on two – partly merging – grounds: First, the mark as such must possess a certain *symbol function*, either by itself – *inherent distinctiveness* – or as a matter of *establishment on the market* – *secondary meaning*. Through use, a sign may acquire a distinctive character which it initially lacked and thus be registered as a trademark. This exception

[30] Agreement on Trade-Related Aspects of Intellectual Property Rights. Annex 1C of the Marrakesh Agreement Establishing the World Trade Organization, signed in Marrakesh, Morocco on 15 April 1994.

[31] First Directive 89/104/EEC of the Council, of 21 December 1988, to Approximate the Laws of the Member States Relating to Trademarks OJ L 040, 11/02/1989 P. 0001 - 0007 (as now replaced by Directive 2008/95/EC of the European Parliament and of the Council of 22 October 2008 to approximate the laws of the Member States relating to trademarks OJ L 299, 8.11.2008, pp 25–33 (Codified version)).

[32] Council Regulation (EC) No 40/94 of 20 December 1993 on the Community trademark Official Journal L 011 , 14/01/1994 P. 0001–0036 (as now replaced by the Council Regulation (EC) No 207/2009 of 26 February 2009 on the Community trademark OJ L78, p1, 24/03/2009 (codified version).

[33] Case C-363/99, [2004] ECR I-1619 (Postkantoor) para 86.

[34] See Maniatis, *Trade Marks in Europe. A Practical Jurisprudence* (Sweet & Maxwell 2006) (cit Maniatis) p 208.

follows from Article 3(3) of the Directive. In the so called *Windsurfing Chiemsee* decision[35] the CJEU stated that a trademark acquired distinctive character following the use which had been made of it where the mark came to identify the product in respect of which registration was applied for as originating from a particular undertaking and thus distinguishing that product from the goods of other undertakings. Second, the requirement of distinctive character is based on the basis of competition to keep generally used signs or non-distinctive words free from exclusive protection – *Freihaltebedürfnis*. The rationale behind this is that the most common words and elementary symbols should not be the subject of a monopoly.

It is clear from case law that the first ground has been the most fundamental one for the assessment of distinctive character. But the latter ground has also been taken into consideration in some cases. In the *Windsurfing Chiemsee* decision the CJEU ruled that Article 3.1 (c) of the Directive did not require a real, current or serious need to leave a sign or indication free[36] and that Article 3.3 of the Directive precluded differentiation regarding qualities of distinctive character by reference to the perceived importance of keeping a word available for use by other undertakings.[37]

The distinctive character of trademarks can be seen as a spectrum with a sliding scale of protection, going from inherently distinctive marks at one end to *generic terms* with no distinctive character at the other. A generic term is the common name for the products or services in connection with which it is used. Within the spectrum lie *arbitrary*, *suggestive* and *descriptive* signs. Unlike descriptive signs, the arbitrary trademarks do not describe the products or services for which they apply, but use common words which are irrelevant to the particular product or service in question. Nothing prevents the use of a common word for another kind of good or service. Thus, the most common words may be distinctive when used for new types of goods or services. While descriptive marks merely designate the kind, quality, quantity or intended purpose of the products or services in relation to the manner in which they are used, suggestive trademarks call for the consumers' imagination. They indicate or allude to the nature, quality, or a characteristic of the products or services. Generic terms as well as descriptive marks are held to be devoid of distinctive character and therefore excluded from the protection. They lack the fundamental symbol capacity as they exclusively, or with only minor changes or additions, denote either the goods or services, or their characteristics.

[35] Joined Cases C-108/97 and C-109/97, *Windsurfing Chiemsee Produktions- und Vertriebs GmbH (WSC) v Boots- und Segelzubehör Walter Huber and Franz Attenberger* [1999] ECR 1999 I-2779 (Windsurfing Chiemsee) at para 45.

[36] Ibid at para 35.

[37] Ibid at para 45.

3. CASE LAW

Today there is a relatively extensive case law from the CJEU on distinctive character of compound trademarks. It is obvious that the CJEU has been influenced or inspired by linguistic features and figures. Great attention has been paid to the well-known *Baby-dry* decision from 2001, the first decision of the Court in respect of registration of a Community Trademark (CTM).[38] Baby-dry was about the distinctive character of the compound '*Baby-dry*' in connection with its use for diapers. The application was initially refused on the basis that the mark consisted exclusively of words that were descriptive for diapers. The appeal to the General Court was refused as keeping a baby dry was deemed to be the main purpose of the good. The CJEU remarked that the descriptiveness must be determined *not only in relation to each word taken separately but also in relation to the whole which they formed*. Any perceptible difference between the combination of words submitted for registration and the terms used in the common parlance to designate the goods or services or their essential characteristics was apt to confer distinctive character on the word combination enabling it to be registered as a trademark.[39] In order to assess whether a word combination such as *baby-dry* was capable of distinctiveness, it was necessary to put oneself in the shoes of an English-speaking consumer. From that point of view, and given that the goods concerned were babies' nappies, the determination to be made depended on whether the word combination in question could be viewed as a normal way of referring to the goods or of representing their essential characteristics in common parlance.[40] Whilst each of the two words in the combination could form part of expressions used in everyday speech to designate the function of babies' nappies, their *syntactically unusual juxtaposition* was not a familiar expression in the English language, either for designating babies' nappies or for describing their essential characteristics.[41] Word combinations like *baby-dry* could therefore not be regarded as exhibiting, as a whole, descriptive character; they were *lexical inventions* bestowing distinctive power on the mark so formed and could not be refused registration.[42]

The case indicates a liberal attitude to the registration of word marks as it seemed to allow registration even of descriptive marks, provided that they possessed a secondary meaning, ie that the mark function as such irrespective of the meanings of its original constituents. Much effort has also been expended analysing the findings by the CJEU, not the least on what was meant by the wordings *syntactically unusual juxtaposition* and *lexical invention*. In grammar *juxtaposition* refers to the absence of linking elements in a group of words that are listed together. Within linguistics the term *lexical invention* has been used

[38] Case C-383/99 P, [2001] ECR 2001 I-6251 (Baby-dry).
[39] Ibid at para 40.
[40] Ibid at para 42.
[41] Ibid at para p 43.
[42] Ibid at para 44.

for lexemes in *interlanguage* which are morpho-phonologically adapted to the target language but which are never used by native speakers.[43] Those wordings had previously never been connected to a trademark law assessment.

The next so-called *Companyline* decision[44] involved the registration of the word *Companyline* for services in the insurance sector. Here the Court came to an opposite conclusion than it reached in the *Baby-dry* decision. The General Court dismissed the action against a refusal by the Board of Appeal (BoA) to allow registration. In its judgment (issued before the publication of the *Baby-dry* decision) the General Court found the mark to be devoid of any distinctive character, since the sign consisted of two generic words simply coupled together. On appeal, the CJEU concluded that the sign was composed exclusively of the word parts *company* and *line*, both of which were customary in English-speaking countries. The word *company* pointed out goods or services intended for companies. The word *line* had various meanings. In the insurance and financial services sector it denoted, amongst other things, a branch of insurance or a line or group of products. They were generic words which simply denoted a line of goods or services for undertakings. *Coupling them together without any graphic or semantic modification* did not imbue them with any additional characteristic such as to render the sign, taken as a whole, capable of distinguishing the appellant's services from those of other undertakings. The sign *Companyline* was therefore held to be devoid of any distinctive character.[45]

It is immediately apparent that the Court abandoned its expressions from the *Baby-dry* decision: *syntactically unusual juxtaposition* and *lexical invention*. Instead it concluded that coupling the word parts *company* and *line* together *without any graphic or semantic modification* did not imbue them with any *additional characteristic*. Although one can assume a change in orientation from the *Baby-dry* decision, it should be noticed that the word *companyline* in the business sector has a clear generic function, and therefore comprises a far lower level of distinctiveness than that of *Baby-dry*. However, case law after the *Companyline* decision indicates not only a more restrictive standard, but also a more elaborate assessment.

The next decision concerned the distinctive character of the mark *Doublemint* for chewing gum.[46] The main issue was how to assess ambiguity. The General Court had found that the mark was not exclusively descriptive. The word *double* was unusual, compared with words like *strong* or *extra*. *Mint* could refer to spearmint, peppermint, or other types of herb. The combination of the two words could convey two messages: either that it contained twice the usual amount of mint or that it was flavoured with two varieties of mint. On appeal

[43] Dewaele, 'Lexical inventions: French interlanguage as L2 versus L3' (1998) 19(4) *Applied Linguistics* pp 471–90.

[44] Case C-104/00 P, *DKV Deutsche Krankenversicherung AG v OHIM* [2002] ECR I-7561 (Companyline).

[45] Ibid para 7; see Maniatis at p 87.

[46] Case C-191/01 P, *OHIM v Wm Wrigley Jr Company* [2003] ECR I-12447 (Doublemint).

the CJEU found it was sufficient ground for a refusal of registration if at least one of the signs and indications composing the mark could be descriptive for goods or services in relation to which the application was filed.[47]

In two decisions of 5 February 2004 the CJEU reconsidered its interpretation and application of Article 3(l) (c) following the *Doublemint* decision.[48] In the first case[49] *Telefon & Buch VerlagsgmbH* had filed two applications for registration of the words *Universaltelefonbuch* and *Universalkommunikationsverzeichnis* for goods and services in Classes 9, 16, 41 and 42.[50] In its findings the CJEU followed the General Court and concluded that the word marks for which registration was sought had specific meanings and were properly formed in accordance with the grammatical rules of a given language and were composed of common words in that language. Since the word marks designated the kind of goods and the intended use of the services for which registration was sought, they could not be registered.[51]

The second case was about registration of *Streamserve* in Classes 9 and 16.[52] This decision seems to consolidate the position of the CJEU regarding the interpretation of Article 3(l) (c) following the line of reasoning adopted in the *Doublemint* decision. The BoA dismissed the appeal on the ground that the word *Streamserve*, which was made up of two English words without any additional unusual or innovative element, was descriptive of the intended use of the goods concerned (in this case a technique for transferring digital data from a server enabling them to be processed as a steady and continuous stream, known as *streaming*). The General Court considered that the word *Streamserve* was made up of a basic verb (*serve*) and a noun (*stream*). It was therefore not unusual for the consumers concerned. An important issue in the decision was the relationship between the mark and the good for which the registration was sought. In this part the CJEU referred to the findings of the Court of First Instance.[53] It was sufficient if at least one of the potential meanings of a word sign designated a characteristic of the goods or services concerned. Regarding goods falling within some categories, such as apparatus for recording, transmitting and reproducing of sounds and images, and data processing equipment including computers, the streaming technique did not merely constitute a field in which those goods were applied but rather was one of their specific functions. Accordingly, there was a sufficiently direct and specific relationship between the term *streamserve* and those goods.[54] Regarding goods in other categories, such as manuals and publications, the

[47] Ibid at para 32; see Maniatis at p 191.

[48] Ibid at p 213.

[49] Case C-326/01 P, *Telefon & Buch VerlagsgmbH v OHIM* [2004] ECR I-1371 (Telefon & Buch).

[50] Referring to the *Nice International Classification of Goods and Services for the Purposes of the Registration of Marks,* 9th Edn, WIPO publication No 500.2/9.

[51] Case C-326/01 P, [2004] ECR I-1371 (Telefon & Buch) paras 30–35.

[52] Case C-150/02 P, *Streamserve Inc v OHIM* [2004] ECR I-1461 (Streamserve).

[53] Case T-106/00, *Streamserve Inc v OHIM* [2002] ECR II-723 (Streamserve).

[54] Ibid at para 44.

streaming technique was, at most, a field of application of that technique but not a technical function of the goods in question. Accordingly, there was not a sufficiently direct and specific relationship between the term *streamserve* and those goods.[55] The Court therefore annulled the contested decision in so far as it refused the application for registration of *Streamserve* for goods within the categories manuals and publications.[56]

In the *Telefon & Buch* and *Streamserve* decisions the CJEU also stressed the so-called *Freihaltebedürfnis* doctrine and concluded that signs and indications which may serve, in trade, to designate the characteristics of the goods or services in respect of which registration was sought were deemed to be incapable, by their very nature, of fulfilling the trademark's function as an indication of origin, without prejudice to the possibility of such distinctive character being acquired through use. By prohibiting the registration the Regulation pursued an aim which was in the general interest, namely that such signs or indications should be freely used by all. That provision accordingly precluded such signs or indications being reserved to a single undertaking as a result of the registration of the trademark.[57]

Two other decisions of the CJEU from February 2004 – the *Biomild*[58] and the *Postkantoor*[59] decisions – seem to resolve several uncertainties from earlier case law. In the *Biomild* case *Campina Melkunie* (*Campina*) applied to the Benelux-Merkenbureau (BTMO) for registration of the mark *Biomild* as a trademark in respect of goods in Classes 29, 30 and 32 for mild-flavoured yoghurt. The BTMO refused the application because it conveyed only that the products were *biological* and *mild*. The sign was held to be exclusively descriptive and without any distinctive character. *Campina* brought an action against the refusal before the Gerechtshof te's-Gravenhage, which dismissed the action. *Campina* appealed to the Hoge Raad der Nederlanden, which referred some questions to the Benelux-Gerechtshof for a preliminary ruling. Taking the view that an interpretation of the Directive was necessary for it to answer three of those questions, the Benelux-Gerechtshof decided to request a preliminary ruling by the CJEU. According to the CJEU a trademark consisting of a *neologism* composed of elements, each of which was descriptive of the goods or services in respect of which registration was sought was itself descriptive, unless there was a perceptible *difference between the neologism and the mere sum of its parts*: that assumed that, *because of the unusual nature of the combination in relation to the goods or services, the word created an impression which was sufficiently*

[55] Ibid at para 50.

[56] Para 17 in the decision by the CJEU.

[57] Case C-326/01 P, *Telefon & Buch VerlagsgmbH v OHIM*, [2004] ECR I-1371 (Telefon & Buch) paras 26–27 and Case C-150/02 P [2004] ECR I-1461 (Streamserve) paras 24–25; the CJEU referred to the Joined Cases C-108/97 and the Joined Cases C-108/97 and C-109/97, [1999] ECR I-2779 (Windsurfing Chiemsee) para 25, and Joined Cases C-53/01 to C-55/01, [2003] ECR 2003 I-3161 (Linde) para 73.

[58] Case C-265/00 [2004] ECR I-1699 (Biomild).

[59] Case C-363/99[2004] ECR I-1619 (Postkantoor).

far removed from that produced by the mere combination of meanings lent by the elements of which it was composed, with the result that the word was more than the sum of its parts.[60]

In the *Postkantoor* decision *Koninklijke KPN Nederland NV* (KPN) lodged an application for registration of *Postkantoor* (ie *post office*) as a trademark in respect of certain goods and services falling within Classes 16, 35 to 39, 41 and 42 with the BTMO. The BTMO refused registration on the ground that the mark was exclusively descriptive of the goods and services mentioned and that it therefore had no distinctive character. KPN brought proceedings before the Gerechtshof te's-Gravenhage, which decided to refer questions to the CJEU, which stated that a mark consisting of a word composed of elements, each of which was descriptive of characteristics of the goods or services in respect of which registration was sought, was itself descriptive of those characteristics for the purposes of Article 3(1)(c) of the Directive, *unless there was a perceptible difference between the word and the mere sum of its parts: that assumed either that, because of the unusual nature of the combination in relation to the goods or services, the word created an impression which was sufficiently far removed from that produced by the mere combination of meanings lent by the elements of which it was composed, with the result that the word was more than the sum of its parts, or that the word had become part of everyday language and had acquired its own meaning, with the result that it was now independent of its components. In the second case, it was necessary to ascertain whether a word which had acquired its own meaning was not itself descriptive for the purpose of the same provision.*[61]

Presumably the *Biomild*- and *Postkantoor* cases were decided with regard to a desire to clarify the earlier rulings in eg the *Baby-dry* and *Doublemint* decisions and to provide some further guidelines, where the starting point being that descriptiveness in the elements of a mark does not automatically result in the conclusion that the compound mark is also descriptive.[62] This also seems to be the state of the law so far as the cases' findings are followed in later decisions by the CJEU and the General Court.

The *SAT.1* decision was about an application for a Community trademark in respect of the term *SAT.2*.[63] The CJEU set aside the judgment of the General Court,[64] because it had based its refusal on the assumption that elements individually devoid of distinctive character could not, on being combined, present such a character. The General Court had examined the impression as a whole produced by that term only as a secondary matter. The CJEU stated that a trademark comprising words or a word and a digit, the distinctiveness of each of those terms or elements, taken separately, might be assessed in part, but

[60] Ibid at para 43.
[61] Ibid at para 100.
[62] Maniatis at p 208.
[63] Case C-329/02 P, *SAT.1 SatellitenFernsehen GmbH v OHIM* [2004] ECR I-8317 (SAT.1).
[64] Case T-323/00, *SAT.1 SatellitenFernsehen GmbH v OHIM* [2002] ECR II-2839 (SAT.1).

must, in any event, depend on an appraisal of the whole which they comprised. Indeed, the mere fact that each of those elements, considered separately, was devoid of distinctive character did not mean that their combination could not present a distinctive character.[65] The manner in which the General Court had applied the Regulation reflected a misinterpretation of that provision.[66] It was clear that the General Court assessed whether the term *SAT.2* had a distinctive character essentially by means of a separate analysis of each of its elements and on the presumption that elements individually devoid of distinctive character could not, on being combined, present such a character instead of, as it should have done, on the overall perception. The General Court had examined the impression as a whole produced by the term only secondarily, refusing to give any relevance to aspects such as the existence of an element of imaginativeness, which ought to be taken into account in such an analysis.[67] The CJEU also stated that the distinctive character should be seen in the light of the general interest. Registration of a sign as a trademark was not subject to a finding of a specific level of linguistic or artistic creativity or imaginativeness on the part of the proprietor of the trademark. It sufficed that the trademark should enable the relevant public to identify the origin of the goods or services and to distinguish them from those of other undertakings.[68]

One decision concerned the registration of a composite mark, containing the word parts *Bio* and *ID*, a full stop and the ®-symbol, for goods and services in classes 9, 38 and 42 (see picture).[69] The BoA refused the application since the mark, seen as a whole, was an abbreviation of the words *biometric identification* and therefore descriptive of the characteristics of the goods and services covered by the application:[70]

BioID®.

According to the CJEU any distinctive character could be assessed, in part, in respect of each of the terms or elements, taken separately, but *that assessment must, in any event, be based on the overall perception of that trademark by the relevant public and not on the presumption that elements individually devoid of distinctive character could not, on being combined, present such character.*[71]

[65] Case C-329/02 P, SAT.1 (SAT.1) at para 28 citing Case C-265/00, [2004] ECR I-1699 (Biomild), paras 40–41, and Case C-363/99, [2004] ECR 2004 I-1619 (Postkantoor) paras 99–100.

[66] Ibid at para 29.

[67] Ibid at para 35.

[68] Ibid at para 41; see Maniatis at p 97.

[69] Case C-37/03 P, *BioID AG, v OHIM*, [2005] ECR I-7975 (BioID).

[70] See Maniatis at p 100.

[71] Case C-37/03 P, [2005] ECR I-7975 (BioID) citing Case C-329/02 P, [2004] ECR I-8317 (SAT.1) at para 35.

The mere fact that each of those elements, considered separately, was devoid of distinctive character did not mean that their combination could not present such character.[72] The CJEU noted that the General Court rightly had held that it was not inconsistent with a successive examination of the different composite elements of the mark to consider the mark as a whole.[73] The General Court had noted that, where it did not appear that there was concrete evidence, such as, eg the way in which the various elements were combined, to indicate that a compound trademark, taken as a whole, *was greater than the sum of its parts, such a trademark was devoid of distinctive character in respect of the goods and services concerned*.[74] In addition, the General Court referred to its detailed analysis first of the elements. In doing so, the General Court integrated the analysis into its examination of the impression produced by the trademark applied for *as a whole*, with a view to determining whether it was of a character such as to render it registerable as a trademark.[75] Finally, the General Court found that the structure of the trademark applied for did not alter the conclusion that the trademark, taken as a whole, was devoid of distinctive character.[76]

In the *Celltech* decision[77] *R&D Ltd* (*Celltech*) had filed an application with the OHIM for registration of the word mark *Celltech* as a CTM for eg. pharmaceutical, veterinary and sanitary preparations, compounds and substances, surgical and medical apparatus and instruments, and research, development and consultancy services in Classes 5, 10 and 42. The OHIM rejected the application as the sign consisted of the grammatically correct combination of the two terms *cell* and *tech* (an abbreviation of *technical* or *technology*) and that, consequently, the mark could not serve as an indicator of origin for the goods and services in respect of which registration was sought. The BoA dismissed the appeal. *Celltech* brought an action before the General Court which held that the BoA had not demonstrated that the word *Celltech* was descriptive of the goods and services in respect of which registration was sought. According to the CJEU it was not sufficient that each of the word elements could be found to be descriptive. The word itself must be found to be descriptive.[78] As OHIM had pointed out, it followed from the Court's case-law that, as a general rule, *a mere combination of elements, each of which was descriptive of characteristics of the goods or services in respect of which registration was sought, itself remained descriptive of those characteristics*.[79]

[72] Ibid at para 29 citing Case C-363/99, [2004] ECR I-1619 (Postkantoor) at paras 99–100, Case C-265/00, [2004] ECR I-1699 (Biomild) paras 40–41, and Case C-329/02 P, [2004] ECR I-8317 (SAT.1) para 28.

[73] Ibid at para 31.

[74] Ibid at para 34.

[75] Ibid at para 35.

[76] Ibid at para 36.

[77] Case C-273/05 P, *OHIM, v Celltech R&D Ltd*, [2007] ECR I-2883 (Celltech).

[78] Ibid at para 76 citing Case C-363/99, [2004] ECR I-1619 (Postkantoor) para 96 and Case C-265/00, [2004] ECR I-1699 (Biomild) para 37.

[79] Ibid at para 77 citing Case C-363/99, [2004] ECR I-1619 (Postkantoor) para 98 and Case C-265/00, [2004] ECR 2004 I-1699 (Biomild) para 39.

However, such a combination could not be descriptive, provided that it created an impression which was *sufficiently far removed from that produced by the simple combination of those elements*.[80] Accordingly, the words' distinctive character should be assessed, in part, in relation to each of its elements, taken separately. It must, in any event, depend on an appraisal of the whole which they comprised.[81] Contrary to OHIM, it did not follow from the Court's case-law that the *prior analysis of each of the elements of which a mark is composed was an essential step*. On the contrary, the assessment of the descriptiveness should be for the mark considered as a whole. In that case, it was not established that the mark was descriptive.[82]

The *Eurohypo* decision concerned an appeal against the decision to refuse to register the word *Eurohypo* in Class 36 for eg financial affairs, monetary affairs, real estate affairs, provision of financial services and financing.[83] According to the CJEU the average German-speaking consumer understood the sign *Eurohypo* as referring to financial services requiring real securities and, in particular, to mortgage loans paid in the currency of the European Economic and Monetary Union. Furthermore, there was no additional element which would allow the view to be reached that the combination, created by the current and usual components *Euro* and *hypo*, was unusual or might have its own meaning which distinguished the services offered by the trademark applicant from those of a different commercial origin. Therefore, the mark should be perceived as providing details of the type of services which it designated and not as indicating the origin of those services.[84]

The General Court

In order to follow the development of distinctive character in compound word marks it is of some interest to examine relevant cases from the General Court. In this part I have selected some of the most relevant cases, the aim of which primarily is to show how the statements of the CJEU have been adopted by the General Court.

In one case, the General Court held that the word *EuroHealth*, which shows significant similarities with *Eurohypo*, was not distinctive with regard to health insurance services.[85] According to the General Court the word, in the English-

[80] Ibid at para 78 citing Case C-363/99, [2004] ECR I-1619 (Postkantoor) para 99 and Case C-265/00, [2004] ECR I-1699 (Biomild) para 40.

[81] Ibid at para 79 citing Case C-329/02 P, [2004] ECR I-8317 (SAT.1) para 28 and Case C-37/03 P, [2005] ECR I-7975 (BioID) para 29.

[82] Ibid at paras 80–81.

[83] Case C-304/06 P, *Eurohypo AG v OHIM*, R [2008] ECR I-3297 (Eurohypo).

[84] Ibid at paras 68–69.

[85] Case T-359/99, *Deutsche Krankenversicherung AG (DKV) v OHIM*, [2001] ECR II-1645 (EuroHealth).

speaking areas of the Community, indicated health insurance services which could be offered at the European level. In those areas the term *Health* was purely descriptive and the prefix *Euro* only indicated the European character of the services concerned. Moreover, there was nothing to suggest that the combination of the prefix *euro* with the noun *health* conferred on the word *EuroHealth* an additional element as a result of which it no longer had a purely descriptive character. The word established immediately and without further reflection a definite and direct association with the health insurance services.[86]

Two General Court cases concerned the similar signs *Carcard*[87] and *Truckcard*[88] in Classes 9, 36–39 and 42. As regards the word *Carcard* for the categories of goods listed as machine-readable data carriers equipped with programs and/or data, in particular magnetic cards and/or chip cards and/or credit cards, the word *Carcard* taken as a whole must be considered as capable of designating both the kind and quality of those goods. The goods actually comprised different kinds of card and the fact that they were linked to a car must be a quality of the goods that constituted an essential characteristic. Therefore there was a sufficiently direct and concrete association between the word *Carcard* and those goods.[89]

The *Best Buy* decision from 2003 concerned registration of a *composite mark* constituted by the shape of a coloured price tag with the words 'BEST BUY' and the ®-symbol (see picture), in respect of services in Classes 35, 37, and 42.[90]

Concerning the word part of the mark, the General Court noted that it was composed of ordinary English words which clearly indicated an advantageous relation between the price of the services covered by the application and their market value.[91] It was therefore immediately perceived as a mere promotional formula or a slogan which indicated that the services in question offered the best *buy* possible in their category or the *best price-quality ratio*.[92] The semantic content of the word mark indicated a characteristic of the service relating to its market value rather than an indication of the commercial origin of the services. The mere fact that the semantic content of the mark *Best Buy* did not convey any information about the nature of the services concerned was not sufficient to make the sign distinctive.[93]

[86] Ibid at paras 26–27.
[87] Case T-356/00, *DaimlerChrysler AG v OHIM*, [2001] ECR II-1963 (Carcard).
[88] Case T-358/00, *DaimlerChrysler AG v OHIM* [2002] ECR II-1993 (Truckcard).
[89] Case T-356/00, [2001] ECR II-1963 (Carcard) para 32.
[90] Case T-122/01, *Best Buy Concepts Inc v OHIM* [2003] ECR II-2235 (Best Buy).
[91] Ibid at para 28.
[92] Ibid at para 29.
[93] Ibid at para 30.

In the *Robotunits* case[94] *HERON Robotunits GmbH*, filed an application for the mark *Robotunits* for eg profiles of metal, guide rails of metal, shaped static elements, shaped connecting elements within Class 6, guides for machines, pressure and linear cylinders with various types of drive system and shaped pneumatic elements within Class 7, and conveyor belts and striking systems with position controls within Class 9. The OHIM refused the application on the basis of Article 7(1) (c) of the TMR on the ground that the mark was descriptive. According to the BoA, which dismissed the appeal, the mark described the intended purpose of the goods, namely the fact that those goods could be used for the assembly of automated and programmed machines, or the fact that they were installed in assembled machines. The General Court stated that since the applicant had not limited its application for registration by excluding the use of the goods referred to as robot parts, the fact that the sign in question might serve to designate one of the possible intended purposes of the goods covered by the trademark, the application was a sufficient basis for refusing registration, on the ground that the mark was descriptive.[95] By reference to the *Carcard* decision,[96] the General Court concluded that the goods referred to in the application might be used in automated or programmed machines was one of the technical functions of those goods. That they might also be used in machines which were not automated or programmed did not preclude their technical function from being precisely the characteristic which rendered the sign *Robotunits* descriptive of those goods.[97] It therefore followed that the sign *Robotunits* could serve to designate essential characteristics of the goods falling within the categories referred to by the application.[98]

In the *Nurseryroom* case[99] from 2004, the General Court referred to the CJEU's *Postkantoor* decision. *Anne Geddes* had filed an application for the mark *Nurseryroom* seeking registration in connection with books, stationery, and cards in Class 16, diaper bags in Class 18, plates and cups in Class 21, hats, booties, baby clothing, shoes and layettes in Class 25, and plush toys, mobiles in Class 28. The OHIM rejected the application on the ground that the mark was descriptive of the intended purpose of the goods pursuant to Article 7.1 (b) and (c) of the TMR. The BoA dismissed the appeal. According to the General Court the words *nursery room* designated a place for use by babies or young children. It must be held, moreover, that the sign in question, in *coupling those two words in the grammatically correct order* in English, did not create *an impression sufficiently removed from that produced by the mere juxtaposition of the words to change their meaning or scope.*[100] The sign was perfectly appropriate

[94] Case T-222/02, *HERON Robotunits GmbH v OHIM* [2003] ECR II-4995 (Robotunits).
[95] Ibid at para 46.
[96] Case T-356/00, [2002] ECR II-1963 (Carcard).
[97] Ibid at para 40.
[98] Case T-222/02, [2003] ECR II-4995 (Robotunits) at para 48.
[99] Case T-173/03, *Anne Geddes v OHIM* [2004] ECR II-4165 (Nurseryroom).
[100] Ibid at para 21 citing Case C-363/99 [2004] ECR I-1619 (Postkantoor) paras 98–99.

to designate goods capable of being used in a nursery and, therefore, for use by babies or young children. Since the goods in question were all capable of being intended, exclusively or potentially, for those users, the relevant public would easily establish a *direct and specific link between the sign and the goods in question.*[101] The action was therefore dismissed.[102]

In the *Rockbass* case from 2005, the General Court referred to the *Biomild* and *Postkantoor* decisions. In this case the mark *Rockbass* was applied for registration in respect of goods in Classes 9, 15 and 18 (eg technical sound equipment, mixing desks, sound effect equipment, amplifiers, loudspeaker boxes, active loudspeaker boxes (combos), containers, cases and bags for the aforesaid goods, musical instruments, in particular guitars, bass guitars, and guitar accessories).[103] According to the General Court the word *rockbass* designated a bass guitar which lent itself to playing rock music or, conversely, a style of music played with a bass guitar. This could not be called in question by the fact that the word did not appear as such in dictionaries.[104] A trademark consisting of a *neologism* composed of elements *each of which was descriptive of characteristics of the goods or services in respect of which registration was sought was itself descriptive, unless there was a perceptible difference between the neologism and the mere sum of its parts; that assumed that, because of the unusual nature of the combination in relation to the goods or services, the neologism created an impression which was sufficiently far removed from that produced by the mere combination of meanings lent by the elements of which it was composed.*[105] In the present case, the sign *Rockbass* did not diverge from English word composition rules, since it corresponded to the *syntactically correct juxtaposition* of the two words. Therefore nothing unusual about the structure of the word which *did not create an impression far removed from that produced by the mere combination of meanings lent by its components.*[106] The Court made a detailed analysis of the distinctive character in relation to the various kinds of goods applied for. It then concluded that it could not be called into question by an individual analysis of the goods, which did not have any intended purpose other than in connection with handling guitars. Thus, if registration of the sign *Rockbass* was claimed solely for containers, cases and bags for guitars, and not for the guitars themselves, it would have to be held that *Rockbass* evoked the sole intended purpose of those goods. In relation also to containers, cases and bags in Class 18, since the applicant had not drawn any

[101] Ibid at para 23.

[102] Ibid at para 28.

[103] Case T-315/03, *Hans-Peter Wilfer v OHIM*, [2005] ECR II-1981 appeal dismissed, Case C-301/05, [2007] ECR I-137 (Rockbass).

[104] Ibid at paras 57–58.

[105] The General Court cited Case C-363/99, [2004] ECR I-1619 (Postkantoor) and Case C-265/00, [2004] ECR I-1699 (Biomild).

[106] Ibid at para 60 citing Case T-356/00, [2002] ECR II-1963 (Carcard) para 29, and Case T-222/02, [2003] ECR II-4995 (Robotunits) para 39.

distinctions within this generic category, the BoA's findings must be confirmed in so far as they related to all goods in that category.[107] For those reasons, the same solution must be adopted with regard to the containers, cases and bags as for the goods for which they were designed. Finally the Court concluded that the link between the sign *Rockbass* and the characteristics of all the goods referred to in the application was sufficiently close to fall within the scope of the prohibition under Article 7(1) (c) of the TMR.[108]

Hence, it can be seen that the General Court in its later cases has made its decisions on similar grounds as the findings of the CJEU in the *Biomild* and *Postkantoor* decisions.[109]

4. ANALYSIS

Indeed, it is surprising that there have been so many decisions from the CJEU with regard to distinctive character in compound word marks. According to *Bezant* all the good names appeared to have been already taken, resulting in the increased use of compound trademarks. Those compound trademarks could lack distinctiveness, both in a trademark sense and to consumers.[110] It has also been pointed out that '[k]eeping different types of compounding apart is essential for psycholinguistic investigations, in order to guarantee compatibility of results both within the same language and in a cross-linguistic perspective.'[111] Even though these are interesting explanations, they do not appear to be exhaustive. Designing trademarks by compounding is probably just a recent trend perhaps founded in a strategy, where it is easier not only to claim distinctive character in a compound than in a single word, but also providing that such a mark is easier to protect against attacks from third parties, such those grounded on degeneration. This does not explain why there have been so many EU cases on compound trademarks in comparison with the many other questions which have traditionally been litigated with regard to the distinctive character of word marks. Questions which in comparison have not been litigated to the same extent in EU case law.

[107] Ibid at paras 69–70.

[108] Ibid at paras 74–75.

[109] See Case T-19/04, *Metso Paper Automation Oy v OHIM*, [2005] ECR II-2383(Paperlab) Case T-190/05, *The Sherwin-Williams Company v OHIM*, [2007] ECR II-1911(Twist & Pour), Case T-207/06, *Europig SA v OHIM*, [2007] ECR II-1961 (Europig), Case T-160/07, *Lancôme parfums et beauté & Cie SNC v OHIM*, [2008] ECR II-1733 (Colour Edition)), appeal dismissed, Case C-408/08 P OJ C 100 of 17.04.2010, para 5, and the Joined Cases T–178/03 and T-179/03, *CeWe Color AG & Co OHG v OHIM*, [2005] ECR II-3105 (DigiFilm and DigiFilmMaker).

[110] Bezant, *The Impact of Permitted Use on Trade Mark Valuation, Trade Marks at the Limit* (Phillips Ed) (Edward Elgar Pub 2006) p 204.

[111] Dressler, *The Representation and Processing of Compound Words* at p 23.

Nevertheless, today there is an extensive body of law which can be analysed in a number of different ways. I would like to take this in three different steps: The first is to analyse the European case law from the *Baby-dry* decision to the *Postkantoor* decision. The second is to analyse the EU case law within the framework of linguistics set out in the beginning of this article. The third is, as mentioned in the introduction, to analyse whether and to what extent linguistics and jurisprudence should go hand in hand, interrelate, or follow different regimes.

Before proceeding into the details of interpretation of the different prerequisites for distinctive character of compound trademarks, it should be noted that a determination of distinctive character must be based upon an *overall assessment*.[112] This is the case not only in the registration stage, but also in the infringement stage. For example, in the so called *Lloyd* decision, with respect to the likelihood of confusion between the marks *Loint's* and *Lloyd* for shoes, the Court stated that

> in determining the distinctive character of a mark and, accordingly, in assessing whether it is highly *distinctive*, the national court must make an overall assessment of the greater or lesser capacity of the mark to identify the goods or services for which it has been registered as coming from a particular undertaking, and thus to distinguish those goods or services from those of other undertakings.[113] ... [T]he global appreciation of the likelihood of confusion must, as regards the visual, aural or conceptual similarity of the marks in question, be based on the overall impression created by them, bearing in mind, in particular, their distinctive and dominant components.[114]

CJEU decisions on distinctive character in compound trademarks have dealt with different questions. One question is whether the concatenation, as such, of common words or word parts makes the compound mark distinctive. This was the main question in the *Baby-dry* decision.[115] From an examination of case-law, it is clear that the CJEU has abandoned the notions of *lexical invention* and *syntactically unusual juxtaposition* from the *Baby-dry* decision. Those concepts can still have validity from a theoretical point of view. On that point it can therefore be observed that the notion *syntactically juxtaposition* has been used by the General Court in case law even after the *Biomild* and *Postkantoor* decisions.[116]

How to combine common words in a new way is another question. This was addressed in the *Doublemint* decision,[117] where an ambiguity related to the constituent parts of the trademarks (a noun and a verb) was held to be devoid

[112] See Case C-37/03 P, ECR 2005 I-7975 (BioID) para 29 and Case C-329/02 P, [2004] ECR I-8317 (SAT.1) para 35.

[113] Case C-342/97, *Lloyd Schuhfabrik Meyer & Co GmbH v Klijsen Handel BV*, [1999] ECR I-3819 (Lloyd) p 22 citing the Joined Cases C-108/97 and C-109/97, [1999] ECR I-2779 (Windsurfing Chiemsee) para 49.

[114] Case C-342/97, [1999] ECR I-3819 (Lloyd) para 25 citing Case C-251/95, *SABEL BV v Puma AG, Rudolf Dassler Sport*, [1997] ECR I-6191 (Sabel) para 23.

[115] See Case C-383/99 P, [2001] ECR 2001 I-6251 (Baby-dry) para 44.

[116] See Case T-315/03, [2005] ECR II-1981 (Rockbass) para 60.

[117] Case C-191/01 P, [2003] ECR I-12447 (Doublemint).

of distinctive character. If at least one of the constituents was descriptive for the good or service, the compound mark should logically be devoid of any distinctive character. The conclusion from the *Doublemint* decision therefore is that the compound must give an entirely new meaning in relation to the good or service. Perhaps, this is too narrow an assessment. Indeed, if there is just one interpretation and it is descriptive for the good or service in question, the mark should be devoid of any distinctive character. However, the greater number of possible meanings of the mark, the more the trademark acquires distinctive qualities. Assuming that a mark may be interpreted, not only in two, but more different ways, would this also mean that the mark is devoid of any distinctive character? From my point of view it is unsatisfying that this question was not more fully elaborated on by the Court.

A third question is whether the combination of common words or word parts makes the compound distinctive in relation to its good or service. This question was addressed by the CJEU in *Postkantoor*, where the Court ruled that a mark consisting of a word composed of elements, each of which is descriptive is itself descriptive of those characteristics, unless there is a *perceptible difference between the word and the mere sum of its parts* ... because of the *unusual nature of the combination in relation to the goods or services.*[118]

From my perspective the answers to those questions to a great extent can be supplied by a combination of EU case law and traditional trademark principles. To some extent the principles elaborated by the CJEU can also be explained by linguistic theory. I also believe that the Court should permit itself to be even more and explicitly inspired by linguistics, because distinctive character is very much about what is going on in the minds of the average consumers, who are reasonably well informed, reasonably observant, and circumspect.[119] Accordingly a fourth question, which has not been so clearly dealt with by the CJEU should be added, namely to what extent the distinctive character of each word part affects the distinctive character of the entire compound mark. The CJEU has concluded that the distinctive character *might* be assessed, *in part, in respect of each of the terms or elements, taken separately*, but the mere fact that each of the elements, considered separately, was held to be devoid of distinctive character did not mean that their combination could not present such distinctiveness.[120] An understanding of a compound word also depends on the transparency or opacity of its constituents. Lexical processing systems do not represent compound words solely in terms of their constituents, but

[118] Case C-363/99, [2004] ECR I-1619 (Postkantoor) para 100; see Case C 265/00, [2004] ECR I-1699 (Biomild) para 43.

[119] See Case C-210/96, *Gut Springenheide GmbH, Rudolf Tusky, and Oberkreisdirektor des Kreises Steinfurt - Amt für Lebensmittelüberwachung v Oberbundesanwalt beim Bundesverwaltungsgericht*, [1998] ECR I-4657 (Gut Springenheide und Tusky) para 31.

[120] See Case C-37/03 P, [2005] ECR I-7975 (BioID) para 29; Case C-329/02 P, [2004] ECR I-8317 (SAT.1) paras 28 and 35; Case C-363/99, [2004] ECR I-1619 (Postkantoor) paras 99–100; Case C-265/00, [2004] ECR I-1699 (Biomild) paras 40–41.

also indicates that they are not semantically transparent in the sense that the meanings of the compounds are fully predictable from the meaning of their constituents.[121] Transparency refers to the extent to which the meaning of a compound word is predictable from its constituents.[122] It follows from the *Doublemint* decision[123] that a compound word may be more or less ambiguous. If this is so, the understanding of the distinctive character in a compound mark should also depend on the transparency or opacity of its constituents.[124] In that respect I think that the CJEU has been too strict in its assessment. As the ambiguity of the word parts makes the meaning of the mark opaque, the mark *Doublemint* should therefore be viewed as distinctive. The same would apply for concatenations of or with unusual word or word parts which, seen separately, are generic or descriptive.

Compound trademarks consist of more than one stem. This occurs when two or more morphemes are attached together to make them function as one new mark. The meanings of the parts interrelate in such a way that a new meaning arises, which is different from the meanings of the word parts in isolation. This is what usually is called *secondary meaning*. Lexical processing systems do not represent compound trademarks solely in terms of their constituents. The interpretation of combined concepts involves an interaction between the two constituents, rather than an additive process.[125] A *maximisation of opportunity* system would allow whole-mark processing as well as morphological processing to occur simultaneously. Thus, a word mark such as *Coca-Cola* would be simultaneously processed as a whole as well as in terms of its constituents *Coca* and *Cola*. This results in bi-directional activation, such that the constituents receive activation from the process of morphological parsing, as well as from the structured representation of the compound in the mental lexicon.[126]

If a compound mark is presented often enough so that it can be lexicalised, it is probably stored as a representation that can be retrieved as a single representation,[127] ie *that the mark has become part of everyday language and has acquired its own meaning, with the result that it is independent of its components*.[128] This, however, does not shut down the process of morphological decomposition for that mark and its constituent morphemes.[129]

Lexicalised compound marks refer to compounds that are familiar and have a common usage. The meaning of lexicalised compounds can therefore be retrieved directly from the lexicon,[130] ie that a trademark has been established on the

[121] See Libben in *The Representation and Processing of Compound Words* at p 11.
[122] Ibid Jarema at pp 48 ff.
[123] Case C-191/01 P, [2003] ECR I-12447 (Doublemint).
[124] See Jarema in *The Representation and Processing of Compound Words* at pp 48 ff.
[125] Ibid Gagné and Spalding at p 149.
[126] Ibid Libben at p 9.
[127] Ibid at p 6.
[128] See Case C-363/99, [2004] ECR. I-1619 (Postkantoor), para 100 and Case C 265/00, [2004] ECR I-1699 (Biomild) para 43.
[129] Libben in *The Representation and Processing of Compound Words* at p 6.
[130] See Gagné and Spalding, above note 21.

market, reputed or well known. In this case, it is *necessary to ascertain whether the mark which has acquired its own meaning is not itself descriptive.*[131] In contrast, the meanings of novel or less familiar combinations must be processed or computed because they are not yet established.[132] Understanding a combined concept involves creating a new concept because a combined concept is *more than a hybrid of its parts,*[133] ie that there is a *perceptible difference between the mark and the mere sum of its parts* and that it *creates an impression which is sufficiently far removed from that produced by the mere combination of meanings lent by the elements of which it is composed.*[134] To interpret a novel compound, one must therefore access the *concepts* denoted by the words and select a relation which links them together,[135] ie that the mark has *inherent distinctive character.*

Taking this reasoning out further from the EU case law in view of the framework of linguistics set out in the beginning of this article, it is clear that it must be easier to obtain distinctive character in a novel compound mark than in a lexicalised one, because the novel compound is the result of a *lexical invention.* For lexicalised compound words their distinctive character will rather rely mainly on their arbitrariness, or establishment on the market. If so, this would result in the principles that the more common parts of which the mark is constructed, the less will be its inherent distinctive character, and as to the opposite, the more opaque the word parts are, the greater will be its inherent distinctive character. The harder it is to process a word or word parts, the greater will be its inherent distinctive character. The more common the lexical invention is the less will be its distinctive character.[136] The more known or reputed a mark, the greater will be its acquired distinctive character.

The conclusion should therefore be that jurisprudence should go hand in hand with, or follow linguistics to the extent that linguistics may explain what is going on in the minds of the average consumer. In this context I would like to revert to the discourse on conceptual combination within linguistic theory. This would probably lead the CJEU into a more liberal manner of interpretation than found in the current case law, but would not necessarily be as lenient as in the *Baby-dry* decision. [137] Under that construction at least at minimum, marks such as *Robotunits*[138] and *Rockbass*[139] would reach the level of inherent distinctive character.

[131] See Case C-363/99, [2004] ECR I-1619 (Postkantoor), para 100 and Case C 265/00, [2004] ECR I-1699 (Biomild) para 43.

[132] See Gagné and Spalding, above note 21.

[133] Gagné and Spalding in *The Representation and Processing of Compound Words* at p 149.

[134] See Case C-363/99, [2004] ECR I-1619 (Postkantoor), para 100 and Case C 265/00, [2004] ECR I-1699 (Biomild) para 43.

[135] Gagné, above note 22.

[136] In the *Companyline* decision (see above note 44) it was concluded that coupling two word parts without any graphic or semantic modification did not imbue them with any additional characteristic such as to render the sign, taken as a whole, distinctive character.

[137] Case C-383/99 P, [2002] ECR I-6251 (Baby-dry).

[138] Case T-222/02, [2003] ECR 2003 II-4995 (Robotunits).

[139] Case T-315/03, [2005] ECR 2005 II-1981 (Rockbass).

5
Protection of Non-Registered Trademarks in Sweden and the EU

ASSOCIATE PROFESSOR ERIKA LUNELL*

Protection through registration is the predominant form of protecting trademarks in Europe. However, in each of the Member States this is complemented by methods for protecting non-registered trademarks, even though the form and scope of protection may vary between them. For example, in some Member States the protection of non-registered trademarks is primarily regulated outside the trademark legislation, via the law of unfair competition or 'passing off', although such marks can be invoked as grounds for refusal or cancellation of another registration under the trademark legislation. In others, the protection of non-registered trademarks has been integrated into the trademark laws, implying that the same protection applies for a trademark whether it is registered or not. This has long since been the case in Sweden, Norway, Finland, and Denmark.

The first Trademark Directive[1] was adopted in order to approximate the trademark laws of the Member States but only to the extent required for a smoothly functioning common market. It was considered best to harmonise the trademark laws in stages, and that the first efforts should relate to those provisions that had the strongest and most direct influence on the establishment and functioning of the common market for branded goods. For registered trademarks indeed, a far-reaching harmonisation took place, including, inter alia, rules about subject matter of protection, scope of protection, user requirement, and relative and absolute grounds for refusal or invalidity.

Such harmonisation did, however, not occur in the field of non-registered trademarks. The reason for this was not that there was no need for harmonisation in this area, but rather that it was considered too complicated to accomplish, on account of the large variation in the laws of the different Member States.

* Associate professor, Karlstad University, erika.lunel@kau.se. This work was supported by a grant from Stiftelsen Längmanska Kulturfonden.

[1] Directive 89/104/EEC of 21 December 1988 to approximate the laws of the Member States relating to trademarks OJ L 40 11/02/1989 pp 1 –7.

As it did not seem possible to find a common solution, this was postponed to the future.[2] Recently, the first Directive was replaced by a new Trademark Directive.[3] This did, however, not lead to any essential modifications and, like the original Directive, it does not effect any harmonisation of the protection of non-registered trademarks. The Member States have thus been able to keep the provisions that give such protection to trademarks through use.

According to certain provisions of the Directive, however, non-registered trademarks that are protected according to national law are taken into account in regard to the relationship between them and trademarks acquired by registration. There are also provisions in the Community Trademark Regulation,[4] which regulate the relation between non-registered national trademarks and Community trademarks. Further, it is for the European Court of Justice (CJEU) to interpret Community trademark law, including those provisions that regulate non-registered trademarks. The CJEU is the court of last instance for registration matters concerning Community trademarks as well as giving preliminary rulings on questions on Community law after referrals from a national court in a specific case.[5]

The questions addressed in this article are: To what extent is the protection of non-registered trademarks a purely national concern? How has Community law influenced the protection of non-registered marks in Sweden? Is there a continued need for non-registered trademark protection whether as it exists today or in modified form?

1. THE DEVELOPMENT OF THE NON-REGISTERED TRADEMARK PROTECTION

Prior to the existence of explicit legislation in Sweden, trademark protection was established when a mark began to be used, ie by first use. When the first Swedish Trademarks Act (*Lag om skydd för varumärken)* was promulgated on 5 July 1884, however, registration became the only way to obtain the protection. Similar trademark legislation was introduced at the same time in the other Nordic countries.[6] The trademark laws arose as a result of Nordic legislative collaboration, inspired by the German system of registration. However, it turned out that the

[2] HP Götting, 'Protection of Well-Known, Unregistered Marks in Europe and the United States' (2000) 31 *International Review of Intellectual Property & Competition Law* pp 389, 392.

[3] Directive 2008/95/EC of the European Parliament and the Council of 22 October 2008 to approximate the laws of the Member States relating to trademarks OJ L 299, 8.11.2008, pp 25–33.

[4] Regulation (EC) No 40/94 of 20 December 1993 on the Community trademark OJ L 11, 14.1.1994, pp 1-36 was repealed by Regulation (EC) No 207/2009 of 26 February 2009 on the Community trademark OJ L 78, 24.3.2009, pp 1-42.

[5] For a recent commentary on the CJEU's interpretation of the Directive, see L Pehrson, 'Interpretation of the Trademark Directive' (2007) 2 *Swedish Studies in European Law* p 157.

[6] In Norway and Denmark, which formally participated in a legislative collaboration with Sweden, trademark laws were promulgated in 1884 and 1890, respectively. Finland issued an ordinance in 1889 on the protection of trademarks, closely related to the above laws.

registration principle did not solve all problems. It was considered to be unfair that someone who had established a trademark through use, but for some reason had not registered the mark or renewed its registration could be prevented from using it if someone else, often in bad faith, had registered the same mark.

The possibility of protecting non-registered marks was a topic for discussion at the beginning of last century. Many countries in Europe, including Germany, began to allow protection of non-registered trademarks to a greater or lesser extent. Norway was the first Nordic country that diverged from the registration principle, through its Trademark Act of 1910. In Finland, trademark acquisition through use and by registration were put on an equal footing as grounds for exclusive rights through the 1953 reform of the Finnish Trademark Act of 1889. In Denmark the Trademark Act of 1936 marked a break with the registration principle. Contrary to the case in the other Nordic countries, where qualified use was required, the mere first use of a mark had legal relevance for the acquisition of protection for a non-registered trademark.

Of special importance for the development of non-registered trademark protection was the *Paris Convention for the Protection of Industrial Property of March 20, 1883, (Paris Convention)*, ratified by Sweden in 1885. A general protection against unfair competition was introduced in 1911 through Article 10 *bis* of the convention. At the Hague conference in 1925, Article 6 *bis* was introduced, which stated that all countries in the Paris union must grant protection for 'well-known marks'. This provision originally obligated the countries in the union to refuse or cancel the registration of a trademark that could be confused with a mark well-known in the country of registration, but which was the property of a person in another country in the union, and used for identical or similar goods. A trademark with a reputation reaching to another country's territory was hence given a certain protection in the latter country, even if it not yet had been registered there. At the Lisbon conference in 1958 this rule was complemented with a prohibition against using a trademark that could be confused with a well-known mark.[7]

Through the *Agreement on Trade-Related Aspects of Intellectual Property Rights (the TRIPs agreement)*,[8] adopted in 1994 and coming into force two years later, which applies to both the EU and its Member States, the protection for well-known marks was further extended. Article 16(2) provides that Article 6 *bis* of the Paris Convention shall also be applied when well-known service marks are concerned and that knowledge within the relevant part of the public shall be considered in determining whether a trademark is 'well-known'. Furthermore, according to Article 16(3), trademark protection can also be extended to dissimilar goods or services for a well-known and registered trademark. Neither

[7] See eg DH Tatham, 'WIPO Resolution on Well Known Marks: a Small Step or a Giant Leap' (2000) 2 *Intellectual Property Quaterly* p 127.

[8] The Agreement on Trade-Related Aspects of Intellectual Property Rights, Annex 1C of the Marrakesh Agreement Establishing the World Trade Organization, signed in Marrakesh, Morocco on 15 April 1994 ('TRIPs').

the Paris Convention nor the TRIPs agreement, however, gives a clear definition of when a trademark shall be considered as 'well known'.[9]

Subsequent to TRIPs work began at the *World Intellectual Property Organization (WIPO)* to further improve the protection of well-known marks. This resulted in a resolution 'Joint Recommendation Concerning Provisions on the Protection of Well-Known Marks', which was adopted by the Paris union and WIPO in September 1999.[10] WIPO's resolution recommends that non-registered marks also be given extended protection.[11] Article 2(1) provides some factors which may be taken into consideration when assessing whether a trademark should be regarded as 'well known'. These are only guidelines which, however, may still be helpful to the authorities of the Member States in particular cases.[12]

Initially, trademarks that had acquired protection through use were accepted only as relative bars to registration in Swedish case-law.[13] In 1934, however, a new provision, motivated by the Hague document, was included in the Swedish Trademarks Act of 1884, under which a trademark could not be registered if it was fully similar to, or could easily be confused with, a mark, which had already been established as a trademark by someone else in Sweden. If a registration was allowed in violation of this rule, it could be declared invalid. The provision, however, only applied to such marks having acquired protection through use as would otherwise be eligible for registration.[14] Therefore only word and pictorial marks, which could be applied to goods or their wrapping, could be invoked against a registration. Further, the person who had established a trademark through use had no protection against someone else using the same mark. In view of this, and the increasing use of packaging to distinguish the products of different undertakings from each other, it was considered that the provision on non-registered trademarks in the Trademarks Act did not give sufficient protection against unfair competition.[15]

The solution originally chosen to this dilemma was to supplement the provisions on trademark law by competition law. The Act of 1931 with certain provisions of unfair competition (*Lagen den 29 maj 1931 (nr 152) med vissa*

[9] Concerning the difficulties in reaching international agreement about what constitutes a 'well-known mark', see, eg, FW Mostert, 'Well-Known and Famous Marks: Is Harmony Possible in the Global Village?' (1996) 86 *The Trademark Reporter* p 103.

[10] Joint Recommendation Concerning Provisions on the Protection of Well-Known Marks, adopted by the Assembly of the Paris Union for the Protection of Industrial Property and the General Assembly of the World Intellectual Property Organization (WIPO) at the Thirty-Fourth Series of Meetings of the Assemblies of the Member States of WIPO September 20 to 29, 1999 Publication 833(E).

[11] Cf Art 2.3 and Art 4.1 b in the Resolution.

[12] See eg A Kur, 'The WIPO Recommendations for the Protection of Well-Known Marks' *IIC* 824 (2000).

[13] The first case dealing with establishment by use in Sweden is *Nytt Juridiskt Arkiv* (NJA) (Supreme Court) (1929) p 44 (*Tengor/Tengax*).

[14] L Holmqvist, 'Om inarbetning av varukännetecken' ('On establishment of marks through use') (1975) 44 *Nordiskt Immateriellt Rättsskydd (NIR)* pp 255, 260.

[15] S Heiding, *Om registrerade varumärken och inarbetade kännetecken* ('On registered trademarks and non-registered marks') (Uppsala, Almqvist & Wiksell, 1946) pp 31 ff.

bestämmelser om illojal konkurrens) was therefore extended in 1942 to cover unregistered marks. The use of a sign that was confusingly similar with an unregistered mark became forbidden.[16] Unregistered marks were considered to include, not only names, trade names and trademarks, but also design and other distinctive features.[17]

The protection of non-registered trademarks was soon integrated into the trademark legislation. The current Swedish Trademarks Act (*Varumärkeslag 1960:644*) also arose as a result of Nordic collaboration. Committees from each of the Nordic countries participated and, once their work was finished, presented proposals for new trademark laws: Denmark in 1959, Sweden in 1960, Norway in 1961 and Finland in 1964. Each country agreed that, in principle, the same rules should apply for the protection of registered and non-registered trademarks. In Sweden, Norway and Finland, essentially similar provisions were introduced where the legal ground for protection of non-registered trademarks was establishment on the market through qualified use. Denmark, however, continued to have first use as an alternative ground for trademark protection.[18]

Since Article 6 *bis* of the Paris Convention only provides a minimum level of protection for well-known marks, it is possible for the Member States to stipulate a lower degree of knowledge than that stated in the Article. A provision explicitly giving protection to well-known marks, in the sense in which the words are used in Article 6 *bis*, was not included in the Swedish Trademarks Act. The protection of well-known but non-registered marks was instead considered to be guaranteed through Section 2(1), the provision which regulates the protection of non-registered marks established on the market *(inarbetning)*, and Section 14(1) No 7, pursuant to which, a trademark may not be registered if it is confusingly similar with a mark, when, at the time of the application, it was used by another economic operator, the applicant knew of this, and it was not the case that the applicant had made use of his mark before the other mark was taken into use. Both provisions make it possible to protect trademarks that have only been used outside Sweden, but have become known in Sweden.

Pursuant to the original definition in Section 2 of the Swedish Trademarks Act, exclusive rights to a trademark were established through use when a mark in Sweden had become *generally known* to designate the goods of the proprietor among the relevant part of the public. Protection was then given against confusingly similar trademarks, independent of whether the infringing party intended to imitate it or not. The rationale given by the Swedish legislator as to why protection acquired through use should be treated equivalently to protection through registration was, foremost, that, as a factual matter, upon infringement the goodwill value that a trademark has acquired through use is exploited, whether the mark in question is registered or not. It was further

[16] § 9 of the Act of 1931 with certain provisions of unfair competition (SFS 1931:152).
[17] *Nytt Juridiskt Arkiv* (NJA) *II* (Supreme Court) (1942) pp 693 ff.
[18] *Betænkning* (Danish Commission Report) 199/1958 pp 26 ff.

stated that certain signs, for purely technical reasons, are not appropriate for registration, for example, all signs that are intended to be perceived by other senses than the visual. As the latter were considered to be no less important to protect than conventional trademarks, it was considered desirable that such signs might acquire trademark protection through use.[19]

The Trademarks Act was amended in 1993, in order to harmonise Swedish trademark law with the Directive. The provisions concerning non-registered trademarks were, however, not altered. A Nordic legislative collaboration, among Finland, Norway and Sweden, was initiated at the end of the 1990s, with the aim of proposing new trademark legislation. The committees in the three countries delivered their final reports in 2001.[20] A common feature of their suggestions is that the dual system with protection through registration or use be maintained.[21]

When the Community Trademark (CTM) was introduced through the Trademark Regulation, an alternative was provided to the existing national trademark laws. By submitting an application to the European trademark authority, the Office for Harmonisation in the Internal Market (OHIM) in Alicante, it became possible to obtain a protection which extends throughout the territory of the EU by way of a single registration.[22] The alternative, acquisition of EU-wide trademark protection through use could not, for reasons of legal certainty, be accepted since the trademark protection is valid throughout the Community.[23] To fulfil the goals of the Treaty, the new trademark system was based on the principles of the *unitary character and autonomous standing of the Community trademark*.[24] The meaning of the first principle is that the protection afforded by a Community trademark shall be the same throughout the Community while the second principle implies that the Community trademark is subject only to provisions in Community law, and that national law is applicable only when explicitly stated.

In the *travaux préparatoires* to the Trademark Regulation it was presupposed that the national trademark laws would continue to exist in parallel to the Regulation. It was pointed out that there always will be undertakings which do not need a protection which extends throughout the EU, that certain word marks which are designed to communicate information to consumers cannot be used outside the language domain in question, and that the Regulation only protects registered trademarks. It was particularly emphasised that there is 'an additional need for the complementary protection of unregistered trademarks,

[19] SOU 1958:10 pp 62 ff.

[20] In Sweden, SOU 2001:26, in Norway, NOU 2001:8 and in Finland, Committee Report 6/2001, ISBN 951-739-595-7.

[21] See eg SOU 2001:26 pp 24, 234. See also P Carlson, 'Något om den svenska varumärkeskommitténs arbete' ('Comments on the work of the Swedish trademark committee') 67 *NIR* 580 (1998).

[22] Art 6, Reg No 207/2009.

[23] Proposal for a Council Regulation on the Community trademark (CTM Proposal), Bulletin of the European Communities, supplement 5/80, p 56.

[24] The principle of the unitary character of the CTM is found in Art 1(2) of the Reg No 207/2009.

and other signs, which must still be guaranteed by national laws on trademarks, unfair competition and the like'.[25]

2. TRADEMARK PROTECTION THROUGH QUALIFIED USE – PROTECTION REQUIREMENTS

He who claims that his mark is protected bears the burden of proving it. The 'to be or not to be' of a non-registered right is often brought to a head in a conflict situation, in connection with either an infringement or a registration process. It then turns out that the proprietor of the registered trademark has in practice, a stronger right. Registration grants the proprietor a right, which is clearly defined as to subject matter, scope and time of origin. He who claims protection acquired through use must, in contrast, provide evidence for this. Therefore a proprietor of a non-registered trademark must show that the mark has been sufficiently used to be established, determine the point of time at which the protection has been acquired, and the geographical territory within which the mark has been established. For the proprietor himself, it may, in many cases, be uncertain whether an exclusive right to the mark exists at all, and to what extent it may be invoked.

The CJEU has stated that the essential function of a trademark is to guarantee the identity of the origin of the marked goods or services to the consumer or end user by enabling him, without any possibility of confusion, to distinguish such goods or services from those with another origin. A trademark must, in other words, have *distinctive character* to be able to be registered. Some trademarks have inherent distinctiveness, in which case it is presumed that they will function as source identifiers for the consumer. According to Section 13 of the Swedish Trademarks Act and Article 3(3) of the Directive, lack of distinctiveness (and descriptive or generic character) is a ground for refusal, which, however, may be overcome if the mark acquires distinctive character through use.

In Swedish law, there is no specific requirement of distinguishing capability for non-registered trademarks, contrary to the situation in Norwegian law.[26] Instead, this is considered to be an intrinsic part of the process of obtaining protection through use. Distinctiveness is a prerequisite to acquiring protection through use and is at the same time a consequence of the use. The mark must always, irrespective of what inherent distinctive character it possesses, be used to such an extent that it receives a certain degree of recognition. The right to a non-registered trademark ultimately depends on the reaction of the relevant part of the public, and it is the experience that a mark serves to distinguish goods or services of one undertaking from those of other undertakings which creates the

[25] See Memorandum on the creation of an EEC trademark (CTM Memorandum), Bulletin of the European Communities, supplement 8/76 p 19.

[26] For Norwegian law, see BS Lassen and A Stenvik, *Oversikt over norsk varemerkerett* ('Overview of Norwegian Trademark Law') (Oslo, 2003 2nd edn) p 43.

exclusive right. The assessment of whether a trademark has distinctive character is, in principle, to be carried out according to the same criteria irrespective of whether the exclusive right has been gained by registration or through use.[27] In Sweden, the relevant part of the public has long been considered to comprise two main groups, one consisting of actual and potential consumers or end users of the goods or services (*the consumers*), and the other consisting of persons, who in their work may deal commercially with the goods during their distribution such as agents, importers, wholesale dealers, merchants and salesmen (*the operators*).[28] It has been considered that a lack of knowledge in the consumer group may be compensated for by a higher degree of knowledge among the operators and *vice versa*. How much relevance should be given to the degree of knowledge of consumers and operators, respectively, must in the specific case depend on the kind of goods concerned and what the target group is. Where a typical everyday product is concerned, the opinion of the general public is most relevant. While knowledge among operators is given less weight in this case, it is more likely to compensate for a lower degree of knowledge among the consumers where a product which usually does not reach the general public is concerned.[29]

In the case-law of the CJEU, the importance of the end users/consumers has usually been emphasised. The distinctive character of a sign is, for example, assessed in the light of how an *average consumer* of the goods or services in question – who is reasonably well-informed, observant and circumspect – perceives the mark which is subject to a trademark application.[30] How the relevant class of persons is to be defined was addressed by the CJEU in a preliminary ruling in the *Bostongurka* case. The dispute in the Swedish court concerned a claim for revocation of the registered trademark 'Bostongurka', which was alleged to have lost its distinctive character, as it was considered to be a generic name for chopped pickled gherkins. A question was referred to the CJEU by the Svea Hovrätt (Svea Court of Appeal in Stockholm) seeking to clarify which class of persons is relevant in the assessment of whether a trademark has lost its distinctive character, in cases where the goods is handled at several levels of the distribution chain before reaching the consumer or end user. The CJEU stated that, in general, the perception of consumers or end users will play a decisive role since the whole aim of the commercialisation process is the purchase of the product by those persons. Accordingly the relevant classes of persons whose views are to be taken into account in the assessment comprise

[27] SOU 2001:26 pp 234 ff.

[28] SOU 1958:10 p 222, Prop. (Swedish Government Bill) 1960/167 p 45. See also L Pehrson, *Varumärken från konsumentsynpunkt – en rättsvetenskaplig studie* ('Trademarks from a Consumer's Point of view') (Stockholm, Liber, 1981) pp 156 ff.

[29] In the case of, eg, spectacle frames, it is likely that it is the opinion of operators which primarily determines which brands of glasses will be sold. See NJA 1937 note. A 343 (*Bonop*).

[30] See, eg Case C-210/96, *Gut Springenheide v Tusky* [1998] ECR I-4657, para 31 and Case C-299/99, *Philips v Remington*, [2002] ECR I-5475, para 63.

principally consumers and end users. The CJEU added, however, that depending on the features of the market concerned, the perception of all those in the trade who deal with the product might also be taken into consideration.[31]

Protection of a non-registered trademark is acquired when the mark has through use reached a certain level of knowledge in the relevant part of the public. Initially, the main rule was that a mark was considered to be established if it was known by at least 50 per cent of the relevant part of the public (was 'generally known').[32] The Swedish legislators found, however, that the changing role of trademarks in today's society implies that marks which are not 'generally known' may represent a significant commercial value and hence need protection. The degree of knowledge necessary to obtain protection was therefore lowered, with the aim of widening the range of marks that could be protected through use. Since 1 January 1995, a mark is considered to have become established on the market according to Section 2(3) of the Swedish Trademarks Act, when it is known to identify goods or services that are marketed under the mark in question within a *significant proportion* of the relevant part of the Swedish public.[33] Since 1995, when the criterion was changed to 'a significant proportion', a rule of thumb is that a mark, which has inherent distinctiveness can normally be considered to be established if it is known by approximately one third (30-35 per cent) of the relevant part of the public.[34] Knowledge in one third of the relevant part of the public is also often quoted as a guideline in the literature.[35]

It should, however, be pointed out that neither older nor newer *travaux préparatoires* state any particular percentage for determining when a mark should be considered to be known in a 'significant proportion' of the relevant part of the public. It has been left to the case-law to decide how this provision should be applied in each specific case. In cases where market surveys have been accepted by the courts there is usually no mention of a determined percentage.[36] Hence, there is no decision, which nails down the rule of one third in an authoritative way. Different factors may also influence the required degree of knowledge in the specific case.[37]

[31] Case C-371/02, *Björnekulla Fruktindustrier AB v Procordia Food AB (Bostongurka)*, [2004] ECR I-5791, paras 23-26.

[32] S Tengelin, 'Inarbetning av kännetecken' ('Establishment of marks through use') 44 *NIR* 371 (1975).

[33] Prop. 1994/95:59 pp 43 ff.

[34] Ö Grundén, 'Skyddet för kända och ansedda kännetecken' ('The Protection of Established and Reputed Trademarks and Names') 64 *NIR* 227, 233 (1995) and SOU 2001:26 pp 220 ff.

[35] U Bernitz, G Karnell, L Pehrson, C Sandgren, *Immaterialrätt och otillbörlig konkurrens* ('Intellectual property and unfair competition') (Stockholm, Jure, 11th edn 2009) 240, M Levin, *Lärobok i Immaterialrätt* ('Textbook on intellectual property') (Stockholm, Norstedts Juridik, 9th edn 2007) p 387, PJ Nordell, *Varumärkesrättens skyddsobjekt. Om ordkännetecknets mening och referens* ('The subject matter of protection in trademark law') (Stockholm, Mercurius, 2004) p 190.

[36] SOU 1958:10 pp 222 ff, Prop. 1994/95:59 p 45, SOU 2001:26 p 221.

[37] L Pehrson, *Varumärken från konsumentsynpunkt* (1981) p 160 and Ö Grundén, *Kända och ansedda kännetecken* pp 227, 233 (1995). See also Case No T 1792/96, *El Molino*, Svea Hovrätt (Svea Court of Appeal in Stockholm) [1997]. Here the court held that the requirements set on the degree

A comparison may be made with the degree of knowledge that is required for a descriptive mark to be registered as a trademark according to the Directive. The CJEU gave some indications in the *Chiemsee* case on how to determine the distinctive character of a mark.[38] The underlying dispute in the national court between Windsurfing Chiemsee Produktions- und Vertriebs GmbH (Windsurfing Chiemsee) and Boots- und Segelzubehör Walter Huber and Franz Attenberger concerned the fact that the latter used the name of the lake, Chiemsee in their sale of sportswear. The same name had already been registered as a pictorial mark, in the shape of different graphical symbols, which were sometimes accompanied with additional information by Windsurfing Chiemsee. The question raised was whether it is possible to have an exclusive right to a geographical name.[39] The Landgericht in München referred a number of questions in this connection to the CJEU, which delivered its decision on 4 May 1999.

The CJEU held that in determining whether a mark has acquired distinctive character following the use made of it, the competent authority must make an 'overall assessment' of the evidence that the mark has come to identify the product concerned as originating from a particular undertaking, and thus to distinguish it from those of other undertakings.[40] In this process, the following may, according to the CJEU be taken into account: '[T]he market share held by the mark, how intensive, geographically widespread and long-standing use of the mark has been, the amount invested by the undertaking in promoting the mark, the proportion of the relevant class of persons who, because of the mark, identify goods as originating from a particular undertaking, and statements from chambers of commerce and industry or other trade and professional associations.'[41]

The CJEU stated that 'if, on the basis of these factors, the competent authority finds that the relevant class of persons, or at least a significant proportion thereof, identify goods as originating from a particular undertaking because of the trademark, it must hold that the requirements for registering the mark laid down in Article 3(3) of the Directive are satisfied'.[42] The Court held that general, abstract data, such as knowledge held by predetermined percentages of the relevant part

of knowledge required for establishment in a significant proportion of the relevant class of persons must be lower on a market where there are an exceptionally large number of brands as is the case of the wine market.

[38] Joined cases C-108/97 and C-109/97, *Windsurfing Chiemsee v Boots- und Segelzubehör Walter Huber and Franz Attenberger (Chiemsee)*, [1999] ECR I-2779.

[39] Geographical names are regulated in Art 3(1) (c) of the Directive. According to this provision, a trademark must not be registered if it consists 'exclusively of signs or indications which may serve, in trade, to designate the kind, quality, quantity, intended purpose, value, geographical origin, or the time of production of the goods or of rendering of the service, or other characteristics of the goods or service'. The required distinctiveness may, however, be acquired through use, according to Art 3(3).

[40] Joined cases C-108/97 and C-109/97, *Chiemsee*, para 49.

[41] Ibid at para 51.

[42] Ibid at para 52.

of the public, cannot be used to decide when the mark has acquired sufficient distinctive character. The Court noted, however, that Community law does not preclude the competent authority, in particularly difficult cases, from using a market survey as guidance for its judgment, subject to its own national law.[43]

In Sweden, it is customary to speak of direct and indirect evidence. To *indirect evidence* belong documented information about sales volume, extent and method of marketing, market investments, and number of years the product has been on the market, etc, ie, different pieces of information showing merely that the mark has been used. It concerns the circumstances that help to create an association between a mark and a commercial origin in the minds of the consumers. However, such evidence cannot prove that a certain mark is indeed understood as an indication of origin by the consumers; this is for the registration authorities or the courts to infer. As *direct evidence*, anything that can show that there is knowledge about the mark in the relevant class of persons is considered, including market surveys carried out by authorised institutes.[44] It is possible to demonstrate by way of market surveys that a mark is understood as an indication of origin and has been established through use.

In Sweden, market surveys are often emphasised as the ultimate piece of evidence. By comparison, in Denmark and Finland, all relevant pieces of evidence, including market surveys, are accepted on an equal footing.[45] In Norway, the attitude to market surveys appears to be sceptical, and it is instead advocated that establishment through use is best demonstrated by 'hard facts', ie, such circumstances as in Sweden are characterised as indirect evidence.[46] The emphasis in the *Chiemsee* case is on indirect evidence, even if the judgment allows the possibility of using market surveys in a specific case, if necessary. Since the CJEU has not clarified what constitutes a 'significant proportion' or defined a norm to follow in determining whether a sign shall be considered to have acquired distinctiveness through use in a specific case, it has been left to the national authorities to decide whether market surveys with percentages should be used and, if so, what percentages should be required.[47]

In the case of a trademark registration, the knowledge must also include its geographical context. In the *Europolis* case the CJEU stated that the registration of a trademark can be allowed on the basis of Article 3(3) of the Directive only if it is proven that that trademark has acquired distinctive character through use *throughout* the part of the territory of the Member State in which there

[43] Ibid at paras 52, 53.

[44] One cannot consider this distinction to be established in Community law.

[45] See eg O Eskildsen, 'Varemaerkerettens stiftelse uden registrering. Danmark' ('Establishment of trademark rights without registration. Denmark') (1996) 65 *Nordiskt immateriellt rättsskydd* pp 515, 517 and T Lydman, 'Grunderna för varumärkesskydd utan registrering: ibruktagande – inarbetning. Finland' ('Grounds for trademark protection without registration: first use – establishment through use. Finland') (1996) 65 *Nordiskt immateriellt rättsskydd* p 520.

[46] For the situation in Norway, See BS Lassen and A Stenvik, *Norsk varemerkerett* (2003) pp 219 ff.

[47] L Pehrson, *Interpretation of the Trademark Directive* pp 157, 168 (2007).

exists a ground for refusal.[48] The CJEU stated further that the linguistic areas in a Member State or, as in the specific case, in Benelux, must be taken into account in the assessment of distinctiveness. The grounds for refusal in the case in the main proceedings existed only in that part of Benelux where Dutch is spoken. The CJEU therefore found that it must be established that the mark had acquired distinctive character through use throughout that linguistic area.[49]

The Swedish Court of Patent Appeals (Patentbesvärsrätten, PBR) has addressed the question whether it is sufficient to claim acquired distinctiveness amongst a geographically restricted class of consumers if the market for the product or service in question is limited to that locality or region.[50] In this case, the applicant applied to register five figure marks consisting of the names of different parts of central Stockholm (including the word mark '*Södermalmsnytt med Gamla Stan*') for newspapers containing information about and relevant to the respective areas of Stockholm. The applicant argued primarily that the marks had inherent distinctive character and, in the alternative, that they had acquired distinctive character amongst a substantial proportion of the relevant class of persons, namely residents of the particular areas of Stockholm, or at least residents of central Stockholm. Only one of the marks was considered by the court to be inherently distinctive.

Concerning the question of acquired distinctiveness through use, the court referred to the *Europolis* case and held that the mark must be perceived as a source identifier throughout the country. The applicant's evidence, consisting of market surveys in particular, was only showing use of the marks in the respective parts of Stockholm. The court found that the market surveys were not representative of the relevant class of consumers, neither with respect to their composition nor to their geographical coverage. Also, the evidence failed to demonstrate that the marks were perceived as source identifiers for the goods or services in question. Accordingly, the marks were not considered to have acquired distinctive character.[51]

It can be difficult to demonstrate acquired distinctive character throughout Sweden in the case of a mark which is primarily important in a local market. One example is provided by the above-described case relating to names of newspapers containing mostly local news. If the applicant fails to show sufficient geographical coverage, the mark cannot be registered, even though it may be known by a significant part of the relevant class of persons. The applicant may, in such a situation, obtain protection through use within the geographical area in question. According to Section 2 of the Swedish Trademarks Act, it is not

[48] Case C-108/05, *Bovemij Verzekeringen NV v Benelux-Merkenbureau (Europolis)* [2006], ECR I-7605 para 19-23.

[49] Ibid at paras 24-28.

[50] Joined cases No 05-404 – 05-407 and 05-410, *Södermalmsnytt med Gamla Stan*, Patentbesvärsrätten (Court of Patent Appeals, PBR) [2008].

[51] See also *Hull Daily Mail Publications Ltd's Trademark Applications* [2009] RPC 8 126(3):199-208. (An English case similarly decided.)

necessary that the mark acquire distinctive character among the relevant class of persons in the whole country to acquire protection. Knowledge within a certain part of the country can be considered and can give rise to a locally limited exclusive trademark right.[52]

Protection through use can be obtained by means of a spectrum of different activities, such as selling, advertising, etc, that may contribute to establish the mark in the minds of the relevant class of persons. In order to obtain protection through use in Sweden, the only requirement is that the mark has become known. It is of no importance how the knowledge has been spread. Hence, it is not necessary that goods have been sold under the mark, it is enough that the mark has appeared in advertising. Neither is it considered necessary that the mark has been used in Sweden, it suffices that it has become known through, say, advertising in another country. In the international literature, the term 'spill-over advertising' has been used to describe this situation.[53] Examples of this phenomenon are that the mark is shown on TV, is seen in international magazines, for example in-flight magazines, or that the general public encounters the mark when travelling abroad.

It is always required that a certain time has passed from the moment the mark began to be used 'as a trademark' until it has acquired protection through use. Buyers must first become acquainted with the mark in a shopping situation or through advertisements. Subsequently, they must begin to associate the mark with certain goods or services and finally expect that the mark serves to distinguish a certain – albeit possibly unknown – commercial origin. The length of time this process takes depends upon a number of factors. How intensely and extensively the mark is being used is of decisive importance. The brand consciousness and perceptivity of consumers is another. Marks of expensive and prestigious goods are considered easier to acquire protection for than marks of cheaper, mass-produced goods. The nature of the mark is also of great importance. As a general rule, a highly distinctive mark normally needs less time to become known than a mark, which lacks or has weak inherent distinctiveness. Other factors of importance are how the mark is used in combination with other distinguishing elements, and how the market for the goods or services in question functions as a whole.

There is a *requirement of use* for registered trademarks, which means that the registration may be revoked in full or in part if the trademark has not been put to genuine use within a continuous period of five years after the end of the registration period or any subsequent five-year period.[54] When a mark is found to have acquired protection through use, it often coincides with its being used, but there is no real requirement of use for non-registered trademarks.

[52] SOU 1958:10 p 221 f and Prop 1960/167 pp 45, 52.

[53] FW Mostert, 'Well-Known and Famous Marks: Is Harmony Possible in the Global Village?' (1996) 86 *The Trademark Reporter* pp 103, 112 ff.

[54] See §§ 25(a) and 25(b), Swedish Trademarks Act, cf Art 10, 12 and 13 Directive 2008/95/EC.

A non-registered trademark retains its protection as long as there is sufficient knowledge about it among the relevant part of the public. As a consequence, a mark that has been established during the registration period may be protected as a non-registered trademark after the registration has expired or been revoked.

Knowledge of a trademark that has acquired a strong reputation can sometimes stay in the minds of the relevant part of the public for a long time after the proprietor has stopped selling and marketing the marked goods. The foremost example in Swedish case-law is the mark '*Ljunglöfs*' for snuff, which retained protection for almost 50 years after it ceased to be used.[55] In another case, the name '*Frukostklubben*' of a radio program was considered to be protected through use and constitute a bar to registration of the same name as a trademark 18 years after the last broadcast of the program.[56] Sooner or later, however, protection is lost due to inactivity. The proprietor must therefore try to ensure that it remains known among the relevant class of persons to such a degree that it continues to fulfil the criteria for protection. This has been described in the literature as a 'natural requirement of use' for non-registered trademarks.[57]

It can be argued whether, in order to retain protection for a non-registered trademark, there should not only be a requirement that the mark continues to be known among the relevant part of the public, but also that this knowledge should be the result of an association with goods that are still available on the market under the trademark. The problem relates to the weight that should be given to the opinion of consumers on the question of whether a certain sign constitutes a trademark, in cases where it is no longer used as such. The problem is brought to a head when the acts or intentions of the proprietor of the mark are not in accordance with the opinion of the customers, ie, when the proprietor has abandoned the mark.[58] Whether it is worth protecting such a mark may be questioned. Where the proprietor has not used his mark for five years this could well lead to a presumption that the mark has been abandoned, which the proprietor would have to rebut in order to keep his rights.

3. TRADEMARK PROTECTION THROUGH QUALIFIED USE – THE SCOPE OF PROTECTION

Under the Swedish Trademarks Act, the proprietor of a non-registered mark can intervene against the use of confusingly similar trademarks within the

[55] *Regeringsrättens Årsbok (RÅ)* (Reports of cases from the Supreme Administrative Court) 1970 p 74 (*Ljunglöfs snus*).

[56] Case No 01-114, *Frukostklubben*, PBR [2002].

[57] L Holmqvist, 'Inarbetning av varukännetecken' (1975) 44 *Nordiskt immateriellt rättsskydd* pp 255, 267.

[58] Cf Judgment delivered by the Norwegian Supreme Court (*Høyesterett*) 16 November 1999 in the case '*Lundetangen*' (2000) 69 *Nordiskt immateriellt rättsskydd* p 449.

geographic area of protection, which coincides with the territory where the mark has been established through use. If the mark has not been established on the market in the entire country, the exclusive right is, according to Section 4(1), only valid within the territory where it has been established. In principle, it is thus not possible to intervene against the use of a confusingly similar trademark outside the limited territory where the mark has acquired protection.[59] Even identical marks, which have acquired protection in different parts of the country, can co-exist simultaneously. This is in accordance with Article 6(2) of the Directive, which entitles a Member State to authorise the usage of an earlier right, which only applies in a particular locality, within the limits of the territory in which it is recognised.

Trademarks that have been established through use in Sweden, may be invoked as grounds for refusal of a national trademark application or revocation of a trademark registration. According to Section 14(1) No 6 of the Swedish Trademarks Act, the proprietor of a non-registered trademark has protection against the registration of that mark, or a confusingly similar one, by a third party. If such a trademark has been registered, and the grounds for refusing the registration still exist, the registration may be revoked, unless the trademark right is allowed to continue under Sections 8 and 9 (as to which, see below).[60] At present, it is also possible under the same provision to bar the registration of confusingly similar trademarks on the basis of a locally acquired exclusive right and to claim revocation if such a trademark has been registered.[61] In practice, it has been considered sufficient if the mark has acquired distinctiveness through use in larger cities/municipalities.[62] In this respect, *Finnish* law differs, since the right of the proprietor of a non-registered trademark to bar or revoke a registration presumes that the mark has acquired protection in the entire country.[63]

Well-known marks, within Article 6 *bis* of the Paris Convention, must, in contrast, be known in a *substantial part* of the territory of the relevant Member State before they can be invoked as relative bars to registration and grounds for invalidity, in accordance with Article 4(2)(d) of the Directive. This provision has been interpreted by the CJEU in its preliminary ruling, *Fincas Tarragona*.[64] Mr Nieto Nuño brought proceedings before a Spanish court against Mr Monlleó

[59] See eg Case No T 106-97, *DRUVAN*, Hovrätten över Skåne och Blekinge (The Scania and Blekinge Court of Appeal in Malmö) [1998].

[60] § 25, Swedish Trademarks Act.

[61] SOU 1958:10 p 221.

[62] See Case No 83-102, *BALLO*, PBR [1984], where a mark used for ladies' wear, which was invoked as a bar to registration, was considered to be established 'at least in Stockholm'. See also, Case No 94-859, *DIN OPTIKER*, PBR [1998] and Case No 97-311, *PIPELINE*, PBR [1998]. See also SOU 2001:26 p 222.

[63] See T Lydman, 'Varumärkesskydd utan registrering. Finland' 65 *Nordiskt immateriellt rättsskydd* 520 (1996). The Norwegian Trademark Committee II has proposed a provision, according to which a locally established right may not constitute a ground for invalidity but only a bar to registration. See B S Lassen and A Stenvik, *Norsk varemerkerett* (2003) p 138.

[64] Case C-328/06, *Alfredo Nieto Nuño v Leonci Monlleó Franquet (Fincas Tarragona)* [2007] ECR I-10093.

Franquet for a finding that the latter had infringed the trademark *Fincas Tarragona*, which Mr Nieto Nuño had registered for different services related to property. Mr Monlleó Franquet, an estate agent in Tarragona, counterclaimed for the annulment of the registration of the trademark. He held that *Fincas Tarragona* was a well-known earlier mark, which he had been using for the purpose of designating his business since 1978 in the city of Tarragona and its surrounding area.

The question referred from the national court concerned the geographical area in which an earlier mark must be well-known to be protected according to Article 4(2)(d) of the Directive. The CJEU stated that a trademark cannot be required to be well-known 'throughout' the territory of the Member State, since Article 4(2)(d) lacks a definition to that effect, and that it is sufficient for it to be well-known in a 'substantial part' of it. The Court further stated that the customary meaning of the words used in the expression 'in a Member State' precludes the application of that expression to a situation where the fact of being well-known is limited to a city and to its surrounding area which, together do not constitute a substantial part of a Member State.[65]

According to Article 4(4)(b) of the Directive a Member State may provide that a trademark is not to be registered or, if registered, is to be liable to be declared invalid where and to the extent that the rights of a non-registered trademark were acquired earlier and that that non-registered mark confers on its proprietor the right to prohibit the use of a subsequent mark. The CJEU has stated that its interpretation of the geographical area in which an earlier mark has to be well-known according to Article 4(2)(d) has no bearing on the respective scopes of Article 4(4)(b) and 6(2).[66] Each Member State accordingly, is free to define the geographical area in which a national non-registered trademark must be known. Community law raises no objection if locally established trademark rights in the Member States can be invoked as bars to registration or grounds for invalidity, as is presently the case under Swedish legislation.

The Swedish Patent and Registration Office does not examine whether there are earlier non-registered rights, which could constitute relative bars to registration. Such rights are usually discovered in connection with an opposition procedure by the proprietor of the earlier right.[67] The interest of the proprietor must be weighed against the demands of legal certainty for third parties. In other words, competitors must have a fair chance to keep informed of owned marks with exclusive rights. In the case of establishment through use it is considered that the interests of third parties are met by the requirement that the mark must possess a certain degree of knowledge. Marks which have been established through use throughout the country, or in a substantial part thereof, are normally also known to competitors.

[65] Ibid at paras 17–18.

[66] Ibid at para 20.

[67] *Departementsserien (Ds)* (Ministry publications series) 2008:28 p 65.

A locally established mark can, however, be established through use in one part of the country while the applicant for a registration resides in another part. The consequences of failure on the part of the applicant to notice a non-registered mark can be far-reaching. This is because non-registered, confusingly similar marks may be invoked at a later stage of the administrative procedure or in court as grounds for revocation or invalidity. From the perspective of a third party, locally established non-registered marks thus create a significant amount of uncertainty.[68]

The right of the proprietor of an established trademark right to intervene can be lost through inactivity, according to the so called preclusion rule of Section 8 of the Swedish Trademarks Act, which is harmonised with Article 9 of the Directive. According to this provision the rights in a confusingly similar registered trademark may, as regards goods for which it has been used, exist side by side with an earlier mark which is established or registered, if the registration was applied for in good faith and the owner of the earlier mark was aware of and accepted the use of the registered trademark in Sweden for a period of five years. There is also a special passivity rule for the situation where the younger trademark is established through use in Section 9. In this case, a confusingly similar established mark may exist side by side with an earlier established or registered trademark, if the proprietor of the earlier right has not, within reasonable time, taken action against the use of the later mark.

There are two provisions in the Regulation, which grant protection to non-registered trademarks as relative bars to registration of a Community trademark, Article 8(2)(c) and Article 8(4). Well-known trademarks, in the meaning of Article 6 *bis* of the Paris convention, can be invoked as relative bars to registration to identical and confusingly similar Community trademarks, according to Article 8(2)(c). The provision thus applies to trademarks whose reputation extends into the territory of a Member State where it is neither registered nor used. This exception covers two types of trademarks: on one hand, marks which have been established through use in one Member State, provided that these marks are well-known in another Member State; on the other hand, marks that exist in a non-member state and have become well-known within the territory of the Community. This provision is, however, not applicable to trademarks which have been established through use in one Member State and are well-known only within this state.[69]

Non-registered national trademark rights fulfilling the conditions of Article 8(4) of the Regulation may also be invoked as relative bars to registration of a Community trademark according to Article 41(1)(c), in an 'opposition procedure' by the proprietor or a person authorised to exercise these rights. The

[68] BS Lassen, 'Krav för skydd av oregistrerade kännetecken och oregistrerade kännetecken som registreringshinder, nationellt och enligt varumärkesförordningen' (1996) 65 *Nordiskt immateriellt rättsskydd* pp 38 ff.

[69] CTM proposal, p 57.

main principle is that if grounds exist for refusal in one single Member State, a mark cannot be registered as a Community trademark. This is true also if the earlier mark is a non-registered trademark. An exclusive right, which fulfils the requirements in Article 8(4), can also be invoked as a relative ground for invalidity pursuant to Article 53(1)(c).

Article 8(4) refers to non-registered trademarks as well as to other signs used in the course of trade. A trademark which has been established through use in Sweden can be assigned to the category 'non-registered trademark' and hence constitute a relative bar to registration. The category 'other signs used in the course of trade' includes, inter alia, 'trade names and company names (corporate names), other business designations like establishment or store names, titles of publications or similar works, as well as any other similar exclusive right falling within the same category or type of right'.[70]

According to the wording of Article 8(4) the opposition is to be based on a sign 'used' in the course of trade. The General Court (formerly the Court of First Instance (General Court)) has, however, stated that the opposing party needs to do no more than show that the sign concerned was used in the context of a commercial activity with a view to economic advantage, and need not prove that the sign has been put to genuine use.[71] A further condition to be observed is that the sign must be of 'more than mere local significance'. The expression does not refer to the geographical extent of the use of the sign but to the geographical extent of its protection.[72] The rationale of this condition is to restrict the number of conflicts between signs, by preventing an earlier sign, which is not sufficiently important or significant, from being able to challenge either the registration or the validity of a Community trademark.[73] It is up to the opponent to show that the earlier trademark has been used in the course of trade and is of more than local significance, whereupon OHIM decides whether the necessary conditions are fulfilled, based on the Regulation and the Community trademark system. The decision is thus made through the application of a unitary European standard and is independent of any national criteria.[74]

The General Court has given some indications how to determine whether the use is of more than local significance. It follows already from a textual interpretation of Article 8(4) that account must be taken of the geographical dimension of the sign's significance, that is to say of the territory in which it is used to identify its proprietor's economic activity. This interpretation was confirmed by the General Court, which held that account must also be taken of

[70] OHIM Opposition Guidelines, 5.3.1. Available at http://oami.europa.eu/ows/rw/pages/CTM/legalReferences/guidelines/guidelines.en.do.

[71] Joined Cases T-225/06, T-255/06, T-257/06 and T-309/06, *Budějovický Budvar, národní podnik, v OHIM*, [2008] ECR II-3555, appeal pending Case C-96/09 P OJ C 113 of 16.05.2009. p 2, paras 163, 166.

[72] Ibid at para 180.

[73] Joined cases T-318/06 – T-321/06, *Alberto Jorge Moreira da Fonseca, Lda v OHIM* (GENERAL OPTICA) [2009] ECR II-649 para 36.

[74] Opposition Guidelines, 5.3.4.

the economic dimension of the sign's significance. This is to be assessed in the light of the length of time for which the sign has fulfilled its identifying function and the degree to which it has been used, of the group of addressees among which the sign in question has become known as a distinctive element, namely consumers, competitors and suppliers, and of the exposure given to the sign, for example through advertising or on the internet.[75]

Under Article 8(4)(a), the rights to the national mark must be acquired before the date of application for registration of the Community trademark, or the date of priority claimed in the application for registration of the Community trademark. As regards national rights, the relevant date of acquisition of exclusive rights under the national law is decisive. Where, under national law, mere use is sufficient, this must have begun before the priority date of the Community trademark. Where recognition in the trade or reputation is required, these must have been acquired before the priority date of the Community trademark.[76]

According to Article 8(4)(b), the law in the Member State where the rights exist must also confer on the proprietor of the earlier right the right to prohibit the use of a subsequent trademark. In other words, there must exist a 'protection in the abstract'.[77] The Office treats the applicable rules and provisions of national law as an issue of fact. Consequently, the burden of proving that the sign concerned confers the right to prohibit use of a subsequent trademark is on the party bringing an opposition before OHIM.[78] The opponent must show which legislation he is referring to and in what way this legislation gives him the right to prohibit the use of a later trademark.[79]

Finally, the prerequisites for a prohibition must be present in the specific case.[80] This means that where the Community trademark is used in the national territory, the prerequisites according to national law which would allow the grant of an injunction against this use must be present. In other words, the Community trademark must fall within the scope of protection of the national mark which is being relied on. The General Court has stated that the opposing party need not establish that he has, in fact, already been able to prohibit use of a subsequent mark but only that he has such a right available to him.[81] Similar cases already decided by competent national authorities may suffice to demonstrate the existence of the right and its scope of protection.[82]

[75] Joined cases T-318/06 – T-321/06, *GENERAL OPTICA*, at para 37.

[76] The Opposition Guidelines, at 5.3.5.

[77] Ibid at 5.3.6.

[78] Joined Cases T-225/06, T-255/06, T-257/06 and T-309/06, *BUD*, at para 185.

[79] Opposition Guidelines, 5.4. See Rule 74(1) IR regarding the obligation of the opponent to present relevant national legislation.

[80] Opposition Guidelines, 5.3.6. According to Rule 16(2) IR the notice of opposition based on any other earlier right than a registered right shall in principle be accompanied by appropriate evidence on the acquisition and scope of protection of that right.

[81] Joined cases T-225/06, T-255/06, T-257/06 and T-309/06, *BUD*, at para 195.

[82] See eg Decision No 920/2000 of the Opposition Division of 28 April 2000 ruling on opposition No B 38564 (*INTERPRINT*).

According to Article 110(1) of the Regulation, both non-registered trademarks and other signs used in the course of trade can also be invoked in infringement proceedings against a Community trademark. The fact that signs, which are only of local significance fall outside the scope of Article 8(4), has as a consequence that Community trademarks and non-registered trademarks or other signs are allowed to exist in parallel. However, according to Article 111(1) the proprietor of a locally established sign has been granted the right to oppose the use of a Community trademark within the geographical territory where his sign has acquired protection, to the extent allowed by national law. This constitutes an exception to the principle of the unitary character of the Community trademark. The right to intervene may, however, be lost due to inactivity during a period of five successive years.[83]

Since the protection of non-registered trademarks is fully integrated into the Swedish trademark law, protection is provided not only with respect to identical marks but also with respect to confusingly similar marks in accordance with Section 6(1) of the Swedish Trademarks Act.[84] Marks are considered to be confusingly similar only if they relate to goods or services of the same or a similar kind. According to Section 6(2) of the Swedish Trademarks Act, a mark with a *reputation* may also be given an extended protection beyond the scope of similar goods.[85] It is clear from the optional provision in Article 5(2) of the Directive that a Member State can decide that the proprietor of a mark with a reputation shall be entitled to prevent all third parties not having his consent from using in the course of trade an identical or similar sign for types of goods or services different from those for which the earlier mark was registered, if the use of that sign takes unfair advantage of, or is detrimental to, the distinctive character or the repute of the trademark. On account of this provision, Swedish legislators modified Section 6(2) in order to give a better protection to marks with a reputation.[86] According to CJEU case-law, as seen in the *Davidoff* case, such protection can also be granted when the younger mark is intended to be used for goods or services that are identical to those goods or services which are covered by the well-known mark and, even though there is no risk of confusion, there is a risk that the distinctive character or reputation of the earlier mark is unfairly taken advantage of or damaged. This must be considered to be in agreement with earlier Swedish practice.[87]

[83] See Art 110(1) and Art 111(2) Reg No 207/2009.

[84] Cf Art 4(1) (b) and 5(1) (b), Dir 2008/95/EC.

[85] See eg RÅ 2001, Case No 4439-1996 (*SAF*), where an established trademark was given extended protection under § 6(2), Swedish Trademarks Act.

[86] The earlier so-called *Kodak rule* in Section 6(2), Swedish Trademarks Act, had in practice small impact due to its strict requirements. See also Prop 1992/93:48 pp 80 ff. See also J Rosén, 'Känneteckens goodwillskydd – från anseende till uppmärksamhetsvärde i svensk känneteckens- och marknadsrätt' ('Protection of the goodwill of marks') in *Festskrift till Mogens Koktvedgaard* ('Essays in honour of Mogens Koktvedgaard') (M Bryde Andersen, C Heide-Jørgensen, J Schovsbo editors, DJØF Forlag 2003) p 473.

[87] Case C-292/00, *Davidoff & Cie SA Zino Davidoff SA v Gofkid Ltd (Davidoff)*, [2003] ECR I-389 paras 24–25, 30; cf Joined Cases No 97-065 and 97-641, Tulosba Akdov, PBR [1999].

In the *Chevy* case, the CJEU gave some guidance as to the scope of Article 5(2) of the Directive, and more specifically on the meaning of the term 'to have a reputation'. After having compared differences in nuances between versions of the text of the Directive in the different languages of the Member States, the CJEU came to the conclusion that the term 'reputation' implies a certain degree of knowledge of the mark among the public.[88] The Court further stated that the degree of knowledge required must be considered to be reached 'when the earlier mark is known by a significant part of the public concerned by the products or services covered by that trademark'.[89] When examining whether this condition is fulfilled, the national court should take into consideration all the relevant facts of the case. The reasoning shows a strong similarity to what is considered necessary in Sweden in order to grant protection through use. A non-registered trademark can often be given an extended protection beyond the similarity of goods or services if all other conditions are fulfilled.[90]

The reputation or knowledge must also be of a certain geographical extent for the mark to qualify for extended protection. Article 5(2) of the Directive states that a condition for protection is that the trademark has a reputation 'in the Member State'. The interpretation given by the CJEU in the *Chevy* case is that a trademark cannot be required to have a reputation 'throughout' the territory of the Member State and that it is sufficient for it to exist in a 'substantial part' of it.[91] It has, however, been left an open question regarding when it should be considered that a trademark is known within a 'substantial part' of a Member State.[92] In the literature it has been suggested that 'substantial' could be interpreted to mean a high degree of recognition in any one location, or a lesser degree of recognition in many cities or towns across the country.[93] A further case, *Pago International*,[94] was referred to the CJEU in June 2007. In this, a national court asked for guidance as to the scope of Article 9(1)(c) of the Regulation, which is a parallel provision to Article 5(2) of the Directive. One of the questions concerns how the expression 'reputation in the Community' should be interpreted in relation to a Community trademark.

The national background was the following: Since 2001, Pago International (Pago) had been the proprietor of a Community figurative mark for, inter alia, fruit drinks and fruit juices. The essential element of the mark was the representation of a green glass bottle with a distinctive label and lid. Pago marketed in Austria a fruit juice called 'Pago' in such bottles and its Community

[88] Case C-375/97, *General Motors Corporation v Yplon SA (Chevy)* [1999] ECR I-5421, para 25.

[89] Ibid at para 26.

[90] See eg Case No 96-695, *ACTU-ELLE*, PBR [2001], where the mark *ELLE* was considered to be established for magazines in Sweden and therefore well reputed at the time of application for registration of the trademark *ACTU-ELLE*.

[91] Case C-375/97, *Chevy*, para 28.

[92] See also L Pehrson, *Interpretation of the Trade Mark Directive* (2007) pp 157, 176.

[93] FW Mostert, *Well-Known and Famous Marks* (1996) pp 103, 121.

[94] Case C-301/07 *PAGO International GmbH v Tirolmilch registrierte Genossenschaft mbH* Judgment of the Court (Second Chamber) of 6 October 2009 OJ C 223, 22.9.2007.

trademark was widely known in that Member State. Tirolmilch marketed, also in Austria, a fruit and whey drink called 'Latella'. That drink, which was initially sold in cartons, was subsequently also sold in glass bottles. Two bottle designs resembled in several aspects the Community trademark held by Pago. In its advertising, Tirolmilch used a representation which, like Pago's trademark, showed a bottle next to a full glass. Pago brought trademark infringement proceedings against Tirolmilch, seeking to prohibit Tirolmilch from promoting, offering for sale, marketing or otherwise using its drink in the bottles at issue and from advertising by means of a representation of the bottles together with a full glass of fruit juice.

The Advocate General delivered her opinion in the *Pago International* case on 30 April 2009,[95] and the CJEU delivered its judgment on 6 October 2009.[96] With regard to the geographical scope over which the trademark must have acquired reputation the Advocate General as well as the Court concluded that the judgment in the *Chevy* case should be applied by analogy. From this it follows that it is not necessary for a proprietor to demonstrate that his trademark enjoys a reputation throughout the Community in order to be granted the protection which is prescribed in Article 9(1)(c) of the Regulation. A 'substantial part' of the territory is sufficient. In order to assess what 'a substantial part' is, the Advocate General applied a similar argument to that in the *Fincas Tarragona* case, and concluded that the 'part' in question must not be insignificant compared to the Community as a whole. The Advocate General further emphasised that knowledge within a substantial part of the Community cannot be determined with reference to any abstract figures or any specific number of Member States, but rather that the national court must consider a number of factors. These factors shall include, but not be limited to, the economic significance of the territory within the Community, the geographical extent of the area where the trademark has a reputation, and the demographics of the public concerned.[97] The CJEU held that in view of the facts of the main proceedings, the territory of the Member State in question, namely Austria, may be considered to constitute a substantial part of the Community.[98]

In summary, one can note that within Community law, a number of different expressions are used to describe the geographical area within which a mark may be considered as known by the public concerned. Different legal results depend on the size of the territory. The demarcations between these different areas are not very distinct. CJEU case-law indicates, however, that in a specific case it is necessary to make an overall assessment of a number of factors to determine the geographical aspect of 'known'. Applying the above-mentioned principles, as set

[95] Opinion of AG Sharpston in Case C-301/07, *Pago International GmbH v Tirol Milch registrierte Genossenschaft mbH (Pago International)* [2009].

[96] Case C-301/07, *Pago International GmbH v Tirol Milch registrierte Genossenschaft mbH (Pago International)* [2009].

[97] Opinion of AG Sharpston in Case C-301/07, *Pago International* paras 32, 34.

[98] Case C-301/07, *Pago International*, paras 27–30.

out in *Chevy* and *Pago International*, to locally established trademark rights one may also draw the conclusion that a locally protected mark will normally not be considered to 'have a reputation'. However, a mark which is known within a limited geographical area may in principle be granted an extended protection if the relevant territory can be regarded as significant, in consideration of its size and commercial importance, and if the relevant part of the public is confined to this area.[99]

4. SUBJECT MATTERS OF PROTECTION

The range of signs that can be registered as trademarks was expanded by the Swedish Trademarks Act of 1960. The previously accepted principle that a trademark must be capable of being attached to a piece of goods or its packaging was abandoned, so that it became possible to also register 'trade dress' or 'get-up' (*varuutstyrsel*), ie the shape, colour or decoration of the product itself or its packaging. The rationale given for this was that self-service in stores contributed to an increased use of trade dress as a means of individualisation. Consumers were therefore assumed to recognise the desired goods as much or more by their appearance or their packaging as by the trademark affixed to it.

Originally, however, a registrable trademark could only consist of a number of explicitly listed signs, namely pictorial elements, words, letters or numbers, or a highly distinctive trade dress. Signs that were not mentioned in the codified legislation could only acquire protection through use. It was also explicitly stated that it was possible to acquire exclusive rights to 'a slogan or other special sign used in the course of trade' through use. While an ordinary word mark functions as a means of individualisation of goods or services, a slogan often acts as an advertisement for goods or services that are already available on the market under a certain word mark. Since a mere slogan plays such a role, it was not considered to be capable of functioning as a means of identification, and it hence could only acquire trademark protection through use.[100]

According to the *travaux préparatoires*, the expression 'other special sign used in the course of trade' primarily refers to design features which cannot be included in trade dress, such as the design of advertisements, business letters, catalogues, signboards, customer carts, business premises, special clothing for the employees, and special arrangements in window-dressings. Further, signs which can only be perceived with senses other than the visual were regarded as belonging to the category of marks that can only acquire protection through use. It was considered that such signs could not function as trademarks until they had been used to such an extent that they had acquired a distinctive character. In addition, a distinction was made between sound marks, which were considered to

[99] Cf Opinion of AG Sharpston in Case C-301/07, *Pago International*, n 24.

[100] See also SOU 1958:10 pp 94, 104, 215 ff and Prop 1960:167 pp 40 ff.

be easier to establish through use, and signs which were intended to be perceived through the senses of smell, taste or touch. The latter were not considered to be very important, but in case someone did succeed in establishing a phenomenon of this type as his distinctive sign, it would, like all other distinctive signs, be entitled to protection.[101]

The entry of the more general concept of a 'mark' (*varukännetecken*) into Swedish trademark law, and the enumeration of signs for which it is possible to acquire protection through use, can be seen as a reflection of a principle then prevailing, namely that trademark protection should be comprehensively regulated by specific legislation (*the principle of the exclusivity of the intellectual property law*).[102] It was considered that there was no need for complementary protection through the law of unfair competition.[103]

Harmonisation within the European Community included the definition of a registrable trademark, which is to be found in Article 2 of the Directive. According to this provision, a registrable trademark can consist of 'any sign capable of being represented graphically, particularly words, including personal names, designs, letters, numerals, the shape of goods or of their packaging, provided that such signs are capable of distinguishing the goods or services of one undertaking from those of other undertakings'. A corresponding provision is found in Article 4 of the Regulation. New to many Member States, though not for Sweden, was that three-dimensional marks were considered to be registrable. An important novelty with respect to earlier Swedish legislation was, however, that the list of registrable signs was non-exhaustive. A proposal from the Commission about a new trademark system for the European Community noted that no type of sign should by its mere nature be excluded from registration. The question whether abstract colours, as well as sounds, scents or tastes, in the future could constitute trademarks, was left open. The responsibility of deciding in a specific case was left to OHIM, the national courts or, in the last instance, the CJEU.[104]

Partial modifications were made to the Swedish Trademarks Act, in force from January 1, 1993, in connection with the implementation of the Directive. A definition of a trademark (*varumärke*) was introduced, implying that a sign must fulfil two criteria in order to function as a registrable trademark: on one hand it must have distinctive capacity, on the other hand it must be capable of being

[101] SOU 1958:10 pp 110, 221 and Prop 1960:167 pp 41 ff.

[102] U Bernitz, 'Skyddet mot illojal konkurrens, särskilt med avseende på efterbildningsskyddet enligt de nordiska marknadsföringslagarna' ('The Protection against Unlawful Competition, Especially Regarding Protection against Copying in the Nordic Acts on Marketing') (1994) 63 *Nordiskt immateriellt rättsskydd* p 590.

[103] In connection with the formulation of the Trademarks Act of 1960, the provision in § 9 of the Act of 1931 and certain provisions of unfair competition were therefore modified so that they would not encompass trademarks. The Act of 1931 was finally repealed in connection with the Swedish Trade Names Act of 1974. See also SOU 1958:10 pp 110 ff, 225, SOU 1966:71 pp 236 ff, Prop. 1970:57 pp 75 ff.

[104] Cf CTM Proposal, p 56.

represented graphically. In accordance with the Directive, the list of registrable signs in Section 1(2) was also made non-exhaustive. The rationale given was that, among other things, the Swedish Trademarks Act should be designed so that it does not preclude colours, sounds, scents and other signs from being capable of being registered as trademarks, if all the other prerequisites for protection were fulfilled. Slogans were considered for inclusion in the new trademark concept, but it was not considered necessary to explicitly list these as an example of signs which can constitute trademarks.[105]

The provision on establishment through use in Section 2(2) now states that it will be possible to grant exclusive rights 'also to other special signs which are used in the course of trade'. From this provision it follows that not only trademarks but also all other types of signs can acquire protection through use. The wider concept of a 'mark' (*varukännetecken*) has thus been retained. It has, however, been given a partly different demarcation, since the requirement of graphic representation has become part of the definition of a trademark. A mark is, in comparison, something that has distinctive capacity, but it need not be possible to represent it graphically. Establishment through use can be considered to constitute a complement to protection through registration.

In addition, protection acquired through use can provide an alternative when the proprietor of the mark in a specific case has 'missed' registering. Doubtless many non-registered trademarks have been created more or less accidentally. The public gets accustomed to a trade dress, and eventually regards it as indicating the commercial origin of the goods. The shape of a bottle may, for example, over time evolve into a distinguishing sign, without the proprietor consciously having intended it.[106] Undertakings may also start to use unregistered signs which lack inherent distinctiveness, such as descriptive words and colours, as secondary marks in addition to the main trademark. Protection acquired through use can then function as a last resort in an infringement situation, before a potential registration has been achieved. The essential condition is that the sign functions as a trademark when the protection is invoked.

It is likely that considerations relating to the law of unfair competition initially influenced the formulation and interpretation of the concept of protectable signs.[107] When the Trademarks Act of 1960 was promulgated, it was more difficult to obtain complementary protection for marks that could not be protected by trademark law under competition law in Sweden than in the other Nordic countries. A general clause against unfair competition was, however, introduced by the Swedish Marketing Act of 1970, which was regarded as a break with the abovementioned exclusivity principle.[108] An overlap between marketing

[105] Prop 1992/93:48 pp 71 ff.

[106] G Schricker, 'Protection of Unregistered Marks and Get-up in the Federal Republic of Germany' (1980) *International Review of Industrial Property* pp 615, 620.

[107] Cf NOU 2001:8 p 13.

[108] U Bernitz, 'Marknadsföringslagen och känneteckensskyddet' ('The marketing act and the protection of marks') (1975) 44 *Nordiskt immateriellt rättsskydd* p 179.

law and trademark law was therefore accepted in the case of trademarks.[109] Within the framework of the general clause a protection against imitation of marks used in the course of trade evolved from the case-law, especially regarding the protection of packaging.[110] A provision was introduced by the Marketing Act of 1995, under which an undertaking is forbidden from using imitations in its marketing which are confusingly similar with the known and distinctive products of another undertaking. This provision is also found in the current Marketing Act of 2008 (*Marknadsföringslag 2008:486*).[111]

The Swedish unfair competition law of today provides stronger protection for objects which function as trademarks on the market. Despite this, the rules which grant protection through use for marks which cannot be registered have been retained as part of trademark law. Even though the principle of the exclusivity of intellectual property law has been abandoned, the relation between competition law and trademark law is still different from that for example, in Danish law. In Sweden, the main rule has been that it is not possible to protect more objects by competition law than by trademark law.[112] In Denmark, by contrast, there is a harmonisation between trademark law and competition law, implying that if a certain object fails to obtain trademark protection, supplementary protection can be obtained under the law of unfair competition.

An adaptation to the Directive has been made by way of the *Danish* Trademark Act of 1991.[113] The requirements for a sign to be capable of being registered as a trademark are therefore that it has a distinctive capacity and can be represented graphically.[114] It is not possible to acquire protection through use of a mark which, by its very nature, is excluded from registration.[115] This means that a protectable sign must fall within the definition of a trademark, ie, it must be capable of being represented graphically and of distinguishing the goods or services of one undertaking from those of other undertakings.[116] As it is not possible to establish exclusive rights by use to a mark that cannot be represented graphically, Danish law can be said to take an opposite stance to the Swedish one as regards objects which can acquire protection through use. Protection through use is only an alternative to registration and not, as in Sweden, a true complement.

[109] However, it is not possible to invoke protection from both trademark law and competition law in the same proceedings, since they are handled by different courts.

[110] U Bernitz, 'Skydd mot illojal konkurrens' (1994) *Nordiskt immateriellt rättsskydd* pp 591 ff.

[111] See §14, Swedish Marketing Act (SFS 2008:486).

[112] See PJ Nordell, 'Skyddet för kommersiellt särpräglade utstyrslar i svensk känneteckens- och marknadsrätt' ('Protection of Commercially Distinctive Get-ups') (1998) 67 *Nordiskt immateriellt rättsskydd* pp 205, 232.

[113] Law No 341 from 6 June 1991.

[114] § 2, Danish Trademark Act.

[115] Ibid § 3(2).

[116] K Wallberg, *Varemaerkeret (*Trademark Law), (København, Jurist-og Økonomforbundets Forlag, 4th edn 2008) p 74.

Likewise, according to the *Norwegian* Trademark Act of 1961, it is only possible to acquire protection through use for signs of the same kind as those which are registrable. After the change in legislation following the implementation of the Directive, the list of registrable signs is now non-exhaustive, and the sphere of protectable signs is ultimately decided by the requirement of graphic representability. As a consequence, the graphic representation barrier arises with respect to all trademarks, including those that acquire protection through use. This is, however, a situation which has been criticised in the literature.[117] It has been proposed that exclusive rights to a trademark or other distinguishing marks should be obtainable without registration when the mark has been established through use. It is explicitly suggested that the law should also apply to other distinguishing marks (*annet varekjennetegn*) and not to trademarks alone. The underlying intention is said to be that protection through use shall be granted to marks that cannot be registered, even though they cannot be represented graphically.[118]

In the *Finnish* Trademark Act of 1964, the categories of signs that could acquire protection through use were originally the same as those which could be registered, with the exception of slogans, which were only considered capable of being protected through use. As a consequence of the incorporation of the Directive into Finnish trademark law, however, a distinction is, as in Swedish law, made between registrable trademarks, which must be capable of being represented graphically, and marks which can acquire protection through use, which also can consist of other signs.[119] There is no longer a separate provision for slogans, as these can be registered under Community law. As justification for introducing the new concept of protectable signs through use, the *travaux préparatoires* state that the Directive recognises establishment through use as a legal ground for trademarks which cannot be registered.[120]

The requirement of *graphic representation* was introduced by the Directive and the Regulation, and there is no corresponding requirement in international conventions. The term 'graphical' normally suggests a picture or description which captures the main characteristics of a sign. The CJEU has not explained in more precise terms what is meant by the term 'graphic representation', except that it must be possible to perceive it visually and that such a representation may, in particular, consist of 'images, lines or characters'.[121] The requirement of graphic representation thus implies that a trademark must be able to be represented visually. It must hence be possible to document it in a public register in such a way that it is clear what is covered by the protection. Marks, which are visually perceived, such as words and pictorial marks, are normally not

[117] Lassen and Stenvik, *Norsk varemerkerett* (2003) p 227.

[118] NOU 2001:8 pp 57 ff.

[119] N Bruun, *Intellectual Property Law in Finland* (Helsinki, Kluwer, 2001) p 101.

[120] RP (Finnish Government Bill) 302/92, p 10.

[121] Case C-273/00, *Sieckmann*, [2002] ECR I-11737, para 46.

problematic in this regard. For marks which are perceived through other senses, however, this requirement may cause problems.

In a preliminary ruling by the CJEU from 2002, the *Sieckmann* case, which concerned the registrability of an olfactory mark, the CJEU explained what should be included in an acceptable graphic representation. The CJEU emphasised that a graphic representation must contain a complete, clear, unequivocal, objective and precise identification of the mark, which in addition must be durable, easily accessible, and intelligible for those who may be interested in consulting the register ('the *Sieckmann* criteria').[122] The *Sieckmann* case is of decisive importance for the possibility of protecting scent marks.[123] The CJEU considered whether it was possible to graphically represent a scent by a chemical formula, a written description, or the deposit of a sample. Applying the above-mentioned criteria the CJEU came to the conclusion that none of the listed manners of representation could be considered as a satisfactory graphic representation, due, inter alia, to lack of precision and intelligibility.[124] As there is no generally accepted system of defining an odour which fulfils the demands of precision as well as intelligibility, the possibility of registration for the whole category of scent marks has been negatively affected. After the judgment in the *Sieckmann* case, opinion in the Member States seems to be that it is problematic – if not impossible – to register scents as trademarks. OHIM has also maintained a restrictive policy after *Sieckmann*. No new scent marks have been registered. Further, the opinion seems to be that there is no margin for interpretation after the *Sieckmann* case.[125]

As to marks, which are perceived aurally, a distinction should be made between musical and non-musical sounds. There is a long practice at OHIM of accepting musical notations as a graphic representation of musical marks. The first registered sound mark in Sweden, the signature of the ice-cream vendor *Hemglass*, was represented in this way.[126] In 2003, in the *Shield Mark* case,[127] the CJEU accepted that if musical notes are given in a musical stave so that the pitch and duration of the sounds are defined – which is a prerequisite for a melody to be identified – such a musical stave fulfils the requirements of a graphic representation. The number of musical sounds registered as

[122] Case C-273/00, *Sieckmann*, [2002] ECR I-11737, paras 46–55. These criteria have been confirmed by the CJEU in later cases.

[123] An analysis of this case is found in E Lunell, 'Dofter och ljud som föremål för varumärkesrätt – några kommentarer kring Sieckmann-fallet' ('Scents and sounds as trademark subject matter – some comments about the 'Sieckmann' case') (2003) 72 *Nordiskt immateriellt rättsskydd* 124 ff.

[124] Case C-273/00, paras 69–72. See also R Sieckmann, *Zum Begriff der grafischen Darstellbarkeit von Marken* ('On the graphic representability of marks') Wettbewerb in Recht und Praxis (WRP) 491 ff (2002).

[125] CTM application No 001807353 (*The smell of vanilla*) was rejected 19 August 2003. See also *Resolución de la Cuarta Sala de Recurso de 12 de diciembre de 2005, en el asunto* R 0445/2003-4 (*El olor a limón*).

[126] Case No 95-491, *Hemglass*, PBR [1998].

[127] Case C-283/01, *Shield Mark BV v Joost Kist h.o.d.n. Memex (Shield Mark)*, [2003] ECR I-14313.

Community trademarks is now considerable, and several such sound marks have also been registered in Sweden. The registration practice is liberal, and as a rule it is not required that distinctiveness acquired through use has to be demonstrated.

In contrast, it has been more difficult to represent non-musical sounds, for example animal cries. In the US, scents as well as non-musical sounds may be represented by a description in words, but such descriptions have thus far not been accepted by the CJEU. An alternative is to use a sound spectrogram (sonogram, time-frequency-amplitude diagram), which, in principle, can provide an exact representation of a sound.[128] In a decision rendered by the Fourth Board of Appeal in 2007, concerning registration of the *Tarzan yell* as a Community trademark, the Board held that a spectrogram is not in itself an acceptable graphic representation since it does not fulfil the *Sieckmann* criteria. It pointed out, however, that an electronic Community trademark application may be combined with a sound file, to fulfil the requirements of being easily accessible and self-contained.[129] It may also be added that a sound spectrogram is intelligible to anyone in combination with a sample in the form of an electronic sound file, which can be downloaded.

Concerning the Tarzan yell, the first application, which only contained a graphic representation of the sound (a sound spectrogram) combined with a written description, was refused. However, a new application was filed, where the spectrogram was combined with an MP3 sound file, and this was accepted. Not only the Tarzan yell, but a number of non-musical sounds, are now registered at OHIM, among them the sound of a bellowing stag for liqueur and Metro-Goldwyn-Mayer's famous roaring lion. In the trademark register, the sound is represented by a sound spectrogram and the sound can be heard directly via a downloadable file. So far, however, no sound marks have been registered in this way in Sweden. The CJEU has not as yet determined whether sound spectrograms and/or sound files should be considered as acceptable graphic representations of sound marks.

The registration of abstract colours, including one or several colours without special demarcations, as trademarks is a relatively new phenomenon. In two cases in 2003 and 2004, the *Libertel* case and the *Heidelberger Bauchemie* case, respectively, the CJEU held that abstract colours can be protected as trademarks. The CJEU has stated that a colour can be graphically represented by designating that colour using an internationally recognised identification code. A sample of a colour combined with a description in words of the colour may also constitute a graphic representation, provided that the *Sieckmann* criteria

[128] See also E Lunell, *Dofter och ljud som föremål för varumärkesrätt* (2003) and E Lunell, *Okonventionella varumärken – form, färg, doft, ljud* ('Unconventional Trademarks – Shape, Colour, Scent, Sound') (Stockholm, Norstedts Juridik, 2007) (Regarding the use of sound spectrograms to represent sounds.).

[129] Decision of the Fourth Board of Appeal of 27 September 2007, in Case R 708/2006-4 (*Tarzan yell*).

are fulfilled.[130] The graphic representation of a combination of colours must, in addition, be systematically arranged by associating the colours concerned in a predetermined and uniform way.[131] In order to have a colour mark registered, however, it is as a rule also required that it be demonstrated that the colour in question in practice functions as an indication of origin among consumers. This makes it comparatively difficult to protect colour marks. The most well-known example in Sweden is a special shade of the colour lilac for coffee.[132]

The statements of the CJEU may be labelled as general guidelines since they leave some latitude to the national courts.[133] It is presupposed that the national authorities decide upon the registrability of sound and colour marks, including also the question of whether the requirement of graphic representation is fulfilled, in the light of the circumstances of each individual case. One can also observe that the requirement of graphic representation has been given different interpretations by the CJEU, OHIM, and national authorities. The CJEU has not yet taken any decision on what concerns other unconventional trademarks, such as taste marks, touch marks and holograms.[134]

The idea of a sign as a 'communicator of information' reflects the potential capability of all signs that can be perceived by the human senses of being protectable as trademarks. The requirement of graphic representation, as it has been interpreted by the CJEU, constitutes, however, an obstacle for certain marks, which in fact may function as trademarks on the market. There is a conflict between the requirements of intelligibility and preciseness for marks that are not perceived visually, and where the mark is an entity separate from its graphic representation. This problem does not arise in the case of non-registered protection, where the mark can be established among the consumers through any one of our senses. A system based on *in casu* decisions provides flexible trademark protection which allows for adaptation to developments on the market.

Since protection through use is not dependent on registration, the graphic representation obstacle does not arise. In fact, one could argue that the requirement of graphic representation is natural only within a system of registration, where the aim is that the subject matter of protection shall be clear to a third party from the register alone. In connection with trademark protection through use, where the focus is on the demonstration of the actual circumstances, however, this is not a natural criterion.[135] It can also be considered to be in line with the core of the trademark legislation that it is the relevant class of the public which decides

[130] Case C-104/01, *Libertel Groep BV v Benelux-Merkenbureau (Libertel)* [2003] ECR I-3793, paras 36-37.

[131] Case C-49/02, *Heidelberger Bauchemie GmbH* [2004] ECR I-6129, para 33.

[132] Case No 03-088, *Löfbergs lila*, PBR [2005].

[133] Cf Opinion of AG Dámaso Ruiz-Jarabo Colomer in Case C-283/01, *Shield Mark*, paras 31 ff.

[134] Regarding these and other unconventional marks see E Lunell, *Okonventionella varumärken* (2007).

[135] See BS Lassen and A Stenvik, *Norsk varemerkerett* (2003) p 227.

what constitutes a trademark, since the requirement of distinctiveness, as well as the risk for confusion, are assessed from the perspective of the average consumer.

5. BAD FAITH PROVISIONS IN SWEDEN AND IN THE EU

In Sweden, first use of a mark alone does not provide grounds for a trademark right. There is no possibility to bringing trademark infringement proceedings with regard to a confusingly similar mark, solely by virtue of an earlier mark that has been put to use. A mark which has been used, but has neither been registered nor has reached the threshold for establishment as an unregistered mark may, however, be given a certain protection against unauthorised registration through Section 14(1) No 7 of the Swedish Trademarks Act. According to this provision, a trademark must not be registered if it is confusingly similar to a mark which on the date of application for registration is used by another person and if the application has been submitted with knowledge thereof and the applicant has not used his mark before the other mark was first used. This provision is often invoked as an alternative ground for revocation by the opponent, in cases where the registration authority or the court is likely to find insufficient proof that the opponent's mark has been sufficiently established through use.

The so called inactivity rules in Sections 8 and 9 only apply to collisions between signs with full trademark protection. This means that the first user of the mark cannot lose his rights due to inactivity and hence has the possibility, with no time limit, of demanding the revocation of a registration which a third party, who knows of the earlier mark, has applied for. Regarding establishment by use, however, there is nothing that the first user can do to intervene.[136]

The signs which are thus protected are trademarks, other marks used in the course of trade, as well as names and trade names which have been used to identify goods or services. There are no requirements of distinctiveness laid down in order to obtain the limited protection of Section 14(1) No 7. The rights of the first user are created when the sign is actually used, whether on the product or its wrapping, or in advertising. If an undertaking has merely engaged in certain preparatory activity relating to the use of the mark, such as ordering some printed matter this will not be sufficient. Account must also be taken of the date of first use. This must have taken place not only before the applicant has applied for registration of the mark, but also before the latter has started to use it – otherwise it is not possible to invoke the earlier mark as grounds for refusal.[137]

The provision covers the situation when the mark has first been used abroad and when its first use has been in Sweden.[138] If the mark has been used abroad,

[136] SOU 1958:10 pp 78 ff, 262.
[137] SOU 1958:10 p 288 and Prop. 1960/167 pp 106, 114.
[138] Prop 1992/93:48 p 79.

it is not required that it be well-known, implying that this provision reaches beyond what is required by Article 6 *bis* of the Paris Convention. As far as foreign marks are concerned, however, it is likely that the provision will be important only for marks that are well established in another country, due to the difficulty of proving that a registration has been applied for in bad faith.[139] Protection is granted against the use of confusingly similar marks, where similarities both of the mark and of the goods or services are considered.

Normally, only those marks are protected, which have been continuously used and are still being used. It is not mandatory that the mark has been used without interruption until the request of revocation or invalidity has been tried. If the interruption has lasted for a short period of time only, or been caused by special circumstances, protection is not excluded. On the other hand, if the mark has ceased to be used under such conditions that it must be considered as abandoned, it is not possible to claim protection.[140]

A necessary condition for the first user to be able to maintain his rights is that the other party has filed his application of registration with *knowledge* of the mark which has already been used. Exceptionally, the applicant will confess that he knew about the use of the mark.[141] A more common situation is that the applicant denies it, in which case it is up to the person who maintains that the applicant had such knowledge to substantiate the fact. Knowledge can be derived from the factual circumstances of the matter.[142] This may be the case if the applicant had previously been employed by the first user or been his agent, or when a well-known foreign mark is concerned, which any person in the trade circles concerned may be assumed to know about.[143]

However, it must be shown that the applicant had positive knowledge about the use of the earlier mark on the filing date of the application. It is not sufficient that it is plausible that the applicant had such knowledge.[144] The difficulties of substantiating such knowledge limit the importance of this provision. The proposed new trademark law would pose higher demands on the applicant by setting up the criterion 'knew or should have known'.[145] If this were enacted, it would be easier to demonstrate that the applicant acts in bad faith. In conclusion, in Sweden, what matters is not the trademark applicant's intention but only his objective knowledge: whether he was (or should have been) aware that another person was already using the same or a similar mark.

In Swedish case-law the expression 'bad faith' is sometimes used, even though the legislation talks about 'knowledge'. 'Bad faith' is an autonomous concept

[139] M Levin, *Noveller i varumärkesrätt* ('Essays in trademark law') (Stockholm, Juristförlaget, 1990) pp 35 ff.

[140] See eg Case T 411-07, RH 2008:29, *GOLDEN GATE*, Svea Hovrätt (Svea Court of Appeal in Stockholm) [2008].

[141] See eg RÅ 1984 para 122, *GOLDEN LIGHTS*.

[142] Prop 1960:167 p 114 and RÅ 1986 note 664, *DAVIDOFF* as a figurative mark.

[143] SOU 1958:10 p 289.

[144] *RÅ* 1984 ref. 2:37, *FÄRGTEMA COLOR TREND*.

[145] SOU 2001:26 p 438.

of EU law but there is, however, no definition of the term in either the Directive or the Regulation.[146] There are two bad faith provisions in the Directive, which are optional for the Member States. One of them, Article 4(4)(g), stipulates that any Member State may provide that a trademark shall not be registered or, if registered, shall be liable to be declared invalid where, and to the extent that 'the trademark is liable to be confused with a mark which was in use abroad on the filing date of the application and which is still in use there, provided that at the date of the application the applicant was acting in bad faith'. The other, Article 3(2)(d), which is more general, permits a Member State to refuse or invalidate a registration if 'the application for registration of the trademark was made in bad faith by the applicant'.

The Swedish bad faith provision, Section 14(1) No 7, is limited to a situation where the trademark applied for is to the knowledge of the applicant confusingly similar to one already in use. It is considered that it is primarily an analogue of Article 4(4)(g) of the Directive. The provision in the Directive is, however, intended to provide protection to trademarks which have been in use abroad, while the Swedish provision also protects trademarks which have been in use in the country. Article 3(2)(d) of the Directive, however, has been interpreted in Sweden as covering marks that have been used in the country of registration. When the Directive was incorporated into Swedish law it was stated that Section 14(1) No 7 would be kept in its present form.[147]

In relation to a Community trademark, bad faith can be raised in proceedings for invalidity under Article 52(1)(b) of the Regulation. According to this provision a trademark shall be declared invalid on application to OHIM or on the basis of a counterclaim in infringement proceedings 'where the applicant was acting in bad faith when he filed the application for the trademark.' According to OHIM's case-law a dishonest intention has often been a prerequisite for bad faith.[148] How the provision of bad faith should be interpreted has recently been the subject of a judgment of the CJEU after a reference from an Austrian court in the *Lindt* case.[149]

The background is as follows: Lindt, which has produced and marketed chocolate Easter bunnies since the early 1950s was granted registration 6 July 2001 of a three-dimensional Community trademark consisting of the form and presentation of an Easter bunny wrapped in gold-coloured foil, with red and brown markings, wearing round its neck a red ribbon with a bell attached, and bearing on its haunch a design including the words '*Lindt Goldhase*'. Following registration, Lindt brought trademark infringement proceedings against

[146] Some guidance may be found in a comparative 'Bad faith case study' made by OHIM, published on January 31, 2003, HOM/02/08. Available at oami.europa.eu/en/enlargement/pdf/badfaithCS3101.pdf.

[147] Prop 1992/93:48 p 79. See also SOU 2001:26 p 438.

[148] See eg Case No C479899/1, *BE NATURAL*, OHIM [2000].

[149] Case C-529/07, *Chokoladefabriken Lindt & Sprüngli AG v Franz Hauswirth GmbH* [2009] ECR I-4893 (*Lindt*).

Franz Hauswirth, GmbH seeking an order directing it to cease producing and marketing its Easter bunnies in a presentation which, Lindt claimed, was likely to be confused with the registered mark. In reliance, inter alia, on Article 51(1)(b) of Regulation No 40/94, Hauswirth counterclaimed that the registration had been made in bad faith and the trademark should therefore be declared invalid.

The Advocate General delivered an opinion on 12 March 2009, after both written and oral submissions had been made by the parties to the main proceedings, by the Czech and Swedish Governments and by the Commission.[150] The meaning of bad faith was examined. The Swedish Government argued that what matters is not the trademark applicant's intention but his objective knowledge: whether he was, or should have been, aware that another person was already using a mark capable of causing confusion. [151] The Advocate General held, however, that the concept of 'bad faith' relates to a subjective motivation on the part of the trademark applicant – a dishonest intention or other 'sinister motive' – which will none the less normally be established by reference to similar objective criteria.[152]

The CJEU delivered its decision on 11 June 2009. It explicitly held that the situation before the Court was limited to a situation in which, at the time the application for registration was filed, several producers on the market were using, identical or similar signs for identical or similar products capable of being confused with the sign, for which registration was sought. The CJEU further stated that whether the applicant was acting in bad faith must be the subject of an overall assessment, taking into account all the factors relevant to the particular case.[153]

As a condition for bad faith, the CJEU first of all mentioned the requirement of *knowledge* and accepted that it is sufficient if the applicant knows or must have known that a third party has long been using, in at least one Member State, an identical or similar sign for an identical or similar product capable of being confused with the sign for which registration is sought. With regard to the expression 'must know', a presumption of knowledge by the applicant may arise, inter alia, from general knowledge in the economic sector concerned of such use, and that knowledge can be inferred, inter alia, from the duration of such use. The CJEU held, however, that knowledge by the applicant is not enough in itself to permit the conclusion that the applicant was acting in bad faith. Consideration must also be given to the applicant's *intention* at the time when he files the application for registration. In accordance with the opinion of the Advocate General, the Court stated that the applicant's intention is a subjective factor, which must be determined by reference to the objective circumstances of the particular case.[154]

[150] Opinion of A G Sharpston of 12 March 2009 in Case C-529/07, *Lindt*.
[151] Opinion, Case C-529/07, *Lindt*, para 55.
[152] Ibid, paras 57–60.
[153] Case C-529/07, *Lindt*, paras 36–37.
[154] Ibid at paras 39–42.

The intention of preventing a third party from marketing a product may, according to the CJEU, be relevant to determining whether the applicant is acting in bad faith in certain circumstances. This may be the case when the applicant applies to register a Community trademark with no intention of using it.[155] The nature of the mark applied for may also be relevant. In a case where the sign for which registration is sought consists of the entire shape and presentation of the product, the fact that the applicant is acting in bad faith might more readily be established. This is explained by the fact that the competitors' freedom to choose the shape of a product and is presentation is restricted by technical or commercial factors, so that the trademark proprietor is able to prevent his competitors not merely from using an identical or similar sign, but also from marketing comparable products.[156] The fact that a third party has long used a sign for an identical or similar product capable of being confused with the mark applied for and that that sign enjoys some degree of legal protection was also a relevant factor.[157]

In comparison with Swedish law, the CJEU requires an additional criterion besides knowledge, namely the existence of some kind of dishonest intention if the bad faith requirement is to be fulfilled. Even though the test for establishing bad faith is primarily objective, as in Sweden, simple knowledge of the use of another mark is not sufficient to establish bad faith. From the presumptions in the *Lindt* case it is clear that the 'bad faith' provision in the Regulation applies to confusingly similar marks. On account of its general character it could also encompass activities that do not at present constitute bad faith in Sweden. However, exactly how far the provision may reach is a matter which requires further guidance from the CJEU.

6. CONCLUDING REMARKS

Whether a Member State should grant protection against registrations made in bad faith or not is a national concern, since the provisions in Article 3(2)(d) and 4(4)(g) of the Directive are optional. However, if a Member State makes use of this possibility and prescribes such protection, CJEU case-law indicates that it would be obliged to follow the CJEU's interpretation of the provisions of the Directive.[158]

In the *Lindt* case, the CJEU gave an interpretation of what constitutes 'bad faith', which indicates that the notion has a moral or ethical element. The bad faith provision in the Regulation is a counterpart to Article 3(2)(d) of the Directive. Given the need for harmonious interaction between the two systems,

[155] Ibid at paras 42–44.
[156] Ibid at para 50.
[157] Ibid at paras 46–52.
[158] Cf Case C-408/01, *Adidas-Salomon AG v Fitnessworld Trading Ltd*, [2003] ECR I-12537, paras 13–22.

there must be a single Community concept of bad faith covering both the Regulation and the Directive. The way the CJEU interprets the corresponding concept in the Regulation will therefore also be relevant when the courts of the Member States apply national bad faith provisions.

However, in Sweden, there is no general bad faith provision in accordance with Article 3(2)(d) of the Directive. Only a partial implementation of the Article has been made. It is important that future legislation enables measures to be taken, not only in the case of a person in bad faith registering a trademark which is confusingly similar to a mark already used by someone else, but also in cases of especially unfair competition, when, for example, one partner in a contractual relation registers the trademark of his adversary for goods or services of another kind or registers a certain trademark with the sole purpose of preventing others from using it.

The situation with exclusive trademarks rights acquired through use is somewhat different. Since the national trademark laws are not harmonised when it comes to these rights, each Member State is in principle free not only to grant protection for non-registered trademarks, thus recognising that the use of a sign gives rise to an exclusive right, but also to define the extent, scope and conditions of such protection as well as its subject matter. One can observe that the trademark protection acquired through use in Sweden is harmonised with Community law in the sense that the assessment of whether a trademark has a distinctive character is carried out according to the same criteria, irrespective of whether the trademark right has been gained by registration or through use.

Locally established non-registered rights are also compatible with Community law, since each Member State is free to define the geographical area in which a national mark must be known to acquire protection.[159] It follows that, in principle, even an earlier non-registered trademark of merely local significance may constitute a bar to the registration of a trademark, or grounds for its cancellation, if there is a provision to that effect in the legislation of the Member State.[160]

One should note, however, that locally established rights are only mentioned in Article 6(2) of the Directive dealing with the relation between trademark rights in the case of infringement, and not in Article 4(4)(b) dealing with the declaration of invalidity. Moreover, according to Article 8(4) of the Regulation, it is not possible to prevent a registration or have it declared invalid on the basis of a locally established right. It has been proposed that it should no longer be possible in Sweden for a locally established mark to constitute grounds for a revocation of a registration. If this were done, one would be more in harmony with Community law and in particular Article 8(4) of the Regulation.[161]

[159] Opinion of AG Mengozzi in Case C-328/06, *Fincas Tarragona*, paras 45–46.
[160] See also Opinion in case C-328/06, *Fincas Tarragona*, at paras 47–48.
[161] See also SOU 2001:26 pp 237 ff.

In Sweden, no difference was previously made between locally and regionally established trademarks. In a case where it is not possible to prevent registration, or declare a registration invalid, by virtue of a locally established trademark, the definition of 'locally established' becomes more important. The assessment of what constitutes a locally established right should then be the same in both Swedish and EU law based situations. To consider geographical aspects only is not sufficient, since a mark which is established within a geographically limited area may possess a significant commercial value and in exceptional circumstances even be entitled to an extended protection. The concept of local establishment should be reserved for such marks, which in comparison with the country as a whole can be considered insignificant. In contrast it does not seem unreasonable that regionally established trademarks may be invoked as bars to registration or grounds for revocation.

Finally, an important question is the extent to which the Member States should allow the definition of a trademark in the Directive to apply to signs which are protected in ways other than registration, and where no harmonisation has occurred.[162] The extent to which national non-registered protection should comprise signs that fail to qualify for registration because the requirement of graphic representation cannot be fulfilled is a matter that merits further discussion.

Differences in case-law between the Member States will always exist. The most uniform practice is likely to be attained if the same underlying rules apply irrespective of whether trademark protection has been acquired by registration or through use.[163] Of importance, however, is how close a concept in a national provision is to a concept in the Directive, and for this reason should be unified, and the extent to which the coexistence of different rules influences trade between the Member States.[164] In this connection one should note that the Swedish concept of a mark (*varukännetecken*) stems from the 1960s, is a purely indigenous construction, and has not been harmonised with Community law. The need for a unitary interpretation is therefore not as urgent as it would be if the concept had been borrowed from Community law.

Marks which have acquired protection through use and which are not registrable are not likely to have a large effect on trade within the Community. They still constitute a small fraction of the total number of trademarks. National, non-registered trademarks that can be invoked as bars to registration according to Article 8(4) or grounds for invalidity according to Article 52(1)(c) of the Regulation are, in practice, probably also limited to signs which would be eligible for registration. Unconventional marks which have been established in Sweden but cannot be registered, such as scents, are therefore likely to be important primarily on the national plane.

[162] See NOU 2001:8 p 12.

[163] See HP Götting, 'Protection of Well-Known, Unregistered Marks in Europe and the United States' (2000) 31 *International Review of Intellectual Property and Competition Law* (IIC) p 407.

[164] See Case C-28/95, *A.Leur-Bloem v Inspecteur der Belastingdienst/Ondernemingen Amsterdam* 2 [1997] ECR I-4161.

One can finally notice that neither the Directive nor the Regulation excludes any specific category of signs from registration as a trademark. The CJEU has also left this question open in its preliminary rulings, even though it did not adjust the requirement of graphic representation so that it could be fulfilled for, say, scent marks.

The current trend is that the number of types of signs that can be registered as trademarks is increasing. The importance of non-registered protection as a complement should therefore decrease. The fact that there still exist signs that constitute a challenge for trademark legislation shows, however, that national non-registered protection continues to have vitality as a complement to registered protection. There is also a need to retain a non-registered type of protection for a sign, which in itself could have been registered, in cases where registration has been overlooked, when a sign has acquired trademark character 'by accident', without this having been a conscious intention of its proprietor from the outset, and for trademarks which are indeed of merely local significance. Non-registered protection will be needed for such cases also in the future. Full harmonisation within the European Community has thus still quite some way to go.

6
Swedish Soda Club Dispute – Competition Law and IPR Intersection

ASSISTANT PROFESSOR ULF MAUNSBACH

1. INTRODUCTION

Early on, the European Court of Justice (CJEU) noticed that the relationship between the functioning of the internal market and the protection of intellectual property rights (IPR) can give rise to conflict between the two interests.[1] When the issue was first addressed the CJEU introduced the distinction between the existence of and the exercise of IPR. The CJEU reasoned that Community competition law would not interfere with the existence of intellectual property rights but in some situations the exercise of IPR could be regarded as a breach of community law.

The first cases dealing with this problem were framed in relation to the rules regarding the free movement of goods and the interpretation of the rules in Article 30 TEC (now Article 36 TFEU), which provide justifications for restrictions on imports and exports.[2] It is not surprising that these developments initially dealt with this article due to the fact that this is the first article in the EC or EU-treaties which expressly provides certain exceptions from internal market rules for industrial and commercial property (which include IPR's.) The CJEU developed the doctrine of exhaustion of rights with the aim of fostering a smoothly functioning internal market and the free movement of goods. The doctrine prohibits IPR from being used to prevent parallel trade within the

[1] One of the first examples where intellectual property right were identified as a potential problem in relation to the functioning of the internal market was in joined cases C-56 and C-58/64 *Établissements Consten S.à.R.L. and Grundig-Verkaufs-GmbH v Commission* [1966] ECR 229.

[2] See case C-78/70 *Deutsche Grammophon Gesellschaft mbH v Metro-SB-Großmärkte GmbH & Co KG* [1971] ECR 487.

Community in relation to goods that have been put on the market by the rights owner or by her consent.[3]

Since the idea of efficient competition is inextricably connected to the free movement of goods and is one of the most obvious elements of a functional internal market, it is not particularly strange that competition law concerns were rose in relation to IPR. In the centre of interest lie Articles 101 TFEU and 102 TFEU (formerly Articles 81 and 82 EU) which govern situations where companies may distort efficient competition in the internal market to the degree that is actionable. Article 101 TFEU deals with the distortion of competition between undertakings and is particularly relevant in relation to IPR licensing. Article 102 TFEU deals with abuse of a dominant position and is of relevance to situations where use of IPR is the core reason for the distortion. The most frequent example of such an abuse is an unjustified refusal to licence. In this sense the applicability of Article 102 is closely connected to the concept of essential facilities although this essay will not analyse questions in relation to abuse of dominant position as a result of refusal to supply an essential facility.[4]

Following its previous practice relating to the free movement of goods, the CJEU has concluded that it is not possible to use competition law to affect the existence of intellectual property rights but it may be possible to regulate the exercise of such rights.[5] Having held that you may act on the exercise of an intellectual property right the next problem is specifying those situations where such exercise may be prohibited under competition law. In order to distinguish the exercise/existence dichotomy the CJEU introduced the concept that there is a certain 'specific subject matter' of each intellectual property right and that its use within the subject matter is justified even if it may lead to a distortion of competition.[6] Consequently a right holder is permitted to use the intellectual property rights within the boundaries of its 'specific subject matter', but when the use is expanded beyond these bounds the exercise may be prohibited by competition law.

The concept of a specific subject matter seems easy to accept and it appears quite reasonable to assume that it ought to be possible to prohibit abuses of intellectual property rights by utilizing competition law. However, on a closer examination, several problems appear among which the most problematic would likely be that fact that it is still unclear how the concept of 'specific subject matter' is to be interpreted.

[3] See eg Case 15/74 *Centrafarm BV and Adriaan de Peijper v Sterling Drug Inc* [1974] ECR 1147 and case C-355/96 *Silhouette International Schmied GmbH & Co KG v Hartlauer Handelsgesellschaft mbH* [1998] ECR I-4799.

[4] For a more comprehensive discussion as to the concept of essential facilities see A Jones and B Sufrin, *EC Competition Law* (Oxford 3d Edn 2008) (Cit Jones/Sufrin) pp 536–53, with further references.

[5] See eg Case 238/87, *AB Volvo v Erik Veng (UK) Ltd* [1988] ECR 6211.

[6] Ibid at para 8.

The question has been briefly touched upon by the CJEU but so far, there are no Swedish court decisions regarding this matter. However, it is likely that the question of how to balance competition and right holder interests will have to be addressed in a dispute regarding different potential infringements in relation to the trademarks of Soda-Club (CO2) SA, presently pending before the Stockholm district court. This dispute provides the motivation for this essay and its purpose is to highlight the problems involved. To begin with I will present the case and the facts as they stand at present (summer 2010). Thereafter I will briefly present the CJEUs position in this matter and then I shall draw some general conclusions regarding the interrelation between competition and intellectual property law. I have no intention in this essay to take sides in the dispute or affect the forthcoming decision. I am simply interested in the issues involved.

2. THE CASE

Soda-Club, as part of the SodaStream Group, is one of the world's largest manufacturer, distributor and marketer of home carbonation systems. The SodaStream Group has an extensive intellectual property portfolio including several trademark registrations world-wide, some of which are germane to the dispute pending before the Stockholm district court, namely; SODA-CLUB®, ALCO2JET® and SODASTREAM®.

One the growing consumer market for home carbonation systems, Soda-Club is the manufacturer of leading brands in the area of drink-makers. A drink-maker works, to put it simply, by dispensing CO2 from a gas cylinder in the back of the drink-maker, into fresh tap water. When a consumer purchases a SodaStream drink maker, a full CO2 gas cylinder is included in the starter pack. As the market for drink-makers grows the aftermarket for gas cylinders grows in parallel. The case before the Swedish court concerns the important aftermarket in which consumers pay to refill their gas-cylinders. The gas cylinders that are distributed together with the SodaStream machine are provided under license, which states that the consumer is permitted to use the cylinder for as long as the machine functions, but that the actual cylinder belongs to Soda-Club. The licence contains further provisions providing how the consumer must handle empty cylinders. One strong condition is that refilling of the cylinder is only to be performed by an authorized SodaStream retailer.

Vikingsoda started its business in 2009 with the ambition to become an actor in the market for refilling gas cylinders. In order to be able to establish the business in the Swedish market Vikingsoda purchased 9200 gas cylinders from a German company most of which were 'Soda-Club' cylinders, having the trademark SODA-CLUB engraved on the top of the cylinder. Vikingsoda commissioned the German company to refill the cylinders and mark them with Vikingsoda label. This required, among other things, that the original SodaStream label had to be removed.

After discovering that Vikingsoda had entered the Swedish market Soda-Club commenced an action before the District Court of Stockholm [Stockholms tingsrätt] claiming that Vikingsoda infringed Soda-Club's trademarks: (1) by using the trademark SODA-CLUB,(2) by removing the original labels from the gas cylinders (containing the trademarks SODASTREAM® and ALCO2JET®),(3) by labelling the gas cylinders with Vikingsoda's new label (including the trademark VIKINGSODA®) and (4) by using that label together with remaining Soda-Club trademarks (in particular, the engraved trademark SODA-CLUB® located on top of the gas cylinders). Soda-Club also moved for a provisional injunction against the use of Soda-Club's trademark.

Vikingsoda objected and argued that its use of Soda-Club's trademarks was not infringing due to the fact that the gas cylinders used by Vikingsoda are put on the market by Soda-Club and consequently that any trademark rights in relation to those cylinders have been exhausted. Furthermore Vikingsoda argued that the procedure of relabeling the cylinders was not an infringing act and finally, that the use of the trademarks VIKINGSODA and SODA-CLUB together did not create the impression of a commercial connection.

After having reviewed the facts of the case the district court pronounced its decision on 5th February 2010.[7] In summary the decision resulted in the imposition of an injunction on the penalty of a fine directed both against Vikingsoda's use of the trademark Soda-Club® and against the removal of Soda-Club's labels from the gas cylinders. The injunction was issued primarily due to the fact that Soda-Club managed to show probable cause in relation to the claimed infringement. In particular, the court found that it was not shown that the use of Soda-Club's gas cylinders was necessary for Vikingsoda to access the refill market. Further, the court concluded that Vikingsoda's use of the trademark SODA-CLUB® in combination with its own trademark VIKINGSODA®, taking account to the fact that trademark rights are broad by nature, could create an impression of commercial connection and consequently such trademark use may be regarded as infringing.[8]

Vikingsoda appealed the interlocutory decision to the Court of Appeals [Svea hovrätt] arguing that the court should vacate the decision of the district court. During the period the case was pending before the Court of Appeals the Swedish Competition Authority [Konkurrensverket] submitted an opinion to the court in relation to the on-going dispute.[9] The Competition Authority viewed it as likely that Soda-Club was to be regarded as a dominant actor on the relevant market and that its use of its trademark could be questioned under competition law.

After this Soda-Club decided to withdraw its claim for an interlocutory injunction and the case was remanded to the district court for a hearing on the merits in the principle dispute regarding trademark infringement. Presently

[7] Decision of the District Court of Stockholm in case No T 17919/09.

[8] Ibid.

[9] See opinion from the Swedish Competition Authority the 25th of March 2010, No 632/2009.

the parties have been urged to finalize their claims before 13th August 2010. Thereafter it can be presumed that the main hearing will commence in the winter 2010/11.

After having said this, it is obvious that there is, as yet, no final Swedish case to write about. Still the case up to this point may be used as an illustration in relation to some of the problems that may arise when intellectual property rights collide with competition interests. These are questions that most certainly will be discussed in the up-coming adjudication of the Soda-Club and Vikingsoda dispute. I shall try to address those questions below from a general point of view.

3. THE PROBLEMS

To begin with it can be concluded that IPR's and Competition Law interact in a number of different ways. One general point is, as mentioned above, that competition interests are not supposed to interfere with the existence of intellectual property rights but that it may be relevant to take account competition interests in relation to the exercise of IPR's. Courts may consequently restrict the use of IPR's when they determine that the use in question distorts competition because the use goes beyond the specific subject matter of the IPR. This is the starting point of the analysis.

In addressing conflicts between competition law and intellectual property law the question is best addressed by dividing them into two parts. First are problems relating to license agreements and technology transfer within the framework of Article 101 TFEU and second, problems in relation to abuses of a dominant position that should be addressed within the framework of Article 102 TFEU.

Article 101 is the most widely applied provision. It is obvious that this rule is applicable in relation to certain types of agreements and that agreements dealing with intellectual property are to be tried according to the same principles applied to agreements in general. If certain provisions of the agreement distort competition it may be challenged from a competition law perspective notwithstanding the existence of IPR's. Because the licensing of IPR's is crucial to the functioning of the internal market in today's global IT-society the application of Article 101 TFEU is subject to a Community regulation creating block exemption that deals with technology transfers.[10] If the parties to such an agreement comply with the block exemption in the manner set forth in the regulation such agreements are justified, and in principal lie outside of the reach of Article 101 TFEU. In summary, the application of Article 101 TFEU in relation to IPR's is comparatively clear and there is quite a lot of practical guidance available.[11]

[10] Commission Regulation (EC) No 772/ 2004 of 27 April 2004 on the application of Article 81(3) of the Treaty to categories of technology transfer agreements OJ L 123, 27/04/2004 p 11.

[11] See Jones/Sufrin at pp 785–855.

The application of Article 102 TFEU in relation to IPR's is much more complicated and the arguments in favour of its application are not that obvious. To trigger the application of Article 102 TFEU there must be a dominant undertaking and this undertaking must abuse its dominant position if the conduct is to be prohibited under Article 102 TFEU. Depending on its definition, mere ownership of an IPR may be regarded as a sufficient prerequisite for dominance due to the fact that IPR's are exclusive rights granting the owner a monopoly over a certain kind of intangible property. From this point of view the exercise of all IPR's may be challenged from a competition law perspective. On the other hand, the core purpose of the intellectual property regime is to enable the owners the ability to monopolize certain kind of rights, asserted in respect of products of the human intellect. In line with this argument there should be no possibility to attack neither the existence nor the exercise of IPR's. This conclusion is supported by the fact that intellectual property law and competition law share the same aim of pursuing the benefits of society by producing greater consumer welfare.[12] Further, the distinction between the existence and exercise of IPR's may be questioned. Considering the fact that if you are prohibited from exercising an IPR it is of no practical use, it is obvious that there is such interdependence between existence and exercise such as to make the distinction less useful.[13] Following this line of reasoning the balancing of interests between the two legal regimes is better achieved within the frames of intellectual property laws, which place limitations on IPR's in different ways (eg by limiting their duration and by allowing certain kind of use).

The determination of the point when the exercise of an IPR may be regarded as abusive is a sensitive question, irrespective of the fact that the issues involved are quite complicated. Courts have had few occasions to address these particular questions and when given the opportunity their answers have generally been quite vague. However, some clarifications have been made and the CJEU have issued a few cases dealing with the exercise of IPR's in connection with the abuse of a dominant position. Some of the most relevant cases are discussed below. These cases have a common denominator in the fact that they generally relate to what can be defined as a refusal to license. In general an undertaking is supposed to have total freedom in relation to its choice of counterparty and it should not be possible to force undertakings into agreements with each other. Such a power contradicts the entire idea of contractual freedom. Still when the undertaking is in a dominant position, compulsory licences may be an option to cure their abuse, particularly when the refusal to license prevents the entry of new actors into the market, eg when barriers to entry are created. This kind of abusive use of IPR's has been regarded as falling outside the elusive boundaries of the above-mentioned specific subject matter.

[12] See Jones/Sufrin at pp 777–79, and references therein.

[13] Ibid at p 781.

The first time the CJEU came into contact with this issue was in the *Volvo* case. The case dealt with the question of whether or not it is an abuse for a car manufacturer to refuse to licence the design rights for spare parts for cars it manufactures to other independent undertakings that are willing to manufacture these spare parts. The Court concluded that 'the right of the proprietor of a protected design to prevent third parties from manufacturing and selling or importing, without its consent, products incorporating the design constitutes the very subject-matter of his exclusive right'.[14] Consequently 'an obligation imposed upon the proprietor of a protected design to grant to third parties, even in return for a reasonable royalty, a licence for the supply of products incorporating the design would lead to the proprietor thereof being deprived of the substance of his exclusive right'.[15] Thus a refusal to license may not, as a principle rule, be regarded as abuse in relation to the application of Article 102 TFEU. However, the Court continued its reasoning to clarify that 'the exercise of an exclusive right by the proprietor of a registered design in respect of car body panels may be prohibited by Article 86 [102] if it involves, on the part of an undertaking holding a dominant position, certain abusive conduct such as the arbitrary refusal to supply spare parts to independent repairers, the fixing of prices for spare parts at an unfair level or a decision no longer to produce spare parts for a particular model even though many cars of that model are still in circulation, provided that such conduct is liable to affect trade between Member States'.[16]

As to the different categories of potential abuse listed by the CJEU the specific question of pricing was further elaborated in the *Renault* case (decided on the same day as the *Volvo* case). The Court clarified '[w]ith reference more particularly to the difference in prices between components sold by the manufacturer and those sold by the independent producers, it should be noted that [...] a higher price for the former than for the latter does not necessarily constitute an abuse, since the proprietor of protective rights in respect of an ornamental design may lawfully call for a return on the amounts which he has invested in order to perfect the protected design'.[17]

As to refusal to licence in relation to design protection for spare parts the CJEU provided some guidance in the above-mentioned cases. We know that the right to control access to exclusive design lies within the specific subject matter of the design protection and we know that there must be an additional abuse before the conduct can be prohibited under Article 102 TFEU. The remaining important question is how to understand the different 'abuse categories', referred to by the CJEU in the *Volvo* case.[18]

[14] Case 238/87, *AB Volvo v Erik Veng (UK) Ltd* [1988] ECR 6211, at para 8.

[15] Ibid.

[16] Ibid at para 9.

[17] Case C-53/87, *Consorzio italiano della componentistica di ricambio per autoveicoli and Maxicar v Régie nationale des usines Renault* [1988] ECR 06039, para 17.

[18] See Jones/Sufrin, at pp 554–56.

The relation between competition and intellectual property law was further elaborated in the *Magill* case. The case involved copyright protection in relation to listings of television programs and the defendant's (Radio Telefis) refusal to provide information about the listings to an independent undertaking (Magill) that wanted to publish a weekly television guide. The CJEU concluded that this constituted an abuse of a dominant position, which inevitably leads to the conclusion that the copyright owners were compelled to provide the demanded information.[19] As to the rationale for its decision the *Magill* Court cited the *Volvo* case for the conclusion that an abuse may exist if there is additional misconduct (ie exceptional circumstances). In the *Magill* case the exceptional circumstances can be divided in four parts: First there was no substitute for the weekly television guide. Second the refusal to supply prevented the appearance of a new product. Third, there was no justification for such refusal and finally, the copyright owners reserved the market for television guides to themselves.[20]

The *Magill*-decision has been widely discussed and it is still referred to as an example where compulsory licences can be used in relation to IPR's.[21] One initial question, related to the *Magill*-decision, was whether the circumstances were to be regarded as cumulative. This specific question was answered in the negative in a subsequent decision by the General Court (GC – former Court of First Instance/CFI). The GC appears to take the position that the listed circumstances in *Magill* are to be regarded as severable, not cumulative.[22] This position was later supported by the European Commission in a decision regarding interim masseurs.[23] However, when the issue finally came before the CJEU, in the *IMS* case, the Court stated that the exceptional circumstances listed in *Magill* are cumulative.

The *IMS* case concerns a refusal to licence copyright in a certain system for representing sales data, which has become close to becoming the industrial standard on the market for pharmaceuticals in Germany. Access to the sales data system was regarded as crucial for new undertakings wishing to compete on this market. When the case came before the CJEU on a reference from the Landgericht Frankfurt am Main, the court referred three questions all of which, in different ways aimed to clarify to what extent a refusal to license might constitute an abuse of a dominant position. The CJEU initially stated, (citing *Magill* and *Volvo*), that 'the exclusive right of reproduction forms part of the rights of the owner of an intellectual property right, so that refusal to grant a licence, even if it is the act of an undertaking holding a dominant position,

[19] See Case C-241-2/91 *Radio Telefis Eireann (RTE) and Independent Television Publications Ltd (ITP) v Commission of the European Communities.* [1995] ECR I-00743.

[20] Ibid at paras 52–56.

[21] See Jones/Sufrin, at pp 557–61.

[22] See Case T-504/93, *Tiercé Ladbroke SA v Commission* [1997] ECR II-00923, para 131. See also Jones/Sufrin, at pp 561–63.

[23] 2002/ 165/ EC: Commission Decision of 3 July 2001 (Case COMP D3 / 38.044 - *NDC Health / IMS Health* OJ L 59, 28/02/2002 p 18 para 180.

cannot in itself constitute abuse of a dominant position'.[24] As to the possibility of applying Article 102 TFEU in relation to IPR's the CJEU concluded that 'in order for the refusal by an undertaking which owns a copyright to give access to a product or service indispensable for carrying on a particular business to be treated as abusive, it is sufficient that three cumulative conditions be satisfied, namely, that that refusal is preventing the emergence of a new product for which there is a potential consumer demand, that it is unjustified and such as to exclude any competition on a secondary market'.[25] As to the question whether those conditions were satisfied in *IMS* the CJEU concluded that this was for the national court to determine in the main proceedings.

In *IMS* the CJEU referred back to *Magill* and confirmed that the '*Magill*-test' is still valid. Further it confirmed that the exceptional circumstances are cumulative but once again not much is said as to how the different circumstances are to be understood. A crucial consideration seems to be that of consumer welfare and the fact that 'in the balancing of the interest in protection of the intellectual property right and the economic freedom of its owner against the interest in protection of free competition, the latter can prevail only where refusal to grant a licence prevents the development of the secondary market to the detriment of consumers'.[26]

4. CONCLUDING REMARKS

In summary it is possible to conclude that the concept 'specific subject matter' is quite versatile and that it is hard to generalise its application due to the fact that the cases decided so far have been of a *sui generis* nature. One observation is that both *IMS* and *Magill* are cases concerning with the exercise of weak copyright protection that is, protection that is not generally based on copyright in all EU Member States. *Magill* deals with compilations or listings of television program schedules and *IMS* deals with a certain kind of information system for sales data. Both products are on the verge of what copyright may be able to protect and it has been stated that the findings from *Magill* and *IMS* might not be applicable in relation to stronger copyright, not to mention that it may be even harder to expand the applicability of this case-law into the fields of patent and trademark protection.[27] In that respect the findings from *Volvo* and *Renault* might be more suitable in relation to the up-coming Swedish dispute regarding Soda-Club, in so far as *Volvo* and *Renault* deal with distortions of competition on the aftermarket for spare parts. In that respect there might be factual similarities with respect to the replacement of gas cylinders in the market for carbonated water.

[24] Case C-418/01, *IMS Health* at para 34.
[25] Ibid at para 38.
[26] Ibid at para 48.
[27] See Jones/Sufrin, at p 570.

In my opinion however, there is little guidance to be found in existing case-law from the CJEU relating to the issue involved in the Soda Club case. Trying to make a general statement that adds to the interpretation of the concept 'specific subject matter' will prove difficult. Still it may be interesting to give it a try. First it can be concluded that it lies within the boundaries of the specific subject matter to put protected property into circulation on the internal market for the first time. As a principle rule, the owner of an IPR also possesses the possibility to control which undertakings may be allowed to benefit from the intellectual property in question. However, this last observation does not apply without exceptions. In exceptional circumstances a refusal to license can be regarded as an abuse of a dominant position and therefore actionable under competition law. Here we confess to being puzzled as to the definition and extent of what might constitute such abusive circumstances. From exiting case-law it can be concluded that arbitrary refusal to licence might be an abuse. We do have the cumulative list from *Magill*, which, to put it simply, states that abuse equals the unjustified prevention of a new product. That does not apply directly in the circumstances of the Soda-Club case, although it indisputably deals with the interconnection between competition interests and intellectual property rights. In my opinion this is a perfect situation in as much as hopefully it will force Swedish courts to try new arguments and create new case-law (most likely with the help of a preliminary ruling from the CJEU). I'm looking forward to that!

7

Copyright Contracts – EU Solutions or National Concern? A Swedish Proposal to Amend the Copyright Act on Individual and Collective Contracts

PROFESSOR JAN ROSÉN

1. INTRODUCTION

Copyright works and related rights have always been licensed in a multitude of markets with very little in common, except that the transactions concern IP rights of a certain kind. The factual circumstances and objects of licensing within the realm of copyright widely differ among each other. The multitude of purposes and uses and very different markets and interests creates thereby such a multifaceted commercial reality that contracts developed and deployed within this prolific area cannot be described and ordered in any completely consistent methodology. This is probably one reason why the EU, over time, has to its Member States to solve contractual matters in this field of law on a national basis. That notwithstanding, harmonization of specific elements of the exclusive rights of copyright owners and their related rights have been accomplished, to a great extent, during the last twenty years, based on seven Community Directives, with various targets relating to copyright and related rights.[1] Actually there is very little material in the European Copyright

[1] Directive 2001/84/EC of the European Parliament and of the Council on the resale right for the benefit of the author of an original work of art; Directive 2001/29/EC of the European Parliament and of the Council on the harmonisation of certain aspects of copyright and related rights in the information society; Directive 96/9/EC of the European Parliament and of the Council on the legal protection of databases; Directive 2006/116/EC of the European Parliament and of the Council of 12 December 2006 on the term of protection of copyright and certain related rights (codified version); Council Directive 93/98/EEC harmonizing the term of protection of copyright and certain related

Directives regarding contractually-based uses of rights, and even that is not presented in a harmonized fashion.

The most important exceptions to this unwillingness vest probably in the Sat/Cab Directive.[2] Article 3 (1) mandates that an author's authorization of communication to the public by satellite may only be acquired by agreement. This is primarily meant to merely stress that the exclusive right of satellite broadcasting may not be made subject to a system of statutory licensing, Despite any authorization found in Article 11bis (2) of the Paris Convention,[3] EU copyright directives normally reject statutory licensing, thus leaving the market open for individuals to negotiate contract terms.

Article 3 (2) of the Sat/Cab Directive leaves it open for Member States to provide that collective agreements between a collecting society and a broadcasting organization concerning a given category of work may be extended to rightholders of the same category who are not represented by the collecting society. Notwithstanding the first paragraph, this system of 'extended' collective licensing, a truly Nordic innovation,[4] may be applied to the right of communication to the public by satellite but only in the case of simulcasting by satellite of a terrestrial broadcast.

Article 8 (1) of the Sat/Cab Directive requires that Member States ensure that cable retransmission of programs in their territory take place on the basis of individual or collective contractual agreements between copyright owners, holders of related rights and cable operators, whereas Article 9 requires that all grants or a refusals of authorization to a cable operator may only be exercised through a collecting society.

These examples show that, in short, the EU has been eager not to expose the world of copyright to systems of statutory licenses, preferring instead that such transactions be based on, and guided by, private law norms or the law of

rights (repealed); Council Directive **93/83/EEC** on the coordination of certain rules concerning copyright and rights related to copyright applicable to satellite broadcasting and cable retransmission; Directive **2006/115/EC** of the European Parliament and of the Council of 12 December 2006 on rental right and lending right and on certain rights related to copyright in the field of intellectual property (codified version); Council Directive **92/100/EEC** on rental right and lending right and on certain rights related to copyright in the field of intellectual property (repealed); Council Directive **91/250/EEC** on the legal protection of computer programs.

[2] Council Directive 93/83/EC of 27 September 1993 on the coordination of certain rules concerning copyright and rights related to copyright applicable to satellite broadcasting and cable retransmission OJ (L 248) 15–21.

[3] Berne Convention for the Protection of Literary and Artistic Works of September 9, 1886, completed at PARIS on May 4, 1896, revised at BERLIN on November 13, 1908, completed at BERNE on March 20, 1914, revised at ROME on June 2, 1928, at BRUSSELS on June 26, 1948, at STOCKHOLM on July 14, 1967, and at PARIS on July 24, 1971, and amended on September 28, 1979.

[4] Cf Kyst, 'Aftalelicens *Quo Vadis*?' (Extended collective licens – quo vadis?) (2009) 1 *Nordiskt immateriellt rättsskydd* pp 56 ff; Rognstad, 'Opphavsrettens innhold i en multimedieverden – om tradisjonelle opphavsrettsbegrepers møte med digital teknologi' (Copyright in a multimedia world – on the junction of traditional copyright concepts and digital technology*)* (2009) 6 *Nordiskt immateriellt rättsskydd* pp 535 ff.

contracts but, in very special cases, also to leave authorization and rightful uses to be transacted under collective agreements.[5] Yet, in spite of a quite extensive *acquis communautaire* in this area, based on the seven copyright Directives, considerable differences still prevail in the national copyright legislations among Member States.

But this does not present the full picture. The Commission has been intensely involved in finding trans-national or, rather, pan-european solutions to on-line licensing of copyright uses or objects covered by related rights during the first decade of this century. In particular those measures have been taken in wake of and evaluation of the Infosoc Directive.[6] In its review of the Single market the Commission highlighted the need to promote free movement of knowledge and innovation as the 'Fifth Freedom' in the single market.[7]

The Commission's efforts in that regard may be observed in some quite telling examples such as its Recommendation on collective cross-border licensing of music.[8] Further, in Autumn 2009, DG INFSO and DG MARKT launched a document called Creative Content in a European Digital Single Market.[9] Former EU information society and media commissioner Viviane Reding said about this paper that it is 'the starting point for new EU actions to support development of innovative business models, cross-border services and consumer-friendly offers'. Reding stated: 'Europe's content sector is suffering under its regulatory fragmentation, under its lack of clear, consumer-friendly rules for accessing copyright-protected online content, and serious disagreements between stakeholders about fundamental issues such as levies and private copying. We should give industry legal certainty, content creators a fair remuneration and consumers broad access to a rich diversity of content online'.[10] Apart from its political rhetoric this statement captures the essence of the contemporary copyright debate within the EU.

The Commission has pointed out in the context of the digital libraries initiative, that digitisation and online accessibility of cultural content require

[5] Cf Art 2 (3) of the Rental and lending Directive **2006/115/EC** (formerly 92/100/EEC) laconically stating that 'The rights referred to in paragraph 1 may be transferred, assigned or subject to the granting of contractual licenses.'

[6] Directive 2001/29/EC of the European Parliament and of the Council of 22 May 2001 on the harmonisation of certain aspects of copyright and related rights in the information society, OJ (L 167) 10.

[7] Communication from the Commission to the European Parliament, the Council, the European Economic and Social Committee, and the Committee of the Regions A single market for 21st century Europe COM(2007) 724 final (November 20, 2007) p 9.

[8] Commission Recommendation of 18 May 2005 on collective cross-border management of copyright and related rights for legitimate online music services (Text with EEA relevance) (2005/737/EC) OJ (L 265) 54.

[9] *Creative Content in a European Digital Single Market: Challenges for the Future*, a Reflection Document of DG INFSO and DG MARKT, 22 October 2009. Available at http://ec.europa.eu/avpolicy/other_actions/content_online/index_en.htm (last visited 19 September 2010).

[10] See S McClelland, 'The Right Policy Mix. An Interview with Viviane Reding' (Intermedia October 2009) available at http://www.iicom.org.

appropriate measures when dealing with so-called orphan works, ie material still in copyright but whose right holders cannot be identified or located. In the recently released Communications 'Europeana – next steps'[11] and 'Copyright in the knowledge economy[12] the Commission indicated that it would examine the orphan works problem in an impact assessment, which would explore a variety of approaches to facilitate the digitisation and dissemination of such works.[13] This was initiated by a recommendation adopted by the Commission in 2006 encouraging Member States to create mechanisms to facilitate the use of orphan works and to promote the availability of lists of orphan works.[14]

In sum, this decade has seen a stream of Commission recommendations, test balloons and recommendations for stepping stones to solve trans-border licensing or rights clearance issues concerning the digital environment. Unfortunately today there exists no element of a common *acquis communautaire* to assist in harmonizing such issues.

Against this background it is understandable that, several years ago, the Swedish Government decided to focus on certain aspects on copyright contract law without any specific reference to EU Law to fulfil the need for contemporary statutory support for licensing, and rights clearance generally. A special commissioner was appointed in April 2008 (the author of this article) to revise the whole Copyright Act (SFS 1960:729),[15] primarily to edit it to provide greater clarity, but also to analyse the effects of all articles of the Act on copyright contracts, not the least regarding extended collective licences.[16]

This is the first time in some fifteen years that amendments to the Swedish Copyright Act were not considered merely in order to effectuate the implementation of EU Law, but more in order to reflect digitisation and the challenges of Internet uses and trans border licenses which had garnered such attention from the Commission and the Parliament. It should be stressed, however, that some of the issues to be considered by the Inquiry, were old leaven, touched upon several times by Nordic commissions, without much result, hopefully to be solved at last or at least carefully and finally analysed. These included such issues as employers' rights to an employee's protected works accomplished within the terms of an employment.

[11] Communication from the Commission to the European Parliament, the Council, the European Economic and Social Committee, and the Committee of the Regions Europeana – next steps COM(2009) 440 final August 28, 2009.

[12] Communication from the Commission, Copyright in the Knowledge Economy COM(2009) 532 final October 19, 2009.

[13] Cf Guibault et al. 'Study on the Implementation and Effect in Member States' Laws of Directive 2001/29/EC on the Harmonisation of Certain Aspects of Copyright and Related Rights in the Information Society', Institute for Information Law, University of Amsterdam, The Netherlands, February 2007. Available at www.ivir.nl/publications/guibault/Infosoc_report_2007.pdf (last visited 19 September 2010).

[14] See Commission Recommendation of 24 August 2006 on the digitisation and online accessibility of cultural content and digital preservation, 2006/585/EC, OJ (L 236) 28.

[15] As amended by (SFS 1995:1274).

[16] See Regeringen direktiv (Dir 2008:37) 10 april 2008 and, adding to the commission, Justitiedepartementet, Kommittédirektiv (Dir 2009:65) 29 June 2009.

The commissioner delivered an interim report in April 2010, SOU 2010:24, Avtalad upphovsrätt, which was concerned mainly with copyright and contracts issues. A final report, concerning the re-editing and rephrasing of the whole Copyright Act, will be published in April 2011, which will contain suggestions for adoption of a new Copyright Act.

The following text refers to and summarises the interim report. Articles of the Copyright Act, mentioned below, are those referred to or proposed in the interim report, if not otherwise indicated.

2. PROPOSALS IN BRIEF

As previously discussed the main tasks of the Inquiry on Copyright in the interim report were to undertake a comprehensive review of the provisions on the transfer of copyright in Chapter 3 of the Copyright Act and to perform a fundamental analysis of issues concerning extended collective licences and related matters. Somewhat paradoxically, the subject matter of the Inquiry stresses the need for norms supporting, on the one hand, the individual author as a party to contracts on transfer of rights as well as, on the other hand, further collectivisation of rights clearances. The latter is to address conceptually all extant markets in broadcasting, Internet uses and other forms of mass market uses where authors' rights simply cannot be handled piecemeal as the Copyright Act presently is formulated.

The proposals presented in the report are summarised as follows. It suggests that many new general provisions regarding contracts be introduced into Chapter 3. At the same time, the special provisions on publishing contracts, introduced in the Act of 1960, should be removed. It should be observed in particular, that a provision is proposed regarding the interpretation of contracts designed to codify and clearly define the 'principle of specification'. In addition, a reference is proposed to be introduced to the general clause on correction of contractual terms in Section 36 of the Contracts Act (SFS1915:218), and a general provision will be proposed on the obligation to use rights acquired exclusively.

Further, provisions are proposed to clarify authors' rights in the event of a transfer by assignment or licence of copyright protected works. A provision is also proposed to create a presumption that the author is entitled to reasonable remuneration when he or she, by assignment or licence, transfers the right to exploit the work to someone who intends to use this right in the framework of commercial activities. Moreover, a provision is proposed, giving an author the right, in the event of a royalty agreement, to receive a settlement once a year and to audit the information upon which the remuneration is based. A further provision is proposed concerning the right of the employer to works created by an employee within the employment relationships, as a result of which the 'rule of thumb', as developed in case-law and doctrine, should be codified and clearly defined. Subject to certain conditions, this provision would give an employer a limited, but exclusive, right to use works created by an employee within an employment relationship.

The proposals on extended collective licences in Chapter 3 a) of the Act on Copyright in Literary and Artistic Works ('the Copyright Act') concern, firstly, fundamental changes in the general provision in Article 42 a) of the Copyright Act and, secondly, changes and extensions in some of the specific provisions on extended collective licences. Among other things, the proposals in Article 42 a) should make it clear that only one organisation in each area will be authorised to enter into agreements under which collective licences have long-term effects. Corresponding amendments are also proposed to be made in the provisions concerning collection of remuneration under Article 26 m) of the Copyright Act, the provisions on collection of resale right remuneration under Article 26 p) of the Copyright Act and the provisions on collection of remuneration under Article 47, third paragraph of the Copyright Act.

The provision on extended collective licences in Article 42 b) concerning the making of copies at the workplace – authorities, companies, organisations – is extended to include digital copies. The provision on extended collective licences in Article 42 d) of the Copyright Act is proposed to be broadened to make it easier for libraries and archives to digitise works in their collections and to make them accessible to the public. A broadening of the provision concerning sound radio and television broadcasts in Article 42 e) of the Copyright Act is also proposed, in order to cover all communication to the public and the making of copies which are necessary to enable the communication to take place. This means that the provision covers cases in which material is made available at the request of individuals. Moreover, a completely new provision on extended collective licences is proposed, allowing the parties to enter into agreements under which collective licences have extended effect in areas other than those specified in the Act. This would be known as a special extended collective licence.

The new general provisions' overall aim is to promote clarity and certainty in copyright contracts, which should be to the advantage of all parties. In addition, these proposals are intended to prevent lock-in effects arising, a problem quite often observed in today's media landscape. The provisions are also intended to clarify authors' rights and to support the principles of copyright in an increasingly complex and many-faceted market for protected works and performances.[17] The amended and new provisions on extended collective licences are designed to facilitate rights clearance in connection with various forms of mass use of works and performances protected by copyright so as to make the massive repertoire of works available in organised form and on terms that are acceptable to users, authors and other rightholders. Significantly, uses in Sweden of works of foreign authors and right holders are also intended to be covered by such extended collective licenses.

[17] Rosén, 'Copyright Control in Sweden and Internet Uses – File Sharers' Heaven or Not?' (2008) 2 *Nordiskt immateriellt rättsskydd* pp 95 ff.

3. REMIT

As discussed above, the main tasks of the Inquiry on Copyright, as set forth by the Government,[18] have been primarily to undertake a comprehensive review of the provisions on copyright transfers in Chapter 3 of the Copyright Act, but also to analyse and make suggestions regarding certain issues concerning extended collective licences and related matters. In addition, on the basis of an added remit in June 2009, a full scale test of the whole system based on statutory extended licenses was added to the scope of review and analysis. This opened up the inquiry to an almost endless number of issues and tasks which potentially fell within the framework of the inquiry. Upon closer examination there are, however, a number of issues which were stressed by the Government in its commission.

Within the framework of the first grouping is the very specific task of investigating and taking a position on whether the role of the author as a contracting party should be *strengthened,* thus based on the assumption that individual authors might have difficulties merely on the basis of their exclusive rights to reach fair contractual terms when they are licensing their rights.

The task of undertaking a comprehensive review has also, in particular, included investigating and taking a position on whether a kind of 'work-for-hire rule' should be introduced. A 'work-for-hire rule' is defined by the Inquiry's terms of reference as a provision entailing that the financial element of the copyright to material produced in the framework of an employment relationship passes to the employer unless otherwise agreed. This was a revisiting of an old task which had not received a successful solution at any point of time in the Nordic countries, but which however, the Government obviously wanted a thorough examination.

The task of reviewing certain issues concerning extended collective licences also included the general and, not least from the purposes of Competition Law, the very difficult, question of what criteria to apply in deciding which organisation or organisations should be authorised to enter into agreements with the effect of extended collective licences, instead of the present criterion that the organisation should represent a substantial number of merely *Swedish* authors. Obviously, the potentially discriminatory effect of the Copyright Act in this respect, may create conflict with basic EU principles.[19]

The general issues of the commission have also included investigating and taking a position on whether only one organisation should be granted the authority to enter into agreements with the effect of extended collective licences or whether several organisations should have that authority.

[18] Dir 2008:37 was quite explicit in listing tasks for the commissioner to deal with, in spite of its basically broad approach, and, eventually by adding to the commission, under (Dir 2009:65), a full scale analysis of the collective licensing system as such.

[19] See eg Arts 18, 45, TFEU and Art 21 ECHR.

With regard to the specific provisions on extended collective licences, the remit has included the issue of whether the provision on the making of copies within public authorities, enterprises and organisations, etc, should be broadened to also include the making of digital copies, and the question of whether a new, extended collective licence should be introduced for making available, on request, works forming a part of radio and television programmes.

The supplementary terms of reference issued to the Inquiry in June 2009 added considerably to the workload of the special commissioner as it presented the additional questions of (i) whether the Copyright Act should be amended to make it easier for libraries and archives to digitise works protected by copyright and make them available, (ii) whether a general extended collective licence should be introduced, and (iii) whether the Copyright Act should be amended to ensure that the remuneration paid to an organisation on the basis of extended collective licences reaches the rightholders, particularly those who are not represented by the organisation.

4. A COMPREHENSIVE REVIEW OF CHAPTER 3 OF THE COPYRIGHT ACT

4.1 New General Provisions on Contracts

The provisions of Chapter 3 of the Copyright Act have remained virtually unchanged since the Act came into existence.[20] Meanwhile, the Inquiry began its work under the burden of knowing that society and the copyright market have undergone sweeping changes since its enactment. Technical developments constantly give rise to new forms of uses of works protected by copyright. Accordingly, the Inquiry's terms of reference emphasised the need to modernise Chapter 3 of the Copyright Act.

The task of the Inquiry has therefore been to undertake a comprehensive review of the provisions in Chapter 3 of the Copyright Act. The terms of reference emphasise, as a general point of departure that the Inquiry was to attempt to propose durable and flexible solutions reflecting the copyright market, giving authors a reasonable opportunity to maintain their rights while also accommodating other legitimate interests. The Inquiry has also been commissioned, as set out above, to consider the question of whether the position of the author as a contracting party should be strengthened and, if so, how.

The provisions on publishing contracts dominate in Chapter 3 of the Copyright Act as it stands today, while there are relatively few general provisions on contracts. The Inquiry came to the conclusion that in many respects, the rules on publishing contracts had lost their relevance. The report therefore

[20] The Swedish Copyright Act (SFS 1960:729) became effective on 1 January 1961. Virtually none of the provisions on individual contracts introduced in it have been amended; indeed, some of these provisions were also part of the previous 1919 Copyright Act.

proposes removing existing special regulations on publishing contracts, but to give general application to certain fundamental principles. This is in line with the introduction of a number of general provisions on contracts. The intention is for these provisions to promote clear and well-defined contracts. The commission assumes that this will be to the advantage of all parties. Freedom of contract should apply as the underlying assumption, so that parties may make contractual arrangements as best suit their particular needs.

The report proposes that the new Chapter 3 of the Copyright Act should contain special provisions on the following subjects.

4.2 Interpretation

It is proposed, that a provision on the interpretation of copyright contracts be introduced into the Copyright Act in Article 27 paragraph 3. This provision involves a codification and clearer definition of the principle of specification and means that the party having a contractual right to exploit a work shall not be considered to have more extensive rights than are stated in the contract or than may be considered to follow from the contract or its purpose.

A similar provision has been a feature of the Danish and the Norwegian Copyright Acts respectively. However, both use a definition that the Inquiry found too narrow or unclear, especially in light of Swedish courts' interpretation and application of this instrument over time. The Swedish proposal thus aims to apply those developments on the so called specification principle as adopted by the courts.[21]

4.3 Modification

It is proposed, that a reference to Section 36 of the Contracts Act (SFS 1915:218) be introduced into Article 29 of the Copyright Act. Further, a special provision is proposed to enable modification of unreasonable contract terms relating to non-material rights, ie moral rights.

The proposal also stresses that no rules other than the general clause in Swedish Private Law, ie on modifying or setting aside a term of a contract or to disregard a contract in its totality due to unreasonable terms or misuse of a party's inferior position in these respects, should be valid in the field of copyright than elsewhere.

Earlier on a specific clause of this kind did exist in the Copyright Act. It was repealed in 1976 when all similar types of correctional instruments were also

[21] Cf J Rosén, *Upphovsrättens avtal: regler för upphovsmäns, artisters, fonogram-, film- och databasproducenters, radio- och TV-bolags samt fotografers avtal* (Stockholm Norsteds Juridik, 3rd edn, 2006) pp 151, 300 ff.

cancelled in all other Private Law Acts valid in Sweden at the time – Section 36 of the Contracts Act then becoming the collective formula. Representatives of authors' groups had never liked that uniform instrument, claiming that the old rule was more strongly supportive of the interests of authors as parties to a contract. However, the Inquiry was not able to detect any situation that would be aided by such a provision which would, per definition, fall aside of Section 36 of the Contracts Act. Hence the importance of stressing, also in the authors' interest, that a direct reference to that provision of the Contracts Act is needed in the Copyright Act.

As for the latter issue the Inquiry concludes that Moral Rights cannot be the object of a transfer based on a contract, but that contractual terms may, nevertheless, relate to such a right, eg to terms relating to moral rights being waived only to a limited extent as to their character and scope, as follows from Article 3 paragraph 3 of the Copyright Act.

4.4 Obligation to Use

It is proposed that a general provision on the obligation to use rights acquired exclusively be introduced into Article 30 of the Act. The provision would be optional and intended to mean that a party to a contract other than an employment contract who has acquired from the author an exclusive right to make a work available to the public is obligated to use this right. If the party acquiring this right has not made the work available to the public within reasonable time or, at the latest within five years from the date on which the author fulfilled her or his part of the contract, the author may cancel the contract.

The basic assumption underlying this proposal is that the idea of an exclusive agreement includes the exploitation of the work or, at least, the public exposure of it. A work or related right should not merely be put on the shelf by the owner of the exclusive right. This assumption also reflects a response to what is quite frequently claimed today, that copyright is used to lock up products of cultural values, hence to block public access. This view is probably slightly exaggerated – authors themselves must generally be said to support public access of their works – but the Inquiry has found it valuable to stress that exclusive licensees must actively plan for the uses allowed by the contract.

4.5 Remuneration, Settlement and Control

A new, general contractual provision concerning remuneration is proposed in Article 31. This provision would give the author a right to reasonable remuneration when the right to exploit a work is transferred by assignment or licence to someone who intends to use the right in the framework of commercial activities. This provision is also optional.

New provisions are proposed to give, in Article 32, the author the right, in the event of a right holder's entry into a royalty agreement, to receive a settlement once a year, together with a right to audit the information on which this is based. These provisions would be mandatory and it will not be possible to waive them by contract.

4.6 Contracts Concerning Communication to the Public

It is proposed to retain a provision on contracts relating to public performance, etc. This would be addressed separately in Article 35. The heading would be amended to *Contracts concerning communication to the public, etc*. Under this provision, a contract concerning communication to the public or public performance of a work will apply for a three-year period and will not confer exclusivity, unless otherwise agreed.

The gravamen of this concept has generally been accepted since the introduction of the Copyright Act in 1960. However, it has been more honoured in the breach than in the observance. At the time of its enactment it was thought merely to relate to contracts between the performing rights societies and authors of musical works. Not even in there has it been of any significant importance. Still, the Inquiry assumes that this concept has gained in importance in the digital age and that it is particularly important in respect of use in the digital environment, such as on the Internet.

4.7 Film Contracts

It is proposed to clarify the presumption rule concerning film contracts, which has for many years been in Article 39 of the Copyright Act. Under this proposal, a contract conferring the right to use a work for purposes of recording it in a film means that an author contributing a work for a film cannot object to copies being made of the film, the film being made available to the public, provided with subtitles, or being translated into another language.

It is proposed that musical works continue to be exempt from the scope of this provision. Under the proposal, however, the provision will also include the rights that performing artists enjoy over their performances in a film.

That would also clarify what, generally speaking, is probably the crux of film contracts, namely that the rights of the contributing and normally comprehensive grouping of authors and performing artists are conferred on the producer of the film without addressing the issue of remuneration to members of that group. This provision offers a presumption facilitating the use of the film, whereas remuneration is a separate issue, not covered by the presumption.

4.8 Copyright to Computer Programs Created in Employment Relationships

It is proposed that the provisions of the Act concerning computer programs created in employment relationships be modified in Article 34 in order that the rights transferred to the employer under the conditions of the provision do not include non-material rights. A presumption is also introduced that employers are entitled to transfer their right to the computer program to others.

The novel feature of Article 34 lies in the fact that it diminishes the scope of an employer's rights to computer programs as expressed in the Copyright Act (Article 40 a), by expunging the moral rights dimension now vested in Article 40 a). The Software Directive, which forms the basis for the just mentioned article, never required Member States to leave authors' rights, with their complete content, to the employers regarding computer programs accomplished within the frames of an employment.[22] To include the moral rights dimension in the employer's acquisition was probably merely a gesture of the legislature in the 1990's to please the U.S. software industry. However, moral rights simply cannot be part of a commercial acquisition, something in full consequence observed throughout this interim report. Hence, this dimension is separated from the employer's position.

On the other hand a very useful and important legal instrument is added to the armoury of the employer. As it stands now, Article 40 a) merely concerns the situation within the employer's realm, ie the first transfer from the author/employee to the employer, not the next and very natural step of the employer, to address third parties on the market via licenses and sub-licenses. Article 28 of the Copyright Act, similar to the provision and content of this proposal, contains a presumption against any transferor's transfer of the right to others or to license it to someone else, or to alter it. The Inquiry now proposes that an employer, having gained the rights to a computer program from his employee, shall also have the right to transfer it to others. This is what generally happens in the marketplace when a software producer manages to introduce novel computer programs, but the present rules, however seemingly so broad in scope, seeks to hinder the employer's marketing of his software.

4.9 A Work-for-hire Rule?

The point of departure in Swedish law is that, initially, the copyright to a work always vests in the natural person who has created it. In the event of employment relationships, copyright is transferred to the employer only to the extent that this

[22] Cf Council Directive 91/250/EEC of 14 May 1991 on the legal protection of computer programs OJ (L 122) 42. See in particular Art 2 (3) which states: 'Where a computer program is created by an employee in the execution of his duties or following the instructions given by his employer, the employer exclusively shall be entitled to execute all economic rights in the program so created, unless otherwise provided by contract'.

is deemed to be explicitly or implicitly prescribed by the employment contract or by a special agreement. Interpretation of a contract would probably generally allow works produced as part of an employee's tasks to be used by the employer in his or her normal activities and to the extent that could be foreseen with reasonable certainty when the work was created.[23]

The Inquiry's analysis states that copyright legislation should be designed to be functional in its practical application. At the same time, it states that introduction of a work-for-hire rule would be a major deviation from the fundamental principle that copyright belongs to the author creating the work. Any need that may exist for a work-for-hire rule must therefore be carefully weighed against the interests of individual authors in being allowed, as far as possible, to make decision with respect to their work, and regarding other interests of relevance.

There is currently no special legislative provision concerning copyright in employment relationships, apart from the one on computer programmes. However, both in case-law and doctrinal 'rule of thumb' has been developed the assumption according to which, within their area of activities and for the purposes of their normal activities, employers may use works created by the employee as a result of employment duties to the employer. The employer's rights refer to use for the purposes foreseen when the work is created. Further, changes in the work are permitted to the extent required to achieve the purposes for which it was created during the employment relationship.

The Interim report concludes that a general and essentially broadly framed presumption rule entailing the total transfer to the employer of the financial element of the copyright of a work produced in an employment relationship does not offer a flexible and durable solution. Some groups, primarily owners of the press or, rather, daily papers, have faced long time disagreements with their journalists regarding allocations of authors' rights, which caused these employers to recommend the broadest possible acquisition of rights for the employer to be incorporated into law. It became obvious to the Inquiry, however, that far from all employers desire vast transfers of rights or even any acquisition at all. Employers eg in the fields of teaching, science and various forms of schooling or knowledge industries were generally reluctant to step into their employees' copyright positions, which would thereby result in facing demands by the authors related to the employers (effective) commercial activity and increases in salaries for the authors. It became clear that the balance between conflicting interests in the whole area of copyright would be weakened by such a provision and would constitute a serious deviation from the fundamental principles of copyright. Instead a provision corresponding to the 'rule of thumb' was proposed.

A number of important prerequisites are defined and set out in proposed Article 33. The interim report's proposal would mean that an employer, within

[23] See Prop 1988/89:85, p 21 and the decision of the Labour Court 2002, No 87.

his or her area of activities and for the purposes of his or her normal activities, may hold exclusive rights to works created by an employee as a part of his or her tasks or following instructions by the employer. The right of the employer covers uses for the purposes foreseeable when the work is created. Where a work must be changed to achieve the purpose for which it was created during an employment relationship, this change is permitted, but only to the extent permitted by proposed Article 3 of the Copyright Act.

As mentioned above there are special provisions on computer programs in Article 34 of the proposal (current Article 40 a). The provision should also apply with respect to rights belonging to performing artists under Article 45 and to photographers under Article 49 a) of the Copyright Act respectively.

5. EXTENDED COLLECTIVE LICENSES

5.1 International Obligations

As already mentioned, the provisions of the Treaty on the Functioning of the European Union governing free movement and non-discrimination and the Treaty of Lisbon have had an impact on the formulation of the new provisions on licenses with extended effects. Another element had further effects in this context, namely the Service Directive.[24] The Service Directive is a horizontal Directive with wide scope of application. It builds on the general principle that services should be freely available within the European Union.

The notion of 'service' is defined in Article 4.1 of the Service Directive as 'any self-employed economic activity, normally provided for remuneration, as referred to in Article 50 of the Treaty' (now Article 57 TFEU). The European Commission has, on numerous occasion alleged that the collective management of rights is the making available of services – in relation to the right-owners as well as users and also in relation to each other – and that organisations that pursue collective management of rights are subject to the provisions on, among other matters, the free movement of services in the European Community Treaty and the Service Directive.

It must be assumed then, that the activities pursued by the managing organisations in accordance with the provisions in the Copyright Act on extended collective licenses and collection of remunerations respectively are covered by the notion of 'services' in the Service Directive and fall under the scope of application of the Directive.

It follows from the Service Directive Article 16 that Member States shall respect the right of service providers to provide services in a Member State other than the one where they are established and that consequently, they must not subject

[24] Directive 2006/123/EC of the European Parliament and of the Council of 12 December 2006 on services in the internal market OJ (L 376) 36.

a service provider established in another Member State to certain requirements. For instance, the Member States must not – in order to permit access to or exercise of a service on their territories – impose obligations that are directly or indirectly discriminating with regard to nationality (Directive 2006/123 Article 16.1 (a)). Nor must the Member States impose obligations that a service provider established in another Member State must obtain authorization from the competent authorities in order for it to be able to provide its services in a Member State (Article 16 2. (b)).

Article 17 contains, however, an enumeration of a number of exceptions from Article 16. Under Article 17.11 it follows, *inter alia,* that Article 16 shall not apply to copyright and certain other intellectual property rights.

During the negotiations concerning the Service Directive, there were discussions on how the exception of Article 17.11 should be interpreted. Sweden, like the other Nordic countries, considered that the exception would apply to provisions related to the collective management of rights while the Commission held the view that the exception would apply only to the rights themselves. In the course of the implementation of the Directive, the Commission has continued to argue for its position while a number of the Member States (including Sweden) have argued that provisions related to the management of rights are covered by the exception in Article 17.11, because the rights in themselves cannot be considered to be services. A Government Bill on the implementation of the Service Directive was submitted to the Swedish Parliament on 26 May 2009.[25] The Parliament adopted the Bill on 4 November 2009.

This Directive also contains, in addition to the provision on free movement of services, general provisions on authorization schemes. Article 9 for instance prescribes that the Member States may make the access to a service or exercise of it subject to an authorization scheme only if it is called for overriding interests relating to public interests.

5.2 Point of Connection to Redeem the Extended Collective License

Chapter 3 a (Articles 42 a–42 f) of the Copyright Act contains comprehensive and quite complex provisions on extended collective licences. Under these provisions, agreements on the exploitation of works may be entered into with an organization that represents a substantial number of Swedish authors in the field concerned. By entering into such an agreement, a user can also acquire the right to exploit works by authors *not represented* by the organization. Without the support of the legislature this would of course not come about. The intention, just as clearly, is to make it easier for a user, such as a major broadcaster or cable distributer of TV content, by agreement with the representative organisation, to

[25] See Prop 2008/09:187.

acquire all the rights the user needs for his or her activities, while enabling the authors concerned to receive reasonable remuneration. The interests of authors not represented by the organization are safeguarded by certain protective rules, eg provisions on the right to remuneration on the same basis as those of members who are contractually represented by the contracting organization, and the possibility of prohibiting exploitation. If there was no possibility for authors to opt out the system of extended collective licenses would stand little chance to comply with the requirements of the Paris Convention.[26]

Article 42 a) is the basic provision for all sorts of statutory extended collective licenses. As previously mentioned a collective licence for the time being only has extended effect in the case of agreements with organisations representing a substantial number of Swedish authors in the field concerned. Corresponding requirements exist also concerning the collection of a 'private copying levy', the so called kassettavgift, (Articles 26 k–26 m) and resale right remuneration, *droit de suite*, (Article 26 j). This requirement is also found in the mandatory licence provision in Article 47 of the Copyright Act (see the third paragraph), on phonogram producers' and performing artists' right to remuneration for public performances and communication to the public of their recordings and performances, a kind of compulsory licence structured by the same collective arrangement as the extended collective licenses in the said respect. However, the focus on Swedish authors (and performers/producers) to trigger the effect of those provisions is of course debatable, to put it mildly, from an EU non-discriminatory perspective. It has already been the subject of contention in connection with the implementation of the EC Directive on Copyright in the Information Society,[27] where it was noted that there was cause to review whether it is a suitable delimitation for organisations to represent a substantial number of Swedish authors.[28]

Denmark amended its equivalent provisions after the European Commission's finding that this was in violation with the prohibition of discrimination contained in the EC Treaty. The other Nordic countries have subsequently made similar amendments. The Inquiry's terms of reference state that there is also cause in Sweden to remove the recited limitation of *a substantial number of Swedish authors* and examine what other criteria are required in order for the systems to work in a way that is transparent, effective and competition-neutral from right holders' and users' perspectives.

According to the terms of reference, the Inquiry was also required to examine equivalent requirements in the provisions on the private copying levy (Article 26 m), resale right remuneration (Article 26 p), and the right to remuneration for performing artists and producers of sound recordings (Article 47).

[26] T Riis and J Schovsbo, 'Extended Collective Licenses and the Nordic Experience- It's a Hybrid but is it a VOLVO or a Lemon?', Available at: http://ssrn.com/abstract=1535230, Forthcoming in *Columbia Journal of Law & the Arts*, Vol 33, Issue IV, (2010) pp 10–12.

[27] See n 6 above.

[28] See Prop 2004/05:110 pp 144 and 247.

Against this background the special commissioner, not very surprisingly, proposed that the general extended collective licence provision in Article 42 a) of the Copyright Act be amended so that an organisation that is the most representative and best situated to represent the authors of the works in the area *exploited in Sweden* be authorised to enter into agreements in which collective licences have extended effect. By adhering to an organization that represents the authors of the works in the area exploited in Sweden, Swedish Law is made conform to the demands of EU-norms on non-discrimination by setting forth the connecting element as works actually *used* in Sweden, whether works created by nationals of Sweden or by foreigners. Equivalent requirements should also of course be introduced into the provisions on collecting remuneration under Articles 26 m), 26 p) and 47 of the Copyright Act.

5.3 Which Organizations are to be Authorized to Enter into Agreements under the Rules on Extended Collective Licenses?

Closely linked, but of a fundamentally different nature, to which criteria should apply instead of the requirement that an organization represents a substantial number of Swedish authors is whether *one* or *several* organizations should be authorised to conclude agreements in the same area of copyright. In the other Nordic countries this issue has been resolved by instituting a system based on a concession from a public authority to an organisation that may enter into agreements executing the extended effect for non-member authors. These apply a policy of only permitting a single organisation to have the concession for a specific area of copyright.[29]

In Sweden the extended collective licence provisions state only that an agreement must have been concluded with an organization representing a substantial number of Swedish authors in the field (Article 42 a). Similar formulations appear in the above-mentioned provisions on the private copying levy (Article 26 m), resale right remuneration (Article 26 p) and the right to remuneration for performing artists and producers of sound recordings under Article 47, third paragraph. Concerning the issue of resale right remuneration, the Supreme Court has ruled in a judgment that this provision means that more than one organisation may be entitled to claim remuneration, but that certain requirements must apply with regard to the organisation's structure and stability.[30] In connection with the implementation of the Directive on Copyright in the Information Society, the Swedish Council on Legislation, Lagrådet, observed that problems could arise as a consequence of several organisations

[29] See J Rosén, *Administrative Institutions in Copyright – notes on the Nordic Countries, Institutions administratives du droit d'auteur/ Copyright – Administrative Institutions* (edn Ysolde Gendreau, Montreal 2001, ISBN 2-89451-601-0).

[30] See NJA 2000 p 178, *BUS v DUR*.

being authorised to claim a private copying levy or sign agreements on extended collective licences.[31]

In light of this, and other matters, the Inquiry's terms of reference stressed that there should be a careful examination into whether several organizations within the same field should be allowed to operate in the extended collective licence area, or whether only one organisation should be authorised to conclude agreements in the area. A similar review was required to be carried out regarding the private copying levy, resale right remuneration and the right to remuneration for performing artists and producers of sound recordings.

The commissioner proposed the following: the new phrasing of 'an organization that is *the most representative and best represents* the authors of the works in the area' makes it clear that under the general provision on collective licences as well as in Articles 26 m, 26 j and 47 third paragraph of the Copyright Act, only *one* organization may be authorised in a given field to enter into agreements in which collective licences have extended effect or to collect the remuneration concerned.

This statement needs some clarification, particularly as the proposal does not foresee a concession system – perhaps executed by the Government itself – as is employed in the other Nordic countries, but rather something to be dealt with by the contracting parties in the marketplace or, in cases of severe disagreement, a civil court. The following observations of the commission address the issue:

As long as the organizations represent authors in different areas or sub-areas and do not compete with each other, normally no problems would arise in determining which one is competent to conclude agreements with extended collective license effect. On the other hand, problems may arise in determining their competence in situations where the organizations compete with each other and represent authors in the same area or sub-area. As mentioned, it might be possible that the organizations might come together to form a party to the agreement, for instance if they are only in such a case representatives. If, in a specific area or sub-area, several organizations exist where they individually may be seen as sufficiently representative, in the opinion of the commissioner, it would be sufficient if an agreement with only one of those be concluded in order for the agreement to have extended collective license effect. The user cannot be required to conclude additional agreements with the other organizations or with one of them. Such an agreement would not provide the user with additional rights or provide additional remuneration for the authors but would only complicate the picture and the payment system. This would conflict with the underlying purpose of the extended collective agreement system. Nor can it have been the intent of the legislator that a user would be required to conclude agreements with each one of the organizations where each one is acting in a representative capacity.

[31] See Prop 2004/05:110, p 563.

Generally speaking, competition is considered to promote administrative efficiency and pricing. In the course of the Inquiry it was been suggested that the new law be designed in such a way to encourage competition. Indeed, the Terms of Reference mention competition as a positive factor that should be balanced against other advantages, such as clarity and transparency.

Competition between two or more organizations that represent authors or other rightholders can arise in two different respects. The organizations may compete with each other on the one hand in relation to the authors or right-owners in respect of the best management of the rights, and, on the other hand, in relation to the users concerning the best agreements relating to the use. In the commissioner's view, free competition should, as a matter of principle, exist in relation to the members. As an author or a rightholder one should be able to select the organization in which an author has the most confidence to manage his or her rights. In practice, under the current regime, which surely allows for more than one organisation in each copyright field, such freedom of choice is present only to a very limited extent as, broadly speaking, *de facto* there is only one organization in each area. In almost fifty years of uses of statutory extended collective licenses in Sweden we have never seen two competing organizations actively working in the same field. The interest in establishing a 'new' organization in addition to the ones already established has so far been extremely low. One reason for this could be that comparatively wide degree of experience, contacts and administration is needed to handle the management of rights in an efficient way. This may, however, change over time. The new provisions should take this into account.

Looking at the competition issue in relation to the users does not provide a clear answer. In other words it is not obvious that users should be free to choose to conclude agreements with the organization that offers the best conditions in relation to the use. Organizations represent their members and have, therefore, only a limited scope when it comes to the agreements that they can offer to users. In principle only the administrative cost related to their management is subject to variation and competition. For users the alternative to an extended collective license would be to negotiate directly with the authors or the rightholders. In relation to those there is no freedom of choice if one wishes to use a certain work or a certain subject matter. The exclusive right in itself constitutes, in consequence, a sort of monopoly to which, however, are linked certain limitations required to satisfy certain public and private interests.

The fact that the organizations hold a certain monopoly position has been accepted within European Community law, and the European Court of Justice has for a long time seen a considerable market concentration – in fact a monopoly position – on the part of right holders as being necessary to obtain reasonable results in relation to negotiating with large user enterprises, such as radio and television corporations and other enterprises in the mass market.[32]

[32] See T Riis, 'Kollektiv forvaltning og konkurrenceretlige spørgsmål' (Collective management and competition law questions) (June 2009) *Nordisk Immaterialrättslig tidskrift* p 621.

An organization considered to hold a dominant position in the market place must, however, not misuse that position by making unreasonable demands. Such a misuse may consist in the application of too high a price which does not reflect a reasonable relation to the economic value of the transaction. The misuse may also consist of the application of a certain remuneration model.[33] No misuse was found in the Kanal 5 case but the application of a remuneration model which was *per se* acceptable, could, according to the CJEU under certain circumstances constitute misuse, namely if another method for calculation of the remuneration to the authors existed which made it possible to more closely identify and quantify the use of copyright-protected material.

The CJEU has, in a number of decisions, shown considerable understanding for authors' problems (and their successors in title) from a practical and administrative point of view in obtaining reasonable remuneration in mass markets.[34] The opinion in the *Kanal 5* case, referred to above and in footnote 33, the CJEU (at para 40) stated that, even if more detailed calculation methods were desirable in order to avoid misuse from a competition point of view, a remuneration model must always be based on fundamental legitimate aims, of safeguarding the authors' interests and that more precise and detailed systems for licensing and collection must not result in an disproportionate increase of costs of administering agreements and controlling use of copyright-protected works. This obviously speaks in favour of a concentrated administration of rights in mass markets.

In practical terms problems rarely appear in the application of the existing legislation. In most areas it is more or less obvious which organization is competent to conclude agreements with extended collective license effect. In the areas of photography and still pictures there are, however, several organizations where each has considered itself competent to conclude agreements under Article 42 c) of the Copyright Act. New organizations may also come into existence and when the limitation to Swedish authors is deleted, foreign organisations may enter the Swedish extended collective license market. Starting from the position that a user for a specific exploitation shall have to conclude only one agreement at each point of time, ie for a certain agreement period, the Inquiry could not see any problems in the concept that several organisations at a time could be competent to conclude extended collective license agreements in the same area.

On the other hand it is to be assumed that a system which requires that only one organization in each area (or part of an area) be competent to conclude agreements with an extended collective license effect has some advantages, for instance as regards clarity. This is obvious especially in relation to the users, but also in relation to the authors, those represented as well as those who stay outside, and in relation to the organisations themselves.

[33] See eg Judgment of December 11, 2008, Case C-52/07, *Kanal 5 Ltd v Föreningen Svenska Tonsättares Internationella Musikbyrå (STIM) upa* [2008] ECR I-9275, in particular paras 28–40 and the references there to earlier decisions.

[34] See case C-395/87, *Ministère public v Jean-Louis Tournier* [1989] ECR 2521.

Legislation in the other Nordic countries contain, as has been said, no explicit provisions related to the number of competent organizations which may conclude agreement with extended collective license effect. The system of concession implies, however, in practice that only one organisation in each field has such competence or that the organisations cooperate. This should speak in favour of a system for Sweden where it is clear that only one organization in each field actually has such a competence.

Consequently, the proposal does not prevent an organization other than the one that has concluded the agreement with extended collective license effect, at a certain point of time, to conclude a subsequent agreement in that field on the next occasion, if that other organisation meets the criteria to be the most representative one and best takes into account the authors′ interests. The proposed system would mean that users may negotiate with only one organization in each field. They would consequently not be able to select the organization that, in their view, gives them the best conditions for use, ie the lowest price. The Copyright Act for the protection of authors' rights really can't, as a matter of principle, provide for a system that would create downward pressure on authors' revenue.

In conclusion, the Inquiry considered that the advantages outweigh the disadvantages resulting from a single organization in each area being deemed competent to conclude an agreement with extended collective license effect. On the basis of those considerations and as the Inquiry did not find any obstacles under EU legislation or EU case law, it concluded that only one organization in each area or partial area should have competence to conclude agreements with an extended collective license effect.

5.4 Distribution of Remuneration under Extended Collective Licenses

The mandate of the commission also requested an overall analysis of how the system for extended collective licensing has functioned in Sweden over the years. Somewhat surprisingly, such an investigation has not ever been performed by a public authority. The analysis was necessary if the Inquiry were also to have suggested, if appropriate, new forms of extended licenses and a widened scope of existing licenses. Such proposals could naturally not be made if the result of such study would have resulted in a negative analysis of the existing system of extended collective licenses

The report makes the judgment that the distribution systems for extended collective licences as currently used by the organizations collecting and distributing remuneration function well, and remuneration paid to right holder organizations on the basis of the extended collective licence provisions does in fact reach the right holders, including those not represented by the organizations. Nothing has come to light to suggest that there are irregularities concerning payments. Therefore, no new provisions have been proposed in the Act to ensure that remuneration reaches the rightholders.

5.5 Making of Digital Copies at Public Authorities and Private Enterprises

The report proposes a simplified and extended arrangement for rights clearance concerning copying carried out at places of work for internal information purposes. It therefore proposes that the extended collective licence provision in Article 42 b of the Copyright Act be broadened to include the production of *digital* copies. Currently, the statute deals only with the making of copies by reprographic means, ie photo copying. By this amendment, copying from the Internet world falls within the framework of an extended collective licensing system which encompasses virtually all entities, organisations and public authorities in Sweden.

In addition, it is proposed to remove restrictions to the effect that the only works of art covered by the extended collective licence provision are reproductions in connection with the text in a literary work. The proposal would also include separate pictures in the statutory licensing system. In line with a step towards digital copying it is also proposed that the provision's current requirement, that works in question must have been *published*, be amended to state that the works must merely have been *made public* (eg *lawfully been posted on the Internet)*.

5.6 Possibility for Archives and Libraries to Digitize Works and Make Them Available to the Public

The report proposes a broadening of the extended collective licence provision in Article 42 d) of the Copyright Act to make it simpler for libraries and archives to digitise works in their collections and make them accessible, for example, by communicating them via the Internet. It is therefore proposed that Article 42 d) of the Copyright Act cover (i) all kinds of production of copies and all forms of (ii) making available of works to the public that cannot be reproduced under to the restrictions (exceptions) in Articles 16 and 21 of the Copyright Act. As a result, libraries would be able to digitize and to communicate their repository of assets on screens, not only to visitors to their premises, but also to make them available online.

Moreover, it is proposed that an amendment be made to the existing exemptions in Article 21 to improve opportunities for archives and libraries to make works contained in their collections available within their own premises, ie if they possess a lawful digital copy they may also display it on screens on their premises in spite of the fact that such a use would be a communication to public and otherwise barred.

5.7 Works and Performances that Appear in Radio and TV Programmes

A major practical problem today in Swedish broadcasting is the fact that no extended collective licenses cover further uses of a broadcast in the Internet environment, ie for what is often called Webb-TV. A broadcasting organization must therefore negotiate individually all copyright elements in a TV-program if that organization would like to post the program on its own web, thus communicating it to the public. Currently, no extended collective license covers on-demand forms of communication to the public, thus not what is available on the web, but merely broadcasting.

The report favours simpler rights clearance for radio and TV companies for programmes made available at the request of individuals, for example via the Internet after the regularly scheduled transmission time. It is therefore proposed to broaden the extended collective licence provision in Article 42 e) of the Copyright Act concerning sound radio and television broadcasts. Under the proposal, the extended collective licence provision would cover all communication to the public and not just broadcasts. In addition, it is proposed that the provision cover such copying as is necessary to enable the communication to take place.

It is also proposed that the provision cover performing artists' performances of certain literary works under Article 45 of the Copyright Act, as well as certain sound recordings under Article 46 of the Copyright Act.

5.8 A Special Extended Collective License

All existing extended collective licenses are valid for very specific purposes and for well-defined areas of works and uses. The underlying basic assumption is that extended licenses should only be executed in areas where ordinary Private Law principles of copyright do not function well, ie if individual contracts cannot be employed for necessary rights clearances. Prior to the proposal, the legislature has decided what would be covered.

Now it is proposed that the general provision on extended collective licences be supplemented with respect to the scope of a potential extended license. This offers the possibility of entering into agreements in which collective licences have extended effect in areas *other* than those specified in the Act. This would be known as *special extended collective licences* or *general extended collective licence*.

The proposal would require the following conditions be met: the agreement must apply to a limited and well-defined area; an agreement under which a collective licence has extended effect must be a precondition for exploitation; the agreement must be in writing and contain information to the effect that the parties' intention is for the collective licence to have extended effect. Special protective provisions will be introduced, under which, among other things, the author will always have the right to file a prohibition against exploitation.

This novelty already exists in the Danish Copyright Act. Obviously, this is a strong mandate for the actors on market and it expresses a strong belief in their capacity to comply with the prerequisites set forth. It must be observed, though, that in Denmark the concessional system offers control by a public authority, whereas the Swedish proposal is built on the assumption that contracting parties on the market may themselves enter into a special extended collective license instrument in an acceptable way.

6. SOME CONCLUDING WORDS

All these amendments to the Copyright Act would, if accepted by the Swedish Parliament, lead to the most comprehensive remake of the Act since 1960. Consequently, a completely new Act is to be proposed by the special commissioner in the Inquiry's final report in April 2011.

It is proposed that the new provisions enter into force on 1 July 2012. The new provisions are also to apply to works and performances originating before the proposed provisions' entry into force. Existing provisions will continue to apply with regard to measures taken or rights acquired before entry into force. This means, among other things, that the new provisions will not affect existing agreements.

As has been demonstrated, the proposed amendments, while certainly not comprising an act of implementation of the *acquis communautaire*, still reflect areas of EU interest, certainly those expressed by the Commission's policy documents and, to some extent, the Parliament. The more unique Swedish approach to these issues lies of course in its focus on amendments to the Copyright Act supportive of authors of literary and artistic works as parties to commercial contracts. This addition to general Contract Law is quite rare in a European context, although eg The Netherlands have recently made proposals for some provisions similar to those discussed here.

As for rights clearances for mass uses of works and objects of related rights, in particular as far as broadcasting and Internet uses are concerned (a truly trans-border or Pan-European phenomenon), these are dealt with in the Swedish proposal utilising the Nordic formula. The extended collective license has proved to be quite successful in the Nordic countries. However, it is not guaranteed to be successful as a vehicle for a simplified licensing system for the entire EU, much less as a system for a one-stop service. Certainly, a principle of EU-wide mutual recognition of a work's status cannot be generated under the Nordic license.[35]

[35] Cf T Lueder, *The Orphan Work's Challenge*, Fordham Int IPL Conference (New York 2010). Available at http://webcache.googleusercontent.com/search q=cache:IBulaLP_J40J:www.fordhamipinstitute.com/ip_conference/documents/TilmanLueder.pdf+Tilman+Lueder+Orphan+Works+challenge+fordham&cd=1&hl=en&ct=clnk&gl=us.

But perhaps it may be that trans-border licensing of mass uses of copyright works and objects of related rights can never be fully harmonised – at least not to the result of not letting licensing of copyright be a national concern.

8
Swedish Copyright Evergreens Mini-Maglite?

PROFESSOR HANS HENRIK LIDGARD

BACKGROUND

On April 9, 2009 the Swedish Supreme Court gave its judgement in the protracted infringement battle between the US Mag Instrument ('Mag') and Sweden's IKEA regarding alleged copyright protection for the Mini-Maglite® torch.[1] The Court determined that Swedish copyright legislation protects artware without any special expression level requirements.

> The distinctive shapes, styles and overall appearances of all Mag® flashlights, and the circumferential inscriptions extending around the heads of all Mag® flashlights are trademarks of Mag Instrument, Inc. The circumferential inscription on the head of every flashlight signifies that it is an original Mag® flashlight and part of the Mag® family of flashlights. U.S. Trademark Registrations for the shape, style and overall appearance trademarks of Mag® flashlights and for circumferential inscription trademarks of Mag® flashlights include Nos. 1,808,998; 2,074,795; 2,687,693; 2,745,460; 2,765,978 and 2,765,979.[2]

The Court held that the overall impression made by the well-known Mini-Maglite torch is still different from that of other similar torches and displays enough independence and originality despite the fact that the functional design properties of the torch are neither new nor original. The Court held that the design is more than trivial and not just an expression of the functionality of

[1] Högsta domstolen (Swedish Supreme Court), Case T 1421-07, *Mag Instrument, Inc v IKEA Svenska Försäljnings Aktiebolag ('IKEA')*, nyp, in the official court report. The case is available on www.domstol.se/.../2009-04-09%20T%201421-07%20Dom.pdf.

[2] http://www.maglite.com/productline.asp.

the different parts. It is rather an example of a consistent and balanced design, deserving of copyright protection. The Court emphasised that this was a borderline case, and that the reach of the copyright protection was limited.

Mag's strategic protection efforts on behalf of its mini-torch had been successful.[3] A hesitant Court could find no support from inconsistent Swedish doctrine. Undoubtedly, the judgement raises questions as to how far intellectual copyright legislation, protecting the expression of what has been termed 'the seven fine arts', can also be used to protect items of design and handicraft. How should copyright be balanced against other industrial property rights? Are there competition concerns that must be considered?

Approaching the crossroads of intellectual and industrial property rights is in itself a difficult task involving issues of subjective aesthetic considerations. What is an artistic work? When is art merely design or handicraft, and when do elegant and functional individual creations become mass-produced industrial goods?

It is even difficult to decide which notions are to be used. This article will turn on the concept of useful art and the use of the term 'artware'. If products are characterized by a certain level of creativity and originality they will have reached what will be referred to as the 'required expression level'[4] and can be protected by copyright. This notion does not cover the core of creativity, such as its subject, idea or factual content.[5] How this expression level should be defined is, of course, the crux of the paper. Does the protection only apply to identical products, or are similar products included – a problem referred to as the 'scope of the protection'.

The discussion does not end with putting copyright law and design law against each other. Design, form and shape can also attract patent and trademark protection. Furthermore, the 'passing off' rules under common law and general unfair trade laws or marketing laws also affect the final outcome and must therefore be addressed.

Addressing these complex questions is not an easy task. First, this paper discusses the interplay between copyright and other IPRs in Sweden and abroad. It also traces Mag's efforts to fend off competition in Sweden and other countries. Eventually it arrives at a discussion on how to strike a reasonable balance in protecting creative efforts against a dynamic and competitive market.

[3] Mag Instruments have been active over the years in a number of cases in different jurisdictions aiming at defending its products. The outcome differs as will be further explained. An important judgment, where the outcome was less happy for Mag, was when the EFTA Court in Case E-2/97, *Mag Instruments Inc v California Trading Company Norway*, [1997] EFTA Ct Rep 129 opted for 'international' exhaustion and thus indirectly allowed parallel importation of the Mini-Maglite from USA to Norway. This case preceded CJEU, Case C-355/96 *Silhouette v Hartlauer*, ECR[1998] I-4799. The EFTA court has now altered its position in Joined Cases E-9/07 and E-10/07, *L'Oreal Norge AS v Per Aarskog AS*, 7 July 2008, [2008] ETMR 60.

[4] In German 'Werkshöhe' and in Swedish 'Verkshöjd'.

[5] SOU 1956:25, Upphovsmannarätt till litterära och konstnärliga verk, s 68.

1. COPYRIGHT PROTECTION

As the European Court of Justice often puts it, 'in the present state of Community law and in the absence of community standardization or of a harmonization of laws' the determination of the conditions and procedures under which copyright protection is granted, is a matter for national rules.[6] Harmonization on the European level at present primarily relates to information technology[7] and the core of copyright law remains a national prerogative.[8]

Roman law did not prevent copying. In England, a society more driven by technological development, copyright protection had its roots in privileges granted by the 1662 Act for the Encouragement of Learning and the 1710 Statute of Anne.[9] Initially only publishers were protected from having their books copied, but with the Statute of Anne the focus was on the author, whose work was protected for a period of 14 to 20 years.[10] The legislation regulated the marketplace where booksellers and publishers operated, but gradually evolved into an instrument that recognised ownership in an author's intellectual labour. In 1787 a revolutionary American development found expression in

[6] See eg CJEU, Case 144/81, *Keurkoop BV v Nancy Kean Gifts BV*, 14 September 1982, [1982] ECR 2853, para 18.

[7] See Council Directive 91/250/EEC of 14 May 1991 on the legal protection of computer programs, OJ 1991 L 122/42 (as amended by Directive 93/98/EEC); Council Directive 92/100/EEC of 19 November 1992 on rental right and lending right and on certain rights related to copyright in the field of intellectual property, OJ 1992 L 346/61 (as amended by Directive 93/98/EEC); Council Directive 93/83/EEC of 27 September 1993 on the coordination of certain rules concerning copyright and rights related to copyright applicable to satellite broadcasting and cable retransmission, OJ 1993 L 248/15; Council Directive 93/98/EEC of 29 October 1993 harmonising the term of protection of copyright and certain related rights, OJ 1993 L 290/9; Directive 96/9/EC of the European Parliament and of the Council of 11 March 1996 on the legal protection of databases, OJ 1996 L 77/20; Directive 2001/31/EC of the European Parliament and of the Council of 8 June 2000 on certain legal aspects of information society services, in particular electronic commerce, in the internal market ('Directive on electronic commerce'), OJ 200 L 178/1; Directive 2001/29/EC of the European Parliament and of the Council of 22 May 2001 on the harmonisation of certain aspects of copyright and related rights in the information society, OJ 2001 L 167/10.

[8] Once harmonization has occurred, the need for uniform application of Community law and the principle of equality require that where provisions of Community law make no express reference to the law of the Member States for the purpose of determining their meaning and scope, they must normally be given an autonomous and uniform interpretation throughout the Community. See CJEU, Case C-5/08, *Infopaq International A/S v Danske Dagblades Forening*, 16 July 2009, [2009] ECR I-6569 nyp. Reference for a preliminary ruling under Article 234 EC from Højesteret regarding Directive 2001/29/EC and reproduction of short extracts of literary works.

[9] R Deazley, *On The Origin Of The Right To Copy: Charting the Movement of Copyright Law in Eighteenth Century Britain* (Hart Publishing, 2004).

[10] The term of protection was prolonged in 1814 to 20 years or the life of the author if longer. Copyright Act 1814, 54 Geo III, c 156 (Eng).

[11] US Const, Art I, §8, cl 8: 'Congress shall have the power to promote the Progress of Science and useful Arts, by securing for limited Times to Authors and Inventors the exclusive Right to their respective Writings and Discoveries.' The 1790 Federal copyright statute protected maps, charts and books. Later amendments granted protection to historical or other print or prints, musical compositions and photographs. In 1870 the list was completed by the addition of paintings,

the US Constitution.[11] U.S. courts have frequently noted that the purpose of US copyright legislation is to promote the interest of the public, rather than to follow the author-centred moral rights view expressed by the Europeans.[12] France followed suit in 1791 with protection that went beyond just economic reward and underlined a work's moral aspects.

In the mid-1700s Sweden granted privileges to printers. Inspired by the French and US developments, an 1810 constitutional enactment (also with a revolutionary origin) protected authors.[13] A general author's legislation was introduced in 1877 and protection was granted for the life of the author plus 50 years, (later reduced to 30 years). Separate legislation was gradually introduced to protect other artistic efforts, but it was only with the Swedish copyright law of 1919 that a unified copyright legislation came about.[14]

National copyright protection only applies to works created within the country in question. Consequently, a work published in one country could be copied elsewhere by anyone and sold there. The 1886 Berne Convention[15] internationalized copyright protection for the benefit of the author in the same way as industrial property rights had been addressed in the Paris Convention.

Article 2 of the Berne Convention protects the 'expression' of literary and artistic works. This includes every production in the literary, scientific and artistic domain, whatever may be the mode or form of its expression. Article 2 also covers writings, lectures, musical works, choreography and cinematography. Drawings, paintings, architecture, sculpture, engraving and lithography and photographic works are also protected. Of special interest is that the same provision now also covers works of applied art.[16] The Member States, now some 160 countries, may prescribe that works in general or any specified categories of works will not be protected unless they have been fixed in some material form.

The Berne Convention left it to national legislation to determine the extent of the application of the law with respect to works of applied art and industrial

drawings, chromos, statues, statuaries and models and designs 'intended to perfect the work of fine art'. See Zimmerman, Dianne Leenheer, 'It's An Original! (?): In Pursuit Of Copyright's Elusive Essence' *(2005)* 28 *Columbia Journal of Law and the Arts* pp 187, 200 n 87 (and references therein.)

[12] See eg *Sony Corp of America v Universal City Studios*, 464 US 417, 429 (1984). (Reward to owner is secondary to benefit to public.)

[13] 1810 Tryckfrihetsförordningen (Constitutional regulation of freedom to print/freedom of the press) § 1 section 8 stipulated that every printing belongs to the author. (Varje skrift vare författarens eller dess laglige rättsinnehavares egendom'.

[14] Lagar den 30 maj 1919 om rätt till litterära och musikaliska verk, om rätt till verk av bildande konst samt om rätt till fotografiska bilder. See SOU 1956:25, Upphovsmannarätt till litterära och konstnärliga verk, pp 35 ff.

[15] Berne Convention for the Protection of Literary and Artistic Works of September 9, 1886, completed at Paris on May 4, 1896, revised at Berlin on November 13, 1908, completed at Berne on March 20, 1914, revised at Rome on June 2, 1928, at Brussels on June 26, 1948, at Stockholm on July 14, 1967, and at Paris on July 24, 1971, and amended on September 28, 1979. Available at http://www.wipo.int/treaties/en/ip/berne/pdf/trtdocs_wo001.pdf.

[16] Ibid, Art 2. The initial Bern Convention did not contain any rules on artware. It was only with the 1908 revision that Art 2 of the Convention stated that it was left to national law to decide on the extent of protection for industrial designs and applied art.

design, as well as the conditions under which they would be protected.

The Swedish history in this area is less than consistent and hardly glorious in so far as concerns the protection of industrial designs and artware.

Swedish Design Protection

The 1899 Swedish Design Act[17] created a five-year protection for new, registered ornamental designs in the metal industry. In spite of numerous regulatory attempts,[18] modern, general, legislation was only introduced in 1970 when protection was granted to industrial designs for a period of 15 years from their registration.[19]

Under the law a 'design' is a prototype for the shape of a product or for an ornament. The person who has created a design may obtain, through registration, an exclusive right to exploit it. Designs may be registered only if they substantially differ from what has become known before the date of filing. Everything that has been made generally available anywhere in the world is considered as 'known'. The right applies only to the goods for which the design has been registered, or for similar goods.

The term of Swedish design protection has now, in line with the EU Directive on Design Protection[20] been extended to cover a period of 25 years from registration. Likewise inspired by EU developments, Sweden has also introduced an abbreviated protection for unregistered designs.

Swedish Copyright Legislation

The 1960 Swedish Copyright Act[21] provides that anyone who has created a literary or artistic work shall have copyright in that work, regardless of whether it is a fictional or descriptive representation in writing or speech. Works of fine arts, architecture or applied art are also protected.

Before the 1960 Copyright Act, protection for artware only lasted for 10

[17] 1899 års lag om skydd för vissa mönster och modeller, (SFS 1899:59).

[18] See SOU 1965:61, Mönsterskydd, pp 34 ff.

[19] 1970 års Mönsterskyddslag (Swedish Design Protection Act)(SFS 1970:485) of June 29, 1970, available at http://www.wipo.int/clea/en/details.jsp?id=3630

[20] Directive 98/71/EC of the European Parliament and of the Council of 13 October 1998 on the legal protection of designs OJ 1998 L 289/28. Amendment of the Swedish design law in 2002. See Prop. 2001/2002:121, Genomförande av Europaparlamentets och rådets direktiv om mönsterskydd m.m.

[21] Swedish Copyright, Act, 30 December 1960, (SFS 1960:729).

[22] The 1919 Copyright Act did not contain any provisions regarding artware. Revisions in 1926 provided 10 year protection from the date of publication, but did not cover clothing and woven materials as Sweden wanted to benefit from freedom in this area and sought an influx of such material from the European continent

years from publication.[22] This protection was provisionally maintained in the new legislation in anticipation of the contemplated design legislation.[23] With the 1970 Design Act the specific treatment of artware in the Copyright Act was eliminated and copyrightable artware became protected for the life of the creator plus 50 (now 70)[24] years.

Unsurprisingly, the preparatory work for the legislation required that the extended protection for artware should be balanced by stiffer expression level requirements.[25] To qualify for copyright protection a work had to be personal, with an artistic presentation[26] in order to eliminate the risk of independent double creation.[27] A certain generosity towards artware with limited expression alternatives was indicated.[28]

The case-law development after 1970 gives limited guidance as to the extent of the protection of artware. Protection has been granted to certain textile products with ornamental elements. A special design for a ladies' tunic was protected as an independent and original design with an individualised and artistic presentation.[29] Protection was accorded to forms or configuration preventing passing off relating to the specific form under review. Thus the Court also underlined the independence and uniqueness of the design in a textile fabric case, where the ornament consisted of a wild strawberry but a similar design consisting of ordinary strawberries was regarded as outside the area of protection even if the new ornament had been inspired by the commercial success of the earlier design.[30] The general impression is, however, that the Swedish courts, in spite of the fairly clear language in the preparatory work, have been reluctant to deny copyright protection. The courts, rather, seem to reach the conclusion that protection applies, but that the scope of protection is limited and confined to the precise configuration.

[23] The proposal for the 1960 Copyright Act, SOU 1965:61, did not contain provisions regarding applied art, but rather suggested that the area be covered by reformed design legislation and not by extending the reach of the copyright legislation. However, in the final legislation a provisional 10 year protection for artware was retained in anticipation of a planned reform of the design legislation.

[24] Long copyright protection has no reasonably explicable explanation when compared to other IPRs. The TRIPs Agreement requires at least lifetime protection plus 50 years. The extension to 70 years was inspired by the 1998 US Copyright Term Extension Act also referred to as the 'Mickey Mouse Protection Act' aimed at protecting some of the most valuable Disney products. The act was introduced after heavy industry lobbying.

[25] Prop 1969:168 p 135 and SOU 1965:61, Mönsterskydd, pp 210 ff.

[26] In NJA 1962:750 – *String*, the Swedish Supreme Court recognised copyright protection for the functional 'String' bookshelf. A holistic approach should be taken – that included functional details. The String shelf was aesthetically sufficiently original to be regarded as artware. This specific case is cited as an example in the 1965 preparatory legislative work of what should not be copyright protected in the future. See SOU 1965:61, *Mönsterskydd*, p 211.

[27] Determining whether or not there is a risk of double creation is a supporting rule used to establish copyright protection and the reach of the protection. This notion does not, however, clarify whether the object has reached the required expression level. See, Swedish Supreme Court, NJA 2004:149 – *Pergo*.

[28] Prop 1969:168 pp 134-136 and SOU 1965:61 p 211.

[29] Swedish Supreme Court, NJA 1995:164 - *Stickad Tunika*.

[30] Swedish Supreme Court, NJA 1994:74 - *Smultron*.

2. COPYRIGHT VERSUS OTHER FORMS OF PROTECTION

Can copyright be used as a tool-box to create protection for ownership interests where that interest is already protected by other, perhaps more appropriate, legal regimes?

Design and Copyright

As a consequence of the Swedish case law, artware may very well be protected as both copyright and registered design. This is in line with § 10 of the Copyright Law, which expressly states that copyright may subsist in a work even if it has been registered as a design.

This double protection has been the subject of discussions throughout the history of the Copyright Law. One view was that the creator had to make an election. If she wanted to benefit from the more precise design protection, copyright protection would then be excluded. This would lead to increased predictability through registration, and the scope of protection would be similar to the scope of patent protection. In general such predictability would facilitate trade and establish a fair trade-off between the public interest and the reward to the designer. This view was, however, not accepted.

The fact that Swedish law opted for a double protection rule was based on several premises. First, there was no reason not to grant the same protection for artware protected by design protection as for those artistic efforts, which could not be subject of design protection. Second, the moral rights of an artist were only protected by copyright law, and the serious designer had an equal right to benefit from this element of the law.[31] A less clearly enunciated reason for not limiting the protection of artware to design protection may be found in Article 2(7) of the Berne Convention.[32] Without double protection in Sweden, Swedish designs would not be protected under copyright law in a foreign country even if double protection were available in that country. Lacking international agreements regarding the precise protection to be offered to artware, Swedish exports should be able to draw the benefit of strong protection on their home turf.

[31] See SOU 1965:61 Mönsterskydd, pp 224 ff.

[32] 1886 Berne Convention for the Protection of Literary and Artistic Works, Article 2(7): '… Works protected in the country of origin solely as designs and models shall be entitled in another country of the Union only to such special protection as is granted in that country to designs and models; however, if no such special protection is granted in that country, such works shall be protected as artistic works.'

Patents and Trademarks

Can an item be both patent-protected and copyrightable? The law is silent on this issue, but does specify that copyright does not subsist in layout designs in semiconductor products. Special provisions apply to rights in such designs.

Patents protect ideas/inventions, which are functional solutions to problems, whereas copyright protects the expression rather than the idea as such. The functional elements expressed in the claims of a patent are not protectable under copyright (or any other IPR).[33] The fact that a patent has been applied for, is an indication of the fact that the item is not copyright protectable.[34] If a patent protected product embodies a form or shape, which in spite of this reservation has reached copyrightable expression level, the functional elements must then be disregarded.

The underlying logic is that the legislator has granted a 20 year protection for patentable functional elements. The protection is carefully designed to strike a balance between the need to promote innovation and the requirements of free access, further improvements being the lifeblood of the economy.

Trademarks are indications of origin. A trademark can be a single word or a phrase. It can also take the form of a shape of a product. Nothing prevents a slogan or shape from reaching an expression level conferring copyright protection. A trademark, which is initially not inherently distinctive may acquire distinctiveness through use. Functional elements can never acquire protectable distinctiveness.[35] It should be noted that trademarks and copyright serve totally different functions – a trademark is intended to prevent consumers from being misled as to the origin of the product, whereas copyright protection is focused on the rights of the creator.

Marketing Law Prevents 'Passing Off'

A further question is whether protection under unfair trade/competition laws, common law passing off rules, or other marketing laws can coexist with copyright

[33] The Swedish Supreme Court has confirmed that drawings in a patent application in principle can be protected by copyright even if the protection did not apply in the specific instance. See NJA 2004:149 – *Välinge*. Cf NJA 1998:563 – *Finnbohus*.

[34] Cf U.S Supreme Court, *Traffix Devices, Inc v Marketing Desplays, Inc*, 532 US 23, 29 (2001) (where the Court held that 'a utility patent is strong evidence that the features therein claimed are functional. … one who seeks to establish trade dress protection must carry the heavy burden of showing that the feature is not functional.').

[35] Article 7(3) of Council Regulation (EC) No 40/94 of 20 December 1993 on the Community trademark, OJ 1994 L 11/1 does not refer to Article 7(1) e of the same Regulation, which excludes acquired distinctiveness for signs which consist exclusively of: '(i) the shape which results from the nature of the goods themselves; or (ii) the shape of goods which is necessary to obtain a technical result; or (iii) the shape which gives substantial value to the goods.' Cf. Case C-299/99, *Koninklijke Philips Electronics NV v Remington Consumer Products Ltd*, 18 June 2002, [2002], ECR I-5475, para 57, recently confirmed in Case C-48/09 P, *Lego Juris A/S v OHIM*, 14 September 2010, nyp.

protection and thereby increase the scope of protection for distinctive products. Conversely should the copyright holder who sees his copyrights infringed be limited to the consequences established by the law governing his property rights?

In general this type of legislation, like trademark legislation, has as its prime object the prevention of marketing activities that mislead end customers. Therefore, an item may very well benefit both from intellectual property rights and these unfair trade rules.[36]

Evergreen Conclusion

The overall conclusion of this brief comparative survey is that Swedish law provides the artist with a whole battery of rules that may be used to fend off competition. The clever artist will probably consider whether anything in his creation may be patent protected. Are there elements meeting the requirements of the design law? May the entire creation reach such a standard that the creator may claim copyright protection? If the form developed is not inherently distinctive, has it acquired distinctiveness at a later stage, which would allow trademark protection? Are competitors infringing unfair competition laws by marketing products which may mislead the public?

To make use of the entire spectrum of protection is a fine legal exercise and if the job is done well, product protection is maintained on an evergreen basis and, accordingly, competition will be restricted.

3. PROTECTING MAGLITE – AN 'EVERGREENING' EFFORT

An Elegant and Functional Device

The Mini-Maglite is a barrel-shaped aluminium flashlight designed to use AA-cell batteries. Similar flashlights for C- and D-cell batteries have been on the market since the early 1970s. The Mini-Maglite was first introduced in January 1984. Earlier larger torches were also produced in aluminium with a cylindrical barrel with a knurled grip and a tail cap. The lenses had a greater diameter than the barrel as well as a separate headpiece with knurling and a face cap. It has therefore been suggested that the Mini-Maglite was primarily a scaled-down version of the larger flashlights.[37] The Mini-Maglite, however, also lacked an external switch.

[36] See eg the treatment of the liqueur Galliano in the Swedish Supreme Court (NJA:1995:635-*Galliano*), and in the Swedish Marketing Court (MD 1996:3 *Galliano*). In Case C-48/09 P, *Lego Juris A/S v OHIM*, n 35, the CJEU held that a functional shape, which cannot be trademark protected may, 'where appropriate, be examined in the light of rules on unfair competition.'

[37] Statement by Meinhardt, Mag's expert witness in the U.S. Trade Commission, Investigation, n 41 below.

The Mini-Maglite was an instant market success and achieved substantial sales in its US home market and abroad. The primary market consisted of sales to professionals such as the police and other security forces.[38] It was also sold as an accessory eg to the sporting goods and aircraft supply markets. In its own early marketing the company claimed that the 'beautiful, functional design is their hallmark'. The Mini-Maglite 'is a study in simplicity', 'the size makes it the ideal professional or personal light' and it easily fits into a pocket or a purse. Its durability including the 'aircraft grade aluminium' and 'anodized finish' preventing corrosion. The knurling on the flashlight provides a 'sure grip' just enough to minimize abrasiveness. Furthermore the shape of the head was convenient for one-handed operations. The absence of an external switch prevents the torch from accidentally turning on while not in use.[39] The marketing success was, as is often the case, a mixed blessing: by 1987 competitors importing mini flashlights had acquired some 57 per cent of the market and it was obvious that Mag had to take action if it wanted to protect itself from these inroads into the mini torch market.

Patent and Trade Dress Protection Questioned in the USA

By 1984 Mag had already applied for and received utility patent protection under US Letters Patent No 4,577,263. In a continuation-in-part application Mag claimed 'A flashlight ... wherein the head assembly includes an outer surface shaped in a gradual taper towards the tail cap and over an extent substantially greater than half the length of the head assembly'. The features thus claimed were the actual configuration of the torch. In addition Mag also applied for three-dimensional trademark protection for the torch.

In 1987 Mag took action against importation of mini flashlights considered by Mag to infringe on its patent as well as its trade dress protection. The U.S. International Trade Commission determined[40] by way of adopting a more than

[38] It is interesting to note that a number of U.S. cases concern policemen applying Maglite products directly to criminal offenders. See eg *Baker v Holcomb,* 2008 WL 4914439 (D Neb Nov 12, 2008) ('Here, the plaintiff alleges defendants ...carried him by his hair and 'repeatedly' hit him with a 'maglite.'... 'The plaintiff alleges these defendants 'lacerated [his] right eye,' caused 'abrasions on his abdomen,' and 'aggravat[ed] ... [his] pre-existing knee fracture.'), *Thorne v Steubenville Police Officer,* 463 FSupp2d 760, 764. (SD Ohio, 2006.) ('Danny asserts that while they waited for Thorne, Sr. to open the side door to the house, Officer Karovic hit Danny three times above his right eye with an approximately eighteen or twenty-inch Maglite flashlight') *aff'd in part rev'd in part sub nom Thorne v Lelles,* 243 Fed Appx 157, 2007 WL 2781151 (C.A.6 (Ohio), *Yarnall v Mendez,* 433 FSupp2d 432 (D Del 2006) ('[P]laintiff alleges that, pursuant to an arrest and after being handcuffed, Mendez struck him twice on the head with a 'Maglite' flashlight.')

[39] The advertising claims are summarized from findings from the ITC Decision337-TA-254, n 41, pp 111 ff.

[40] The US International Trade Commission (the 'ITC') handles customs matters.

200 page long,[41] that the patents were unenforceable as the invention had been made public more than one year before the registration application. The ITC went as far as to conclude that Mag's failure to disclose prior art was inequitable conduct by gross negligence, at the very least.[42]

With respect to the trade dress claim,[43] the ITC concluded that Mag had failed to prove that the overall shape, style and appearance of Mini-Maglite was not primarily functional; that it had acquired a secondary meaning; or was likely to lead to customer confusion.[44] The ITC concluded that 'the Mini-Maglite does indeed have a sleek design, but each and every component of its design is fully functional; and certainly the overall configuration of the flashlight is, in terms of utility, the best or one of the best designs available.'[45] The features were 'obviously utilitarian'. The sum of the components added up to the total configuration, which determined the functionality. Furthermore, the ITC held that configuration claimed in a utility patent was strong evidence that the configuration was functional.[46] The only design feature that was potentially non-functional was the tapering of the head from the lens to the barrel. This feature was, however, also claimed in the utility patent application.

No Inherently Distinguishable Trademark

The ITC also considered whether or not trademark protection applied to the mini-torch product itself. Under US law a configuration is inherently distinctive if it can be presumed that the average consumer will recognize it to be a trademark.[47] However, the evidence was against Mag. No customer survey confirmed any such distinctiveness while the fact that others copied the product could not as such support trademark protection. Mag had not demonstrated by a preponderance of evidence, that the overall shape and appearance of the

[41] *In The Matter of Certain Small Aluminium Flashlights and Components thereof.* U.S. Trade Commission, Investigation No 337-TA-254, (Mathias ALJ) p 109, point 484, (unreported) (adopted by the ITC) (the 'ITC Decision'). (A copy of the ITC Decision is on file with the author.)

[42] This finding of gross negligence and inequitable conduct was overturned by the Federal Circuit in an unpublished decision, *Mag Instruments, Inc, v ITC*, 868 F2d 1278 (Fed Cir 1989) (remanded on rehearing to hear intervener's patent invalidity claims.) 878 F2d 1443, 1989 WL 49202 (Fed Cir March 21 1989) (unpublished).

[43] For a discussion of the US position on the interface between trade dress and design see Groff, Bradley, K, 'Bare-Fisted Competition or Palming off? Protection of Product Design as Trade Dress under the Lanham Act', 23 *AIPLA Quarterly Journal* 65, 97.

[44] ITC Decision, n 41, point 607.

[45] Ibid at p 181.

[46] Ibid at p 184 with reference to *New England Butt Co v ITC* 756 F.2d 874, 878 (Fed Cir 1985); *In re Morton-Norwich Products, Inc*, 671 F.2d 1332, 213 USPQ ,15 (CCPA 1982), and *Best Lock Corp v Schlage Lock Company* 413 F.2d 1195 (CCPA 1969)

[47] *Seabrook Foods, Inc v Bar-Well Foods, Inc*, 568 F.2d 1342, 196 USPQ 289,291 (CCPA 1977).

Mini-Maglite flashlight enjoys such secondary meaning as to be protected by trademark.

Unfair Commercial Methods

Mag also alleged before the ITC that importation and sales of foreign products constituted unfair acts and unfair methods of competition in violation of Section 337 of the 1930 Tariffs Act. Such activities may not seek to destroy or substantially injure an industry that is efficiently and economically operated in the United States.

The ITC did not accept the allegation. It emphasised the basic rule that 'it must not be forgotten that there is absolutely nothing legally or morally reprehensible about exact copying of things in the public domain'.[48] It is only when the copier is trying to deceive the public by inferring that the product comes from another manufacturer that rules on unlawful 'passing off' may be invoked.

No Trademark Protection in Europe

In 1996 Mag also unsuccessfully advanced trademark protection claims for the three-dimensional torch in Europe under the EC Trademark Regulation[49]. The examiner at OHIM refused the application made under Article 38 of the Trademark Regulation[50] on the ground that the trademarks were devoid of distinctive character. The Board of Appeal[51] agreed and held that for the shape of the goods alone to constitute a distinctive indication of origin the shape must display features sufficiently different from the usual shape of the goods for potential buyers to perceive it as an indication of the origin rather than a representation of the goods themselves. The Board stated that the fact that Mini-Maglite was attractively designed does not by itself make its features inherently distinctive.

In its appeal to the General Court,[52] Mag submitted that even a small degree of distinctiveness suffices to overcome the bar to registration. The Mini-Maglite was, according to Mag, 'a striking example of goods of high technical quality whose aesthetically pleasing shape, as the main feature, embodies their semantic function, one of their leading features'. The torch had been so displayed in various books, in museums and had won international awards. Copying created

[48] ITC Decision, fn 37, at p 191.

[49] Council Regulation (EC) No 40/94 of 20 December 1993 on the Community trademark, OJ 1994 L 11, p 1.

[50] Ibid.

[51] Second Board of Appeal of the OHIM, Cases R-237/1999-2 to R-241/1999-2 of 14 February 2000, http://oami.europa.eu/legaldocs/boa/1999/EN/R0237_1999-2.pdf.

[52] Case T-88/00, *Mag Instruments Inc v Office for Harmonization in the Internal Market ('OHIM')*, 7 February 2002, [2002] ECR II-467.

confusion and copiers exploited the 'cult Mag Lite torch design.' Trademark protection had also been granted in several EU Member States.[53]

The General Court held that regard must be had to the presumed expectations of an average consumer, who is reasonably well informed and reasonably observant and circumspect. Mini-Maglite is cylindrical and opens out at the end where the bulb is. The application corresponds to shapes commonly used by other manufacturers and only provides the consumer with an indication of the nature of the product without distinguishing it from the shapes of similar products. The attractiveness does not draw the consumer's attention to the good's commercial origin.[54]

On appeal[55] the EUCJ basically agreed with the General Court, but added that it may be more difficult for the average consumer to assess three-dimensional marks.

> In those circumstances, the more closely the shape for which registration is sought resembles the shape most likely to be taken by the product in question, the greater the likelihood of the shape being devoid of any distinctive character for the purposes of Article 7(1)(b) of Regulation 40/94. Only a mark which departs significantly from the norm or customs of the sector and thereby fulfils its essential function of indicating origin, is not devoid of any distinctive character for the purposes of that provision.[56]

A mere variant of a common shape is not sufficient to establish distinctiveness. In spite of certain aesthetic features claimed by Mag, the Mini-Maglite did not possess an 'inherently' distinctive character. This did not prevent Mag from demonstrating that the *use* made of the aesthetic, non-functional features could lead to an 'acquired' distinctiveness. This was, however, not Mag's intention in the case. Mag wanted recognition that the excellence of the design of the torches and their aesthetic and functional qualities were sufficient to create a distinctive trademark. Mag has subsequently obtained trademark protection for the configurations based on the use made of them:[57]

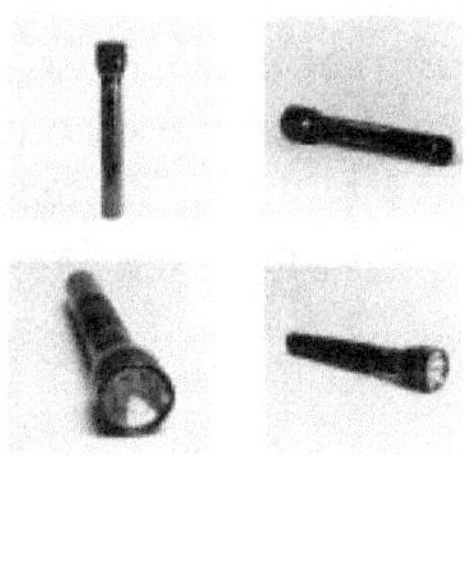

[53] Ibid at para 16–23.

[54] Ibid para 35–40.

[55] Case C-136/02 P, *Mag Instruments Inc v OHIM*, 7 October 2004, [2004] ECR I-9165.

[56] Ibid at para 31 citing CJEU, Joined Cases C-456/01P and C-457/01P), *Henkel KgaA v OHIM*, [2004] ECR 1-5089, para 39.

[57] Trademark number CTM 002351831, http://oami.europa.eu/CTMOnline/RequestManager/en_DetailCTM_NoReg. The Mini-Maglite was also the first 3D mark to be protected in Japan in spite of considerable resistance. See, http://www.jonesday.com/pubs/pubs_detail. aspx?pubID=S4538.

Sweden Applies its Market Law

Mag introduced the Mini-Maglite in Sweden in 1984 and more-or-less identical imitations were introduced on the Swedish market during the 1990s. In 1999 Mag instigated proceedings under the Swedish Marketing Act against Libro – a Swedish marketing company selling an unmarked mini torch produced in Taiwan.[58] Mag relied on Section 8 of the Marketing Act, which prohibits deceptive and misleading marketing.[59]

Mag claimed that each of its torches has an individual character, while still fitting into the Maglite family. They are produced to meet professional requirements and have been used in spaceships and the Iraq war. Mini-Maglite's design was not just a reduction in size, but characterised by elegance and the lack of any interruption in its external configuration. The aesthetic features had no equivalents. Mini-Maglite together with the Volkswagen Beetle and Levi's 501-jeans were the most sold consumables. The torch is easily recognized due to its inherent distinctiveness and considerable worldwide marketing efforts. The design reflects the designer, Mr Maglica's personality. It has been designed from the outside towards the inside. It is not the result of functional requirements, but rather of aesthetic and artistic considerations, which had been endorsed by Föreningen Svensk Forms Opinionsnämnd – a private institution, which provides advice on design. In 1996 it was one of the most copied consumables and copies did not have to use the word or the mark Mini-Maglite®. The form was enough to mislead consumers.

The district court found that Mini-Maglite was known to Swedish consumers. It determined that the product was characteristic in a non-functional way as suggested by Svensk Forms Opinionsnämnd and that there were infinite ways of designing mini torches. The Libro torch demonstrated substantial resemblance to the Mini-Maglite (even if there were differences) and it was incumbent on Libro to prove that it was not an imitation. As to the likelihood of confusion, the court underlined that the test was a 'quick-look' one. If the quick-look provides the same impression to the consumer when he sees the original and the copy there is a likelihood of confusion. Minor deviations did not prevent the risk of confusion. Accordingly, the court established there was infringement. On appeal the Swedish Market Court[60] only increased the damages payable by Libro.

[58] Stockholms Tingsrätt (Stockholm District Court), Case T 17705-99, *Mag Instrument, Inc v Libro Invest Aktiebolag*, 29 October 2003.

[59] Section 8 of the Swedish Marketing Act, (SFS 1995:450), regarding misleading imitations, provides: 'When marketing a businessman may not use imitations which are misleading as they can easily be confused for another businessman's known and characteristic products. However, this does not apply to imitations of the design which primarily serve to make the product functional. 'In the alternative reference was made to the general stipulation in section 4 of the Act, which provides that 'Marketing must be compatible with good marketing practice and also in other respects be fair towards consumers and businessmen. When marketing businessmen must provide such information as is of particular importance from the consumer perspective'.

[60] The Swedish Market Court, Case 2005:6 Dnr C 29/03, *Mag Instrument, Inc v Libro Invest Aktiebolag*, 2 October 2005.

German Unfair Competition Law Not Applicable

The outcome, however, in earlier German procedures was quite different. Mag brought proceedings against the importation of mini flashlights under the trademark TopShop[61] alleging that the Mini-Maglite's design was characteristic ('eigentümlich') and different. The design was elegant and light, emphasising the slim barrel, which opens out at the end in a tulip-shaped head and which is underlined by the selection of production material. Mini-Maglite had become a status symbol and the TopShop product was, in conflict with the German Unfair Competition Law,[62] and, Mag alleged, an out-and-out copy.[63]

Both the Landesgerichts München and the Oberlandsgericht München[64] disagreed with Mag and only required that the TopShop torch be marked to avoid consumer confusion. The matter was unsuccessfully appealed to the German Bundesgerichtshof,[65] which carefully considered all the elements of the torches from both an unfair trade and a copyright perspective. In order to be protected by the rules on unfair competition the lamp had to have characteristics, which consumers identify as indications of origin.[66] The Court found that all the elements of the Mini-Maglite were functional in a way that could not be monopolised and that the TopShop lamp, in any event, differed sufficiently from the Mini-Maglite on points where such a distinction could be made. Accordingly, the law on unfair competition could not be invoked against the sale of the competing product.

[61] Judgement of Landgerichts München, in *Mag Instrument Inc, v Eduscho GmbH & Co KG*, 24 July 1996. Mag appears to have been involved in several disputes in Germany with different outcomes regarding its Mini-Maglite. See eg Landgericht Köln, case 81 O 117/99 *Firma Mag Instrument Inc v Firma Ampercell Vertriebsgesellschaft für elektronische Erzeugnisse mbh*, 29 September 2000.

[62] The German Unfair Competition Law (Gesetz gegen den unlauteren Wettbewerb), 7 June 1909 as last amended by the Law of June 22, 1998. Consolidated text by WIPO at http://www.wipo.int/clea/en/text_html.jsp?lang=EN&id=1034.

§ 1 UWG states: 'Any person who, in the course of trade and for the purposes of competition, commits acts contrary to honest practice may be enjoined from such acts and held liable for damages.'

[63] Ibid, at § 3: Any person who, in the course of trade and for the purposes of competition, makes misleading statements concerning business circumstances, in particular the nature, the origin, the manner of manufacture or the pricing of individual goods or commercial services or of the offer as a whole, price lists, the manner or the source of acquisition of goods, the possession of awards, the occasion or purpose of the sale or the size of the available stock, may be enjoined from making such statements.

[64] 29 Zivilsenats des Oberlandesgerichts München, Case 29 U 4906/96, *Mag Instrument Inc, v Eduscho GmbH & Co KG*, 17 April 1997, an appeal from a judgment by the Landesgerichts München, 24 July 1996.

[65] Bundesgerichtshof, Case I ZR 142/97, *Mag Instrument Inc v Eduscho GmbH & Co KG*, 7 May 1998.

[66] Ibid, Entscheidungsgründe 1.1: Eine danach erforderliche wettbewerbliche Eigenart kommt den Erzeugnissn der Klägerin nur dann zu, wenn deren konkrete Ausgestaltung geeignet ist, für die interessierten Verkehrskreise auf die betriebliche Herkunft oder auf Besonderheiten des Erzeugnisses hinzuweisen. … Eine solche Eignung kann allgemein üblichen Gestaltungen die sich am bekannten und zugänglichen Formenschatz anlehnen, nich zukommen'.

The Bundesgerichtshof determined that the German Marketing Law[67] was inapplicable as there was no customer confusion and that Mag could not invoke the German three-dimensional trademark protection it had received for the torch configuration. The functional elements prevented legal protection applying, but other elements could still indicate origin as they had been made known through consistent marketing efforts. However, several other similar products had also been brought to the market and the configuration of the mini torch was no longer unique to Mag.

Copyright Protection Denied in Germany

In the TopShop case[68] Mag also invoked the German copyright legislation.[69] According to the Bundesgerichtshof the Mini-Maglite could not be protected as a copyrightable 'work' under the law.[70] The lamp is 'artware' and copyright protection will be awarded only if the result is a personal design expression, which reaches a level of art according to the opinion of experts. The court expressly emphasized that these aesthetic requirements are clearly higher than for items protected by design legislation.[71] The court, noting the smooth tapering of the head

[67] Act Against Unfair Competition of June 7, 1909 amended on June 22, 1998. (Gesetz gegen den unlauteren Wettbewerb), http://www.wipo.int/clea/en/details.jsp?id=1013.

[68] Bundesgerichtshof, Case I ZR 142/97, n 65.

[69] Law on Copyright and Neighboring Rights (Copyright Law) of September 9, 1965. (Gezetz über Urheberrecht und verwandte Schutzrechte –Urheberechtsgesetzes). Consolidated text by WIPO at http://www.wipo.int/clea/en/text_html.jsp?lang=EN&id=1034.

[70] Ibid, at §2 Abs. 2: 'Protected literary, scientific and artistic works shall include, in particular,

1. works of language, such as writings, speeches and computer programs;
2. musical works;
3. works of pantomime, including choreographic works;
4. works of fine art, including works of architecture and of applied art and plans for such works;
5. photographic works, including works produced by processes similar to photography;
6. cinematographic works, including works produced by processes similar to cinematography;
7. illustrations of a scientific or technical nature, such as drawings, plans, maps, sketches, tables and three-dimensional representations.

(2) Personal intellectual creations alone shall constitute works within the meaning of this Law.

[71] Bundesgerichtshof, Case I ZR 142/97, n 65, Entscheidungsgründe 3: Die Taschenlampen der Klägerin (Mini-Maglite) sind Gebrauschsgegenstände. Als solche können sie im Werk der angewandten Kunst darstellen, bei dem andere Masstäbe als bei einem Werk der Zweckfreien Kunst bei Prüfung der Werksqualität nach §2 Abs. 2 UrhG anzuwenden sind. ... Von einem Werk der angewandten Kunst kann danach nur ausgegangen werden, wenn es eine eigenpersöhnliche Schöpfung darstellt, die mit den Darstellungsmitteln der Kunst durch formgebende Tätigkeit hervorgebracht ist. Dabei muss der ästetishe Gehalt des Werkes einen solchen Grad erreichen, dass nach Auffassung der für Kunst empfänglichen und mit Kunstanschauungen einigermassen vertrauten Kreisse von einer kunstlicheren Leistung gesprochen werden kann. Der erforderliche Grad ästetischen Gehalts ist ein höherer, als er bei nur gesmacksmusterfähigen Gegenständen verlangt wird, da sich bereits die geschmacksmusterschutzfähige Gestaltung von der nicht geschützten Durchsnittsgestaltung, dem rein Handwerksmässigen und Alltäglichen abheben muss. Die zwischen urheberrechlichem Schutz und Geschmacksmusterschutz bestehende Grenze darf nicht zu niedrig abgesteckt werden.'

from the lens to the barrel, agreed that the Mini-Maglite expressed a compact and elegant design. This did, however, not satisfy copyright protection requirements.[72]

4. SWEDISH COPYRIGHT PROTECTS MINI-MAGLITE

While proceedings were still pending in the Swedish Market Court[73] under the Marketing Act,[74] Mag initiated proceedings against IKEA in the Stockholm District Court[75] in 2004 under Swedish copyright legislation.[76] Mag alleged that it had, in accordance with section 1 paragraph 1 of the law, created a work of architecture or applied art. Under section 2 (1), it had the exclusive right to control the Mini-Maglite torch by reproducing it and by making it available to the public, be it in the original or an altered form, in translation or adaptation, in another literary or artistic form, or by other technical means. IKEA had infringed Mag's exclusive rights by introducing an almost identical torch – even if marked 'Design and Quality IKEA of Sweden, Made in Taiwan'. The matter was tried in the district court, appealed to Hovrätten[77] and subsequently to the Swedish Supreme Court.[78]

Mag in all three instances argued that the torch was copyright protectable by referring to the artistic efforts of Mr Maglica, who was called as a witness in the proceedings. He testified that the design development had lasted for several years. The torch had been created from 'outside and in' – ie the form was not dictated by functional or ergonomic requirements but out of artistic and aesthetic considerations. Mr Maglica had aimed at a configuration, which was visually unique, reflecting his own personality – 'A Work of Art that Works'. The result was an unmatched elegant form, perfectly balanced, soft fleeting unbroken contours between the barrel and head undisturbed by exterior switches. Nothing in the configuration was self-evident or functionally mandated. It had changed the torch industry, had obtained design rewards, and been displayed in design publications and museums. Svensk Forms Opinionsnämnd had on two occasions also determined that the Mini-Maglite was copyrightable.[79]

[72] Similarly, Landgericht Köln, n 61, denied Mini-Maglite copyright protection as the torch was regarded as an everyday use object, which could only be copyright protected if the presentation substantially exceeded the average, which was not the case. The court emphasized that the competing torch differed in essential non-functional elements.

[73] See Swedish Market Court, Case 2005:6, n 60.

[74] The Swedish Marketing Act, (SFS 1995:450).

[75] Helsingborgs Tingsrätt (District Court), Case T 1696-99, *Mag Instrument, Inc, v IKEA Svenska Försäljnings Aktiebolag*, judgment 11 March 2005.

[76] Swedish Copyright, Act, 30/12/1960, (SFS 1960:729).

[77] Hovrätten över Skåne och Blekinge (Appellate Court), Case T 916-05, 16 February 2007.

[78] Högsta domstolen, Case T 1421-07, n 2.

[79] Svensk Forms Opinionsnämnd is a private (impartial) institution organized by the Swedish Society of Crafts and Design, which provides design opinions on request. The opinions are non-binding, but often carry a persuasive effect in Swedish courts. Opinion 166 in case 11/1993 established that the torch was copyrightable. In the second opinion, requested by Helsingborgs Tingsrätt, the prior

IKEA, on the other hand, argued that the Mini-Maglite configuration was too trivial to meet the requirements of originality and independence required for copyright protection. The Mini-Maglite lacked the required expression level in comparison with earlier torches and the risk of independent double creation was due to the functionality of the torch. All essential elements of the torch were functional. If functionality could be copyright protected then competition would be unreasonably restricted.

Both parties referred to expert opinions from a divided Swedish academic copyright elite as to whether 'a certain level of independence and originality'[80] was required and how high this level had to be. The three judgments are also related to this notion:

Helsingborgs Tingsrätt[81] (the district court) held that the configuration of the Mini-Maglite, disregarding its functional elements, had reached the required level for copyright protection. It was unlikely that another designer would independently arrive at the same 'tulip-like' form. The scope of the protection, however, was narrow.

Hovrätten[82] (the appellate court) came to the opposite conclusion. Based on the preparatory discussions related to the introduction of the 1970 Design Law and a reading of the expert opinions, the court reached the conclusion that the evaluation of the artistic efforts should be rather stringent in order to confer copyright protection. Prior art indicates the existence of torches with a similar configuration to the Mini-Maglite. Even if Mini-Maglite conferred a pleasant total impression, this was not enough to satisfy the rather stringent requirements necessary to protect a work of artware.

Högsta domstolen[83] (the Swedish Supreme Court) reversed Hovrätten. It held that before 1970 the required expression level for copyright protection was low. With the introduction of the design legislation and the elimination of the specific 10 year protection for artware under the Copyright Act, artistic requirements had increased. The same requirements should apply as they did to other artistic works. The copyright protectable work had to be personal and involve an artistic presentation and the risk for independent double-creation must be limited. The court underlined the need for 'generosity' for artware since configuration alternatives were often limited[84] and balanced increased protection against a limited scope.[85]

decision was confirmed. Mini-Maglite had an artistic independent and original configuration. The institute underlined that functional considerations did not prevent copyright. With respect to a torch the possible forms are infinite.

[80] The law only refers to words like 'create' and 'works'. The preparatory works (SOU 1956:25 p 66) adds as a fundamental criterion 'a certain level of independence and originality'. As a rule of thumb it should be considered was whether it was conceivable that the same work would be produced by two persons independently – 'a double-creation-test'.

[81] Helsingborgs Tingsrätt (District Court), Case T 1696-99, n 75.

[82] Hovrätten över Skåne och Blekinge (Appellate Court), Case T 916-05, n 77.

[83] Högsta domstolen, Case T 1421-07, n 2.

[84] Ref to preparatory works: Prop 1969:168 pp 134 ff and SOU 1965:61 pp 210 ff.

[85] The Supreme Court also referred to the fact that computer programs, photographs and databases were covered by copyright if the result was original and a personal creation.

According to the Court, past case law had allowed copyright for designs since design protection has not been sufficient to protect certain works. Copyright should give incentives to competent and serious designers and at the same time create an obstacle to far-reaching passing off and copying. The protection did not just cover outright imitations but also other configurations which were strikingly similar.

The Court agreed that liberal application of copyright protection might affect the competitive climate. This was, however, the aim and anticipated result of the exclusivity copyright. Protection should cover the right to produce copies and make available to the general public the protected work in its original, or an altered form. A work should be worthy of protection, based on its originality, independence and uniqueness. The Court concluded that the required expression level had been lowered over time. When a product satisfies these requirements without expressing any higher level of originality the scope of protection is limited to pure copy protection.

The Mini-Maglite design was held by the Court to be new, but a new barrel-shaped lamp could not be protected as such. None of the elements could independently be regarded as new or original. It resembled earlier bigger torches. In spite of this, the Mini-Maglite gave a different overall impression, which was a sufficient expression of independence in relation to its prior art. The configuration was more than trivial and not the result of routine efforts. It was more than a functional object and had acquired its own identity with a consistent and balanced design. The Mini-Maglite deserved copyright protection – even if it was a borderline case.

5. DISCUSSION AND CONCLUSION

Intellectual and industrial property rights are exceptions to the fundamental freedom to trade in an unrestricted and competitive market. Like all exceptions they should be narrowly interpreted.

No one denies that Mr Maglica, with his Mini-Maglite, has created a uniquely elegant and highly functional mini torch. This torch has unquestionably won consumer acceptance and become a worldwide market success sold in the millions. Mr Maglica's design development is, as the Swedish Supreme Court puts it, worthy of protection.

The question is, however, what type of protection? Is it an invention that should be the subject of the 20-year patent protection? Is it rather, a shape that should be design protected for some 20 to 25 years? Or is the shape a sign, which identifies the origin of the product and should thus be trademark protected for renewable periods of 10 years at a time? Yet again, is it an expression of a personal idea subject to copyright protection during Mr Maglica's lifetime plus another 70 years? Can Mini-Maglite benefit from unfair competition laws, including marketing laws or common law rules on passing off, to prevent imitations? Or is it, as Mag seems to infer, possible to use all of these rules to make the protection evergreen and fend off competition for a basically unlimited period?

Mag Instrument has been active in different fora and invoked one or the other sets of legislation based on the specific situation and the circumstances of the case. The overall impression is that much effort has been put into creating an ever greening strategy and it is noteworthy that Mr Maglica himself spends considerable time in courts as a witness testifying to the personal artistic efforts that he has put into the design of his mini torch.

From a legal perspective it seems clear that some of the Mini-Maglite functional elements satisfied patent requirements and such protection has been available and granted in the USA.[86] In addition, there is little doubt that the shape of the torch is such that it could have been protected by design legislation if that option were to have been chosen. The combination of these two sets of protections would have granted Mini-Maglite strong protection, (also covering equivalent or similar products), during a 20-25 year period and allowed Mag to capitalize from its original and creative work. Thereafter both the creative invention and the original shape would have been open to future competitors. That is the trade-off created by industrial property rights.

In addition, the Mini-Maglite today also most likely benefits from acquired trademark protection for its overall appearance. Functional features are not included and considering the design alternatives for a barrel-shaped mini torch, not too much should be required to come outside the trademark protected area. It is not the product, a small torch that is protected, but the specific form – perhaps the tulip-shaped head – which should be subject to protection. The protection should, in theory, be very restricted, only covering direct copying of the non-functional form elements.

Can an idea or a form, which has been protected by patents or designs, also invoke unfair trade rules after the expiration of this protection? The argument could at least be made that the originator should be entitled to benefit from form protection under other laws only if she has forgone patent and design protection. Conceptually, a matter that was protected by IPR during a defined period of time should thereafter be free and open to everyone – even for exact copies. Like trademark protection, the potential protection granted by unfair trade laws must also be very narrow, only covering intentional direct copying of all the formal elements with the intention of deceiving customers. The general 'informed customer's quick look test' appears to be much too general to be workable. It is only the precise, slavish imitation of the product with the intention to mislead that should be subject to protection once patents or design protections have expired. Otherwise the scope of the protection would be too far-reaching.

[86] As stated above, the ITC Decision originally invalidated the patent, but the decision was reversed. Rumour has it, that there were a number of other problems involved with the patent, but they have not been verified.

Customer protection may sometimes have to yield to the fundamental interest of unfettered competition and free access.

Mag never applied for patent or design protection in Sweden. The Swedish Supreme Court, however, provided Mag with far-reaching protection for the overall configuration based on Swedish copyright legislation. According to the Court, serious designers are entitled to protection not always granted by design legislation. The Supreme Court emphasised that it was a borderline case and that none of the individual elements were protectable. It, however, emphasized that the overall impression created by the torch merited protection. The wisdom of this approach can be questioned. Of course, serious designers are entitled to the protection provided by the design legislation. If the effort is not serious it is probably not protectable. The design legislation has struck a reasonable balance and providing additional protection by reference to copyright seems misplaced. Furthermore, the overall impression of Mini-Maglite is that of a small torch and chances are that other mini-torches will, at a glance, give the same overall impression in spite of the fact that there are differences in the detail. Indeed the Bundesgerichtshof did not accept this view and the detailed differences were what prevented copyright protection in Germany.

There is much to be said in favour of the German approach. It is odd to protect a functional torch as an artistic item. It is an industrially mass-produced item and should be protected as such for a reasonable period of time. It is more natural to reserve copyright protection for artistic efforts of an individualized character and not subject to mass production. Mass production could even be fixed numerically.[87] The artistic expression requirements should be substantially higher than for design protection.

It is interesting to note that a number of Swedish academics have provided conflicting views on how high the expression requirements for independence, originality and creativity should be set. Swedish case law during the last century also leads to diverging results. Uncertainties create obstacles for further development and trade. It is the excessively long term copyright protection that causes problems.[88] On this view, unregistered copyright protection should only apply in restrictive circumstances for individualised products, which have not been subject of mass production and where there is little doubt that both subjective and objective elements confirm an artistic expression.

Mini-Maglite has been mass-produced. A product like the Mini-Maglite should be entitled to the exclusivity provided by industrial property rights for a

[87] This solution was considered in Sweden but refused in the end as the 50 piece figure chosen was arbitrary; the solution did not fit Swedish tradition; and would deny copyright protection in certain clearly protectable situations. See SOU 1965:61 at p 204.

[88] These uncertainties also pose problems for music, information technology, telecommunications and biotechnology.

period of 20–25 years, but this ought to disqualify it from copyright protection. It also appears reasonable to protect the Mini-Maglite from slavish imitation where competitors' use of the precise form and other marketing activities which mislead the public. Trademark protection in combination with unfair trade laws provides this protection, but it is important that the focus is on whether the circumspect customer is misled, rather than on protecting an intellectual or artistic effort. Usually some clear marking of the product, like 'Design and Quality IKEA of Sweden, Made in Taiwan', should be sufficient to avoid consumer confusion.

European Harmonization Is Required

Uncertainties and conflicting European judgments are of major concern and create obstacles for trade in a single European market. Maglite amply demonstrates the problem. In Sweden Maglite benefits from what may appear as an evergreen protection against copying where the copy would present the same overall impression. In other countries the protection may be non-existent or very narrow.

If a near copy of the well-known US mini-torch is advertised over the internet for sale in the Community and the case brought in Sweden, should the Swedish court apply 27 sets of European copyright legislation to determine the lawfulness of the sale?[89] The task is overwhelming. As we have seen, the problems arising from applying the different relevant laws in one Member State are already challenging enough.[90] The litigation tangle becomes exorbitant if copyright claims must also be litigated along with patent, design and trademark infringement claims.[91]

It is therefore natural to propose that the core of copyright law must be harmonized on a European level. It is likely that more countries than Sweden have had an eye on the Berne Convention and the fact that copyright protection

[89] Council Regulation 44/2001/EC of 22 December 2000 on jurisdiction and the recognition and enforcement of judgments in civil and commercial matters, OJ 2001 L 12/1, Art 2(1) (Persons domiciled in a Member State shall be sued in the courts of that Member State.) Cf Regulation 864/2007 of the European Parliament and the Council of 11 July 2007 on the law applicable to non-contractual obligations, OJ 2007 L 199/40 ('Rome II'). Art 8 (2) states that: 'In the case of a non-contractual obligation arising from an infringement of a unitary Community intellectual property right, the law applicable shall, for any question that is not governed by the relevant Community instrument, be the law of the country in which the act of infringement was committed.'

[90] As indicated earlier, different courts in Sweden handle IPR infringements and unfair trade rules and may very well end up with conflicting outcomes. Patent cases regarding infringement and patent cases regarding invalidity are also initiated and tried in separate courts in many countries.

[91] European harmonization efforts as found in Directive 2004/48/EC of the European Parliament and of the Council of 29 April 2004 on the enforcement of intellectual property rights, OJ 2004 L 157/45 are not sufficient to address the problems. The directive basically satisfies TRIPS enforcement requirements, but offers little assistance where the substantive laws of the Member States differ.

in one country will not be extended to another if the originating country does not grant the same protection for artware. It is only through a coordinated joint effort that a reasonable result can be achieved.

Fundamental rules on competition and free movement of goods require that the same protection be available in different countries. It should not be possible to utilise inequalities in national intellectual property legislation to upset competition rules or to prevent the free circulation of products in the European market.

It may be possible to achieve a coordinated result where outstanding artware and design would receive protection against copying similar to that granted for other creative intellectual efforts. The lifetime plus seventy year rule should – if at all applicable – be reserved for cultural features with limited commercial impact.

9
Swedish Copyright Law Ends The Pirate Bay

JUR DR JONAS LEDENDAL

1. INTRODUCTION

The Pirate Bay trial has attracted a great deal of media attention around the world. Prior to the judgment, Swedish copyright law had come under attack for being unable to deal with Internet piracy and file sharing in particular. Although there are some objective reasons for claiming that Swedish copyright law might be 'less supportive to copyright owners than most of its neighbours', the main problem has been lack of enforcement.[1] The harsh verdict in The Pirate Bay case probably ended the view of Sweden as a haven for pirates. However, it has also been suggested that the verdict helped the Swedish Pirate Party ('Piratpartiet') to gain new members and win a seat in the European Parliament. Whereas it is often predicted that file sharing will bring an end to copyright law, the real question is whether Swedish copyright law has indeed managed to end The Pirate Bay. This article begins with the factual and technical background of the case. It then examines the central issues concerning contributory infringement under Swedish copyright law as treated by the district court in The Pirate Bay case. It is submitted that the district court judgment leaves some loose ends behind which, during the pending appeal, should be given more attention by the court.

2. FACTUAL BACKGROUND

The Pirate Bay (TPB) is a web site that features indexing and tracking of computer files, which can be shared using the BitTorrent protocol (see section 3 below on Technical Background). Files can technically be of any type and

[1] J Rosén, 'Copyright Control in Sweden and Internet Uses – File Sharers' Heaven or Not?' (2008) 2 *Nordic Intellectual Property Law Review* p 95.

content, but the most common files indexed on or shared using The Pirate Bay BitTorrent tracker are films, music and computer programs. The site was originally founded by the Swedish anti-copyright organization Piratbyrån in 2003.[2] In 2004, the site was transferred to a separate organization. The domain name 'thepiratebay' was registered in the top domains '.org', '.com' and '.net' by PRQ Internet Kommanditbolag (PRQ), a company owned by Fredrik Neij and Gottfrid Swartholm Warg.

In the beginning, operations were relatively modest and the site mainly targeted Swedish users.[3] In October 2004, Mr Neij and Mr Swartholm Warg came into contact with Swedish businessman Carl Lundström. Mr Lundström, the founder of telecom company Rix Telecom AB (Rix Telecom), proposed to them that they host two servers at his company's premises, giving The Pirate Bay access to more Internet bandwidth.

According to the prosecutor's indictment, Mr Lundström, Mr Neij and Mr Swartholm Warg further agreed to cooperate on the internationalization of the site and its tracker function. Mr Lundström was to provide additional computer hardware, Internet bandwidth and financial funding. The cooperation involved a company in which Mr Neij and Mr Swartholm Warg were to own 30 per cent respectively and Mr Lundström 40 per cent.[4] Mr Lundström has denied this involvement in TPB, admitting only that his company rented Internet access to PRQ on commercial terms, which are no different from those offered to Rix Telecom's other customers.[5]

It was during the internationalization and commercialization of the site that the fourth defendant, Mr Sunde Kolmisoppi, became engaged in the operations. Mr Sunde Kolmisoppi, by way of his company HAIQ Sweden AB (HAIQ), was contracted to design of the web site and its search function. Mr Swartholm Warg also got in contact with Oded Daniel, who was to sell advertisements for the site. In June 2005, the new web site was deployed. In July of the same year, the Swedish Copyright Act was amended to implement Directive 2001/29/EC of the European Parliament and of the Council of 22 May 2001on the harmonisation of certain aspects of copyright and related rights in the information society (the Infosoc directive).[6] In an e-mail to Mr Swartholm Warg, Mr Lundström expressed his concerns that the July amendment would make The Pirate Bay illegal, suggesting that the operations should be moved to another country. Mr Lundström also had contacts with the Swedish embassy and a lawyer concerning the possibility of moving The Pirate Bay to Argentina. However, the site continued to operate from Sweden.

[2] The District Court Judgment, March 17, 2009 (B 13301-06) (hereinafter the TPB Judgement), para 42.

[3] Ibid at para 29.

[4] Ibid at para 30.

[5] Ibid at para 20.

[6] Directive 2001/29/EC of the European Parliament and of the Council of 22 May 2001 on the harmonisation of certain aspects of copyright and related rights in the information society, implemented in Swedish law by (SFS 2005:359).

On the initiative of Mr Daniel, a company, Random Media, was formed by Mr Neij, Swartholm Warg, and Sunde Kolmisoppi in 2005. Transworld Advertising Group, represented by Mr Daniel, invested US $40 000 in the company, and the three defendants contributed the web sites that they controlled. A fourth party, who remained unnamed in the agreement, but was referred to as the 'hoster', was also to receive 8.25 per cent of the stock in Random Media.[7] The agreement was signed, but the defendants have disputed that it was never carried out.

Transworld Advertising Group continued to sell advertising on The Pirate Bay during 2005 and 2006. Payments for 'purchase of media' were made to Mr Swartholm Warg, Mr Neij, and to Morca AG, a company wholly owned by Mr Lundström. The defendants have disputed that all such payments were related to The Pirate Bay. The right to sell advertisements in the Nordic countries was held by Crystone AB and Eastpoint Media AB. Invoicing for these companies was prepared by Mr Sunde Kolmisoppi's company HAIQ.[8]

On May 31, 2006 the Swedish police raided the premises where The Pirate Bay's servers were located seizing servers and other equipment. Prior to the raid, plaintiff companies had secured evidence by performing several downloads of films and music recordings using torrent files found on The Pirate Bay.[9] The extensive police investigation that followed eventually led to an indictment in January 2008. In 2009, the District court delivered its verdict, finding the four defendants guilty of contributory infringement of copyright. The Pirate Bay moved to a new service provider and was operational within days of the verdict. In 2009, the court ordered the service provider (Black Internet AB) to shut down the site. On appeal the Appeals Court (Svea Hovrätt) affirmed the preliminary injunction.[10] The district court's ruling in the original Pirate Bay case has also been appealed by both defendants and plaintiffs, and is pending trial in the Court of Appeals.

3. TECHNICAL BACKGROUND

Technology plays an important part in the TPB judgment. The Pirate Bay is built around the BitTorrent protocol. BitTorrent is a peer-to-peer file sharing protocol, which is primarily used for distribution of large data files. Both the BitTorrent protocol and peer-to-peer file sharing are commonly associated with illegal distribution of copyright protected films and music recordings, but the technology as such has many other applications. BitTorrent technology is constantly improving. This technical background focuses on describing BitTorrent technology as it relates to The Pirate Bay judgment. Technologies

[7] TPB Judgment at paras 30–32.
[8] Ibid at paras 32–33.
[9] Ibid at paras 33–34.
[10] Court of Appeal Decisions, May 21, 2010 (Ö 7131-09, Ö 8773-09 and Ö 10146-09).

like distributed trackers ('trackerless torrents'), peer exchange (PEX) and other features are now commonplace in most BitTorrent clients.

Client-server

centralised structure

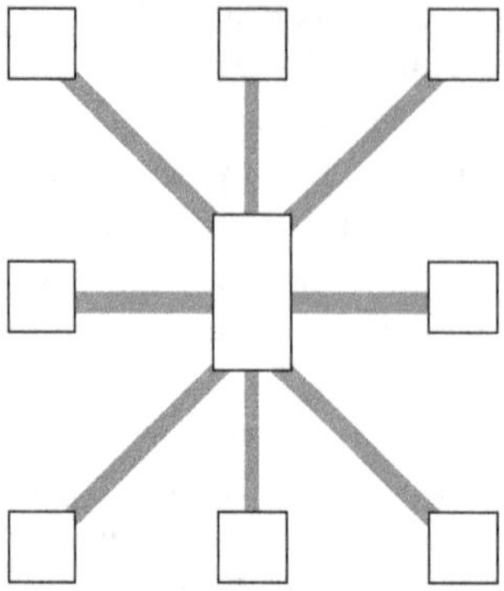

Client receives file sequentially from central server.

Peer-to-peer

decentralised structure

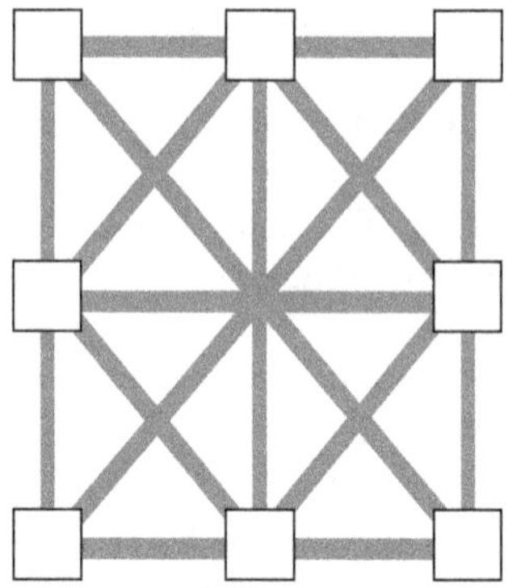

Peer receives file out of order in small parts from different peers, and reciprocates by sending parts that it has already received to other peers.

The main difference between traditional client-server file sharing and peer-to-peer file sharing is that the latter conserves network bandwidth at the source. In a client-server-based file sharing network all resources, including bandwidth, is provided to client computers by a centralized server. The centralized nature of the network causes resources to be depleted as more clients connect to the server. Eventually the system will come to a halt as system resources dry up. The cost of providing access in a client-server-based network increases with the number of concurrent users. The cost accrues at the server-side of the network. To service more users, the supplier must ultimately purchase more system resources like bandwidth. The collaborative nature of peer-to-peer file sharing spreads this cost across all users of the network.

Supply of large files in a peer-to-peer network therefore becomes relatively inexpensive. The technological progress made by peer-to-peer file sharing protocols also affects the natural monopoly that exists in distribution of large files like digital films, sound recordings or computer games. The prohibitively large investments in servers and bandwidth that are necessary to distribute large quantities of data in a client-server network are mitigated by peer-to-peer file sharing to an extent where small companies or even individuals can compete with large film and music distributors. This is unrelated to the fact that many individuals use this possibility to distribute copyright protected material illegally.

The BitTorrent protocol is merely one type of peer-to-peer file sharing protocol, but it is currently the most widely used for distribution of large files over the Internet. BitTorrent was created by Bram Cohen in 2001.The protocol uses three related components: a torrent file (also simply known as a 'torrent'), a BitTorrent client and a BitTorrent tracker. A BitTorrent client is a computer program that implements the BitTorrent protocol. A client constitutes a peer in the peer-to-peer network. In order to know how to connect to other peers the client needs to contact a BitTorrent tracker. The tracker is a centralized server that keeps track of peers and tells the client which other peers have data that the client is interested in downloading.

Hence, the tracker is using a client-server-based model to connect peers. Trackers have the same problems as other client-server networks. Popular trackers eventually run out of system resources. However, the tracker does not distribute any files, so each client only uses a minimum of resources like network bandwidth. Once the client has established a connection to another peer, the tracker is no longer needed. The distribution of the file as such only takes place between the peers that are interested in the file (the 'swarm').

The peers that take part in the 'swarm' exchange data by requesting and sending data in small parts between different machines. Hence, unlike a client-server network the whole file is not sequentially downloaded from the same source. A peer can start sharing a piece of data as soon as it has received it. Pieces are shared in a rarest-first or random order to ensure high availability. The more pieces a peer has received the more efficient it becomes as an uploader. The original uploader (also known as the 'original seeder') must only ensure that a sufficient number of other peers have as many pieces of the file as possible. When enough other peers have the ability to upload ('seed') the file to other peers, the BitTorrent network becomes very efficient. Hence, all clients taking part in a 'swarm' are both uploaders and downloaders.

The BitTorrent tracker participates in establishing a connection between peers, but it does not participate in the transfer of actual content. However, the BitTorrent protocol does not include any indexing of files. Clients cannot use the tracker to search for a specific file. The tracker understands the concept of a torrent and keeps track of which computers that take part in a torrent. The tracker does not know anything about the content that is being shared. This information is stored in torrent files. A torrent file consists of info, meta-data and the Internet address of the tracker. The info section contains a list of files, their names and lengths, file pieces and piece length. The torrent file also contains a checksum for each file piece. The checksum of a particular piece is later compared to the recorded checksum to test that the piece is error-free.

A user who wants to download a file must first obtain a torrent file, which informs the client software where to look for other peers that have that particular file or pieces of the file. The torrent file can be obtained from any source. However, a number of web sites provide indexing and uploading of torrent files to facilitate the exchange of torrent files. The Pirate Bay is such an indexing site, which also provides a tracker. The torrent file contains no actual content and only works as an indirect link to the downloadable content. Providing access to torrent files is analogous to telling someone where the file can be located. Users who want to share files using BitTorrent must create a torrent file and upload it to a site that indexes torrent files, or to another web site.

Ordinary search engines can be used to locate torrent files almost as efficiently as specialized torrent indexing sites. For example, files indexed by sites like The Pirate Bay show up as part of Google search results using keywords like 'torrent [name of a movie]'. An important aspect of contributory copyright infringement analysis is where to draw the line. It has been suggested that the standard of proof in the TPB case could very well include use of evidence of the activities of general search engines. However, the main difference between, for example, Google and The Pirate Bay is that Google merely locates torrent files and does not provide a tracker. The TPB judgment is not clear as to whether the objective side of the offence of contributory infringement is completed by providing only the first step in facilitating file sharing of copyright protected material.

4. THE DISTRICT COURT JUDGMENT

In January 2008, the public prosecutor charged Fredrik Neij, Gottfrid Swartholm Warg, Peter Sunde Kolmisoppi and Carl Lundström with contributory infringement of copyright and preparations to commit infringement of copyright.[11] The right holders, six Swedish record companies, two Nordic and five U.S. film companies also brought actions against the defendants claiming damages amounting to € 2,118,071 and SKR 99,800,080.[12] The District Court found the defendants guilty of contributory infringement, but not of preparation to commit infringement. The court sentenced the four defendants to one year of imprisonment each and awarded the plaintiffs damages in excess of 30 million SKR.[13]

4.1 Direct infringement

The court found that the works and recordings in suit were protected by copyright or neighbouring rights under the Swedish Copyright Act,[14] and that the plaintiffs had provided sufficient proof of ownership of the copyright in these works and recordings. The defendants had not disputed these facts.[15] The defendants had, however, disputed that the prosecutor and the plaintiffs had managed to provide evidence that the copies, which were made available through

[11] TPB Judgment, paras 26 ff.
[12] Ibid at para 40 ff.
[13] Ibid at para 1.
[14] Lag om upphovsrätt till litterära och konstnärliga verk; Act on Copyright in Literary and Artistic Works (No 729, of December, 30, 1960) (SFS1960:729).
[15] Ibid at paras 53–55.

The Pirate Bay, were illegal. None of the direct infringers had been identified. The defendants therefore argued that it could not be known whether a work or a recording was made available without permission of the rights holders.[16] The court, nevertheless, found that it had been demonstrated that the rights holders had not authorized the acts covered by the indictment.[17]

Regarding the question of whether the works and recordings had been made available to the public within the meaning of Article 2 of the Copyright Act, the court found that the manner in which the files had been handled by the original seeder and other users that had obtained those files, in part or in whole, had constituted communication to the public. Pursuant to Article 2, a copyrighted work is, *inter alia*, made available to the public when the work is being communicated to the public. This is deemed to include any making available of the work to the public by wire or by wireless means that occurs from a place other than that where the public may enjoy the work. Communication to the public also includes acts of communication that occur in such a way that members of the public may access the work from a place and at a time individually chosen by them. The court found that by being connected to the Internet and having their BitTorrent client software activated, users made it possible for other users to have access to files being shared and enabled them to make copies of these files. The court held that there was no substantial difference between such arrangements and making a file available for direct download.[18]

The indictment only covered the period from July 1, 2005 to May 31, 2006. Regarding the question of whether the works and recordings in suit had in fact been made available at the occasions specified in the indictment, the court found that it was sufficient that the prosecutor had proved that the works had been made available during a considerable extent of the time period in question. It had also been proved that the works had been made available at several occasions, when representatives of the rights holders had used The Pirate Bay to successfully download the works subject to the suit.

The court acknowledged the defendants' claim that counters available on the site were unreliable and did not give an accurate account of the total amount of downloads. Some downloads could have been initiated using torrent files that had been obtained from other sites than The Pirate Bay. In the event that such files had ultimately been shared using The Pirate Bay's BitTorrent tracker, the court still held such acts to be relevant to the direct infringement in question. The court found that, although the exact number of files that had been made available through The Pirate Bay's file sharing service could not be established, it had been demonstrated that a very large number of files had been made available in relation to the time period.[19]

[16] Ibid at paras 35–36.
[17] Ibid at para 55.
[18] Ibid at paras 55–56.
[19] Ibid at paras 56–60.

The applicability of Swedish criminal law requires that the direct infringement has been completed in Sweden. Regarding this question, the court found that when the infringement constitutes of making the work available to the public, it is sufficient that a copyright-related effect of the act occurred in Sweden. In the opinion of the court, the material was made available in any country from which an Internet user had access to the material. The hosting of the file sharing service and the fact that the service was available in Swedish further underlined that the infringement had been completed in Sweden.[20]

4.2 Contributory Infringement

Having established that direct infringement had been committed and that Swedish law was applicable to these acts, the court turned to the question of whether the defendants could be held liable for contributory infringement. Under Swedish copyright law contributory infringement requires proof of material contribution (the objective element of the crime) and intent (the subjective element of the crime). In relation to material contribution, the question was whether the defendants had aided direct infringers by making it possible for users to upload torrent files to The Pirate Bay's file sharing service, providing a searchable database of torrent files, and making it possible for users to download torrent files and establishing contact using The Pirate Bay's BitTorrent tracker. The question was also whether the defendants could be held jointly liable for the organization, administration, development, funding and operation of The Pirate Bay. In relation to proof of intent, the question was whether the defendants had knowledge of the direct infringement.

Regarding the question of material contribution, the court found that the activity, which constituted the organization of The Pirate Bay's file sharing service, amounted to a material contribution in relation to contributory infringement within the meaning of Swedish copyright law. The defendants had raised the objection that liability for contributory infringement was excluded when the direct infringer had not been identified. The court held that it was sufficient that the prosecutor had established that direct infringement had been materially completed. It was not necessary to identify the direct infringer. The court argued that liability for contributory infringement was not excluded due to insufficient proof of intent with regard to the direct infringer. Provided that a certain action had materially contributed to the direct infringement, the contributor could be held liable for contributory infringement. The court found that the file sharing services provided by The Pirate Bay had facilitated and hence contributed to the making available of copyright protected material.

It was also not required that the activity constituted a necessary condition for the direct infringement. Hence, it did not matter that the works and the

[20] Ibid at para 61.

recordings could potentially have been made available to the public using a file sharing service other than The Pirate Bay. The defendants had objected that their alleged contribution had not taken place before the direct infringement had been completed. The court found that the crime was in progress during the entire time the work was made available. The acts constituting the material contribution were therefore related to the time before the direct infringement had been concluded.[21]

Having established that operating the file sharing service constituted material contribution, the court had to determine whether each of the defendants had taken such part in the operation that they could be held jointly liable for the contributory infringement. For the parties to have joint liability, they must have held such a position within the organization that they can be held responsible for the enterprise, and that each had knowledge (intent) about the activities that constitute the direct infringement and the material contribution.

The court noted that when several persons contribute to the performance of a crime, it is sometimes hard to determine whose actions caused the criminal effect. The nature of contributory infringement is such that no one person has committed all of the acts necessary to complete the crime. In such circumstances, all of the persons involved in the criminal activity can be held liable for the crime, provided that they acted in cooperation and with mutual understanding. The question was whether each of the defendants had taken part in the facilitation of making the works available to the public. The court found that Mr Neij and Mr Svartholm Warg had taken such a part in the operations of the file sharing service. Mr Sunde Kolmisoppi and Mr Lundström disputed having taken such part in the site that they could be held liable for facilitating the direct infringement. The court found that the latter, nevertheless, had been able to influence the development and funding of the file sharing service so that they could be held jointly responsible with the other defendants. The defendants' activities were characterized by collaboration where each member had knowledge of the other's actions.[22]

Having determined that each of the defendants had intent, which covered the objective element of the facilitation (contribution), the court had to determine whether each of the defendants also had intent to infringe. The defendants disputed that they had knowledge of the illegal material that was shared using The Pirate Bay. Citing a recent criminal tax case,[23] the court held that knowledge of each specific infringement was not required. It was sufficient that the contributor knew of the existence of copyright protected material being file shared on the site. It was obvious that the defendants knew of the fact that the web site and the tracker were used to illegally distribute copyright protected material. The defendants had received several cease-and-desist letters from

[21] Ibid at paras 62–64.
[22] Ibid at paras 64–68.
[23] NJA 2007 p 929 (Nytt juridiskt arkiv).

rights holders, including the plaintiffs. The Pirate Bay had become notorious for posting such letters and its reply on the web site. Despite this knowledge neither of the defendants had taken any measure to prevent the direct infringement. The court concluded that they had cooperated in such a manner as to constitute contributory infringement of copyright.[24]

4.3 Preparation to Commit Infringement of Copyright

The TPB indictment also included allegations of preparation to commit infringement of copyright. Pursuant to Chapter 23 Section 2 of the Swedish Penal Code ('Brottsbalken')[25], anyone who, with the intention of committing or promoting a crime, presents or receives money or anything else as pre-payment or payment for the crime or who procures, constructs, gives, receives, keeps, conveys or engages in any other similar activity with poison, explosive, weapon, picklock, falsification tool or other such means, shall, in cases where specific provisions exist for the purpose, be sentenced for preparation of crime unless he is guilty of a completed crime or attempt. The court found that the torrent files could be used as means to commit a crime, but held that liability for preparation was consumed by the completed contributory infringement offence.[26]

4.4 Exemptions from Liability Pursuant to the Act on Electronic Commerce

The defendants had raised the defence that pursuant to the Swedish Act on electronic commerce, they could not be held liable for the direct infringement committed by The Pirate Bay's users. The Act provides exemptions from liability for service providers.[27] The defendants claimed that The Pirate Bay was a service provider in the meaning of the Act on electronic commerce.[28] The Act is based on Directive 2000/31/EC on electronic commerce.[29] Hence, Mr Lundström had also petitioned for a reference for a preliminary ruling by the European Court of Justice (CJEU).[30] The Directive provides exemption from liability only in cases where the activity of the information society service provider is limited to the technical process of operating and giving access to a communication network over which information made available by third parties is transmitted or temporarily stored, for the sole purpose of making the

[24] Ibid at paras 68–69.

[25] English translation available at http://www.sweden.gov.se/sb/d/3926/a/27777.

[26] TPB Judgment at paras 72–73.

[27] Lagom elektronisk handel och andra informationssamhällets tjänster (SFS 2002:562).

[28] Ibid at paras 73 ff.

[29] Directive 2000/31/EC of the European Parliament and of the Council of 8 June 2000 on certain legal aspects of information society services, in particular electronic commerce, in the Internal Market. OJ L 178 , 17/07/2000 P. 0001 – 0016.

[30] TPB Judgment at para 76.

transmission more efficient. This activity is of a merely technical, automatic and passive nature, which implies that the information society service provider has neither knowledge of nor control over the information which is transmitted or stored.

The court found that The Pirate Bay constituted an information society service provider in the meaning of Article 2 of the Act on electronic commerce, but held that the exemptions from liability in Articles 16–19 were not applicable. The exemption in Article 16 is applicable to services that consist of the transmission in a communication network of information provided by a recipient of the service, or the provision of access to a communication network ('mere conduit'). The exemption in Article 17 is applicable to services that consist of the transmission in a communication network of information provided by a recipient of the service, where the storage of that information, is performed for the sole purpose of making more efficient the information's onward transmission to other recipients of the service upon their request ('caching'). Article 18 is applicable to storage of information provided by a recipient of the service ('hosting'), whereas Article 19 is applicable to both transmission and storage. Pursuant to the provisions of Article 19 liability requires intent.[31]

The Pirate Bay file sharing services did not constitute temporary or automatic storage or storage made for the sole purpose of making more efficient the information's onward transmission to other recipients of the service upon their request. The court found that the type of service that The Pirate Bay was providing was consistent with the kind of hosting that is specified in Article 18 of the Act on electronic commerce. Exemption from liability is available when such a service provider does not have actual knowledge of illegal activity or information and, as regards claims for damages, is not aware of facts or circumstances from which the illegal activity or information is apparent; or the provider, upon obtaining such knowledge or awareness, acts expeditiously to remove or to disable access to the information. The court held that that the defendants must have had such knowledge and did not act to prevent the illegal activity. Further the exemption in Article 19 was not applicable, because the court had already determined that the defendants were guilty of intentional contributory infringement.[32]

The court also held that the Swedish Act complied with the Directive on electronic commerce, and that a request for preliminary ruling was not necessary. The Swedish implementation of Article 14 of the directive had not resulted in any unclear points of law.[33]

[31] Ibid at paras 73 ff.
[32] Ibid at para 76.
[33] Ibid at para 77.

5. CONCLUDING REMARKS

The District court's ruling has been appealed by both the defendants and the plaintiffs. The appeals trial, which was originally scheduled to begin in November 2009, has been postponed due to allegations of judicial bias against several judges. These allegations have primarily centred on the question of whether membership in special interest organizations that are allegedly closely related to the rights holders figuring in the trial comes into conflict with judicial impartiality.[34] On this ground the defendants moved for a retrial, but the Court of Appeals found the trial judge had not been biased and denied retrial.[35] Allegations of conflict of interest continued in the Court of Appeals. Both the appeals judge and the chief judge were accused of being biased for previously having been members of the same organization. Allegations of judicial bias were also raised against a lay judge for being an employee of Swedish music service Spotify, which is a legal alternative to The Pirate Bay. In a decision, the Court of Appeals came to the conclusion that the two judges were not disqualified to preside over the case.[36] On appeal the Supreme Court affirmed the Appeals Court decision, making it possible for the appeals trial to continue.[37] The Court of Appeals, however, disqualified the lay judge based on judicial bias.[38] Further, whereas most Swedish legal scholars anticipated a guilty verdict, the ruling has been criticized for being too harsh. However, the District court's judgment also deserves scrutiny in other respects.

The central question of liability for contributory infringement deserves more attention from the Court of Appeals. It is the high number of alleged infringements that resulted in the severe punishment and the high award of damages and it is this high number that is the central issue in the case. Outcome would have been significantly different if the court had not allowed the evidence of direct infringement to be viewed on an aggregate basis. The problem is not that the law requires proof of intent on the part of the direct infringer, but that proof of the identity of the direct infringer must reasonably be part of the objective element of the crime.

Lack of relevant precedent makes it uncertain whether the court is allowed to treat this element on an aggregate basis. The principal objection against allowing this kind of evidence is that it might not be consistent with the high

[34] The trial judge is a member of Svenska Föreningen för Upphovsrätt (The Swedish Association for Copyright) and a board member of Svenska Föreningen för Industriellt Rättsskydd (The Swedish Association for Industrial Property), which are part of Association littéraire et artistique internationale (ALAI) and The International Association for the Protection of Intellectual Property (AIPPI). Members sponsoring these organizations have taken a stance against The Pirate Bay.

[35] The Court of Appeal (Svea Hovrätt) Decision, June 24, 2009 (B 4041-09); published in Judgements of the Court of Appeals as RH 2009:39.

[36] The Court of Appeal (Svea Hovrätt) Decision, June 24, 2009 (B 4041-09).

[37] The Supreme Court (Högsta domstolen) Decision, May 12, 2010 (Ö 5095-09).

[38] The Court of Appeal Decision, September 25, 2009 (B 4041-09).

standard of proof in criminal law. Further, the sources that the court cites in support of this argument are not conclusive. A more stringent assessment of the evidence, or rather the lack thereof could change the outcome of the case. A recent Court of Appeals decision, which reversed a district court ruling in a file sharing case based on insufficient evidence, suggests a potential move in that direction.[39] A change in attitude towards the use of aggregate evidence could potentially render Swedish copyright law a less effective weapon in the fight against Internet piracy.

[39] Court of Appeals (Svea Hovrätt), 2009-10-13, Ö Ä 6091-09, reversing the District Court's (Solna tingsrätt) decision, 2009-06-2, Ä 2707-09.

10

Illicit File Sharing and Intermediary Services Within the Framework of the E-Commerce Directive

ASSISTANT PROFESSOR KRISTOFFER SCHOLLIN

> Any harmonisation of copyright and related rights must take as a basis a high level of protection, since such rights are crucial to intellectual creation.[1]

> ... it would be really quite remarkable if the evolution of legal institutions concerning patents, copyrights, and trade secrets had somehow resulted in a set of instruments optimally designed to serve either public policy purposes or the private economic interests of individuals and firms seeking such protections.[2]

> Now, back to Rome for a quick wedding and some slow executions![3]

1. INTRODUCTION

The market for online access to music and movies in digital format is steadily growing. The form of services taking advantage of this growth is provoked and shaped by the existence of the diverse, and mostly illicit, ways that Internet users share these works of entertainment and culture amongst each other. The techniques for sharing files online are in constant flux and development, but one factor remains constant: there must be a point of

[1] Directive 2001/29/EC of the European Parliament and of the Council of 22 May 2001 on the harmonisation of certain aspects of copyright and related rights in the information society, OJ L 167, 22.6.2001, p 10–19 recital (9).

[2] PA David, 'Intellectual Property Institutions and the Panda's Thumb: Patents, Copyrights, and Trade Secrets in Economic Theory and History' in MB Wallerstein, ME Mogee, R A Schoen (eds), *Global Dimensions of Intellectual Property Rights in Science and Technology*, Office of International Affairs National Research Council (National Academy Press Washington 1993) p 21.

[3] F Melvin and M Pertwee, *A Funny Thing Happened on the Way to the Forum* (Quadrangle Films, 1966).

initial contact between the users. To this end there is a need for a 'Forum': an intermediary service where the supply and demand of uncountable estranged users can be coordinated and managed. Like the fora of the ancient world, the new Internet forums are teeming meeting spaces where all sorts of transactions are initiated and agreed. Technology has made them diverse, specialized and ephemeral to the point of frustration for those who attempt to create taxonomies, but their essential meeting- and handshaking-function remains unchanged.

The Internet site, the 'The Pirate Bay', provides one such forum and four men holding various positions in the site's administration have recently appealed the judgment of the Stockholm district court of April 2009 wherein they were found jointly guilty of accessory copyright infringement through their actions, inactions and the user connectivity provided by the site. Such forum sites are a common and popular phenomenon, though their value-offerings differ in the details. Sometimes they merely offer the users the ability to share links, sometime also they share larger files, or even make content viewable through direct streaming. Regardless, the selling point of forum sites lies in the contact they provide with other users.

Copyright law grants to its rights holder a position of exclusivity. Though this exclusivity is not without its exceptions, it does confer a strong controlling position when it comes to the use, reproduction and distribution of created works of art and entertainment. In these days of online distribution, the most economically important right is becoming that which governs the act of making the work available to the public through digital networks. In this case, Internet users who congregated in The Pirate Bay shared works in such a way that they were held to have communicated those works to the public. But their role is not the direct issue here. Rather, the case revolves around the middleman function: the intermediary physical or juridical person.

The Pirate Bay case has three major points of interest. How should we treat technologies and services that facilitate or assist in copyright infringements?[4] How should we calculate an equitable account of profits? And how do we estimate actual damage to the rights owners in the digital media landscape? To these three points was added a fourth one when the district court decided that the defendants should be considered joint perpetrators, thus fully sharing the responsibility for any secondary infringements.

When it came to the further issue of being an accessory to infringements the district court found that The Pirate Bay was an effective tool in sharing copyrighted material, that the defendants were aware that a large percentage of the site's users were committing illicit sharing of copyrighted material and that

[4] The term 'secondary infringement' will be used as a wide concept throughout this paper to cover all those actions that an intermediary service can perform, since they provide a technical platform which can be used in various ways by the primary infringer, including making infringing copies, making works available to the public or illicitly performing works.

the defendants held positions within The Pirate Bay such that they should be held responsible. Regrettably this does not assist the framing of guiding principles when it comes to distinguishing one Internet service from another as any CEO of an Internet search engine or user-driven site can quite easily fulfil these criteria. This conundrum is highlighted in Directive 2000/31 on electronic commerce in Europe[5] where the various services in the information society, such as search engines and data hosting-service are recognized as having a particularly important, but also complicated, role as mediators between the online users on the European common market. The directive tries to limit disincentives to the development of new Internet technologies having the potential for cross-border activity by providing a sort of safe harbour limitation on intermediary liability.

What needs exploring is that which is needed to allow differentiation between the different forms of middleman services that are used by users in committing intellectual property infringements. In the judgment of the district court, such things as the abrasive language and belligerent behaviour of The Pirate Bay are mentioned, as is the site's refusal to remove torrents despite being prompted to do so. Other factors in the case includes the absence of any notice and take down policy, the question of exactly how integral the service was to the principal infringements committed by the users, and certainly the level of knowledge of these principal acts that can be attributed to the middleman. While the focus lies on examining the liabilities of internet intermediary services under the E-Commerce Directive, this paper makes an effort to systematize criteria regarding both action and inaction as well as the technological capabilities that are relevant in accessory copyright piracy cases and, further, to come to terms with the idea of accessory infringement in an online, networked market. Finally, this paper notes a discrepancy of purpose between the E-Commerce Directive and the more recent IPR enforcement directive.

2. INFRINGING ACTS

2.1 The Primary Infringement

The typical primary copyright infringement takes place when two users illicitly share copyrighted material between themselves. Due to the nature of the technology they are most likely both illicitly copying the work and making it available to the public (see further below). Since the users on the network are typically strangers to each other and since the sharing is typically done in an open environment with hundreds of other users, the criteria of making the work

[5] Directive 2000/31/EC of the European Parliament and of the Council of 8 June 2000 on certain legal aspects of information society services, in particular electronic commerce, in the Internal Market. OJ L 178, 17.7.2000, p 1.

available to the public is quite easily fulfilled. In accordance with 2 § of the Swedish Copyright Act, an act of making a work available to the public entails making it available through with or without wires at a remote location where the public can take part of the work. This category of infringement was created in Swedish copyright legislation when the Act was updated in 1 July 2005. Typical examples include TV or radio transmissions, or making material accessible through the Internet.

The primary infringers were not heard in the case, being only known by their IP-addresses and their forum nom de plumes. No one contested the charge that these nameless individuals had illicitly made copyrighted material available to the public. Though the users making the work available were, to a large extent, not Swedish, or at least not located in Sweden at the time of making the material available, the district court deemed the infringement to have taken place in Sweden because the recipients of the work made available could be located in Sweden, due to the fact that the material was made available through the Internet.[6]

The other primary infringement charge was however dropped during the proceedings.[7] Though making an illicit copy of the work that has come via an open file sharing network is in principle an infringement, the documented copies that had been made in the process had been prepared by a person working for the prosecutor, and could not therefore have been made illicitly. Other copies made by other users were not documented.

2.2 Secondary Infringement

As a general rule, those who aid or abet the primary perpetrator of a crime can be found equally guilty. The main rule found in chapter 23, 4 § of the Swedish penal code is equally applicable to crimes outside of the penal code itself, where the penalty includes imprisonment; this includes copyright infringements. As with the primary offence, the secondary one has both an objective and a subjective requirement, both of which must be present in order for there to be an offence. The objective component requires the facilitation of the primary infringement to actually be effective. However, the level of effectiveness required is very low. For example in penal law, it suffices to hold someone's coat when that person is beating up a third party in order to be guilty of facilitating the assault.[8] The aiding, abetting or general facilitation of the primary act can be physical (by providing tools or assistance) or mental (by providing advice or encouragement). It is not required that the facilitation be a necessary

[6] The District Court Judgment, March 17, 2009 (B 13301-06) (the 'TPB Judgement'), at para 61.

[7] 2 § of the Swedish copyright act prohibits the illicit copying of the protected work in whole or in part. This is the action committed by the users who download, even if the copies are unfinished.

[8] See Swedish Supreme Court, case NJA 1963 s 574.

requirement for the primary infringement. All Internet intermediaries, such as search engines, hosting services, web hotels and Internet access providers are facilitating users' copyright infringements and fulfil the objective component.

The subjective requirement is twofold. First it requires secondary infringers to have some form of awareness of the primary infringement. Obviously, the intentionality of the secondary perpetrators must cover their own actions, meaning an awareness of the functionality of the service provided and how it can be put to use by their users. This – the first part of the subjective requirement – is also likely to be fulfilled by all the types of Internet intermediaries exemplified above.

But the intent must also extend to cover the acts of the primary crime.[9] This is the second part of the subjective requirement, entailing intent with respect to the concrete deed that constitutes the primary crime. Though it is necessary that the accessory be aware of there being an actual and concrete chain of events in which the facilitating actions constitute a part, it is not required that the facilitator's intent cover the course of actual events in precise detail, nor that he or she is aware of the identity of the primary perpetrators, nor is it even required that he or she understands that the primary deed is criminal in nature.[10] The second part of the subjective requirement therefore requires some degree of awareness on the part of the intermediary concerning the concrete deed whereby the primary infringers are illicitly making a copyrighted work available to the public. Here then stands revealed the rational watershed at which forums guilty of secondary infringements can be separated from those that are not.

As an aside, if one wants to make a better approach to secondary infringement, it is possible that a future interpretation of the second subjective requirement should focus not on the awareness of the concrete act, but rather on factors such as collusion and encouragement, as was done in the US Grokster case.

The US Grokster Case

In these days of constantly new, innovative technologies for communication, it is easy to get lost in the fascinating capabilities of the technology rather than the actual acts of facilitation or encouragement engaged in. In the case of a company manufacturing a piece of software that enabled the users to share files among themselves, the highest US Court ruled that it was the

[9] L Holmqvist, M Leijonhufvud, P-O Träskman and S Wennberg, *Brottsbalken En Kommentar Supplement* 20 (Norstedts juridik 2008) ('Holmqvist') paras 23:57–58.

[10] See Swedish Supreme Court, case NJA 2007 s 929, pp 939–40. The case concerned an individual who had withdrawn and deposited money as part of a tax evasion scheme. It was not shown that he was explicitly aware of being party to this crime, but he was obviously aware of withdrawing and handing over the money as well as being aware that his actions were a part of a larger deed and he must have been aware of the likelihood that this cash management was part of an activity intended to deprive the Swedish state of taxes and levies, a result as to which he showed indifference. See also Holmqvist at para 23:58.

behaviour of the company itself that amounted to an inducement to commit copyright infringement. The technology could have both infringing and non-infringing uses, and as such it was not in itself relevant to the rationale and outcome. The court held that: 'One who distributes a device with the object of promoting its use to infringe copyright, as shown by clear expression or other affirmative steps taken to foster infringement, is liable for the resulting acts of infringement by third parties'.[11]

Predictable Application of Law

The legal uncertainty surrounding secondary copyright infringement by intermediary services on the Internet raises the issue of legal predictability. Reading the 2004 correspondence between The Pirate Bay administrator and legal counsel representing a rights owner whose work had been linked to, it shows quite clearly that they were convinced that their activity was not illegal under Swedish Law. The uncertainty about the extent to which forums that do not in themselves post copyrighted material but do assist their users to infringe are liable certainly raises doubts on how far a court can go in applying penalties when it comes to precedent-setting cases in situations such as these. Law is a social construction, and its inherent mutability is most clearly displayed in cases where a court is asked to interpret old concepts so as to apply them in a new setting where technology has made deeds possible that were unthinkable at the time when the concepts were originally conceived. But this mutability also makes it difficult to predict decisions and outcomes under these novel circumstances.[12]

This uncertainty in itself poses a danger to technological innovation by providing potential legal troubles for entrepreneurs who wish to explore technology-based new businesses. Even entrepreneurs are averse to risk when it becomes too high. This leads us, after an initial review of how the Pirate Bay worked as a forum site, to the EC E-Commerce Directive, which aims to do away with (at least some of) this uncertainty for intermediary technologies and services.

3. THE PIRATE BAY DECONSTRUCTED

The capability of The Pirate Bay site on the Internet can be characterized by using a taxonomy of three types of capabilities: the technical capabilities, actions made by the users and actions committed by one or more of the principals of

[11] *Metro-Goldwyn-Mayer Studios Inc v Grokster, Ltd,* 545 US 913,918 (2005). See also Olsson, H *Copyright Svensk och internationell upphovsrätt* (Norstedts juridik 2006) p 319.

[12] U Petrusson, *Intellectual Property & Entrepreneurship: Creation of Wealth in an Intellectual Economy* (Center for Intellectual Property Studies 2004) pp 199–201. Petrusson stresses the extreme complexity that comes to light when legal concepts are to be honestly applied in new settings. When judges validate and accept intellectual claims, it may open matters up for the assertion of new interests.

The Pirate Bay. Making these distinctions is necessary if one is to judge an intermediary's position within the framework of the E-Commerce Directive below.

3.1 Technical Capabilities of BitTorrent in General

BitTorrent was developed in the United States and released for the first time in 2001. It is a free standard maintained by Bittorrent Incorporated, explaining a technical protocol for information-sharing via the Internet. Its model is of the peer-to-peer type, differentiated from the client-server type. The main difference between these types is that the information-sharing is a flow directly between the users (the peers), rather than through a central storage.

The efficiency advantage to BitTorrent is that it is not vulnerable to bottlenecks in distribution, something that normally occurs when a piece of popular information is only available through central storage. To avoid this, BitTorrent creates a distributed networking logic. It uses the other users who are also downloading the file to effectively act as servers to one another, simultaneously uploading the parts of the file received to others requesting the file. Hence, when downloading a file through BitTorrent, several connections will be made to allow reception of 'segments' of the file that combine to create the entire file. Meanwhile, as you are downloading these segments you are also uploading them to anyone else that needs the parts you are receiving. Once the entire file is received it is considered polite to keep your client connected to act as a seed. A 'seeder' refers to a user that has the entire file available.

Since each new user add storage and bandwidth of his or her own when they connect to the other users, the bottleneck problem is practically eliminated. This has made the protocol popular for large information-pushes, such as simultaneous global software updates of popular products. The protocol is also used by global communication services such as Skype, by public service broadcasting corporations such as Canadian CBC[13] or Norwegian NRK,[14] or by private companies such as CBS, Fox, Viacom or New York Times.

Torrent Links

In order to download a primary file[15] from another user, a file called 'a torrent' or 'a torrent link' is needed. This file provides a link to all the other users that

[13] See Canadian Broadcasting Corporation, *CBC to BitTorrent Canada's Next Great Prime Minister*. Available at www.cbc.ca/nextprimeminister/blog/2008/03/ canadas_next_great_prime_minis.html (last visited 23 July 2009).

[14] See NRK – Norwegian Public Service Corporation, *Norsk Rikskringkasting, On BitTorrent*. Available at http://nrkbeta.no/bittorrent (last visited 23 July 2009).

[15] The term primary file or primary work will be used to signify the material shared by the user so as to distinguish it from the torrent link files that are available through the intermediary Forum site.

have a copy of the same. Activating the link allows the user to participate in the sharing by connecting directly to other users. The torrent link is a very small file, easy to send by e-mail. It takes less than a second to download if the user has a standard Swedish broadband connection.

A group of users that have activated the same torrent is known as a 'swarm'. Users that only have the link and no part of the primary file yet cannot initially properly 'share', since they are only downloading. But once they have parts of the primary files downloaded, these parts will be shared with the other users.[16]

The Forum's Database

Any Internet user could (and still can) create a user identity on The Pirate Bay and upload a torrent link. The user can index the file by choosing from a number of headings, including 'movies', 'music' or 'TV-series'.

Any other Internet user can, without needing to create an identity, search the database by browsing it, or by entering keywords. As mentioned, downloading the torrent is a matter of seconds.

The Tracker Function

In order for a torrent file to successfully link up to other users, a tracker function is employed. The tracker in this case is an Internet computer on which the activation of a torrent is announced. As long as the torrent is active and the user is connected to the Internet, the tracker computer will show his or her address to other users who activate their copy of that torrent. Once the users find each other's addresses through the tracker service, their subsequent communication is done directly.

A torrent often makes its activation known on a variety of tracker services. The addresses for these are included inside the torrent itself.

3.2 Actions Taken by the Users

Creating Torrents

A user having access to the primary work in digital form creates a torrent file at his or her home computer. The process takes a matter of minutes, but can increase if the primary work is large, like an entire season of a TV series. The user also enters the addresses of one or more trackers. A torrent does in itself not contain any copyrightable matter. As explained above, it is a link to other users.

[16] Some users do use software that only pretends to share, but does not actually allow any uploading of data to the swarm. Such 'leeching' behaviour is frowned upon within the filesharing community.

Posting Torrents

Users add and index torrent files to the central database. This is done by choosing what headers to add the file under and entering into the database a personal description of what the torrent links to, or just a nonsensical message.

Downloading and Activating Torrents

Users search and download torrents from the forum's database. Once the torrent is downloaded onto the user's computer, it can be activated. In the same manner that normal web-links require a web-browser in order to perform their function, activating a torrent requires a BitTorrent client program in order to work. The BitTorrent Client is a piece of software that the user runs from his computer. Since BitTorrent is a freely available protocol, there are hundreds of available BitTorrent clients. Popular ones include mTorrent, Vuze, BitComet and many more.

3.3 Actions taken by the Principals

The determination of who is or was a principal of The Pirate Bay seems, in practice, quite hard to apply. Over the course of years, many different individuals seem to have had access to posting in the name of The Pirate Bay and to have had access to the html- and database-code that made up the site. The details may prove a headache to the police- and prosecutor authorities, but the principles remain the same.

Running and Maintaining the Database

At least some of the principals of The Pirate Bay ran and maintained the open database for torrent link files. Doing without any notice- and takedown policy, there was deliberately no screening or filtering of the torrents whatsoever. In 2008, a user posted a torrent file linking to the preliminary investigation concerning the murder of two children in Arboga, Sweden. The material contained autopsy photos. Even though it was within their power, the principals refused to remove the torrent. During the trial, the principals testified that they would remove a torrent only on grounds of misleading labelling by the users.

The principals behind The Pirate Bay are responsible for designing the database in the concrete form and shape it takes, with the current headings and categorizations, focusing largely on different kinds of media, such as movies, TV-shows and handheld media.[17] The system of categorization is updated sporadically.

[17] The main headings available to a user who wishes to enter a torrent into the database are: audio, video, applications, games, porn and other. Each main heading has a choice of up to nine sub-categories. For example the video heading includes: movies, movies dvdr, music videos, movie clips, TV shows, handheld, highres-movies, high res-TV shows, and other.

Running and Maintaining a Torrent Tracker

At least some of the principals of The Pirate Bay ran and maintained a tracker service that enabled torrent users to find each other in accordance with what was explained above.

Views and Opinions

The Pirate Bay posts texts regarding copyright, Internet and freedom of information. Often they have a very provocative attitude, quite critical of copyright and openly insulting to representatives of rights owners.[18] The most eloquent of the principals, Peter Sunde, has also, on numerous occasions, expressed his opinions on the issues at hand in television and newspapers.

Signals to the Users

The decision to call the site the 'The Pirate Bay', and the use of the pirate-ship logotype, are not without importance. Doubtlessly these send certain signals to the user collective that are, at least to some extent, an encouragement to post links to illicit material? Exactly how the term 'pirate' and other such signals sent out by the principals are being interpreted by the user collective at large has not been very well documented or studied.

3.4 A Causal Effect of Lawsuits on Technology Design?

Just as it is hard to imagine an iTunes without a Napster,[19] it is difficult to imagine DRM-free downloads or all-you-can-eat services such as Spotify without the existence of illicit peer-to-peer activity ('P2P'). While it is uncontroversial that unlawful services provide a powerful incentive to create new legal alternatives, the details of how this influence works are hard to research.[20] Even more

[18] K Schollin, *Digital Rights Management –The Future of Copyright* (PhD Thesis 2008) pp 105–107.

[19] Prior to the launch of Apple's iTunes Store, the big record labels were finding it very hard to sell any significant amount of music online. At the same time, they were finding increasing numbers of users were growing accustomed to downloading music without having any concept of paying for it. These desperate circumstances led them back to negotiations with Apple. Napster and its various offspring file sharing services were used as leverage by Apple Computer in their licensing negotiations with Universal, Sony BMG, Warner and EMI. The result was the iTunes music store, which practically created the music downloads business. See R Levine, 'Napster's Ghost Rises', *Fortune Magazine*, March 2006. Available at money.cnn.com/magazines/fortune/fortune_archive/2006/03/06/8370610/index.htm (last visited 27 July 2009). See also DE Dilger, 'Rise of the iTunes Killers Myth', *Roughly Drafted Magazine* (2007). Available at www.roughlydrafted.com/2007/10/13/rise-of-the-itunes-killers-myth (last visited 30 June 2009) for an overview of the climate for online music in the years 1998–2003.

[20] See L Barfe, *Where Have All the Good Times Gone? The Rise and Fall of the Record Industry* (Atlantic Books, 2005) pp 327–28.

intriguing, but possibly just as challenging to research, is how laws and legal actions directed at file sharing services are influencing the design of the next-generation file-sharing technologies. A project such as Washington University's OneSwarm[21], builds on the existing BitTorrent legacy but does away with the central Forum site and also adds a layer of privacy by obscuring all sources outside of your own circle of friends. Such technologies, while not directly targeted at copyright owners, will make it much harder to detect and track infringements.[22] In an interesting development regarding The Pirate Bay site, the brunt of the link collection was downloaded into one file, which was then itself shared through a torrent. In essence, each user could download their own archive of The Pirate Bay, or use the downloaded material to quickly set up an identical site on an internet server of their own choosing.[23] These centralization/decentralization effects seem to make for an exciting area of future research.

4. THE E-COMMERCE DIRECTIVE[24]

> It is important ... [to establish] ... a clear framework of rules relevant to the issue of liability of intermediaries for copyright and relating rights infringements at Community level.[25]

In order to do away with many of the uncertainties sketched above, the E-Commerce Directive has as one of its purposes the provision of additional clarity as to the accessorial position of Internet services acting as intermediaries.

4.1 Purpose: Free Movement of Information Services

Directive 2000/31/EC, also known as the EC E-commerce Directive, sets out to protect the growth potential of online trade and services. It is observed that the development of electronic commerce within the information society offers significant employment opportunities in the European Community, something that will stimulate economic growth and investment in innovation by European companies, and can also enhance the competitiveness of European industry.[26] The Directive recognizes the growth potential in the way information society

[21] Oneswarm.cs.washington.edu.

[22] See Oneswarm P2P Screencast, http://oneswarm.cs.washington.edu/screencasts_overview.html#screencast_overview.

[23] P Goss, 'Pirate Bay Clone Site Surfaces', *Techradar.com* Aug 20. Available at www.techradar.com/news/internet/pirate-bay-clone-site-surfaces-627692 (last visited 31 August 2009).

[24] Directive 2000/31/EC of the European Parliament and of the Council of 8 June 2000 on certain legal aspects of information society services, in particular electronic commerce, in the Internal Market OJ L 178 , 17/07/2000 P. 0001 – 0016.

[25] Directive 2000/31/EC, Recital (50).

[26] See Directive 2000/31/EC, Recital (2).

services makes it possible to commercialize goods and services through new business models and in new markets. However, the development of information society services within the Community is hampered by a number of legal obstacles to the proper functioning of the internal market, some of which make less attractive the exercise of the freedom of establishment and the freedom to provide services. These obstacles arise from divergences in legislation and from the legal uncertainty as to which national rules apply to such services.[27]

Legal Predictability for Information Services

It is the purpose of the E-Commerce Directive to move towards a legal framework that is clear, simple, predictable and consistent with the rules applicable at international level. This is in order to allow the unhampered development of electronic commerce. Otherwise it is feared that the uncertainty provided by an unpredictable legal framework will adversely affect the competitiveness of European industry or impede innovation in that sector.[28]

Definition of Information Society Services

The definition of information society services already exist in Community law in Directive 98/34/EC,[29] and in Directive 98/84/EC.[30] This definition covers any service normally provided for remuneration, at a distance, by means of electronic equipment for the processing (including digital compression) and storage of data, and at the individual request of a recipient of a service.

Certain services, referred to in the indicative list in Annex V to Directive 98/34/EC that do not imply data processing and storage, are not covered by this definition. Excluded are such services as are not provided either at a distance, by electronic means, or not supplied at the individual request of a recipient of services.

Recital (18) contains a more in-depth definition of what these services entail. Information society services span a wide range of online economic activities.

[27] Ibid Recital (5).

[28] Ibid Recital (60).

[29] Directive 98/34/EC of the European Parliament and of the Council of 22 June of 1998 laying down a procedure for the provision of information in the field of technical standards and regulations and of rules on information society services. OJ L 204, 21.7.1998, p 37. Directive as amended by Directive 98/48/EC OJ L 320, 5.8.1998, p 18. See point 2, Art 1: 'service': any Information Society service, that is to say, any service normally provided for remuneration, at a distance, by electronic means and at the individual request of a recipient of services.

For the purposes of this definition: 'at a distance': means that the service is provided without the parties being simultaneously present, 'by electronic means': means that the service is sent initially and received at its destination by means of electronic equipment for the processing (including digital compression) and storage of data, and entirely transmitted, conveyed and received by wire, by radio, by optical means or by other electromagnetic means, 'at the individual request of a recipient of services': means that the service is provided through the transmission of data on individual request.'

[30] Directive 98/84/EC of the European Parliament and of the Council of 20 November 1998 on the legal protection of services based on, or consisting of, conditional access.

These activities can, in particular, consist of selling goods on-line. Activities such as the delivery of goods as such or the provision of services off-line are not covered. Information society services are not solely restricted to services giving rise to on-line contracting but also, in so far as they represent an economic activity, extend to services that are not remunerated by those who receive them, such as those offering on-line information or commercial communications, or those providing tools allowing for search, access and retrieval of data. Information society services also include services consisting of the transmission of information via a communication network, in providing access to a communication network or in hosting information provided by a recipient of the service. Traditional television and radio broadcasting within the meaning of Directive EEC/89/552 are not information society services because they are not provided at the individual request of the recipient, though on-demand video services can be.

Recipients of these Services

The definition of 'recipient of a service' does cover all forms of usage of information society services, both by persons who provide information on open networks such as the Internet and by persons who seek information on the Internet for private or professional reasons.[31]

Liability of Intermediary Service Providers

Providers of information services play an important role in the development of the information society, and by extension of the rationale of the 2001/31/EC Directive an equally important role in the growth and innovation of the European market. Information collation services such as Google have become invaluable for consumers and corporations alike, as well as providing a valuable tool for academic research. Price comparison services have provided a revolutionary tool for consumers and helped bolster cross-border trade within the Common Market. Predicting the value of innovative services is hard due to the unpredictability inherent in innovation itself. Even harder is to predict how the recipients will make use of a certain service, or what value they will find in it. To add to this, information services are tools for the users' own purposes and as such they work as intermediary to a wide variety of activities. Additionally, these services invariably span multiple jurisdictions when the users are spread across different nations. 'Both existing and emerging disparities in Member States' legislation and case-law concerning liability of service providers acting as intermediaries prevent the smooth functioning of the internal market, in particular by impairing the development of cross-border services and producing distortions of competition.'[32] Thus we find the need for a clear, simple and

[31] Ibid Recital (20).
[32] Ibid Recital (40).

predictable legal framework that allows for the safeguarded development of information society services unhampered by the fear of unpredictable legal repercussions.[33] In particular this requires a safe harbour for service providers that act as intermediaries.

Section 4 of the 2001/32/EC Directive contains provisions to limit the liability of intermediary service providers for the information conduced or hosted for their customers. Articles 12 and 13 detail the situation where a service provides a 'mere conduit', a simple transmission of the information of its users with no residue or traces of the conduit. Internet service providers who simply furnish their users with an access to the Internet fall within this category. Temporary information storage, lasting no longer than what is reasonably necessary for the transmission, is considered as providing a mere conduit.[34] Article 13 regulates the situation of a service that is not a hosting service but may require pieces of information to be temporarily stored ('cached') for technical efficiency, though the purpose of this transient storage is to provide a transmission of information. The intermediate information storage in mind is automatic and temporary and covers such services provided by Internet service providers as well as information collation services, such as search engines. The latter case though is not entirely applicable since the cached information on a search engine's servers will very likely be modified by the service provider.[35]

Mere Conduit Services

Where the intermediary does not host the exchanged subject matter itself but simply transmits it onwards, or merely provides the access to the communication network in which the matter is exchanged, the service is considered as a mere conduit. Article 12 states:

> 1. Where an information society service is provided that consists of the transmission in a communication network of information provided by a recipient of the service, or the provision of access to a communication network, Member States shall ensure that the service provider is not liable for the information transmitted, on condition that the provider:
>   (a) does not initiate the transmission;
>   (b) does not select the receiver of the transmission; and
>   (c) does not select or modify the information contained in the transmission.
>
> 2. The acts of transmission and of provision of access referred to in paragraph 1 include the automatic, intermediate and transient storage of the information transmitted in so far as this takes place for the sole purpose of carrying out the transmission in the communication network, and provided that the information is not stored for any period longer than is reasonably necessary for the transmission.

[33] Ibid Recital (60).
[34] Ibid Art 12.2.
[35] Ibid Art 13.1 (a).

3. This Article shall not affect the possibility for a court or administrative authority, in accordance with Member States' legal systems, of requiring the service provider to terminate or prevent an infringement.[36]

Caching services

In the digital world, straight transmission is often not the case. What looks like a traditional transmission can be a series of briefly existing copies. Article 13 states:

> 1. Where an information society service is provided that consists of the transmission in a communication network of information provided by a recipient of the service, Member States shall ensure that the service provider is not liable for the automatic, intermediate and temporary storage of that information, performed for the sole purpose of making more efficient the information's onward transmission to other recipients of the service upon their request, on condition that:
> (a) the provider does not modify the information;
> (b) the provider complies with conditions on access to the information;
> (c) the provider complies with rules regarding the updating of the information, specified in a manner widely recognised and used by industry;
> (d) the provider does not interfere with the lawful use of technology, widely recognised and used by industry, to obtain data on the use of the information; and
> (e) the provider acts expeditiously to remove or to disable access to the information it has stored upon obtaining actual knowledge of the fact that the information at the initial source of the transmission has been removed from the network, or access to it has been disabled, or that a court or an administrative authority has ordered such removal or disablement.
> 2. This Article shall not affect the possibility for a court or administrative authority, in accordance with Member States' legal systems, of requiring the service provider to terminate or prevent an infringement.'[37]

Mere Conduit and Caching: Non-involvement With Data or Users

A service provider can only benefit from the exemptions for 'mere conduit' and for 'caching' when he is not actually involved with the information transmitted. This entails, for example, that the information transmitted or provided access to be in no way modified. This requirement does not cover manipulations of a technical nature which take place in the course of the transmission as they do not alter the integrity of the information contained in the transmission.'[38]

An intermediary must not have contact or coordinate with any of its users regarding their use of the service for illegal acts, or they will forfeit the protection afforded by the Directive. A service provider who deliberately collaborates with one of the recipients of his service in order to undertake illegal acts goes beyond the activities of 'mere conduit' or 'caching' and as a result cannot benefit from the liability exemptions established for these activities.[39]

[36] Ibid Art 12.
[37] Ibid Art 13.
[38] Ibid Recital (43).
[39] Ibid Recital (44).

It must be noted that, in a case from the District court of Brussels, these provision have been interpreted as still allowing an Internet service provider to be seen as a secondary infringer and therefore required to filter their digital traffic. Whether this interpretation will last remains to be seen.[40]

Hosting Services

Article 14 of section 4 provides for limited liability for those information society services that provide their users with some form of information storage.

> 1. Where an information society service is provided that consists of the storage of information provided by a recipient of the service, Member States shall ensure that the service provider is not liable for the information stored at the request of a recipient of the service, on condition that:
>
> (a) the provider does not have actual knowledge of illegal activity or information and, as regards claims for damages, is not aware of facts or circumstances from which the illegal activity or information is apparent; or
>
> (b) the provider, upon obtaining such knowledge or awareness, acts expeditiously to remove or to disable access to the information.
>
> 2. Paragraph 1 shall not apply when the recipient of the service is acting under the authority or the control of the provider.
>
> 3. This Article shall not affect the possibility for a court or administrative authority, in accordance with Member States' legal systems, of requiring the service provider to terminate or prevent an infringement, nor does it affect the possibility for Member States of establishing procedures governing the removal or disabling of access to information.

The definition of hosting services includes many of the Internet services that engage in the business of so-called 'user generated content'. Contemporary examples include all kinds of Web-hotel services, portal services such as MSN and Myspace, forums for chat and media-sharing sites such as Youtube.

One common factor in all such services is the service provider's control of the digital storage space on which the information is being stored. This requires the physical control of computer servers, or the contractual control of computer servers provided by a third party.

The requirement in 14.1(a) that the provider should not have actual knowledge of illegal activity or information must reasonably be understood to indicate user activity taking place or information stored on this controlled digital space.

No General Obligation to Monitor

The Directive clarifies that intermediaries should not be given the burden of conducting general monitoring regarding the information flows through or via

[40] *SABAM v s.a. Scarlet (anciennement Tiscali),* Brussels Court of First Instance (TGI), 29 June 2007, N° 04/8975/A. Available at http://www.juriscom.net/documents/tpibruxelles20070629.pdf. The so-called SABAM v. Tiscali case. The court ordered the Internet access provider to block all p2p traffic through their servers in spite of the mere-conduit position that they held, referencing Recitals (40) and (45) to support its decision.

their service, since Member States are prevented from imposing a monitoring obligation on service providers only with respect to obligations of a general nature. However, this does not concern monitoring obligations in specific cases.[41]

Analysis of Torrent-Sharing Forums

A provider of information society services can be a physical or juridical person in charge of providing any of the services within the wide swath of the information society. Even though these services can often be characterized as being provided for remuneration, the definition also extends to services that do not give rise to online contracting in so far as they represent an economic activity at all. Furthermore such services are provided at a distance, through electronic means and at the individual request of the recipient of the service. The service provided by torrent- and link-sharing sites such as The Pirate Bay is to be a forum for Internet users to upload their links to information, and through this uploading be able to link up with other users interested in that particular information. Even if the users do not pay for this service or enter into a contract with the owners of The Pirate Bay, such services cost resources to run and are paid for by on-site advertising or through otherwise leveraging its traffic for economic gain, and as a rule these kinds of sites are information society services.[42]

The grounds for limitations on the liability of such service providers are found in Articles 12–14 of Directive 2000/31/EC corresponding to §§16–19 of the Swedish implementation. §§16–18 deal with claims for compensation while §19 covers criminal culpability.[43]

In technical detail, the services provided by the torrent-sharing sites such as The Pirate Bay include among other things making space available on computer servers for the users to upload, label and store torrent-links on. The services entailing the storing of such links do not commonly include the storing of the information linked to. In The Pirate Bay case, this was certainly not something that the service offered since it was a pure collection of torrent-links. The act for which a service provider could be liable as an intermediary is the copyright-infringement taking place when a recipient of the service unlawfully makes a copyrighted work available to the public. Since the infringed works that are the basis of liability are at no point stored on the server space provided by the torrent-sharing site, Article 14, which describes hosting services, is the least appropriate label for this kind of service.[44]

[41] See Directive 2000/31/EC, Recital (47) and Art 15.

[42] See ibid at Recital (18) and Prop 2001/02:150. Lag om elektronisk handel och andra informationssamhällets pp 56–58.

[43] *Lag om elektronisk handel och andra informationssamhällets tjänster* (SFS 2002:562).

[44] Mistaking the mere torrent-link for the actual information transmitted between the users might have led the Stockholm district court in The Pirate Bay judgment to come to this conclusion at para 75. There are clear indications that this matter was not fully understood, such as the claim in para 69 that 'It suffices that the [defendants] were aware of the fact that copyrighted matter had occurred on the website.'

In the process of transmitting the information between the users, the recipients' access to the torrent-link performs an initial brief and purely transient role. The information is provided by the recipients of the service and passed onto other recipients without actually ever being stored on any space controlled by the service provider. The second role performed by the service happens at the very brief moment when two file sharing users locate each other through the service's tracker. This transient but necessary feature of the service in the file-sharing process needs to be considered in more detail.

Comparison with Search Engines

Similar to a link-sharing forum, Internet Search engines are frustratingly hard to place in any of the three categories of the E-Commerce Directive. Within the mere taxonomy of 'mere conduit', 'caching' and 'hosting', there is little assistance to be found. The only one that offers any tangible help is Article 12: 'mere conduit'. But whereas it would fit with the spirit of the Directive to include search engines under this heading the fit would be difficult under the precise wording. Certainly Recital 18 of the Directive specifically includes services that 'provides tools allowing for search, access and retrieval of data', but there are technical issues that makes the case a hard fit. Allgrove and Ganley point out that this is not a case of the transmission of information provided by the recipient of the service; although the search query is initiated by the recipient, the information against which the defence would need to apply is the search results transmitted from the search engine's servers – clearly not information provided by the recipient. Further, the content of the transmission is selected and arguably modified by the search engine, something that is contrary to the provisions of the mere conduit category of intermediaries.[45]

Torrent Forums as Mere Conduits

It is quite evident that a site where users can connect and share torrent links is an information society service in the sense of the E-Commerce Directive.[46] But, just as with search engines, the drafters of the Directive did not foresee the details of technological development and the three main categories given do not seem to cover the array of services very convincingly. Within a forum site, at least, the infringing work does not pass through the intermediary itself, but instead circulates entirely within the swarm network created by the users.[47] If anything, the torrent forum and the tracker functionality appear most akin to a provision of access to a communication network, working as a gateway to the swarm. Both by the method of elimination, and by the wording of Article 12, this is the most fitting category for forum sites where users exchange torrent-links that link to works on the users' own computer or that of another user. This

[45] B Allgrove and P Ganley, 'Search Engines, Data Aggregators, and UK Copyright Law: A Proposal' (2007) p 17, available at SSRN: http://ssrn.com/abstract=961797 (last visited 24 July 2009).

[46] Compare with The Swedish Pirate Bay judgment at para 74.

[47] Ibid.

would put sites such as these in the same category as Internet access providers and other gateway services who do not in themselves host the material, but do instead provide an important way of gaining access to the network where the material is hosted, in this case the user swarm described above.

The Actions of the Pirate Bay Principals

Did the actions of the principals of The Pirate Bay cause them to forfeit the protection of the E-Commerce Directive? If a forum site such as this can be seen to in any way initiate the transmission between the users, then the exoneration provided by the Directive is forfeit. Are their database design, their site layout, their name or their provocative texts such as to provide a level of collaboration and encouragement that would make them party to the users' copyright infringements? There is certainly room for discussion, but on that issue this paper must suspend judgment. The relevant actions have been separated from the capabilities of the service itself and of its users. That a link-sharing forum site can, in principle, be within the protection of the E-Commerce Directive is uncontroversial.

Whether the principals in the particular case of The Pirate Bay forfeit this protection through their actions is a decision for the courts to make. Further, the E-Commerce Directive states that liability limitation under its Articles will not affect the possibility of a court or administrative authority requiring the service provider to terminate or prevent a particular infringement.[48]

5. A BRIEF NOTE ON THE IPR ENFORCEMENT DIRECTIVE

EC Directive 2004/48 on the enforcement of intellectual property rights[49] (hereafter the Enforcement Directive) focuses on the fact that the modern information- and communication technologies have left intellectual property rights[50] without effective means of enforcement.[51] Increasing use of the Internet enables illicitly copied works to be distributed instantly around the globe.[52]

[48] Arts 12.3, 13.2, 14.3 and 15.2 of Directive 2000/31/EC.

[49] Directive 2004/48/EC of the European Parliament and of the Council of 29 April 2004 on the enforcement of intellectual property rights. OJ L 157, 30.4.2004, p 45. Corrigendum to Directive 2004/48/EC of the European Parliament and of the Council of 29 April 2004 on the enforcement of intellectual property rights. OJ L195, 02.06.2004, p 16.

[50] According to Commission Statement 2005/295/EC. *Statement by the Commission concerning Article 2 of Directive 2004/48/EC of the European Parliament and of the Council on the enforcement of intellectual property rights.* OJ L 94 13.4.2005, p 37.The Commission considers that at least the following intellectual property rights are covered by the scope of Directive EC/2004/48: copyright, rights related to copyright, *sui generis* right of a database maker, rights of the creator of the topographies of a semiconductor product, trademark rights, design rights, patent rights, including rights derived from supplementary protection certificates, geographical indications, utility model rights, plant variety rights, trade names, in so far as these are protected as exclusive property rights in the national law concerned.

[51] See Directive EC/2004/48 Recital (3).

[52] Ibid Recital (10).

Without ways of enforcement, innovation and creativity will be discouraged and investment diminished. It is therefore seen as necessary to ensure that the substantive law on intellectual property is applied affectively within the European Community. This effective protection is of importance not only to promote innovation and creativity, but also for developing employment and improving competitiveness.[53] The Enforcement Directive is without prejudice to national legislation that goes further in protecting the rights owner and to the specific provisions on the enforcement of rights and exceptions on copyright contained in Community legislation.[54]

In order to effectively combat infringement on the Internet the judicial authorities may order that information on the origin and distribution networks of the infringing services or goods be provided by persons other than the infringer who provides services used in the infringement, ie any intermediary services.[55]

5.1 Conflicting Values?

Despite the attempts to create a safe-harbour through the E-Commerce Directive, the Internet intermediaries are still stuck in the middle between their users and copyrights-holders. Though Directive 2004/48 should likely yield when it comes into direct conflict with the older E-Commerce Directive,[56] the conflict between the opposing interests of i) keeping the intermediary away from the conflict and ii) involving him just seem unlikely to be settled in such a facile way.

In 2009 the English High Court referred two questions to the CJEU concerning intermediary liability, ranging from Internet access providers, electronic billboard operators and newsgroup servers to companies such as eBay that are hosting third-party content. One question concerns Article 14 of the E-Commerce Directive and when an information society services provider qualifies as a 'host' exempt from liability within the meaning of that Article. Another question concerns the balance between Article 11 of the Enforcement Directive and Article 15 of the E-Commerce Directive – which kinds of injunctions can be imposed on an online intermediary in order to prevent trademark infringement, when Article 15 of the E-Commerce Directive explicitly prohibits any general obligation of surveillance or monitoring?[57]

In a 2008 judgment, The European Court of Justice affirmed that Community law does not require Member States to oblige Internet service providers to

[53] Ibid Recital (1).

[54] Ibid Art 2.

[55] Ibid Art 8.

[56] Ibid Recital (16).

[57] English High Court of Justice: *L'Oreal SA & Ors v EBay International AG* [2009] EWHC 1094 (Ch). See pending Case 324/09 *L'Oréal SA, Lancôme parfums et beauté & Cie SNC, Laboratoire Garnier & Cie, L'Oréal (UK) Limited v eBay International AG*, eBay Europe SARL, eBay (UK) Limited, Stephan Potts, Tracy Ratchford, Marie Ormsby, James Clarke, Joanna Clarke, Glen Fox, Rukhsana Bi. OJ C 267 of 07.11.2009, p 40.

disclose personal data of its subscribers in civil proceedings initiated by copyright holders.[58]

It would seem likely that this war is just in its infancy. While the E-Commerce Directive focuses on the values of leaving the middle-man alone, as noted above, the gist of the Enforcement Directive is that effective enforcement of intellectual property rights will not be practically possible unless the intermediaries, and especially the internet service providers, are made to cooperate and to provide assistance in the form of information-filtering and or information-monitoring. This matter bears deeper scrutiny, but will have to be the topic of another paper.[59]

6. CONCLUSIONS

It is nearing ten years since the lawsuit against Napster.[60] What should have been a quick wedding between the culture/entertainment industry and the Internet has instead become a painfully slow execution. But it is an execution without any foreseeable end – as long as it is the forum that is being focused on rather than the users that frequent its digital cobblestones and colonnades. New forums will always spring up, whether in the form of services that mediate between users, or in the form of technologies that enable the users to do without a third party.

Professor of law and sociology, Håkan Hyden is part of a research project called 'cyber norms', aiming to research the social and juridical processes of creating norms that arise in the wake of the information society.[61] He describes the tension between different norms and worldviews existing in what he terms 'a transition society': a time of unrest and upheaval between the overripe industrial society and the information society still in the making. The tensions between holders of the different worldviews are manifest. Eventually, new patterns in society are developed as a result of political groupings opposing the old norms, but this may take a very long time. The established systems can only be changed in part, and will linger on as obsolete constructs to eventually depart when their usefulness have long since passed.[62] The very norms governing copyright are

[58] Case C-275/06 *Productores de Música de España (Promusicae) v Telefónica de España SAU*, [2008] ECR I-271).

[59] On the issue of balancing copyright interests and fundamental rights of an ISP's users, see F Coudert and E Werkers, 'In The Aftermath of the Promusicae Case: How to Strike the Balance?' in *International Journal of Law and Information Technology Advance Access: 10.1093/ijlit/ean015* (Oxford University Press 2008). Available at ijlit.oxfordjournals.org/cgi/content/ full/ean015 (last visited 31 July 2009).

[60] *A&M Records, Inc v Napster, Inc* 284 F.3d 1091 (9th Cir 2002) The first big lawsuit against a file sharing intermediary. As noted earlier, Napster was hugely popular, and the lawsuit caused waves in the media.

[61] See www.cybernormer.se.

[62] See H Hydén, *Från samhällsutveckling till samhällsförändring – om behovet av att tänka nytt* in Hydén, Töllborg, Larsson *Framtidsboken* Volym 1.0. (2008) p 89, pp 91–93 Available at www.soclaw.lu.se (last visited 30 July 2009).

changing due to the way that young people are now being brought up in the midst of massive flows of information. This has created a true generational gap that is clearly felt by some of the generation raised with the ubiquitous presence of Internet access.[63]

Thus the focus on the technologies providing the distribution or on the intermediary services providing the connection can be seen as nothing more than a distraction. Granted, the costly legal battles against such intermediaries provide great entertainment as they offer the same kind of recurring frisson as Heracles' battle against the Hydra, with new heads sprouting after old ones are lopped off. They also offer a wide space for analysis and musing by legal commentators and scholars. But it would be deeply tragic if all of this amounts to nothing more than benefitting legal counsel, academic commentators and sensationalist journalism. We risk avoiding facing that the real issue lies with the users of these technologies and services, not the intermediaries themselves. By taking the middleman out of the picture, we can focus properly on the rifts in the norms of the old and the new generations. Thus the question of what to do with the changed norms and expectations of young consumers should be laid bare so that it can beg for a concrete answer. In other words, what should the copyright holders do with the forum users?

As long as there are people to populate them, the forums are not going to cease to exist. Here's hoping for the peaceful and productive forums of a Better Tomorrow instead.

[63] E Claesson, *Normdelning – en rättssociologisk intervjuundersökning om fildelares normer och normskapande*. Master's thesis in law (2009) pp 53–57. Available at https://gupea.ub.gu.se/dspace/handle/2077/20470 (last visited 21 July 2009).

11
The Unfair Commercial Practices Directive and the Legislation Implementing it in Sweden: A Comparison

PROFESSOR ULF BERNITZ

1. INTRODUCTION

The 2005 Unfair Commercial Practices Directive (in this article referred to as the 'UCPD' or the 'Directive')[1] is a major new piece of European legislation. Few EU directives in the consumer law field have such a broad range and represent such a high level of legislative ambition. The Directive is intended to create a high common level of consumer protection[2] and eliminate the barriers stemming from the previous fragmentation of the rules on unfair commercial practices.[3] It aims at full harmonization and will compel Member States to bring their legislation fully in line with its provisions. In Sweden, the Directive was transposed into law by the enactment of the new Marketing Act of 2008, which took legal effect on 1 July 2008.[4] The Directive was found to require such extensive revision of the legislation in force that its terms were rewritten and considerably expanded in the new Act. An English translation of the text of the

[1] Directive 2005/29/EC, OJ L 2005 149/22. 2007. See Weatherill & Bernitz (eds), *The Regulation of Unfair Commercial Practices under EC Directive 2005/29. New Rules and New Techniques* (Hart Pub, Oxford 2007). See also Stuyck et al, 'Confidence Through Fairness? The New Directive on Unfair Business-to-consumer Commercial Practices in the Internal Market' (2006) 43 *Common Market Law Review* pp 107 ff., Anagnostaras, 'The Unfair Commercial Practices Directive in context: From legal disparity to legal complexity?' (2010) 47 *Common Market Law Review* p 147 ff, Micklitz, Reich and Rott, *Understanding EU Consumer Law* (Oxford 2009) ch 2. For an overview in Swedish, Bakardjieva Engelbrekt, EG-direktivet om otillbörliga affärsmetoder: En stundande omdaning av svensk marknadsrätt? Europarättslig Tidskrift 2005 s 236 ff.

[2] Directive 2005/29, Recital 11.

[3] Ibid Recital 12.

[4] The Marketing Act is based on the Government Committee Report Otillbörliga affärsmetoder (Unfair Commercial Practices), SOU 2006:76 and the subsequent Government Bill to Parliament 2007/08:115.

Act is annexed to this article. The enactment of the new act is entirely explained by the need to implement the UCPD. There was general consensus in Sweden that the previous Marketing Act of 1995 was functioning well.

The Swedish marketing law and its counterparts in the other Nordic countries have long been directed primarily at consumer protection and are designed to function in a pro-competitive, open market. Basically, these aims fit very well with the ambitions behind the UCPD. Although the Directive presents itself primarily as a consumer protection measure aiming at establishing a high level of protection for consumers across the Union, on looking at its legislative history, one sees this is not entirely correct. It is also aimed at liberalising and enhancing open markets. A particularly important factor, which explains the Commission's strong interest in the Directive, has been the desire to achieve deregulation of national unfair competition law in those member states where the standard applied was regarded as too strict and restrictive, thus eliminating barriers to the further development of the internal market. As stated in the recitals, the laws of the member states relating to unfair commercial practices have shown marked differences which can generate appreciable distortions of competition and obstacles to the smooth functioning of the internal market.[5] The primary target in this regard has undoubtedly been the traditionally restrictive German unfair competition law as interpreted in the case law. On the other hand, the Directive has probably introduced stricter standards of protection in certain other member states. The fundamental idea behind the UCPD is to create a level playing field throughout the Union for advertising and marketing, making it possible for firms to apply basically the same advertising and marketing methods all over the Union.

Similarities in basic aims did not make the Nordic EU Member States particularly strong supporters of the proposed UCPD as they foresaw the risk of a lowering of the consumer protection standard already established under their national laws. Thus, they supported the decision not to include the Commission's original proposal to base the Directive on the country of origin principle. In particular, the Swedish government did not consider that the Directive offered sufficient protection in the area of advertising directed towards children and youth. The risk of lowered consumer protection standards was the reason why the Danish and Swedish governments (the only dissenters) voted against the adoption of the Directive in the Council. The Finnish government decided, reluctantly, not to follow suit.

There are certain important limitations on the scope of the Directive. Without these, it would probably not have been able to reach acceptance by the majority in the Council. The Directive is confined to collective consumer interests and does not interfere with contract law and is without prejudice to individual actions brought by a consumer.[6] Thus, the relation between the pre-contractual marketing and advertising stage and European contract law as established by

[5] Directive 2005/29 Recital 3.

[6] Ibid Art 3 (2) and Recital 9.

existing consumer protection Directives has been left open to be developed by case law, normally as a matter for national courts.[7] Specific EU directives containing provisions on marketing continue to apply and take precedence within their specific fields of application (*lex specialis derogat lex generalis*).[8] The most important examples are the Television Without Frontiers Directive,[9] and the E-Commerce Directive.[10]

The Directive is also without prejudice to EU or national law relating to the health or safety aspects of products.[11] Examples are national provisions in relation to alcohol, tobacco and pharmaceuticals, eg, specific advertising bans in the member states related to health and safety. However, such bans must be legitimate under general Union law rules on free movement of goods and services. It follows from the case law that such national provisions must basically satisfy three tests, viz. that they are truly non-discriminatory, that they pursue important public health or safety interests and, thirdly, that they are proportionate, ie appropriate to ensure their aim and do not go beyond what is necessary to achieve such an objective. On the proportionality test, the *Gourmet* case on the Swedish ban on alcohol advertising, a preliminary ruling requested by the Stockholm City Court, already constituted an important precedent.[12] The judgment by the CJEU forced Sweden to admit, albeit within strict limits, advertising for beer and wine. There are other exemptions and derogations which contributed to making the UCPD acceptable to member states. The most important one is that member states were allowed a limited, six year transition period to dismantle national provisions which are more restrictive or prescriptive than the Directive, provided the specific national measures applied are proportionate.[13]

[7] On this point, the Draft Common Frame of Reference (DCFR), published in 2009, has drafted a set of contract law rules under the heading Marketing and pre-contractual duties (in Book 2 Ch 3).

[8] Directive 2005/29 Art 3.4.

[9] Council Directive 89/552/EEC of 3 October 1989 on the coordination of certain provisions laid down by Law, Regulation or Administrative Action in Member States concerning the pursuit of television broadcasting activities (OJ L 298, 17.10.1989, p 23), as changed by Directive 2007/65 of the European Parliament and of the Council of 11 Dec 2007 (OJ L 332, 18.12.2007, p 27). On the interpretation of this Directive, the well-known De Agostini case is based on a request for a preliminary ruling by the Swedish Market Court, Case 34-36/95, *Konsumentombudsmannen (The Consumer Ombudsman) v De Agostini (Svenska) Förlag AB and TV-Shop i Sverige AB*, [1997] ECR I-3843. The Television Without Frontiers Directive will be replaced by the Audiovisual Media Services Directive (Directive 2010/13/EU, OJ L 95, 15.4.2010, p 1).

[10] Directive 2000/31/EC of the European Parliament and of the Council of 8 June 2000 on certain legal aspects of information society services, in particular electronic commerce, in the internal market, OJ 200 L 178/1.

[11] Directive 2005/29 Art 3 (3).

[12] Case C-405/98, *Consumer Ombudsman v Gourmet International Products*, [2001] ECR I-1795, see also the subsequent Bacardi cases, C-262/02, *Commission v France, C-429/02, Bacardi France v Télévision Francaise 1 (TF1) et al*, [2004] ECR I-6569.

[13] Directive 2005/29 Art 3 (5). A derogation from the national rules on commercial practices by the regulated professions has been admitted, without time limitation, Art 3 (8). Member States may also impose more restrictive or prescriptive national rules on financial services and immovable property, ie these areas are within the ambit of the Directive but not covered by the full harmonization principle, Art 3 (9).

The aim of this article is to present and discuss the new Swedish marketing legislation and its relation to the UCPD and show how it has been influenced by the implementation requirements. Rather than giving an overall description, it focuses on comparing the Directive and the Swedish legislation regarding four particularly important aspects namely:

In Part 2 the choice of legislative structure,

In Part 3 the assessment of misleading advertising,

In Part 4 the assessment of passing off and

In Part 5 the supervision and enforcement mechanisms.

Finally, conclusions will be drawn in Part 6.

For ease of reading, the text of the Swedish Marketing Act of 2008 (in an English translation) is *annexed* to this article.

2. THE CHOICE OF LEGISLATIVE STRUCTURE: THE DIRECTIVE AND THE SWEDISH LAW COMPARED

The scope of the UCPD is limited to business practices directed towards consumers, ie business to consumer relations (B2C), the consumer being defined as a natural person acting for non-business purposes.[14] By concentrating on consumer protection, the UCPD forged a strong link with other consumer law directives such as the E-Commerce Directive[15] and makes the Directive part of the rapidly developing European consumer law. The Directive as such does not comprise business practices directed to commercial or other non-consumer purchasers, often described as business to business relations (B2B).[16] However, as will be discussed in part 4, *infra*, the Directive offers some indirect protection to B2B.

As mentioned, national legislation on unfair commercial practices in the EU countries follows different legislative models.[17] The German Act on Unfair Competition (*Gesetz gegen den unlauteren Wettbewerb*, UWG), now of 2008, is the primary and historically most influential representative of the unitary, unfair competition model of legislation, which combines B2B and B2C protection against unfair commercial practices within one and the same statutory

[14] Ibid Art 2 (a).

[15] Directive 2000/31/EC.

[16] Directive 2005/29 Recital 6 states that the Directive neither covers nor affects the national laws on unfair commercial practices which harm only competitors' economic interests or which relate to a transaction between traders.

[17] On national unfair commercial practices law in the EU member states see in particular Schulze and Schulte-Nölke, *Analysis of National Fairness Laws Aimed at Protecting Consumers in relation to Commercial Practices*, June 2003, study for the EU Commission (with further references). Available at ec.europa.eu/comm/consumers/cons_int/.../unfair_practices_en.pdf. The study includes a number of national reports, among them the Bernitz, Report on Sweden. See also eg Micklitz – Kessler, *Marketing Practices and Consumer Protection in the EC Member States and the US*, Baden-Baden (Nomos) 2002, Howell, Micklitz, Wilhelmsson, *European Fair Trading Law –The Unfair Commercial Practices Directive* (Ashgate, 2006).

framework. French law is a good example of another model: B2C protection against unfair commercial practices is regarded as part of general consumer law and included in the broadly framed French *Code de la Consommation* of 1992. The French B2B protection against unfair commercial practices is in part the object of specific legislative acts, in part a matter of case law based on the general tort provisions of the *Code civil*. In the United Kingdom, on the other hand, no coherent legal principles regarding unfair competition were ever developed and legislation on unfair practices is scattered and lacks systematization.[18]

Given this lack of European coherence, the fairly quick and smooth acceptance by the European Parliament and the Council of the Commission's proposal for the Directive must be regarded as remarkable. The Commission was probably able to succeed due to the decision not to follow the legislative model of any particular EU country but to place the Directive[19] on a new systematic foundation, based on functional considerations fitting existing EU law. In this way, the Commission was able to adapt its model to the particular needs of removing barriers to cross-border advertising and marketing, thus furthering European integration.

The UCPD requires full harmonization on the basis of what is now Article 114 TEUF (the functioning of the internal market),[20] aiming at a single framework regulating, in principle, all aspects of unfair commercial practices across the EU.[21] The commercial practices concept has been given a broad definition which includes all types of advertising, marketing and commercial communication.[22] However, as already mentioned the Commission had to compromise and drop its original proposal to introduce the country of origin principle relying on the control mechanism of that country. The main thrust of the original Green Paper on Commercial Communication in the Internal Market of 1996[23] was the liberalization of commercial communication and promotion of free movement of advertising and marketing services throughout the Community, using the principles of country of origin and mutual recognition as the main instruments.[24] However, although retained in the Green Paper of 2001 on EU Consumer Protection[25] and in the proposed text of the Directive as first presented, the country of origin principle attracted strong criticism from certain member states, including the Nordic ones, which found it too far-reaching. The critique is in part also explained by the weak structure of the supervision and enforcement mechanisms, see Part 5.

[18] Weatherill, 'United Kingdom Report' in Schultze and Schulte-Nölke, *Analysis of National Fairness Laws* (see n 5), same author, *EU Consumer Law and Policy*, 2005 pp 191 ff.

[19] COM (2003) 356 final, 18 June 2003.

[20] Former Art 95 ECT.

[21] Directive 2005/29 Recital 12.

[22] Ibid Art 2 (d).

[23] Commission Green Paper on Commercial Communications in the Internal Market COM(96) 192 final 08.05.1996 final.

[24] This principle has been accepted in the E-Commerce Directive: 'Member States may not, for reasons falling within the coordinated field, restrict the freedom to provide information services from another Member State', Art 3.2 of the E-Commerce Directive (2000/31/EC).

[25] COM (2001) 531 final.

Turning to Sweden, the unitary legislative approach of the previous Marketing Acts, was retained in the new Marketing Act of 2008 and, there was not even any debate on this point. In Sweden, the unitary approach is regarded as preferable as many important types of commercial practice are considered as unfair both from a consumer and a business point of view. However, certain provisions in the new Marketing Act are specific for B2C-relations. Denmark and Norway have also kept their former unitary approach. In Finland, on the other hand, marketing legislation aiming at consumer protection has been part of Finland's comprehensive Consumer Protection Act since the 1970s, while B2B marketing is subject to a separate Act. Finland kept this division when implementing the UCPD.

A reason why the unitary approach was considered preferable in Sweden, among other countries, is the existence of a second directive in the field, namely the 2006 Directive on Misleading and Comparative Advertising, the MCAD.[26] This combines two texts with different background and structure into one legislative act with only slight revisions. One is the older and far less ambitious 1984 EC Directive (84/450/EEC) on misleading advertising (applicable only to B2B relations after the enactment of the UCPD), and the other is the former 1997 EC Directive on comparative advertising (97/55/EC). The rules on comparative advertising aim at full harmonization and cover B2B as well as B2C relations, while the B2B rules on misleading advertising provide for minimum harmonization. The unitary approach chosen in Sweden, Denmark and Norway has made it possible to implement both directives in their entirety in the Marketing Act. This is considered as a clear advantage and the most rational legislative approach.

However, the Swedish unitary model differs from the German model. Historically, the German unfair competition concept focused on protection against unfair competition in B2B relations, but has gradually been widened and the new German Unfair Competition Act of 2008 aims at offering B2B and B2C protection on the same level, at least in principle, while balancing conflicting business and consumer interests. In Sweden, on the other hand, the first modern Marketing Act of 1970 had a very pronounced emphasis on protection of the consumers, albeit covering B2B relations as well. This emphasis has been gradually reduced over the years, but the new Marketing Act of 2008 should still in the first place be regarded as a piece of consumer law.[27] This is largely true of the Danish and Norwegian Marketing Acts as well.

Basically, the architecture of the substantive provisions of the Directive is based on a division into four parts:

[26] Directive 2006/114/EC, OJ L 2006 376/21.

[27] For a comparative study of the German and Swedish development, Bakardjieva-Engelbrekt, *Fair Trading Law in Flux? National Legacies, Institutional Choice and the Process of Europeanisation*, Stockholm University (Ac Diss), 2003.

(I) A general clause prohibiting unfair commercial practices contrary to the requirements of professional diligence, provided the practice is able to distort consumers' economic behaviour (Art 5),
(II) A prohibition on misleading commercial practices, divided into two statutory provisions, one on misleading actions (Art 6) and another on misleading omissions (insufficient information, Art 7),
(III) A prohibition on aggressive commercial practices, likewise divided into two statutory provisions, one directed against the use of aggressive commercial practices (art 8) and the other against the use of harassment, coercion and undue influence (Art 9),
(IV) A Black list comprising 31 types of commercial practices considered to be prohibited *per se*, ie, unfair in all circumstances (Annex I).

The prohibited practices described in II-IV are particularly important examples of unfair commercial practices. It seems unclear to what extent the general clause in Art 5 is intended to be applicable to practices which fall outside the scope of the specific prohibitions, in particular in cases where the commercial practice would be of a distinctly different type. This is probably an issue which will have to wait for clarification by the CJEU. It would be perfectly possible for the CJEU to find the general clause applicable to other types of commercial practices regarded as contrary to the requirements of professional diligence, especially if the Court finds support in the unfairness of the practice being a widely held view in the member states.

Generally speaking, it was not difficult to transpose the UCPD and the MCAD into Swedish law. The maximum harmonization requirement did not cause particular problems. A general clause has since long been part of Swedish marketing law as has also been the case with obligations to give consumers positive information. However, Swedish marketing law did not previously have any special provisions on aggressive commercial practices. The inclusion in the Act of the Directive's provisions on this point constitutes a clear improvement.

Unlike the UCPD, the Swedish Marketing Act does not use the term 'commercial practice' (Sw: *affärsmetod*) as the basic term to describe the legislation's scope of applicability but has kept the term 'marketing' (Sw: *marknadsföring*) which was used previously. It is stated in the Government Bill that the term is to be understood as covering the same commercial activities as 'commercial practice' as used in the UCPD,[28] thus including all types of advertising, marketing or commercial communication.[29] Sales arguments put forward to individual consumers are included. In order to comply with the UCPD, the scope of applicability of the Marketing Act has been expanded in so far as it also covers delivery of products and, in particular, after sale activities, eg, the handling of complaints.[30]

[28] Government Bill p 63. On this point, the Government Bill took a different position than the Committee Report which had proposed changing the terminology to commercial practice.

[29] Directive 2005/29 Art 2 (d).

[30] Ibid Art 2 (d) UCPD, cf the definition of marketing in s 3 of the Swedish Act.

The UCPD covers all kinds of products. It embraces any goods or service including immovable property, rights and obligations, Art 2 (c) UCPD. The Swedish Act has a similar broad product definition, which also mentions employment opportunities (Section 3).

The UCPD is limited to unfair commercial practices harming consumers' *economic* interests (Art 1); a limitation well in line with its primary harmonization objective. Thus, the Directive excludes practices affecting matters of taste and decency where the requirements are said to vary widely between the Member States.[31] This limitation fits well with the scope of the Swedish Marketing Act which is limited to marketing practices having a commercial purpose and character. This limitation indicates a desire not to intrude on the constitutional protection of the freedom of the press and of free expression. In this field Sweden has a comprehensive Freedom of the Press Act, held in high regard and enjoying constitutional status.

On most points, the substantive provisions of the Marketing Act regarding Unfair marketing, in particular the general clause on Good marketing practice (Section 5 and 6) and the prohibitions on Aggressive marketing (Section 7) and Misleading marketing (Sections 8 – 12), closely follow the text of the UCPD (see the statutory text in the Appendix).[32] Annex 1 to the UCPD, the Black List of commercial practices, has been implemented unchanged and *in extenso* into Swedish law by way of an annex to the Marketing Act and, to satisfy constitutional requirements, as a separate Government announcement. The black-listed practices are prohibited *per se* and, thus do not require any assessment of their effects in individual cases. The provisions of the Black List have also been made applicable as *per se* prohibitions to marketing in B2B relations (Section 4.3 of the Act). This particular feature of the Swedish Marketing Act is explained by the fact that the Act also covers B2B transactions.

In addition, the Marketing Act contains some specific provisions targeting specific types of misleading advertising. These have been transferred from the 1995 Act and comprise, among others, misleading packaging dimensions (Section 13) and misleading use, as specified, of the terms bankruptcy sale, clearance sale, discount sale and the like (Sections 15 – 17). The special provisions on misleading copies will be discussed in Part 4.

There is a specific provision on comparative advertising (Section 18). It adheres closely to the above mentioned text of the MCAD managing to set out the criteria of that text in a single provision.[33]

[31] Ibid Recital 7.

[32] The decision not to include the average consumer concept in the statutory text is commented upon in below Part 3.

[33] The provision on comparative advertising was implemented in Swedish law in the year 2000 within the framework of the 1995 Marketing Act and has been transferred unchanged into the 2008 Marketing Act. On this provision see Bernitz, The EC Directive on Comparative Advertising and its Implementation in the Nordic Countries: Especially in relation to Intellectual Property, 42 *Scandinavian Studies in Law*, Stockholm 2002 pp 11 ff (reprinted in U Bernitz, European Law in Sweden, Stockholm 2002 pp 201 ff.).

The different derogations and exemptions to the UCPD, mentioned in Part 1, do not include any relating to sales promotion practices. Promotions are included in the definition of commercial practices.[34] This is noteworthy as, traditionally, the unfair competition legislation of many continental EU countries included specific prohibitions of particular types of promotional practices, eg different types of combined offers, gifts, advertising lotteries etc. Normally, these prohibitions are primarily aimed at offering protection to small businesses against practices applied by the big chain stores. A specific Commission proposal for a regulation on sales promotion activities was dropped.[35] In two important recent cases the CJEU struck down a Belgian prohibition on combined offers[36] and a German prohibition on marketing lotteries.[37] The court stated there are no prohibitions on promotions other than those specified in the Black list.

The position on sales promotions taken in the Directive is in line with Swedish marketing law. The Marketing Act prohibits no specific types of promotions or special sales methods. Earlier provisions prohibiting specific kinds of combined offers were repealed by the 1995 Act. Thus, action against promotional activities can only be taken in Swedish law to the extent they involve misleading or aggressive marketing or a practice covered by the Black list.

3. THE ASSESSMENT OF MISLEADING ADVERTISING: A COMPARISON

As described in Part 2, the provisions of the UCPD on misleading commercial practices have been incorporated into the Swedish Marketing Act. The application of the Act is intended to be in line with the Directive's requirements. However, two basic problems thus arise. First of all, there is still considerable uncertainty as to the correct interpretation of the requirements of the Directive in the absence of CJEU case law. Much will depend on its forthcoming development, in particular the extent to which differences related to national, cultural and social factors will be accepted. Secondly, Sweden is still at an early phase in the application of its new Act. Having these caveats in mind, it is of interest to compare the assessment of misleading practices under European law and in Swedish practice. The text will concentrate on the most important type of misleading commercial practice, ie, misleading advertising.

[34] Directive 2005/29 Art 2 (d). The Black list explicitly prohibits two types of promotions: making persistent and unwanted solicitations (para 26) and creating the false impression the consumer has won a prize or equivalent benefit (para 31).

[35] Proposal for a European Parliament and Council Regulation Concerning Sales Promotions in the Internal Market, COM (2002) 585 final, see Stuyck, 'The Unfair Commercial Practices Directive and its Consequences for the Regulation of Sales Promotion and the Law of Unfair Competition' in Weatherill – Bernitz, *The Regulation of Unfair Commercial Practices under EC Directive 2005/29* s 159 ff, Stuyck, op. cit., (2006) 43 *Common Law Market Review* p 141.

[36] Cases C-261/07 and C/299/07, *VTB-VAB v Total Belgium and Galatea v Sanoma Magazines,* decided April 23, 2009 [2009] ECR 2009 I-2949.

[37] Case C-304/08, *Zentrale zur Bekämpfung unlauteren Wettbewerbs eV v Plus Warenhandelsgesellschaft mbH*, decided January 14, 2010, OJ C 179 from 03.07.2010, p 3.

It is natural to start looking at the established case law of the CJEU which formed the basis for the drafting of the Directive. These judgments of the CJEU reflect a reaction, based on a freedom of competition approach, against the traditionally restrictive German case law which tended to favour the protection of small business. A few examples will be mentioned.

An early misleading advertising case in the CJEU was the Nissan case[38] on parallel import from Belgium to France of Nissan cars which were being sold in France by a small retailer at cut price. The cars, sold as 'new', had never been driven but were registered for import purposes. They had fewer accessories than the basic models sold in France. A French court requested a preliminary ruling whether or not the marketing of the cars was in conformity with the 1984 Directive on Misleading Advertising. The CJEU found it correct to advertise the cars as 'new' as they had not been driven on the highway and found the claim the cars were cheaper to be misleading only if it could be established that the decision to buy, on a part of a significant number of consumers to whom the advertising was addressed, was made in ignorance of the fact that the lower price of the cars was matched by a smaller number of accessories. The CJEU demonstrated a remarkably tolerant attitude towards the advertising claims made and succeeded in reconciling the 1984 Directive with the overall EU aim of keeping parallel import channels open. In this early case the principles to be applied were not yet clearly formulated.

Another illustrative case is Estée Lauder[39] about the labelling of a firming cream as 'lifting'. The Estée Lauder Cosmetics Co argued before a German court that the use of the term 'lifting' was misleading because it gave the impression that the use of the firming cream would obtain results identical or comparable to surgical lifting. The CJEU, asked for a preliminary ruling, was obviously not impressed by the argument and cited another well-known case in the same area, Gut Springenheide:[40]

> ...when it has fallen to the Court, in the context of the interpretation of Directive 84/450 [on misleading advertising] to weigh the risk of misleading consumers against the requirements of the free movement of goods, it has held that, in order to determine whether a particular description, trademark or promotional description is misleading, it is necessary to take into account the presumed expectations of an average consumer who is reasonably well informed and reasonably observant and circumspect.[41]

The CJEU continued:

> Although, at first sight, the average consumer – reasonably well informed and reasonably observant and circumspect – ought not to expect a cream whose name incorporates the term 'lifting' to produce enduring effects, it nevertheless remains for

[38] C-373/90, *Criminal Proceedings against X*, [1992] ECR I-131.

[39] C-220/98, *Estée Lauder Cosmetics v Lancaster Group*, [2000] ECR I-117.

[40] C-210/96, *Gut Springenheide and Tusky*, [1998] ECR I-4657.

[41] Case C-220/98 para 27.

> the national court to determine, in the light of all the relevant factors, whether that is the position in the case.[42]

A third example is the Hartlauer case[43] on the interpretation of the provisions on comparative advertising, nowadays part of the 2006 MCAD Directive, applicable to both B2B and B2C advertising. The Hartlauer Company, a well-known price-cutter marketing spectacles in Austria, made a direct price comparison with spectacles sold by the Pippig Co at a much higher price. Without going into details, the CJEU, asked by the Austrian court for a preliminary ruling, basically accepted the type of comparative advertising at issue and underlined that member states were precluded from applying stricter standards as far as the form and content of the comparison was concerned. Referring to the Estée Lauder case, the CJEU noted the national court should take into account the presumed expectations of an average consumer who is reasonably well informed and reasonably observant and circumspect.

Characteristic of the cases mentioned, and others, is the pro competition approach taken by the CJEU and its tendency not to apply too strict a standard. These basic features of the case law have been carried forward into the UCPD which also uses the average consumer as benchmark. The general clause on unfair commercial practices and the prohibitions in the Directive on misleading and aggressive practices all refer to the average consumer as the person likely to be misled, having his freedom of choice restricted etc.[44] The Recitals refer to the notional, typical consumer and the benchmark is described as:

> The average consumer, who is reasonably well-informed and reasonably observant and circumspect, taken into account social, cultural and linguistic factors, as interpreted by the Court of Justice.[45]

As is explicitly stated in the Recitals to the UCPD, the average consumer benchmark is not a statistical test.[46] National courts and authorities will have to exercise their own faculty of judgment to determine the typical reaction of the average consumer.[47] This is fully in line with existing case law in the Nordic countries but certainly different from what had been the common approach in Germany. In German unfair competition case law consumer research polls or other statistical market surveys have been used as evidence and it has often been considered sufficient that some 10 – 15 per cent of consumers, or the relevant group of specific addressees, have been misled by the advertising. However,

[42] Ibid at para 30.

[43] C-44/01, *Pippig Augenoptik v Harlauer Handelsgesellschaft et al,* [2003] ECR I-3095.

[44] Directive 2005/29 Arts. 5 (2) (b), 6 (1) first sentence and 8.

[45] Ibid Recital 18.

[46] On the development and application of the average consumer concept see Weatherill, 'Who is the "Average Consumer"' in Weatherill – Bernitz, *The Regulation of Unfair Commercial Practices under EC Directive 2005/29* pp 115 ff.

[47] Directive 2005/29 Recital 18, last sentence. The CJEU gave certain hints in this direction in the Estée Lauder case.

the EUJ has taken a reserved attitude towards this type of evidence in both the Gut Springenheide and Estée Lauder judgments and the Directive confirms this sceptical position. The average consumer is to be considered as a legal concept.

Further, in order to curb over-excessive use of fairness standards, the Directive requires material distortion of consumer economic behaviour as a prerequisite for considering a commercial practice to be unfair.[48] This requirement functions as a threshold and constitutes a *de minimis* rule. It requires that a commercial practice causes or is likely to cause the average consumer to take a transactional decision he would not have taken otherwise.[49] The requirement excludes misleading representations of an irrelevant or petty character. Taking a tolerant position, the text of the Directive talks explicitly about

> The common and legitimate advertising practice of making exaggerated statements or statements which are not meant to be taken literally.[50]

Likewise, the material distortion requirement is applicable to omission of relevant information. According to the text of the Directive omission of information is prohibited only if the omission causes or is likely to cause the average consumer to take a transactional decision he would not have taken otherwise.[51]

To conclude, the primary aim of the Directive is to continue and further develop the basic, pro competition principles of assessment already formulated by the CJEU. The Directive believes in the informed consumer, 'reasonably observant and circumspect' to quote the often used phrase of the CJEU, who is able to take exaggerations in advertising *cum grano salis*.

How do these principles relate to the assessment in practice of misleading advertising in Swedish marketing law? Has the principles of assessment laid down in the Directive reduced the level of consumer protection under the Swedish law? We are at an early stage but the preparatory works behind the new Swedish Act and the emerging new case law provide some guidance.

Section 10 of the Swedish Marketing Act contains a general prohibition of misleading marketing which largely follows the text of the Directive (Article 6, in particular), albeit somewhat shortened. In line with the Directive, it is required that the marketing practice affects or probably would affect the recipient's[52] ability to make a well-founded decision, the transaction test (Section 8, in particular). However, the implementation of the text of the Directive is not precise as the latter text (in Article 6.2) refers to a practice which 'causes or is likely to cause the average consumer to take a transactional decision that he would not have taken otherwise'. As one can see, the Swedish text is missing a reference to the concept of the average consumer, the other threshold developed

[48] Ibid Art 5 (2) (b).
[49] Ibid Art 6.1 first sentence.
[50] Ibid Art 5.3 *in fine*.
[51] Ibid Art 7.1.
[52] The term recipient is used instead of consumer as the Act also comprises practices addressed to non-consumers, primarily business firms.

by the CJEU as described *supra*. Indeed, references to the 'average consumer' are nowhere to be found in the Swedish statute. In both the provisions which transpose the text of the general clause in the Directive (Article 5.2 b) and the article on aggressive commercial practices (Article 8) itself, references to the average consumer which are to be found in the Directive are missing.[53]

In the preparatory works to the new Swedish Marketing Act it was argued that it would be unnecessary to include a reference to the average consumer as such a test was already applied in the case law.[54] However, there is reason to believe that the concept of the average consumer was unpopular in governmental circles, as the concept could be taken as indicating the desire to lower the standard of protection. In Swedish case law the emphasis has generally been on determining whether or not a specific statement or practice should be considered misleading or not and on this point, quite strict standards were normally applied. Statements made are generally understood literally and there has been little scope for accepting exaggerations. In Swedish case law, there has seldom been any discussion of how well-informed and observant consumers should be considered to be.[55] So far, these strict standards, well-established by the previous case law, seem to be being carried on in the application of the new Marketing Act by the Market Court. There are references in recent judgments to the transaction test, albeit satisfied very easily.

It is possible under the Directive to offer extended protection to particularly vulnerable target groups, eg, children and sick people. The Directive text speaks of clearly identifiable groups of consumers who are particularly vulnerable to the commercial practice or the underlying product because of their mental or physical infirmity, age or credulity. The need for special protection of particular groups of consumers in a weak position was particularly stressed by the Nordic countries during the deliberations of the text of the Directive.[56] On this point, Swedish case law is in line with the Directive, but there is no explicit provision inserted in the statutory text.

Normally, traders carry the burden of proof as to the accuracy of factual claims they have made.[57] This reversed burden of proof has been well established in Swedish case law since the enactment of the first Marketing Act of 1970 but has not found statutory expression in the new Act.

[53] Another peculiarity in the Swedish text should be noted. According to Section 5, the general clause, and Section 6, aggressive marketing, the recipient's ability to make a well-founded transaction decision has to be affected *appreciably* (Swedish: *i märkbar mån*). In Section 8, misleading advertising, the word 'appreciably' is missing, indicating the test shall be applied less strictly. This differentiation between the statutory provisions has no counterpart in the UCPD and the Government Bill offers no clear reasons for it. One might assume the legislator wanted to preserve the status quo in the case law.

[54] Government Bill 2007/08:115 p 68.

[55] The issue is discussed in Steen, *Genomsnittskonsumentens snedvridna ekonomiska beteende – konsekvenser av svenskt införlivande av direktivet om otillbörliga affärsmetoder*, Europarättslig Tidskrift 2009 s 617 ff.

[56] Directive 2005/29 Recitals 18 and 19 and Art 5.3 (the general clause).

[57] Ibid Recital 21, second sentence.

As the Directive prescribes total harmonization within its ambit of application, there should be no room for differences among the member states in the assessment of what constitutes misleading advertising, save for cases in which actual differences can be established in consumers' perception or understanding of a certain type of marketing practice.[58] However, the realities as expressed in legal traditions and evaluations, seem somewhat different. It remains to be seen whether the continuing development of EU case law will lead to the introduction in Swedish statutory or case law of the 'average consumer' and whether this will indeed lead to a certain lowering of the standards presently applied in Sweden in relation to the correctness of advertising statements and practices.

4. THE ASSESSMENT OF PASSING-OFF: A COMPARISON

As explained in Part 2, the UCPD and the Swedish Marketing Acts have different legal structures; the Directive only covers B2C relations while the Swedish Act also covers B2B relations and has as one of its basic purposes to prevent marketing that is unfair to traders (Section 1 of the Act). However, this difference is not as radical and total as one might think.

Many unfair business practices can be seen as such from the viewpoints of competitors or other businesses as well as from a consumer protection perspective, albeit with a different emphasis in the assessment of the character of the unfairness. Such practices are normally covered by the Directive; the view that the Directive excludes B2B transactions is therefore only partially correct. It is noted in the recitals that unfair advertising, which directly harms consumers' economic interests, indirectly harms the economic interests of legitimate competitors as well.[59] This indirect protection of the interests of competitors has different aspects. Often, advertising or other marketing practices are directed at consumers but in such cases national law based on the Directive will, in effect, offer protection covering a broader circle of addresses or parties interested. Misleading advertising, addressing both end consumers as well as commercial purchasers, are the obvious example. Another aspect is the indirect beneficial effect on those competitors who stick to honest practices. As stated in the recitals, the Directive indirectly protects legitimate businesses from competitors who do not play by its rules.[60] This approach which treats the interests of competitors indirectly or in a manner complementary to the interests of consumers has much in common with the structure of Nordic marketing legislation but was unfamiliar to the German unfair competition law tradition which focused on protection of the honest and law-abiding competitor.

[58] The issue is discussed in J Stuyck et al, 'Confidence Through Fairness?' (2006) 43 *Common Market Law Review* pp 107 ff, 115 ff.

[59] Directive 2005/29 Recital 6 first sentence.

[60] Ibid Recital 8.

The object of the Directive to offer, within its general limits of application, some protection for the interests of competitors and the business community in general is further demonstrated by the provision that competitors, as well as organizations, shall be regarded under national law as having a legitimate interest in combating unfair practices. This includes the right to take legal action against such practices and to initiate other appropriate legal proceedings.[61] Orders for the cessation of unfair commercial practices are available remedies.[62]

There are certain practices, explicitly included in the Directive, which have a particularly strong link to the interests of competitors and which might even be regarded as inclusions of protection of unfair B2B practices in the Directive. Thus, the use of brands, trade-names, packaging (get-up) of products etc which mislead the average consumer about the commercial origin of the products and cause him or her to purchase the products on the basis of that misconception (passing off in a general sense) is covered by the Directive.[63] The Black list includes as a prohibited practice the promotion of a product similar to a product made by a particular manufacturer in such a manner as deliberately to mislead the consumer into believing that the product is made by the same manufacturer when it is not (para 13). Of particular practical importance is misleading advertising or misleading exposure of products or their packaging in sales outlets causing consumers to purchase look-alikes.

The standard of assessment is touched upon in one of the Recitals which declares it is not the intention of the Directive to reduce consumer choice by prohibiting the promotion of products which look similar to other products unless this similarity confuses consumers as to the commercial origin of the product and is therefore misleading.[64] This recital can be read as a pronouncement in favour of a rather restrictive view of the scope of protection offered, indicating the priority of consumer perception and thus possibly reducing the application of the Directive to instances of clear deception of consumers looking for a particular brand or the like. In this economically important area, it will be the task of the CJEU to clarify and develop the legal standards to be applied. Most likely the CJEU will use its present trademark law jurisprudence on confusion and deception as an important point of departure. The Court's recent decision in the Oréal case clearly points in that direction.[65]

Misleading use of attributes, qualifications, connections to other undertakings, ownership of intellectual property rights and similar misleading actions all

[61] Ibid Art 11 on enforcement.

[62] Ibid Art 11 (2) (a).

[63] See, in particular, Directive 2005/29 Art 6 (2) (a) which covers 'any marketing of a product, including comparative advertising, which creates confusion with any products, trademarks, trade names or other distinguishing marks of a competitor'. See also Art 6 (1) (b), referring to misleading information about commercial origin of a product.

[64] Ibid Recital 14.

[65] Case-487/07, *LÓréal SA et al v Bellure* NV et al, decided June 18, 2009 [2009] ECR I-5185.

constitute typical examples of unfair B2B practices.[66] They also fall under the Directive if they are contrary to the standards laid down in the Directive as to what is misleading to the consumer and having an economic effect. However, misleading practices addressed exclusively to business customers clearly fall outside the scope of the UCPD. Here, as mentioned in Part 2, only the far less comprehensive Directive on Misleading and Comparative Advertising (MCAD) is applicable.[67]

The Swedish Marketing Act contains a special provision on passing-off (Section 14) which functions as the core provision in this area with the caption Misleading copies. It reads:

> A trader may not, in the course of marketing, use copies that are misleading in that they can easily be confused with another trader's known and distinctive products. This does not, however, apply to copies the design of which is primarily intended to render the product functional.[68]

The term 'copy', used in the English translation, should be understood broadly. The Swedish term used is *efterbildning*[69] which includes imitations and look-alikes in a broader sense. Thus, it comprises what is normally understood by passing-off. Within the ambit of marketing, the provision is intended to satisfy the requirements of the Paris Convention for the Protection of Industrial Property in the field of protection against acts of competition contrary to honest practices.[70] The Swedish provision on Misleading copies has a broader scope than Paragraph 13 of the Black list; under Section 14 it is unfair to promote a product similar to a product made by a particular manufacturer in such a manner as deliberately to mislead the consumer into believing that the product is made by the same manufacturer when it is not.[71] Contrary to the Black list provision, the provision on Misleading copies does not require an intentional deception but only that there be a risk of deceptive effect. However, the transaction test still has to be fulfilled as well. There has to be a probable effect on the recipient's ability to make a well-founded decision. The provision covers different types of deception as to the commercial origin of products. These can involve the design of the product itself as well as different marks or other trade symbols used in

[66] Directive 2005/29 Art 6 (1) (f) reads: 'The nature, attributes and rights of the trader or his agent, such as his identity and assets, his qualifications, status, approval, affiliation or connection and ownership of industrial, commercial or intellectual property rights or his awards and distinctions.'

[67] Other types of unfair B2B commercial practices, not affecting consumers and thus falling outside the scope of the UCPD, are normally not subject to harmonized EU law. An example would be denigrating statements in advertising about other businesses (normally competitors) which are not misleading and have no bearing on consumer interests.

[68] SMA (SFS 2008:486) §14.

[69] German: *Nachahmung*.

[70] Art 10 *bis* of the Convention has a list of prohibited acts which include: 'All acts of such a nature as to create confusion by any means whatever with the establishment, the goods, or the industrial or commercial activities of a competitor.'

[71] In Swedish law, the provisions of the Black list are applicable also in B2B-relations (Section 4, Marketing Act).

connection with the product. Thus, the term 'product' used in the statutory text is also to be understood in a very broad sense. However, to enjoy protection against misleading copying, the product has to be distinctive and known to the public. The protection does not cover elements which are primarily intended to render the product functional. There is much Swedish case law on passing-off which, so far, has been maintained under the new Marketing Act without change. In practice, the Marketing Act functions as a primary tool for stopping the use of all types of designations which are apt to deceive the public.

There is also a significant body of case law under the general clause of the Marketing Act (Section 5) on taking unfair advantage of the reputation of well-known trademarks or other trade symbols of other traders.[72] This case law is not restricted to comparative advertising, where it has a statutory basis following the requirements of the MCAD,[73] but has general application as well. Thus, the Act fulfils an important supplementary role in relation to intellectual property, primarily trademark law.

In comparing passing-off under the Directive and in the Swedish marketing law there are obvious similarities. In both systems the main focus is on competition and consumer protection. Practices are assessed in terms of their effects on consumers rather than competitors, the protection offered the latter being basically indirect. The use of copies and look-alikes does not constitute unfair commercial practice as such; an element of misleading of the consumers is also required. In the area of passing-off the Directive actually follows a pattern which was already well established in Swedish marketing law.

5. THE SUPERVISION AND ENFORCEMENT MECHANISMS: A COMPARISON

The UCPD primarily deals with the substantive law. There is a clear discrepancy between the full harmonization provided for in the area of substantive law and the meagre provisions on supervision and enforcement. From the viewpoint of Sweden and the other Nordic countries, this constitutes an important weakness in the European system.

It is primarily the organization of its enforcement which gives the Swedish legislation on unfair commercial practices, like its Nordic counterparts, its particular emphasis on consumer protection. There is a central governmental body responsible for supervision in each of the Nordic countries. In Sweden, this body consists of the Consumer Agency (*Konsumentverket*) and, as an integrated part of the Agency, the Consumer Ombudsman (*Konsumentombudsmannen*). The person holding the office of Consumer Ombudsman is also the Director

[72] Swedish: *renommésnyltning*.

[73] Section 18 of the Act, see n 33.

General of the Consumer Agency.[74] For the day to day application of the Marketing Act, there is a special secretariat dealing with legal matters within the Agency, which is headed by the Deputy Consumer Ombudsman. This is an efficient system of supervision which has been in place since the 1970s. The enactment of the 2008 Marketing Act did not involve any changes in the structure of this supervision and enforcement system.

The responsibility for the enforcement of the marketing legislation being primarily in the hands of a Consumer Ombudsman, is a special feature of the Nordic EU and EEA countries. On the other hand, private consumer organizations only play a rather marginal role in the application of the legislation. The system has to certain degree a counterpart in the United Kingdom, where the Office of Fair Trading (OFT) supervises both the competition law on restrictive practices and monopolies and marketing legislation. However, in the continental EU countries there is normally no generally applicable system for government supervision and enforcement of unfair commercial practices legislation. This consumer related enforcement lies primarily in the hands of consumer associations organized as private law bodies. The scope and effectiveness of enforcement by consumer associations probably varies between different member states and types of economic activities. In practice, the emphasis in most continental member states is on private enforcement by competing enterprises and trade associations. In most cases, the result seems to be a less comprehensive and efficient enforcement, often unsurprisingly having its primary focus on B2B relations.

It should be added that the application of the Marketing Act in B2B-relations is in the hands of private enforcement. In Sweden and the other Nordic countries, there are every year a considerable number of such law suits, a competitor in most cases acting as the plaintiff. Most of these cases concern misleading advertising or passing-off.

The UCPD is vague when it comes to enforcement; it had, after all, to respect the basic procedural autonomy of the member states. Article 11.1 on Enforcement states that the Member States shall ensure that adequate and effective means exist to combat unfair commercial practices. However, it is left to the states to have in place either a private law system based on persons or organizations, including competitors,[75] taking legal action or to have a public law system based on an administrative authority competent to decide complaints itself or to initiate appropriate legal proceedings. It is for each member state to decide which system shall apply and also whether to combine the systems. Thus, the implementation of the UCPD did not require the member states to change their enforcement systems. In most cases, they seem to have implemented the

[74] The basic provisions on the task of the Consumer Ombudsman in applying the Marketing Act are to be found in the Act itself (S 28, Ss 42 ff etc). Supplementary provisions related to the Consumer Ombudsman are to be found in the Government Instruction for the office. Within specific areas, such as food, pharmaceuticals and financial services, the Consumer Ombudsman cooperates by way of different specialized agencies.

[75] On the position of competitors, Part 4 at n 61.

Directive within their already existing legal framework; which may have been to the detriment of homogeneity in the application of the rules based on the UCPD. Thus, this aspect of the Directive has been left open to the widely varying ways of possible transposition into national law.

In relation to legal remedies, the UCPD is somewhat more precise. The member states have to have a judicial or administrative system to which powers are conferred to order the cessation of unfair commercial practices (Article 11.2). There has also to be an accelerated procedure available, eg, interim measures. Also, the member states are obligated to lay down penalties for infringements of national provisions adopted in application of the Directive and make sure these are enforced and effective (Article 13). The Directive is mute on the issue of payment of damages.

Fulfilling these requirements has not been a problem for Swedish law. The transposition of the UCPD did not change the legal situation in the field of remedies and sanctions. Swedish marketing law contains no criminal provisions. The main sanction is prohibition from continuing a marketing practice found to be unlawful subject to a conditional financial penalty on default, ie, injunctions (Sections 23 and 26). It is possible to obtain interim orders (Section 27). Normally, injunctions and interim orders are issued by the court but in cases of minor importance the Consumer Ombudsman may issue either of them (Section 28). Most of the specific provisions in the Marketing Act and the provisions in the Black list are also sanctioned by administrative fees, so-called market disruption charges, provided the provisions have been contravened intentionally or negligently (Section 29 ff). No charge shall be imposed in minor cases. Only the Consumer Ombudsman can institute proceedings in respect of a market disruption charge. There are possibilities for traders and consumers to obtain damages when they suffer damage caused by intentional or negligent violations of the specific provisions of the Marketing Act (Section 37). In practice, damages play only a limited role as a legal remedy in relation to marketing practices in Sweden. It should be noted that the general clause in Section 5, stating marketing shall be consistent with good marketing practice, is only sanctioned by way of prohibition orders, normally issued subject to a fine in default.

Most cases on infringements of the provisions of the Market Act are handled by a specialized court, the Market Court, situated in Stockholm. In cases involving market disruption charges or damages, the Stockholm City Court acts as the court of first instance with the possibility of an appeal to the Market Court.

There is a well-established cooperation between the Consumer Agencies and Ombudsmen in the Nordic countries, ie, Sweden, Denmark, Finland and the EEA countries Norway and Iceland. This cooperation was already in existence in the 1970s and 1980s and involves regular meetings and exchange of information and experience, including exchange of information of actions taken in relation to unfair commercial practices having a cross-border dimension. This inter-Nordic cooperation is efficient and works smoothly.

On a general EU level, there is the 1998 Directive on Injunctions for the Protection of Consumers' Interests ((98/27/EC) and the 2004 Regulation on Consumer Protection Cooperation (2006/2004/EC). The 1998 Directive is implemented in Sweden by a special Act of 2000 on The Right for Certain Foreign Consumer Authorities and Consumer Organizations to Bring Legal Action. The Act gives certain authorities and organizations in other EU/EEA countries, as listed in the Official Journal of the EU, standing in Swedish courts in cases concerning the application of the Swedish Marketing Act. So far there have been no reported Swedish cases under the Act. The 2004 Regulation deals with mutual assistance and enforcement coordination. In Sweden, the Consumer Agency is the designated authority for the cooperation envisaged in the Directive.

There has also been some cooperation between the Swedish Consumer Ombudsman and the Office of Fair Trading (OFT) in the United Kingdom. However, outside the Nordic countries and Britain, there has so far been rather little cooperation with other Member States. The primary reason seems to be that in many EU countries there is a lack of consumer authorities with the capacity to fulfil a well-functioning supervisory role.[76] This hampers the possibilities of coordinating investigations and actions involving economically important cases of unfair commercial practices which have a European dimension and involve cross-border marketing of goods or services. An obvious example would be a multinational company using Internet marketing containing misleading or aggressive elements.

6. CONCLUSIONS

The UCPD is a far-reaching Directive aiming at a single European regulatory framework governing unfair commercial practices. It requires full harmonization and is based on the twin purposes of opening up the internal market in the advertising sector and enhancing consumer protection. How has the Swedish marketing legislation, basically formulated in the 1970s, and its kin in the other Nordic countries, fared when meeting the requirements of the Directive?

As this article demonstrates, the transposition of the Directive has not caused any major difficulties in Sweden, although the implementation of a number of new provisions made it desirable to draft a wholly new Swedish Marketing Act. The Directive and the Swedish marketing legislation have a fundamental thrust in common, namely, consumer protection. Another factor facilitating the transposition has been the existing pro-competitive bent of Swedish legislation; it has never regarded the protection of competitors as a primary purpose. The protection offered to competitors against misleading advertising and passing-off has always been linked to the protection offered to consumers. In relation to these aspects the Directive and the Swedish legislation have a similar structure.

As discussed in Part 3, the Swedish legislator has taken a cautious position in relation to the concept of the average consumer, used as the benchmark in

[76] Micklitz, 'Transborder Law Enforcement – Does it Exist?' in Weatherill – Bernitz, *The Regulation of Unfair Commercial Practices under EC Directive 2005/29* pp 235 ff.

the Directive and in the case law of the CJEU. Fears have been expressed that the application of the average consumer test might lead to a lowering of the protective standard established in Swedish marketing law. On this point, it will be interesting to follow forthcoming developments, both in EU and national law.

The primary weakness of the Directive, as seen from a Swedish and Nordic perspective, is the structure of the supervision and enforcement system. There are only weak mechanisms available on the European level to tackle situations in which, for example, a large European company is using Internet advertising containing misleading or aggressive marketing elements in a number of countries. It seems that action will have to be taken separately in each national jurisdiction where the practice takes place. From this point of view, it is easy to understand why the member states on the Council opposed the Commission's original proposal to base the Directive on the country of origin principle. The introduction of such a system would require there to be a reliable and well-functioning system of supervision and enforcement of the unfair commercial practices legislation throughout the EU, which did not seem to be the case. The establishment at the EU level of a more elaborate network for cooperation between consumer authorities and organizations in the Member States in the field of marketing law would indeed be strongly welcomed. The European Competition Network (ECN), set up by the Commission in collaboration with the competition authorities in the member states for the enforcement of European competition law, could here be mentioned as a possible model.

Will there be a quick and full harmonization of the unfair commercial practices law in Europe as actually applied in the member states? That is hard to foresee because of the different legal traditions in the field and the structure of the supervision and enforcement mechanisms. Most likely, companies will find that even after the successful implementation of the Directive in all member states, identical advertising and marketing practices will meet legal hindrances in certain member states while being considered acceptable in others. It will probably be necessary to have had a considerable number of cases referred to the CJEU for preliminary rulings, and possibly also Commission infringement proceedings, before a level playing field will emerge. It can be anticipated that the Swedish courts will play an important role in furthering this development.[77]

[77] On 3 Dec 2009, the European Commission has issued as a Commission Staff Working Document Guidance on the Implementation/Application of Directive 2005/29/EC on Unfair Commercial Practices, SEC (2009) 1666. This comprehensive document is non-bindning but addresses a number of issues of interpretation of the Directive. It aims at providing guidance and ensuring uniform interpretation and consistent enforcement in the Member States. Recently, in its decision 2010 No 20 of 8 July 2010, Specsavers Sweden v Synoptik Sweden, the Swedish Market Court, citing the Guidance, has changed and liberalized its long established case law related to the use in marketing of the words 'free' and 'gratis' in connection with promotions in order to comply with paragraph 20 of the Black List as interpreted in the Guidance, paragraph 3.4. According to the new rule it will be possible in Sweden to use promotions of the type 'buy one get one free' provided the quality or composition of the paid-for items has not been reduced, the 'free' item is genuinely separate and the price has not been increased.

12

Two Novelties in Swedish Competition Law: Fine Order and Trading Prohibition – A Critical Review

PROFESSOR LARS HENRIKSSON

1. ENFORCEMENT OF COMPETITION RULES IN SWEDEN

Two major changes of the Swedish Competition Act have been introduced in order to improve enforcement efficiency. In this article I analyse these changes and the challenges that lie ahead for the application of competition law in Sweden.

Some of the Swedish Competition rules are now designed to be harmonised in accordance with EU Law and the 2008 Competition Act[1] introduces several changes to the previous act[2] to provide further harmonisation with EU law. Experience revealed some major problems with the previous Competition Act. There had been few cases in which large administrative fines have been awarded and there had been substantial reductions in the fines awarded by the Courts in relation to the amounts requested by the Swedish Competition Authority, Konkurrensverket (KKV). Further, there had been no successful cases on prohibitions regarding concentrations since the first EU-based competition act entered into force in 1993.

Complex and Lengthy Processes Causing Low Efficiency in Enforcement

Since 1993, the application of the Competition Act and enforcement of the prohibitions contained in the competition rules has led to long and drawn out proceedings before the Swedish courts. The time between the first summons and

[1] Konkurrenslag (SFS 2008:579) amended by (SFS 2009:1280) effective 8 December 2009, and (SFS 2010:642) effective from 28 June 2010 (incorporating references in Swedish competition law and EU Regulations into the provisions of Arts 101 and 102 TFEU).

[2] Konkurrenslag (SFS 1993:20).

final judgment has, in many cases, been several years, and in some cases, several years before cases have even been heard in the first instance.[3]

This in itself is a serious problem. Generally, competition law cases are perceived to be very complex and involve difficult economic-legal considerations, and in most cases numerous witnesses have to be heard. The process material, documents and pleas that the parties submit to the Court etc are extensive and since trials, which may lead to administrative fines, are subject to oral proceeding, all materials submitted must be orally presented during the trial. Taken together, all these factors lead to a time consuming process.

Underlying Problems and Main Reasons for Inefficiency

The Government pointed out several reasons for the lengthy procedure in the preparatory works for the updated Competition Act of 2008. There appears to be a natural inertia in the system affecting both KKV and the courts. Cases involving administrative fines are hard-to-grasp in the early stage of the process. A public inquiry also identified problems related to poor case handling by KKV, which was deemed to have had a negative influence on their handling by the courts.[4] The Swedish Code of Judicial Procedure contains several remedies for speeding up the process which permits, *inter alia*, a means of preparing trials and the active governance of the court during litigation. However, according to the public inquiry, these means have not been fully utilised. All these problems were regarded as demonstrating a need for changes to the enforcement rules.[5]

This inefficiency is problematic for several reasons. Lengthy processes before the Courts may raise concerns from the point of view of legal certainty. Companies are entitled to expect swift, efficient, and legally correct justice when the state brings actions against them. Poor handling by the courts may also be counter-productive in relation to the objectives of the law and, in a worst case, may lead to reducing respect for the law itself. On the other hand, competition law cases generally involve highly complex economic-legal issues that should not be taken lightly. In most cases there are simply no short answers to the complicated and multifarious legal questions posed.

Competition law cases will always be subject to extensive investigations and assessment by KKV and the materials to be considered by the courts will usually be voluminous. Most questions are also open to litigation by the parties, albeit not to the extent that competition litigation may be regarded as a defender's

[3] See Prop 2007/2008:135, *Ny konkurrenslag m.m*, p 76. As an illustrative example, in the pending *TeliaSonera ADSL*-case, case, T31862-04 KKV filed the claim in 2004. The Stockholm City Court eventually referred the case to European Court of Justice (CJEU) *for a preliminary ruling* in January 2009. See Case C-52/09 *Konkurrensverket v TeliaSonera Sverige AB*, OJ C 90 of 18.04.2009, p 12. AG Mazak's Opinion in the case was only delivered on 2 September 2010.

[4] See Prop 2007/2008:135, p 76.

[5] Ibid; SOU 2006:99, p 185.

paradise. However, the law has to strike a delicate balance between fierce competition that is to the benefit of consumers and actions and co-ordinations that are detrimental to the good of society in general, and consumers in particular.

2. THE NEED FOR CHANGES TO THE COMPETITION ACT

On the one hand, efficiency in the enforcement of competition rules is deemed to be of the utmost importance and, as posited by the government, the judicial system must be designed and organised to provide swift, fair and correct justice.[6] Since the old system clearly had serious drawbacks, a major issue for correcting them was whether to change the foundations of the procedural rules to empower KKV to award administrative fines in the first instance, which might then be appealed to the courts. The public inquiry did identify one clear way to improve enforcement, that is, the quality of the decisions and claims of KKV which was to utilise the time-saving instruments already enshrined in the procedural rules.[7] The government agreed with the point but did not take any clear position on the delicate issue of suspected poor case handling by KKV. It could be argued that this was not to be expected in a bill changing the rules because improvement within the current system was ultimately the responsibility of the government itself. It cannot be ruled out that such shortcomings resulted from inadequate funding, budgetary restrictions, formulation of the governmental approval documents etc. Any critique of the application of the law was, therefore, not to be expected.

However, as the Government did propose changes to the existing Competition Act, there appeared to be something wrong either with the system itself or the application of the system taking into account the constraints of budgets, organisation etc.

3. OVERVIEW OF THE CHANGES

I focus here on two procedural changes that entered into force on 1st November 2008. These are the new administrative fine order and the disqualification order. In addition, the new Competition Act also included review permits, now needed for a party to be able to appeal to the Market court, changes in the method of setting of fines and, finally, amended rules on concentration control. By and large, the latter are now more fully harmonised with EU-rules.

One of the major changes discussed in the preparatory works was empowering KKV to adopt decisions on infringements and sanctions in

[6] See Prop. 2007/2008:135, p 83.
[7] See SOU 2006:99, p 187.

the first instance. The current system under Chapter 3, Section 5 of the Competition Act, requires KKV to request that the Stockholm District Court order an undertaking to pay an administrative fine if the undertaking, or a person acting on behalf of the undertaking, intentionally or negligently has infringed the prohibitions in Chapter 2, Section 1 or 7 of the Competition Act or Article 101 or 102 TFEU. Entrusting KKV with such powers would naturally call for a major organisational change and possibly a budgetary change, as the authority would have to act and organise itself in a manner more or less identical to the EU Commission. Such a change would also force KKV to act more in more of a judicial role including the obligation to adopt decisions of such quality as would withstand the full judicial review by the courts. Naturally, such a change would bring about demands for separation of the functions within the authority in order to ensure fair handling and due process. This could eliminate any potential need for mere prosecutorial tactics on behalf of KKV. On the whole, such a change would, I submit, have had merits that cannot be overlooked.

3.1 Changes Violating Fundamental Human Rights?

In the end, the Government decided not to implement any major changes in the procedural system. It pointed out as the main reason for not changing the current system that granting KKV the right to impose administrative fines in the first instance could raise concerns from a legal security point of view in general and which could be contrary to Article 6.1 of the European Convention for the Protection of Human Rights and Fundamental Freedoms (ECHR) in particular.[8] Such a system, in addition, was considered to have the potential for violating Article 2 in Protocol No 7 to the EHCR.[9]

In order to make an assessment of the appropriateness of any change in the awarding of fines, one must first consider the very nature of administrative fines, as this may have an effect upon the manner in which enforcement should be organised. Referring to the European Court on Human Rights, the CJEU stated in *Hüls* that the administrative fines used as sanctions for violating the competition rules are to be considered as equal to 'criminal' sanctions within the

[8] See Prop 2007/2008:135, p 84. Art 6 of the European Convention for the Protection of Human Rights and Fundamental Freedoms(acceded to by Art 6(2) TEU, and Protocol No 8 to the TEU), states, *inter alia*, that everyone is entitled to a fair and public hearing within a reasonable time by an independent and impartial tribunal established by law.

[9] See Prop 2007/2007:135 p 84. The Article referred to covers right of appeal in criminal matters. It states that' [e]veryone convicted of a criminal offence by a tribunal shall have the right to have his conviction or sentence reviewed by a higher tribunal. The exercise of this right, including the grounds on which it may be exercised, shall be governed by law'. Further, '...this right may be subject to exceptions in regard to offences of a minor character, as prescribed by law, or in cases in which the person concerned was tried in the first instance by the highest tribunal or was convicted following an appeal against acquittal.'

meaning of Article 6 of the ECHR.[10] However, it is also explicitly made clear in Regulation 1/2003 that decisions on fines are not of a criminal law nature.[11] In *Boehringer Mannheim* the Court further ruled that the purpose of the sanctions is to stifle unlawful behaviour of undertakings and to prevent recurrence of antitrust conduct.[12]

It is therefore clear that the fine system must be in line with general rules on human rights and consequently must give enterprises a right to appeal as well as a fair and public hearing within a reasonable time.

Such concerns about such a major procedural change, as expressed by the Swedish Government, appear rather surprising as the Government immediately thereafter made clear that any change of this sort would in fact provide for not one but two levels of appeal. Hence, it is difficult to see any human rights concerns related to any such changes. In fact, enabling KKV to award fines in the first instance would, on the contrary, provide for another instance which would permit appeal first to the Stockholm City court and subsequently to the Market Court. Under the current system, there is only one court of appeal, the Market court, which is also the final appellate level.

All in all, the Government concluded in 2008 that there was no need to make any substantial change to the procedural rules in order to enhance the efficiency of the procedure. Instead, it called for only some 'minor adjustments'.[13] Although notably, the Government regarded the proposed changes as not seriously significant, this appears to be the end product of a careful balancing act. On the one hand there appears to be an obvious need to tighten up flawed enforcement by structurally amending remedial measures. On the other hand any critique of either the authorities, or the courts' application of the law would have been awkward, although it was likely to be the main cause of the problem at hand. The key questions are, therefore, whether the proposed changes really target the actual problems and whether the new remedies are likely to provide the foundation for better outcomes in applying competition law. If not, there is a risk that that approach may divert attention from the real issues and sweep the real problems under the carpet provided by a new remedy.

[10] Case C-199/92 P, *Hüls AG v Commission*, [1999] ECR I. 4287. The Court held that '[i]t must also be accepted that, given the nature of the infringements in question and the nature and degree of severity of the ensuing penalties, the principle of the presumption of innocence applies to the procedures relating to infringements of the competition rules applicable to undertakings that may result in the imposition of fines or periodic penalty payments' (para 150). The CJEU here cited the judgments of the European Court of Human Rights of 21 February 1984, *Öztürk v Germany*, Series A No 73, and of 25 August 1987 *Lutz v Germany*, Series A No 123-A. See also, WP J Wils, *Efficiency and Justice in European Antitrust Enforcement*, (Hart Oxford, 2008), p 160.

[11] Council Regulation (EC) No 1/2003 of 16 December 2002 on the implementation of the rules on competition laid down in Arts 81 and 82 of the Treaty, OJ L 1, 4.1.2003, paras 1–25, Art 23(5).

[12] Case 45/69, *Boehringer Mannheim GmbH v Commission of the European Communities*, [1970] ECR 769, para 53.

[13] See Prop 2007/2008:135 p 85.

4. INTRODUCTION OF THE FINE ORDER

One of the major changes to the Competition Act was the introduction of a new remedy; namely the fine order. Pursuant to Chapter 3, section 16, instead of instituting proceedings regarding an administrative fine by bringing the case before the Stockholm City Court KKV may, in uncontested cases, order an undertaking to pay such a fine. A fine order may only be used if several criteria are met. First, the material circumstances regarding the infringement must be clear. Secondly, the undertaking must have conceded the action of KKV. The fine order is therefore voluntary for undertakings, at least insofar as it provides the alleged infringer with a choice between accepting the fine order and proceeding to adjudication.

To some extent the fine order can be viewed as a compromise. The Government decided not to give KKV the power of imposing fines in the first instance for the reasons explained above. However, as the Government points out, in some cases it would not be efficient to bring a fine claim to court, either for KKV, or for the undertaking in question. The fine order would therefore give undertakings an opportunity to put an infringement behind them and allow KKV and courts to utilise scarce resources for other and more important cases.[14]

4.1 Fine Order Applicable to All Infringements

It should be noted that the Government considered whether or not to introduce a special cap on fine orders, but in the end, decided not to do so. Instead, the 10 % maximum of annual turnover also applies to fine orders. Fine orders can be used in any case which may be subject to administrative fines in general and is, therefore, not reserved to petty infringement or simpler cases. From a legal security point of view, a fine order hinges on the fact that there cannot be any considerable uncertainty regarding the outcome of the alternative process before the Stockholm City Court. Although uncertainties may materialise in many different forms, the only limitation on the use of the fine order laid down in the preparatory works refers to cases where the material circumstances are unclear and cases which KKV considers have the potential to become precedents. In such cases, trial is mandatory and no fine order may be made.[15]

[14] See Prop 2007/08/137, p 87.
[15] See Prop 2007/08/137, p 88.

4.2 Evaluation of the fine order

Empowering KKV with Full Competence or Introducing Other Sanction Measures?

The fine order appears to be the end result of a compromise between maintaining the current system and giving KKV the possibility of deciding cases in the first instance. Arguments were made that it would not be advisable to grant KKV such a power on the grounds that – at least not in short run – this would not enhance the efficiency of enforcement insofar as total time to resolve cases would not actually be shortened by introducing yet another instance.[16] There were also legal security concerns because such a change would mean that KKV's role would be mixed. KKV's authority would comprise both investigative and adjudicatory aspects if no organisational changes were made to it.[17] Change of this nature would in fact call for a major change of the administration of the authority, and most likely a budgetary change as well. Apparently, the government was not ready to take this step.

I find it regrettable that this change was not made. Any concerns about KKV deciding cases in the first instance has obviously not been perceived as a major issue in the European Commission's own exercise of such powers under Articles 101 and 102 TFEU and Regulation 139/2004[18] in accordance with Regulation 1/2003. Empowering KKV with similar powers would, on the contrary, tend to make the public enforcement rules more harmonised. The legal security concerns thus appear to be minor.

The overall impression of the arguments justifying the introduction of the fine order is that it would provide a speedy way of closing cases that would otherwise be subject to lengthy court proceedings. Bearing in mind that the preparatory works explicitly state that the application of the law is the main problem, it appears illogical that improvements in the application of the law by the courts and KKV are not implemented first and then evaluated from an efficiency perspective. Although such improvements may well be made in due course, it is still a question as to why a real change, which might have forced KKV to act in a different way, was not effected at the start. The positive effects sought would then materialise as a result of changing the role of KKV and allowing it to become the real guardian of the competition rules.

The Objective of the Sanction System and Deterrence of Infringements

When evaluating a system of sanctions their major objectives must be borne in mind. What is the real purpose of the sanctions? So far as EU law is concerned,

[16] See Prop. 2007/08:137 pp 82 ff.

[17] Cf Prop. 2007/08:137 pp 82 ff.

[18] Council Regulation (EC) No 139/2004 of 20 January 2004 on the control of concentrations between undertakings (the EC Merger Regulation) OJ L 24, 29.01.2004, pp 1–22.

Article 103 TFEU provides that appropriate regulations or directives to give effect to the principles set out in Articles 101 and 102 TFEU shall be laid down by the Council and Article 104 TFEU requires Member State authorities to enforce them. In particular, such regulations or directives are to be designed, *inter alia*, to *ensure compliance* with the prohibitions laid down in Article 101(1) TFEU and in Article 102 TFEU by making provision for fines and periodic penalty payments. Rules on penalties for infringing the EU competition prohibitions are found in Articles 5, 23 and 24 of Regulation 1/2003. As early as the *ACF Chemiefarma* case, the CJEU stated that the object of administrative fine was to suppress illegal activities and to prevent any recurrence.[19] The Court also held in *Musique Diffusion francaise* that the Commission in its setting of fines must take into consideration not only the particular circumstances of the case but also the context in which the infringement occurs and must ensure that its action has the necessary deterrent effect.[20] The Commission points out that its task not only involves the investigation and sanction of individual infringements of the prohibitions, but it must also 'pursue a general policy designed to apply, in competition matters, the principles laid down by the Treaty and to steer the conduct of undertakings in the light of those principles'.[21]

From an economic perspective, enforcement mechanisms should be evaluated in relation to their ability to deter violations of the law.[22] In doing so, Van den Bergh and Camesasca argue that sanctions must be designed and applied in such a manner that '... a genuine dissuasive effect and ensure that firms have an incentive to avoid any kind of unlawful anti-competitive agreement or practice' is achieved.[23] When evaluating fine orders, it appears that one must ask whether or not they will actually contribute to such an effect.

It follows from settled case-law, described above, that deterrence is of the utmost importance. Wils also identifies three other effects of administrative fines; they may raise the cost of setting up and running cartels, have a moral effect by boosting commitment to antitrust prohibitions and serve as a corrective measure by way of the disgorgement of unjust enrichment.[24]

Any sanction system is likely to have a low deterrence effect if the real likelihood of being fined is very low. Therefore, the authorities must be able to detect and successfully bring legal actions against unlawful behaviour. In order to ease the investigatory burden of the Commission, the EU leniency system has

[19] See Case 41/69, *ACF Chemiefarma NV v Commission* [1970] ECR p 661, para 173.

[20] Joined cases 100 to 103/80, *SA Musique Diffusion française and others v Commission* [1983], ECR p 1825, para 106. See also CW Bellamy, Graham D Child, Peter M, Vivien Rose, *Bellamy & Child: European Community Law of Competition* (6th edn, Oxford University Press 2008) p 1280.

[21] Guidelines on the method of setting fines imposed pursuant to Art 23(2)(a) of Regulation No 1/2003,[2006] OJ C 210 p 2, para 4.

[22] R Van den Bergh, P D Camesasca, *European Competition Law and Economics: A Comparative Perspective*, (Sweet & Maxwell London, 2nd edn, 2006) p 311.

[23] Ibid at p 312.

[24] See *Efficiency and Justice in European Antitrust Enforcement*, at p 81. See n 10 above.

been introduced.[25] In short, it may for example give immunity against fines to the first member of cartel that cheats on the other cartel members and works together with the Commission and providing it with necessary evidence. The system is therefore design to make illegal cartels unstable and provide all its members with an incentive to cheat on one another.

When the sanction system therefore is coupled with a leniency programme it becomes apparent that the deterrent aspect is very important. Severe sanctions operating in conjunction with a leniency programme may be perceived as 'unfair' by infringing firms. However, when instituting such a 'prisoners' dilemma' it is never the intent to be fair to infringing firms; cartelisation is unfair to society and instituting this system, based on economic game theory, gets the message across that the ultimate strategy for players of the cartel game is not to play the game at all. The overall objective is therefore to make undertakings abstain from cartel behaviour and abuses of dominance. Whish underlines the importance of not undermining the central importance of deterrence; any leniency programme must not 'reduce the incentive for members of a cartel to 'blow the whistle' in return for immunity from penalties or a significant reduced penalty: this incentive is itself linked to the issue of deterrence.'[26] The deterrence factor is therefore of the highest significance and any leniency programme must work to enhance this negative incentive – not to counteract it.

In Sweden, the public inquiry found that criminalisation of infringement would not be appropriate.[27] One of the main reasons was that it might jeopardize the functioning of the leniency system, which has no counterpart in Swedish penal law. Criminalisation could therefore risk making firms – or rather executives – abstain from co-operating with KKV and admit anti-competitive behaviour rather than working together with KKV and taking advantage of the lenience programme as is presently the case. However, having decided to follow this route, it becomes even more important that the remaining sanctions indeed have the desired effect in the marketplace. In this respect, one should also bear in mind that setting fines at an extremely high level could – at least in theory – result in winding-up of companies, which may, in turn, lead to less competition on the market (although the actual effects will naturally depend on the nature of the market and number of undertakings etc).[28] The discussion in the legal

[25] See eg Commission Notice on Immunity from fines and reduction of fines in cartel cases (Text with EEA relevance) [2006] OJ C 298 p 17.

[26] R Whish, *Competition Law* (6th edn, Oxford University Press 2009) p 259 (footnote omitted).

[27] SOU 2006:99, p 516

[28] See eg J Faull, A Nikpay, *The EC Law of Competition* (2nd edn, Oxford 2007) pp 1011, 1119. For a discussion on 'impossibly high fines', see W PJ Wils, 'EC Competition Fines: *The Deter or Not to Deter*' in W PJ Wils, *The Optimal Enforcement of EC Antitrust Law – Essays in Law and Economics* (Kluwer 2002) pp 22–44. See also, Speech 10/335, 23 June 2010, Joaquín Almunia, Vice President of the European Commission responsible for competition policy, *Bathroom fittings cartel*, ('But we would not want to provoke a company's bankruptcy. Competition policy is about promoting competition, not eliminating firms from the market place. In the case of the bathroom fittings cartel, we have first granted the reductions under the Leniency Programme that you can see in the press release:...') Available at http://europa.eu/rapid/pressReleasesAction.do?reference=SPEECH/10/335&format=HTML&aged=0&language=EN&guiLanguage=en (last visited 23 August 2010).

literature is not whether there is a risk of over-deterrence, but rather whether the current system is robust enough to stifle unlawful behaviour by firms. The current sanction system is indeed not flawless and it is clear that fine orders will not undermine its functioning.

Fine Orders in Relation to Criminal Law

Fine orders have their counterpart in Swedish criminal law; the summary imposition of a fine. This measure can be used where the sanction is limited to either ordinary fines or a suspended sentence. It is not applicable to offences that would normally lead to imprisonment. The rationale behind summary imposition is that petty crimes such as pilfering, certain traffic offences, minor damage etc may be dealt with swiftly so as not to waste the resources of the legal system with cases that in reality do not require court scrutiny. The system could also be beneficial to the defendant for several reasons.

First, as already indicated, the sanctions liable to be summarily imposed are by their very nature at the lowest end of the sanction scale, so the demand for legal certainty is normally satisfied. Secondly, and perhaps most important, it provides for swift out-of-court final settlement of cases. Arguably, court trials are not warranted in these cases. Instead, such clear cases create a risk of overloading the courts to the detriment of efficiency of justice. Thirdly, the summary procedure is much less public than a court process and those defendants preferring to escape the embarrassment of a public trial are thus given an attractive alternative. The drawbacks are naturally that there will be no actual adjudicatory examination of the case and the deterrent factor is very low, as the general public would normally know little – if anything – about individual summary impositions.

Up to August 2009, the fine order had been used in Sweden in only one case, *Rundvirke poles*.[29] The fine that was ordered amounted to the comparatively low sum of 2 million SEK (about €190 000), imposed as a result of the company having engaged in a cartel by rigging bids and dividing the market for power line electrical in the so-called 'Asphalt Cartel'. According to the fine order, the company and Scanpole Sverige AB agreed to divide quantities of purchased orders between them, colluded on business terms and entered into market sharing agreements for public procurement contracts.

Infringing the competition rules is a form of severe economic crime. Breaking the rules endangers the competitive process and can have very negative effects for the end consumer and society in general. As a result, the seriousness of this form of economic crime is deemed to be very high, all of which motivates the severe sanctions. The sanction system is, as mentioned above, in place to ensure

[29] KKV Case dnr 237/2007, *Rundvirke Poles AB* of June 30, 2009. The comparatively low level of the fine could in part be explained by the fact that KKV took into consideration that it had not implemented the guidelines on the setting of fines at the time of the fine order.

compliance with the rules. Given the complexity of competition law cases, there are also important legal certainty issues to address, while considering the comparatively very severe sanctions that can be triggered.

In relation to the previous system of sanctions there are several general caveats enshrined in the fine order system that may in fact render the procedure counterproductive in relation to the objectives of the competition law sanction system. I will discuss below these pitfalls below.

Arbitrary Setting of Fines or Breeding Ground for Bargaining and Taking the Easy Way Out?

The first pitfall relates to legal certainty. Bringing cases on administrative fines to court will require a considerable amount of resource expenditure by both KKV and alleged infringing undertaking. It is not surprising to find that the limited resources of KKV in Sweden have so far been expended on enforcing the rules against larger cartels. However, anticompetitive co-operation entered into by smaller undertakings that are significant enough to be caught by the competition rules that do not qualify for *de minimis* exceptions, or unilateral actions carried out by a dominant undertaking on a small relevant market, may involve just as complex legal-economic questions as cases involving relatively larger companies or larger scale collusions.

I submit, at the very outset, that the administrative fine should be the same regardless of whether it is ordered by the Court or KKV. Hence, there should be no doubt that differences in fine levels only reflect the seriousness of the infringement, all aggravating and mitigating circumstances taken into due consideration. It is therefore of utmost importance that any fine order procedure not be reduced to a bargaining process where both parties may have improper incentives for settling a case. Under the threat of a full trial with a risk of severe sanctions, undertakings may be tempted to settle for certain, but lower sanctions if given the opportunity. This in turn could create a corresponding incentive for KKV insofar as this could produce a better success rate on cases won and thereby ostensibly increased efficiency in enforcement. To satisfy the demands of legal certainty KKV must be prevented from 'cutting corners' in its investigation and ordering of fines. At a minimum, any decisions taken that result in a fine order would have to be of the same quality as would eventually lead to a successful outcome before the Courts.

Fine orders therefore carry the inherent risk that swift justice may come at an unattractive price. There is a risk that the general level of the fines might be reduced as a result of the bargaining process and/or that companies may wrongfully feel forced to settle claims brought against them based upon investigative material that would not hold up in a court. Smaller undertakings with fewer resources may be intimidated or subdued into settling, even if they might prefer to take their case to court. This may create a double standard for undertakings in the marketplace.

It must be observed that the current Swedish Competition Act does not provide any specific legislative safeguards against this problem. However, it follows from Chapter 3, Article 8 of the Competition Act that all fines must be set according to the sanction value of the infringement, whilst account must also be taken of its gravity and duration. The preparatory works make it clear that fines must be set in order to have a restraining effect on the infringing company and that the fine set also act as a deterrent to other companies.[30] In this respect, the Swedish rules appear to be well in line with the objectives of the fines laid down by the CJEU.

KKV is therefore obliged by law to set fines in this way and may be prevented from entering into any kind of bargaining with alleged infringing undertakings about the level of the fines. Naturally, bearing in mind the leniency programme, KKV has some leeway in the fine setting procedure but the principle of how to calculate fines is clear.

It should also be noted that the leniency programme is governed by Chapter 3, Articles 12–15 of the Competition Act, which also sets the outer limits of what factors may be taken into account by KKV when reducing the fine. It must be noted that the Swedish sanction system – including leniency – is now designed with a view to creating a more harmonised and uniform application of the setting of fines throughout the European Competition Network (ECN) and in terms of the corresponding rules on setting of fines under EU rules – especially the Commission's guidelines in setting of fines.[31] Therefore it appears most unlikely that KKV would deviate from the principles set out in the law, the preparatory works and the EU rules and the bargaining effect will most likely not materialise. Although one might argue that this is bound to happen in any plea bargaining system, it must be borne in mind that plea bargaining does not yet exist in Sweden, either for administrative fines, or for criminal offences. It therefore appears inappropriate to introduce rules whose application may become inconsistent with the functioning of the current administrative procedures.

No Judicial Review of the Infringement

The problem remains that a fine order is not normally open to appeal once accepted by the undertaking, with the exception for example in cases of manifest

[30] See Prop. 2007/2008:135 p 120 and the preparatory works to the first competition act in Sweden, Prop. 1992/93:56, p 93. KKV reiterated this in *Rundvirke Poles*, at para 133.

[31] See Prop. 2007/2008:135, pp 119. See also Guidelines on the method of setting fines imposed pursuant to Art 23(2) (a) of Regulation No 1/2003 note 21. See also the older rules, Information from the Commission - Guidelines on the method of setting fines imposed pursuant to Art 15 (2) of Regulation No 17 and Art 65 (5) of the ECSC Treaty, OJ C 9, 14.1.1998. The Swedish Guidelines for setting of fines and leniency is covered by KKV regulation, KKVFS 2008:3 on the general guidance on leniency and reduction of fines (Konkurrensverkets allmänna råd om eftergift och nedsättning av konkurrensskadeavgift) of October 17, 2008. Guidance on the actual setting of fines in Sweden has thus far been covered by a KKV memo, dnr 394/2009 of June 25, 2009, whose legal standing is somewhat unclear.

error of law. Even if the actual setting of fines, ie the calculation of how much shall be paid as a consequence of the infringement, seems to be covered by rules that ensure uniform application regardless of summary imposition or court trials, the sanction will be based on the fact that the undertaking has voluntarily accepted not only the calculation of the fine, but even more important, KKV's evaluation of the infringement itself. Cases involving administrative fines are normally subject to the provisions of the Code of Judicial Procedure concerning disputes where settlement out of court is not permitted (*indispositiva tvistemål*), which, *inter alia*, allows the court *ex officio* to take evidence into account that has not been referred to by the parties. Also, admissions or confessions by the undertakings are not binding on the court and failure to appear before the court does not lead to entry of judgment by default. Bearing in mind the severity of the sanction, this can be considered to be a judicial safeguard as trials on administrative fines are still akin to criminal proceedings.[32] The significant part of the process is perhaps not the calculation of the fine but rather whether the behaviour or action involved can be regarded as an infringement at all. The awarding of a fine order hinges on the fact that the company really has violated the competition rules. By introducing the fine order, a one instance procedure has effectively been instituted. One might argue, naturally, that even under the old system the alleged infringing undertaking could always admit the claims of KKV and thereby avoid lengthy and costly processes. It should not be forgotten, though, that such admissions were and are still not binding on the court. This particular feature of the law works as a safeguard against defective investigative work or ill-formulated or ill-managed claims against undertakings which, for the wrong reasons, are forced to admit an infringement. Under the normal sanction system KKV will have to plead its case if it is to be successful; the case argumentation, evidence etc must hold up on appeal to the Market court. The task of the court is to analyse whether the claims of KKV are well-founded and whether the undertaking in question can indeed be regarded as having infringed the competition rules. However, if the system were to change and KKV given the possibility of making decisions – including administrative fines – at the first instance, these safeguards would not be lost; the decision (instead of the claim) would have to survive two appeals (assuming the review permit is granted for the court of last instance).

The normal procedure therefore ensures that an undertaking that wrongfully admits a violation will still be acquitted, at least in principle. However, under the fine order procedure, such safeguards are not in place at the start. Instead of the neutral and objective trial examination, the alleged infringing undertaking will be subject to KKV's interpretation of its actions. Naturally, it would be presumptuous to insinuate or suggest that KKV's decision making procedure is inadequate, biased or shoddy. There is nothing to suggest otherwise than that

[32] See also the preparatory works in the Ministry bill Ds 1992:18, *Ny konkurrenslag*.

KKV endeavours to maintain a high quality in its decisions. The fact remains that undertakings will still be left to the judicial acumen of KKV regarding the infringement and there is a risk that the absence of court examination, or, in practice, the possibility of an appeal to a court, could lead to fines based upon materially inadequate admissions. Although the risk of this problem ever materialising is arguably low, in my view, the fine order is not in line with the basic demands of legal certainty and it is highly questionable to create a new sanction system carrying any such risk.

The Deterrent Effect of the Public Trial

Although it is not mentioned in the law, one should not overlook another deterrent effect of the old Swedish principle of publicity in competition law cases.[33] There is a major difference in bringing cases to court, or acting as the court of first instance on the one hand, and settling out of court and acting as a surveillance authority. Competition law cases normally receive considerable media attention, which actually serves to enforce the deterrent effect insofar as this will have an effect on the undertaking. A successful claim by KKV might too easily depict the undertaking as morally inferior and could affect its business negatively.

The same effect naturally applies to criminal law. Being prosecuted and appearing before a court of law in an open trial naturally entails some amount of discomfort, embarrassment and humiliation for the accused. Some of this could be avoided by accepting a summary imposition of a fine, as there would not be a public hearing. The same applies naturally to fine orders. Avoiding public court processes could be an incentive for accepting such an order regardless of whether KKV's evaluation of the infringement has merit or not. It cannot be overlooked that a court process might have adverse effects on the share price of publicly traded undertakings. Because the publicity surrounding competition law can be viewed as a part of the sanction system, there is a risk that fine orders would receive less attention in the media, which could work against the desire of having a deterrent effect. It should be noted that so far KKV has made the fine orders public for downloading – at least in part. The question remains whether this will be enough to achieve the same deterrent effect as court proceedings.

Other Means of Achieving the Same Objective

In my view, the solution *de lege ferenda* to increasing the quality of decision-making and reducing process time, thereby increasing efficiency in enforcement would be, to permit KKV to make all decisions on infringements and sanctions in the first instance. This would force KKV to make decisions that must hold up in court and would be more in line with basic demands for legal certainty.

[33] Cf Ulf Bernitz, *Den nya konkurrenslagen* (Stockholm Juristförlaget 1993) p 16.

As mentioned above one of the main reasons for not instituting this change was that major changes to the internal organisation of KKV would have had to be made and perhaps more staff would have been required. The fine order does not solve the problem of inferior quality decisions – it takes the situation from bad to worse. Albeit the fine order appears to speed matters up, it is questionable as to whether it addresses the real problems.

Comparison with the Settlement of Cases by the EU Commission and Conclusion on Swedish Fine Orders

A comparison can be made with the Commission's power of taking first instance decisions. Under Article 7 of Regulation 1/2003, where the Commission, acting on a complaint or on its own initiative, finds that there is an infringement of Article 101 or 102 TFEU, it may, by decision, require the undertakings and associations of undertakings concerned to bring such infringement to an end. The regulation provides that the Commission may impose on such undertakings any behavioural or structural remedies which are proportionate to the infringement committed and necessary to bring the infringement effectively to an end. It further follows from Article 23 of Regulation 1/2003 that the Commission is empowered to make decisions regarding administrative fines and periodic penalties. However, judicial control is provided by Article 31 of Regulation 1/2003, according to which the Court of Justice shall have unlimited jurisdiction to review decisions whereby the Commission has fixed a fine or periodic penalty payment. Thus, the General Court or the CJEU may cancel, reduce or increase any fine or periodic penalty payment imposed. The Commission does not enter into any bargaining regarding the finding of infringements, but can settle cases by reducing any fine if the members of a cartel work together with the Commission.

In a Commission Notice the role of the Commission is explained:

> Whilst the Commission, as the investigative authority and the guardian of the Treaty empowered to adopt enforcement decisions subject to judicial control by the Community Courts, does not negotiate the question of the existence of an infringement of Community law and the appropriate sanction, it can reward ... cooperation ...[34]

The settlement procedure laid down by the Commission[35] is therefore organised much differently than its Swedish counterpart. The main difference lies in the judicial control of the decision taken. Under Chapter 3, Article 19 of the Competition Act, a fine order for which consent has been given can be set aside only under the conditions specified in Chapter 59, Section 6, first paragraph of the Code of Judicial Procedure. That provision of law only concerns such grave

[34] Commission notice on the conduct of settlement procedures in view of the adoption of Decisions pursuant to Art 7 and Art 23 of Council Regulation (EC) No 1/2003 in cartel cases, 2008/C 167/01, OJ C 167, 2.7. 2008, para 2.

[35] See Commission Regulation (EC) No 622/2008 of 30 June 2008 amending Regulation (EC) No 773/2004, as regards the conduct of settlement procedures in cartel cases, OJ L 171, 1.7.2008, p 3.

procedural errors that the admission could not be viewed as a valid declaration of intent. The possibilities of judicial review or control of fine orders are therefore limited.

The EU settlement procedure has the same objective as the fine order in Sweden, namely to 'enable the Commission to handle faster and more efficiently cartel cases'[36] and to 'handle more cases with the same resources, thereby fostering the public interest in the Commission's delivery of effective and timely punishment, while increasing overall deterrence'.[37] The settlement procedure under EU law is to be regarded – just like the leniency programme – as a reward or incentive to companies helping to avoid unreasonable delays in the decision making process which might otherwise be caused by unwarranted confidentiality concerns, not providing the Commission with necessary material or obstructing the investigation. There is essentially no such corresponding reward system in place for the settlement of cases. Instead the fine order gives companies the possibility of choosing between accepting the proposed decision – including sanctions or going to trial. To all intents and purposes the overall effect appears to be limited to saving time and avoiding the embarrassment of a public trial. It may indeed increase efficiency in terms of closing more cases, but only at the expense of legal certainty, which was the main reason for introducing this procedural measure in the first place.

5. THE DISQUALIFICATION ORDER

A novelty in Swedish market law is the introduction of trading prohibition or disqualification orders against executives of infringing companies. Chapter 3, Article 24 provides that the Swedish Trading Prohibitions Act (SFS 1986:486) contain provisions on the issue of disqualification orders for certain infringements of the prohibitions contained in Chapter 2, Article 1 or in Article 101 TFEU. Disqualification orders are limited to cases where the trader or executive has grossly ignored their obligations as executives and thereby violated the prohibitions contained in Chapter 2, section 1 of the Competition Act or Article 101 TFEU. However, further limitations also apply. A disqualification order may only be made if the public interest makes this generally called for and if the infringement is made by undertakings active in the same level of the distribution chain and involves fixing prices, limiting or controlling production or dividing markets (Section 2 a of the Trading Prohibitions Act).

The disqualification order can also be viewed as a compromise as the legislature did not choose to introduce penal sanctions for violating the Competition Act.

[36] Ibid at para 4.

[37] Commission notice on the conduct of settlement procedures in view of the adoption of Decisions pursuant to Art 7 and Art 23 of Council Regulation (EC) No 1/2003 in cartel cases, 2008/C 167/01, OJ C 167, 2.7. 2008, para 1.

Instead the new sanction was introduced. However, there was widespread scepticism about its introduction and the Government pointed out that there are some major drawbacks with disqualification orders. The sanction is, by its very nature, a measure that is directed towards an individual and not towards an undertaking. From a corporate governance perspective this may send mixed messages insofar as cartels may be organised by middle management who will then be personally liable for their actions whereas the top or senior management should have the direct or indirect obligation to organise the activities of the undertaking in such a way to avoid violations of the competition rules. However, such a sanction also sends a clear message to the market that violations of the competition rules are never acceptable, regardless of whether the sanction affect the persons who should have taken actions to prevent infringements or those who actually engaged in the illegal activity on behalf of the undertaking.[38] This could, no doubt, have a deterrent effect.

Hughes emphasizes that directors, as a result of the danger of being disqualified, will be forced to show greater respect for competition law, which in turn should affect trading practices and corporate strategies. This could reinforce and enhance boardroom compliance with competition law. Another compelling argument for disqualification orders is that, in smaller companies, directors and individuals may in fact be undertakings themselves (the physical person and legal person are the same, eg independent professionals) and if such natural persons may be deemed undertakings – why should different rules apply to executives of larger companies with limited liability?[39] Disqualification orders may erase the difference between such undertakings and introduce a form of personal liability.

The question remains whether the disqualification order is be in line with the current sanction system. It appears at this point not to pose any serious concerns from a legal certainty point of view. The normal safeguards that surround the use of disqualification orders on the grounds of gross misconduct in tax matters will also apply to violations of the competition rules. Recently, KKV announced that the leniency programme for fines will also extend to disqualification orders, ie executives of companies may also be granted leniency.

Similar sanctions are in force in the UK through the provisions of the Company Directors Disqualification Act from 1986 (as amended), the CDDA. Under Section 9 a of the CDDA the court must disqualify a director from acting as such for a period of up to 15(!) years if the company of which he is a director breaches competition law and the court considers that he is unfit to be concerned in the management of a company. In the UK, the Office of Fair Trading (OFT) has the power to apply to the Court for such a Competition Disqualification

[38] For a detailed rationale of the introduction of the disqualification order – see Prop 2007/08:135, p 158.

[39] P Hughes, 'Directors' Personal Liability for Cartel Activity under UK and EC Law – A Tangled Web' (2008) 29.11 *European Competition Law Review* pp 645–48.

Order, CDO. The application of the CDO is currently under review by the OFT, but generally, the authorities believe that CDOs are important deterrents to anticompetitive behaviour, precisely because the sanction is directed towards individuals rather organisations.[40]

In contrast to imprisonment, the disqualification order may not appear to be a severe sanction. Wils points out that the force of the sanction may vary among individuals. Some senior managers may find this to be a convenient time to step down and move into comfortable retirement whilst being fully economically compensated by the undertaking for any loss. However younger persons at the beginning of their careers may perceive them as a real threat and they may be a more effective deterrent for such managers.[41] It should also be borne in mind that effective application and a multitude of disqualification orders may, as noted by Hicks, have a chilling effect on risk-taking and stigmatise entrepreneurs, thereby creating a less competitive society as firms and managers may be dissuaded from even pro-competitive co-operation that could qualify for exemption under Article 101 (3) TFEU.[42] Consequently, it must be made clear to the business society exactly what behaviour is to be punished and that the sanction will be applied to illegal behaviour alone. To this end, guidelines will be necessary.

Notwithstanding the fact that disqualification may have different effects for individuals it must be noted that it remains a complement to the Competition Act's main sanctions and may increase their deterrent effect. So long as criminal sanctions and penal procedure may jeopardise the full functioning of the leniency programme it is highly unlikely that Sweden will introduce penal sanctions, which is why the disqualification order can be viewed only as a second best choice. It remains to be seen how its actual application will function. KKV is currently drafting guidelines, which have not, as yet, been published.

6. THE ROAD AHEAD – WHAT IS MISSING IN THE SWEDISH COMPETITION ACT?

The 2008 procedural changes to the Swedish competition act did not entail empowering KKV to adopt decisions in first instance. Instead, other measures were introduced in order to enhance efficiency in enforcement of Swedish competition rules. The introduction of the fine order and the disqualification order are two novelties in the field of competition law. The above analysis demonstrates that there are questions regarding whether the fine order will have the desired effect. It may even have counterproductive effects so far as the overall

[40] See OFT, 'Competition disqualification orders. Proposed changes to the OFT's Guidance, A consultation paper', August 2009, OFT1111con. Available at https://www.iod.com/MainWebSite/Resources/Document/oft1111con.pdf.

[41] See n 10, *Efficiency and Justice in European Antitrust Enforcement*, Oxford 2008, p 188.

[42] See A Hicks, 'Director Disqualification: Can It Deliver?' (2001 September) *Journal of Business Law* p 459.

objectives of the sanction system is concerned. The director disqualification order is a complement to the current sanctions and may be viewed as a compromise measure resulting from penal sanctions not being introduced into Swedish competition law.

I submit that many of the drawbacks analysed in this article could have been solved by taking the procedural changes several steps further and indeed empowering KKV to adopt decisions on infringement and sanctions in first instance. This would naturally require a major organisational change, staff recruitment and perhaps budgetary changes. However, this would make the national system more harmonised with its EU counterparts and more capable of overcoming the inefficiencies previously identified by the Government.

13
Refusal to Supply in the EU Pharmaceutical Sector under the Rule of Reason

ASSOCIATE PROFESSORS TU THANH NGUYEN, XAVIER GROUSSOT AND ASSISTANT PROFESSOR TIMO MINSSEN

1. INTRODUCTION

At the end of 2008, the Court of Justice of the European Union ('CJEU') delivered its much awaited preliminary ruling in *Sot. Lelos kai Sia*[1] clarifying crucial issues relating to the application of Article 102 TFEU (formerly Article 82 EC) to a dominant pharmaceutical company's refusal to supply, which was aimed at the restriction of parallel trade. These issues had already been raised in 2005 in *Syfait*[2] but, on procedural grounds, the CJEU refused to give any specific answers at that time. Yet, like a boomerang, the issues returned to the CJEU, and the Court has now provided some interesting guidelines. Taking into account the Member States' varying regulation of the pharmaceutical sector, the CJEU held that a refusal to supply by a dominant undertaking affecting parallel trade may in principle violate Article 82. However, the Court also recognized that dominant pharmaceutical companies are entitled to protect their legitimate commercial interests provided they do so reasonably and proportionately. According to the CJEU, a dominant undertaking may refuse to meet an order if it is not ordinary in terms of its size in relation to the requirement of the market or the business relation between the dominant undertaking and the prospective purchaser.

A closer analysis of the CJEU's judgment and of the opinions of two Advocates General (AG), namely the opinion of AG Ruiz-Jarabo Colomer in *Sot. Lelos kai Sia* and that of AG Jacobs in *Syfait,* nevertheless reveals some differences

[1] Joined Cases C-468/06 to C-478/06 *Sot. Lelos kai Sia EE v GlaxoSmithKline AEVE* [2008] ECR I-7139. This case has also been referred to as *Syfait II*.

[2] Case C-53/03 *Syfait v GlaxoSmithKline* [2005] ECR I-4609. This case has also been referred to as *Syfait I*.

regarding how to deal with the conduct of a dominant pharmaceutical company's refusal to supply which is aimed at restricting parallel trade. However, it seems that they all try to apply the rule of reason, or at least a more economic and effect-based approach, to deal with the issues in question, rather than simply considering a refusal to supply as a per se (in itself) violation. This approach is similar to the one presented in the guidance on the Commission's enforcement priorities in applying Article 82 EC to abusive exclusionary conduct by dominant undertakings (Article 82 Guidance),[3] which was officially enacted in February 2009.

Using *Sot. Lelos kai Sia* as a starting point, the main purpose of this paper is to investigate the tendency to apply the rule of reason under Article 82 EC/102 TFEU with respect to a refusal to supply in the European Union (EU) pharmaceutical market. Some procedural issues deriving from this case and from *Syfait* will also be analysed in the beginning. Section 2 of this paper considers the procedural concerns raised by those two cases with regard to the functioning of Regulation 1/2003.[4] Section 3 then examines the application of the rule of reason under Article 82 EC/102 TFEU to refusal to supply both before and in *Sot. Lelos kai Sia.* and section 4 identifies the issues which are left open by this case. Section 5 considers potential developments leading towards a full-fledged rule of reason under Article 102 TFEU. Finally, section 6 draws implications for the pharmaceutical industry.

2. PROCEDURAL ISSUES: NATIONAL COMPETITION AUTHORITIES AND THE PRELIMINARY RULING PROCEDURE

The *Sot. Lelos kai Sia* litigation is of particular interest for the national competition authorities so far as procedural matters are concerned. Indeed, it resurrects the issue raised in *Syfait* as to the capacity of these authorities to make a preliminary reference to the CJEU within the framework of Regulation 1/2003. It is worth noting here that in 1992 the CJEU admitted a reference from the Spanish competition authority, the Tribunal for the Defence of Competition.[5] That body shared many of the same features as the Greek competition authority (Epitropi Antagonismou) appearing in the national proceedings in both *Syfait* and *Sot. Lelos kai Sia*: it was a permanent body established by law with responsibility for applying competition rules following an adversarial procedure. Additionally, the national authority acted after receiving a report, in the Spanish case from a separate body. At the same time, it appears that, under

[3] [2009] OJ C45/7.

[4] Council Regulation (EC) No 1/2003 of 16 December 2002 on the implementation of the rules on competition laid down in Arts 81 and 82 of the Treaty, [2003] OJ L1/1.

[5] Case C-67/91 *Dirección General de Defensa de la Competencia v Asociación Española de Banca Privada and Others* [1992] ECR I-4785.

CJEU case law, administrative bodies, as a general rule, do not have the right to refer questions for preliminary rulings under Article 234 EC (now Article 267 TFEU).[6] Two exceptions may be found, namely where an administrative body is performing its tasks as an independent judicial authority,[7] and where an appellate body is reviewing a decision of an administrative body even in the absence of the exercise of a clearly defined judicial function. The second is the so-called *Job Centre* exception.[8] However this exception is inapplicable to national competition authorities in the EU since their decisions are judicially reviewable before a national court of tribunal.

In *Sot. Lelos kai Sia*, the national procedure appears rather complex and knotted. In January 2003, the Greek competition authority asked the CJEU a series of questions relating to the interpretation of Article 82 EC in a reference for a preliminary ruling, the reference being lodged at the Court's Registry under the number C-53/03, also known as the *Syfait* case. The CJEU did not address the substance of the dispute since the Court declared the reference inadmissible on the grounds that that the competition authority in question was not a court or tribunal within the meaning of Article 234 EC. In September 2006, the competition authority ruled against a subsidiary of GlaxoSmithKline (GSK) in Greece and found that GSK held a dominant position in respect of Lamictal, one of GSK's three patented medicinal products in dispute; that the GSK had infringed Article 2 of the Greek Law on competition during the period from November 2000 to February 2001 but not subsequently; and that it had not infringed Article 82 EC. The validity of that decision was challenged before the Administrative Court of Appeal.

[6] M Broberg, 'Preliminary References by Public Administrative Bodies: When Are Public Administrative Bodies Competent to Make Preliminary References to the European Court of Justice?' (2009) 15 *European Public Law* pp 207–21. The author also argued that the independence criterion is surrounded by considerable uncertainty. See also G Anagnostaras, 'Preliminary Problems and Jurisdictions Uncertainties: The Admissibility of Questions Referred by Bodies Performing Quasi-Judicial Functions' (2005) 30(6) *European Public Law* pp 878–90.

[7] See Case C-134/97 *Victoria Film* [1998] ECR I-7023, para 14; Case C-195/98 *Österreichischer Gewerkschaftsbund* [2000] ECR I-10497, para 25.

[8] See Case C-55/96 *Job Centre Coop. arl* [1997] ECR I-7119; Case C-210/06 *Cartesio Oktató és Szolgáltató bt,* [2008] ECR I-735. In *Job Centre*, the CJEU was seized of an application for confirmation of the memorandum of association of a company in a non-contentious procedure. Since the decision sought from the Tribunale civile e penale di Milano was an order to register the company, the CJEU ruled that there was no judicial activity. However, where a reference for a preliminary ruling in a quasi-judicial procedure is thus ruled inadmissible, there may be a risk that the system of appeals against the decisions of the court concerned is also unusual in nature. In such situations, the reference for a preliminary ruling might never reach the CJEU. Though the procedure was not *inter partes* and the decision resolving that procedure was not judicial in nature, the CJEU applied the *Job Centre* exception in *Cartesio*, in an appeal against a decision to refuse registration adopted by a commercial court. As put by AG Colomer in Case C-14/08 *Roda Golf & Beach Resort SL,* [2009] ECR I-5439 Opinion of 5 March 2009, para 59, '[t]hat alteration of case-law has a laudable purpose, since, where a reference for a preliminary ruling in a quasi-judicial procedure is ruled inadmissible, there is a risk that the system of remedies against the decisions of the court concerned is also unusual in nature. In those circumstances, the reference for a preliminary ruling would never reach the Court, regardless of its importance to the dispute and to the consistency of Community law'.

At the same time, civil proceedings were started before the national court of first instance in Athens in 2001 and 2002. The claimants argued that GSK's conduct in interrupting supplies and distributing its products by itself or through another company (Farmacenter) constituted acts of unfair competition and an abuse of GSK's dominant position. The Athens court delivered judgment in these actions in 2003, and dismissed them – with the exception of the claim for loss of profits – as unfounded, deciding that the refusal to supply was justified and that consequently the accusation of abuse of GSK's dominant position was invalid. The claimants appealed these decisions to the Athens court of appeal, which, having waited unsuccessfully for the answer of the CJEU on the questions referred to it by the Greek competition authority in *Syfait*, decided to stay the proceedings and refer identical questions to the CJEU for a preliminary ruling under Article 234 EC.

Article 234 EC/267 TFEU provides that any court or tribunal may make a reference to the CJEU/CJEU. In the early years, the CJEU interpreted the issue of whether a body making a reference was a court or tribunal for the purposes of Article 234 EC rather broadly, in order to enhance the use and effect of the preliminary ruling procedure. The main factors, taken into consideration, have been, inter alia, whether: (i) the jurisdiction is compulsory, (ii) it involves a public authority, (iii) it is an adversarial procedure, and (iv) the decision must be considered as final. Independence then appeared as a new criterion at the end of 1990s.[9] All these criteria were listed by the CJEU in *Dorsch Consult,* which established a non-exhaustive list, including: the body is established by law, the body is permanent, its jurisdiction is compulsory, its procedure is *inter partes*, the body applies rules of law, and the body is independent. [10]

One year after the *Dorsch Consult* ruling, in 1998, another new criterion, ie the body must issue a decision of a judicial nature, was added by the *Victoria Film* judgment.[11] As discussed below, this condition – together with independence – is particularly useful in assessing whether a quasi-judicial/administrative body, like a competition authority, may refer a question to the CJEU. Problematically, not all of the above criteria constitute absolute requirements but are rather mere guidelines.[12] One consequence of this is that the jurisprudence of the CJEU appears to be inconsistent. In 2001, AG Ruiz-Jarabo Colomer vigorously criticized the lack of objective criteria for determining whether national bodies fall under the scope of Article 234 EC. Referring ironically to Cervantes and

[9] See Case 14/86 *Pretore di Salò* [1987] ECR 2545; Case C-24/92 *Corbiau v Administration des Contributions* [1993] ECR I-1277.

[10] Case C-54/96 *Dorsch Consult Ingenieurgesellschaft mbH v Bundesbaugesellschaft Berlin mbH* [1997] ECR I-4961, para 23; Joined Cases C-110/98 to C-147/98 *Gabalfrisa and Others* [2000] ECR I-1577, para 33; Case C-17/00 *De Coster v Collège des bourgmestre et échevins de Watermael-Boitsfort* [2001] ECR I-9445, para 10; *Gewerkschaftsbund* (n 7), para 24; Case C-516/99 *Schmid* [2002] ECR I-4573, para 34.

[11] *Victoria Film* (n 7), para 14; *Österreichischer Gewerkschaftsbund* (n 7), para 25.

[12] In *Dorsch Consult* (n 10), the CJEU for instance ruled that the procedure *inter partes* was not necessary.

Don Quijote de la Mancha, the AG considered that '[t]he case-law is casuistic, very elastic and not very scientific, with such vague outlines that a question referred for a preliminary ruling by Sancho Panza as governor of the island of Barataria would be accepted'.[13] He proposed, instead, a new test in the light of the requirements deriving from the definition of 'tribunal' in Article 6(1) of the European Convention on Human Rights and the substantive standards of justice. According to the proposed test, a body which does not form part of the domestic judicial system and lacks the competence to 'state the law' in judicial proceedings must not be considered a court or a tribunal. In other words, the body must have exclusive jurisdiction to give judgment since this element reflects both independence and submission to the law.[14] This interpretation is very restrictive and may impede the possibility of administrative bodies making preliminary rulings in most situations.

It is also clear that this area is marked by disagreements between Advocates General and the CJEU as to the scope of application of the criteria.[15] This was demonstrated once again when the CJEU refused to follow AG Jacobs in *Syfait*. Just like the European Commission and the Greek competition authority, AG Jacobs argued for allowing the national competition authorities to make a preliminary ruling.[16] The AG considered that the Greek competition authority satisfied many of the criteria which the CJEU has identified in the past as relevant when considering whether a given body may be classified as a court or tribunal. In his opinion, this administrative enforcement agency boasted all the attributes of a judicial authority: it was permanent, the jurisdiction compulsory, and the proceeding *inter partes*. Yet, he also emphasized that a more detailed analysis is required in order to determine whether its structure and composition are consonant with those of a judicial authority, and in particular with the structural guarantees of independence which are the core identifying features of such authorities.[17]

The main issue at stake was therefore whether the Greek competition authority constituted an independent judicial authority. In that respect, AG Jacobs raised two specific doubts. The first one, regarding its judicial nature, arises in relation to the structure and composition of the competition authority (only two lawyers out of nine members).[18] The second one, regarding its independence, related to the structural links which exists between the competition authority and its secretariat.[19] It is apparent from the CJEU judgment in *Gabalfrisa* that

[13] Opinion of AG Colomer in De Coster delivered 28 June 2001 [2001] ECR I 09445 at para 14.

[14] Ibid at paras 84–86.

[15] See eg, *Dorsch Consult, De Coster, Gabalfrisa* (n 10); Case C-407/98 *Abrahamsson et al v Elisabet Fogelqvist* [2000] ECR I-5539.

[16] *Syfait* (n 2), para. 19.

[17] Opinion of AG Jacobs, paras 20–22, in *Syfait* (n 2).

[18] Ibid at paras 23–25.

[19] Ibid at para 25. Attached to the Greek competition authority is a secretariat, the task of which appears to be to investigate cases arising before the authority and to make written proposals to it as to how they should be resolved. According to the order for reference OJ C 101, 26.04.2003

operational separation between a judicial body and an administrative authority is a prerequisite for judicial independence.[20] In *Syfait*, the functions of the Greek competition authority and the secretariat could be considered separate, in line with the formula in *Gabalfrisa*, provided that the investigation of alleged infringements of the Greek Law on competition, carried out by the secretariat, was distinguishable from the competition authority's adjudicatory role.[21] On balance, the AG considered that, though the body was very close to an administrative authority having certain judicial characteristics, it was sufficiently judicial in character to qualify as a court or tribunal for the purposes of Article 234 EC.[22]

However, the CJEU came to a different conclusion. As to the independence criterion, the Court made three remarks. First, it stated that the Greek Minister for Development, which supervises the competition authority, was empowered to review the lawfulness of the decision of the competition authority. Second, the Court noted that there were no particular safeguards concerning the dismissal of the authority's personnel. Third, the President of the competition authority was the immediate superior of the personnel of the secretariat and exercises disciplinary power over them. There was thus an operational link between the competition authority and its secretariat, a State body which may be akin to a party in the course of competition proceedings.[23]

As to the judicial criterion, the Court relied heavily on Article 11(6) of Regulation 1/2003. In that regard, the Greek competition authority is required to work in close cooperation with the European Commission and may be relieved of its competence by a decision of the Commission.[24] Relying on the *Victoria Film* line of jurisprudence, the CJEU ruled that when the Commission so relieves a national competition authority, the proceedings initiated before the latter authority will not lead to a decision of a judicial nature.[25]

In the light of these two criteria, the CJEU ruled that the Greek competition authority was not a court or tribunal within the meaning of Article 234 EC and, therefore, the Court had no jurisdiction to answer the questions referred by that body.[26] It seems to us that the CJEU has interpreted the independence

page 1, the President of the competition authority coordinates and directs the secretariat as an administrative superior exercising disciplinary power. The competition authority nonetheless attested to the full operational separation of its secretariat, indicating that neither the President nor the rest of the competition authority had any involvement in the secretariat's proposals.

[20] *Gabalfrisa* (n 10) (the CJEU admitted a reference from a regional body in Spain responsible for the hearing of fiscal complaints partly on the basis that a separation existed between its functions and those of the State Tax Administration Agency whose departments adopted the decision forming the subject-matter of the complaint).

[21] Ibid at para 28.

[22] Ibid at paras 31–32.

[23] *Syfait* (n 2), paras 30–33.

[24] Art 11(6) of Regulation 1/2003 maintains the rule of Art 9(3) of Regulation No 17 of 6 February 1962, repealed by Regulation 1/2003, under which the competition authorities of the Member States are automatically relieved of their competence where the Commission initiates its own proceedings.

[25] *Syfait* (n 2), paras 34–36.

[26] Ibid at paras 37–38.

criterion rather restrictively by thus focusing on a mere operational link between the competition authority and its secretariat and has thus limited the number of national competition authorities that can use Article 234 EC. In doing so, the Court also brings considerable uncertainty as to the assessment of the criterion of independence as a whole.[27] Further, it is argued that the CJEU effectively resorts to a policy-based rationale when it comes to the assessment of the judicial nature of a decision. Indeed, in paragraph 34 of the *Syfait* judgment, the Court, by relying on Article 11(6) of Regulation 1/2003, appears not only to take too much account of the aim and objectives of this Regulation but also seems to automatically exclude any of the now 27 competition authorities of the Member States from making a preliminary ruling. In other words, by preventing all national competition authorities from making preliminary references to the CJEU, the Court would like to preserve the competition network, including the national competition authorities, national courts, and the Commission, all as governed by Regulation 1/2003. It appears here preferable for the CJEU to rebuff the admissibility rather than sidestepping the Regulation network with a potential Commission intervention and a would-be involvement of the Court of First Instance (General Court).[28]

Indeed, it is important to keep in mind that the purpose of Regulation 1/2003 is to promote the effective enforcement and the coherent application of EU competition rules through the use of a sophisticated network.[29] The effectiveness of this system depends on the interaction and coordination of both the centralized and decentralized authorities competent to apply EU competition law.[30] In its report on the functioning of Regulation 1/2003 in April 2009, the Commission highlighted the success of this network which has boosted the enforcement of the competition rules notably via the use of national competition authorities.[31] This report also noted that the procedure under Article 11(6) of Regulation 1/2003 has never been used.[32] Yet there is no reference to the *Syfait* litigation and to its impact on the competition network, ie the total exclusion of the national competition authorities from the procedure for making a preliminary ruling to the CJEU/CJEU under Article 234 EC/267 TFEU.

Arguably, the CJEU – for policy reasons – has shaped an 'all-out' network system where the national competition authorities must collaborate with the Commission. If the Court in *Syfait* had followed AG Jacobs and his hybrid solution, it would have opened the gate to 'forum shopping' by the

[27] Broberg (n 6), at p 221.

[28] AP Komninos, 'Article 234 EC and National Competition Authorities in the Era of Decentralization' (2004) 29 *European Law Review* pp 106, 113.

[29] See Art 11 of Regulation 1/2003 (n 4).

[30] DJ Gerber and P Cassinis, 'The Modernisation of European Community Competition Law: Achieving Consistency in Enforcement-Part II' (2006) 27 *European Competition Law Review* pp 51, 57.

[31] See the Communication from the Commission to the European Parliament and the Council – Report on the Functioning of Regulation 1/2003, 29 April 2009, COM (2009) 206 final, paras 23–26.

[32] Ibid at para 28.

national competition authorities and endangered the effectiveness of the network established by Regulation 1/2003. It may be maintained that an 'all-in' alternative might be more appropriate a response to the criticism based on procedural economy as exemplified by the procedural imbroglio, or boomerang effect, in the *Sot. Lelos kai Sia* case. There is, however, a considerable risk that such a solution would damage the integrity of the CJEU's case-law on the administrative authorities' ability to use the preliminary ruling procedure.

3. THE APPROACH TO A RULE OF REASON UNDER ARTICLE 82 EC

3.1. Prior to Sot. Lelos kai Sia

For the purpose 'that the internal market as set out in Article 3 of the Treaty on European Union includes a system ensuring that competition is not distorted,',[33] EU competition law, and in particular Articles 101 and 102 TFEU, is regarded as a fundamental tool controlling the functioning of the internal market.[34] While Article 101 TFEU prohibits agreements or concerted practices between undertakings affecting trade between Member States and restraining competition, Article 102 TFEU regulates the unilateral conduct of undertakings by prohibiting the abuse of a dominant position.

Article 101(1) prohibits anti-competitive agreements in general. However, Article 101(3) exempts such agreements from prohibition if they cumulatively satisfy the following four requirements: (i) efficiency gains – improving the production or distribution of goods or promoting technical or economic progress; (ii) a fair share for consumers – allowing consumers a fair share of the resulting benefit; (iii) indispensability – not imposing on the undertakings concerned restrictions which are not indispensable to the attainment of the objectives; and (iv) no elimination of competition – not affording the parties the possibility of substantially eliminating competition.[35] The assessment of an anti-competitive agreement under Article 101 TFEU thus consists of two main steps: first, determining whether or not there are appreciable restrictions on competition under Article 101(1);[36] and second, balancing anti-competitive

[33] TEU Protocol No (27). See also (now repealed) Art 3(1)(g) EC'[T]he activities of the Community shall include,...a system ensuring that competition in the internal market is not distorted'.

[34] Case C-126/97 *Eco Swiss China Time Ltd v Benetton International NV* [1999] ECR I-3055, paras 36–39; Case C-453/99 *Courage v Crehan Ltd* [2001] ECR I-6297, paras 20–22.

[35] For more detail, see Commission Guidelines on the application of Article 81(3) of the Treaty, [2004] OJ C101/97; R Whish, *Competition Law* (Oxford, Oxford University Press, 2009) pp 151–60; J Faull, and A Nikpay (eds), *The EC Law of Competition* (Oxford, Oxford University Press, 2d ed. 2007) pp 300–12.

[36] Art 101(1)TFEU requires that four criteria, namely the undertaking criterion, the agreement criterion, the effect on trade criterion, and the competition criterion, be met in the actual (economic and legal) context of the restraint.

effects and pro-competitive benefits of the agreement found to be restrictive under Article 101(3).[37] Consequently, if an agreement falls into Article 101(1), a rule of reason, or a balanced analysis, is applied under Article 101(3) in order to determine whether such restrictions are objectively justified. However, when assessing an agreement under Article 101(1) without paying regard to 'the rule of reason',[38] the competent authorities must still consider the economic and legal conditions (the actual context) in which the agreement is to be applied,[39] ie even if the agreement consists of a hard-core restriction, which is excluded from the benefit of block exemption regulations. This implies that 'account should be taken of the economic context in which the undertakings operate, the products or services covered by the agreements, the structure of the market concerned and the actual conditions in which it functions'[40] in order to determine whether or not the agreement does indeed fall under Article 101(1).[41] A number of factors thus must be taken into account in the assessment of an allegedly anti-competitive agreement under Article 101(1), none of which is considered determinative. These include the nature of the agreement; the market position of the parties, of competitors, and of buyers of products; entry barriers; and the maturity of the market.[42]

Article 102 TFEU, however, contains no textual basis similar to Article 101(3) regarding the application of the rule of reason. Article 102 is 'intended to prohibit a dominant undertaking from strengthening its position by recourse to means

[37] Guidelines on the Application of Art 81(3) EC (n 35), para 11.

[38] See, eg Case T-112/99 *Métropole Télévision (M6) v Commission* [2002] ECR II-2459, paras 72 and 76–78 (holding that it is not obliged to weigh the pro- and anti-competitive aspects of anti-competitive agreements outside the specific framework of Art 81(3) EC); Case T-65/98 *Van den Bergh Foods Ltd v Commission* [2003] ECR II-2707, para 106 (appeal dismissed by CJEU in Case 552/03 *sub nom. Unilever Bestfoods (anciennement Van den Bergh Foods Ltd) v Commission* [2006] ECR I-9091 ('Masterfoods Ltd'); holding that an interpretation of Art 81(1) EC under the rule of reason is difficult to reconcile with the structure of the rules prescribed by Art 81 EC); Case T-328/03 *O2 (Germany) GmbH & Co OHG v Commission* [2006] ECR II-1231paras 69–70.

[39] See eg Case 56/65, *Société Technique Minière v Maschinenbau Ulm GmbH* [1966] ECR 235 pp 248–250(Eng); Case 22/71, *Béguelin Import Co v S.A.G.L. Import Export* [1971] ECR 949 para 13; Case C-309/99, *Wouters* [2002] ECR I-1577 para 97; Joined Cases T-374/94, T-375/94, T-384/94 and T-388/94, *European Night Services et al v Commission* [1998] ECR II-3141 paras 136–137.

[40] Case C-399/93 *H G Oude Luttikhuis and others v Verenigde Coöperatieve Melkindustrie Coberco BA* [1995] ECR I-4515, para 10.

[41] Owing to the analysis of the economic and legal conditions of an agreement under Art 101(1) TFEU, some legal scholars contend (under Art 81(1) EC))that 'limited application of the rule of reason' should also be made under Art 101(1) TFEU. See eg Opinion of AG Léger delivered on 10 July 2001, paras 103–104, in *Wouter* (n 39); R Nazzini 'Article 81 EC between Time Present and Time Past: A Normative Critique of 'Restriction of Competition' in EU Law' (2006) 43 *CML Rev* 497; P Manzini, 'The European Rule of Reason- Crossing the Sea of Doubt' (2002), 23 No 8 *ECLR* 392; O Black, *Conceptual Foundations of Antitrust* (Cambridge, Cambridge University Press, 2005) p 62.

[42] See eg Regulation No 772/2004 of 27 April 2004 on the application of Art 81(3) of the Treaty to categories of technology transfer agreements, OJ 2004 L 123/11, paras 8 and 12 of the Preamble; Commission Guidelines on the application of Article 81 of the EC Treaty to technology transfer agreements, OJ 2004 C 101/2, paras 132–40; TT Nguyen, *Competition Law in Technology Transfer under the TRIPS Agreement – Implications for Developing Countries* (Thesis Lund, Lund University, 2009) pp 102–03. Available at SSRN: http://ssrn.com/abstract=1431117.

other than those based on competition on the merits'.[43] To prove a violation of Article 102, two requirements must be cumulatively satisfied: the existence of a dominant position,[44] and its abuse. The abuse of a dominant position by an undertaking is defined as conduct capable of restricting competition. Such conduct must influence the structure of a market by methods different from those which condition normal competition and hinder the maintenance of the degree of competition still existing in the market or the growth of that competition.[45]

On the basis of a literal interpretation of Article 102, it might be argued that if those two requirements are met, the dominant firm in question violates this article per se. In other words, the rule of reason may not be applied under Article 102. The case law of the CJEU has shown that a dominant firm's refusal to supply an existing customer could in fact be considered to be such a per se violation of Article 102, although the Court might accept 'objective justifications' to rebut such a per se analysis.[46] However, it was not clear which justifications could be considered and how the Court would in practice weigh and balance such justifications and anti-competitive effects.

In *Commercial Solvents*[47] – the first refusal to supply case decided under Article 82 EC/102 TFEU – the CJEU held that an undertaking which not only had a dominant position in the upstream (raw material) market but also sought to control the downstream market, where upstream products would be used as input for producing downstream products, could not refuse to supply upstream products to its former customer so as to reserve the upstream products for its downstream market operation. Such a refusal would eliminate competition in the downstream market and was regarded as per se illegal under Article 102 TFEU. The CJEU even ruled that the fact that the customer had cancelled purchases from the dominant firm for a period of time did not affect the court decision, because the dominant firm planned to terminate business relations with

[43] Case T-201/04 *Microsoft Corporation v Commission* [2007] ECR II-3601, para 1070; *Van den Bergh Foods* (n 38), para 157; Case T-229/94 *Deutsche Bahn AG v Commission* [1997] ECR II-1689, para 78 Appeal dismissed Case C-436/97 [1999] ECR I-2387 ; Case C-62/86 *AKZO Chemie BV v Commission* [1991] ECR I-3359, paras 69–70.

[44] A dominant position is 'a position of economic strength enjoyed by an undertaking which enables it to prevent effective competition being maintained on the relevant market by affording it the power to behave to an appreciable extent independently of its competitors, its customers and ultimately of the consumers'. It depends on the market position of the undertaking in question and its competitors, expansion and entry barriers, and countervailing power. See Case C-202/07 P *France Télécom SA v Commission* [2009] ECR I-2369, para 103; Case C-52/07 *Kanal 5 Ltd, TV 4 AB v Föreningen Svenska Tonsättares Internationella Musikbyrå* [2008] ECR I-9275, para 25; Article 82 Guidance (n 3), paras 9–12.

[45] *France Télécom* (n 44), para 104; *Kanal 5* (n 44), para 25 (emphasis added). See also Case 85/76 *Hoffmann-La Roche & Co AG v Commission* [1979] ECR 461, paras 6 and 91, *Microsoft Corporation v Commission* (n 43), para 867.

[46] See eg Joined Cases 6/73 and 7/73 *Istituto Chemioterapico Italiano S.p.A. and Commercial Solvents v Commission* [1974] ECR 223, para 25; Case 27/76, *United Brands Company and United Brands Continentaal BV v Commission*, [1978] ECR 207, paras 183–184; Case C-95/04 P *British Airways plc v Commission* [2007] ECR I-2331, para 69.

[47] *Commercial Solvents* (n 46), para 25.

the customer in any event. In *United Brands*,[48] the CJEU held that a dominant firm 'cannot stop supplying a long-standing customer who abides by regular commercial practice, if the orders placed by that customer are in no way out of the ordinary'. However, the Court did not confine itself to the strict per se rule. It weakened the rule by recognizing the right of dominant undertakings to take reasonable steps to protect their commercial interests; but such conduct would not be accepted if 'its actual purpose is to strengthen [the] dominant position and abuse it'.[49] Such conduct must be 'based on criteria of economic efficiency and consistent with the interests of consumers';[50] and a refusal to supply may be applied to occasional customers, rather than traditional ones, particularly in a period of supply shortage.[51] Accordingly, objective economic justifications have been accepted by the CJEU when the Court scrutinizes refusal to supply by dominant undertakings. This was upheld in *Télémarketing*.[52] In this case, a refusal to supply a service was ruled to be incompatible with Article 102 TFEU when the refusal was implemented by a dominant firm in one market whose services was indispensable for activities of another firm in an adjacent market, without any 'objective necessity' and with the sole purpose of the elimination of competition in the second market.[53]

The duty to supply in EU competition law is applied not only to the termination of an existing supply relation but also to a first-time refusal. In *Bronner*, the CJEU listed four requirements for the enforcement of this duty, namely: (i) indispensability of input, which the dominant undertaking has refused to supply, for competitors in the downstream market to carry on their business; (ii) lack of reasonable possibilities to duplicate the input due to technical, legal, or economic obstacles; (iii) elimination of competition in the downstream market due to the refusal; and (iv) no objective justifications.[54] The CJEU went even further with respect to refusal to license intellectual property rights (IPRs). Basing itself on the case law on refusal to supply, the CJEU in such judgments as *Volvo*,[55] *Magill*,[56] and *IMS Health*[57] has

[48] *United Brands* (n 46), para 182.

[49] Ibid, para 189.

[50] Case T-228/97 *Irish Sugar plc v Commission* [1999] ECR II-2969, para 189. Appeal dismissed Case C-497/99 P [2001] ECR I-5333.

[51] Case C-77/77 *Benzine en Petroleum Handelsmaatschappij BV and others v Commission* [1978] ECR 1513 (holding that a dominant undertaking cannot be accused of having applied to occasional customers during the crisis less favourable treatment than that which it reserved for its traditional customers).

[52] Case C-311/84 *Centre belge d'études de marché-Télémarketing v SA Compagnie luxembourgeoise de télédiffusion and Information publicité Benelux* [1985] ECR 3261.

[53] Ibid, para 27

[54] Case C-7/97 *Oscar Bronner GmbH & Co, v Mediaprint [1998] ECR I-7791*, paras 38–44.

[55] Case C-238/87 *AB Volvo v Erik Veng (UK) Ltd* [1988] ECR 6211, paras 8–9. See also Case C-53/87 *Consorzio italiano della componentistica di ricambio per autoveicoli and Maxicar v Régie nationale des usines Renault* [1988] ECR 6039, paras 11 and 15–16.

[56] Joined Cases C-241/91 P and 242/91 P *Radio Telefis Eireann (RTE) and Independent Television Publications Ltd (ITP) v Commission* (*Magill*) [1995] ECR I-743, paras 50 and 53–56.

[57] Case C-418/01 *IMS Health GmbH & Co OHG v NDC Health GmbH & Co KG* [2004] ECR I-5039, paras 38–52.

consistently ruled under Article 102 TFEU, that a refusal to license IPRs by a dominant firm is not in itself an abuse violating competition law, but could be regarded as such in 'exceptional circumstances'. The cumulative exceptional circumstances relating to a refusal to license by a dominant firm that may lead to an abuse are: (i) the refusal to license relates to a product indispensable to the exercise of a particular activity on the secondary (downstream) market; (ii) it prevents the emergence of a new product for which there is a potential customer demand; (iii) it excludes all competition on the secondary market; and (iv) it is not justified.[58] Again, the CJEU did not elaborate on the concept of objective justifications; but at least it clarified that the mere existence of IPRs would not automatically provide objective justification for a refusal to supply or license if the first three circumstances apply.

Perhaps due to the ambiguity of the concept of objective economic justification, such justification is not easily taken into account.[59] The General Court has even stated explicitly that since there is no exception in Article 102 TFEU, 'abusive practices are prohibited regardless of the advantages which may accrue to the perpetrators of such practices or to third parties'.[60] Additionally, in order to raise and justify a justification claim, the burden of proof plays a very important role, although this was not previously spelt out by the CJEU (or the General Court). Due to the lack of a provision equivalent to Article 101(3) in Article 102 TFEU, it may nevertheless be argued that competition authorities have the exclusive duty to provide evidence regarding such justifications. This is reflected in Regulation 1/2003, which states that:

> [T]he burden of proving an infringement of Article 81(1) or of Article 82 [EC] shall rest on the party or the authority alleging the infringement. The undertaking or association of undertakings claiming the benefit of Article 81(3) [EC] shall bear the burden of proving that the conditions of that paragraph are fulfilled.[61]

However, in *Microsoft Corporation v Commission*, when applying the IPR-related four pronged test for scrutinizing a refusal to license recognized by CJEU case law, the General Court held that:

> [A]lthough the burden of proof of the existence of the circumstances that constitute an infringement of Article 82 EC is borne by the Commission, it is for the dominant undertaking concerned, and not for the Commission, before the end of the

[58] *Magill* (n 56), paras 53–56; *IMS Health* (n 57), paras 38–52.

[59] See S Kingston, Joined Cases C–468/06 to C–478/06, *Sot. Lelos kai Sia EE, Farmakemporiki AE Emporias kai Dianomis Farmakeftikon Proionton and Others v GlaxoSmithKline AEVE Farmakeftikon Proionton, formerly Glaxowellcome AEVE, Judgment of the Grand Chamber of the Court of Justice of 16 September 2008* 46 *CML Rev* 683, 695 (2009); C Desogus, 'Parallel Trade and Pharmaceutical R&D: The Pitfalls of the Rule of Reason' (2008) 11 *European Competition Law Review* pp 649, 655 (arguing that Community courts have been reluctant to take economic considerations into account or have tended to narrow down the relevance of economic arguments).

[60] Joined Cases T-191/98 and T-212/98 to T-214/98 *Atlantic Container Line AB v Commission* [2002] ECR II-3275, para 1112.

[61] Art 2 of Regulation 1/2003 (n 4).

> administrative procedure, to raise any plea of objective justification and to support it with arguments and evidence. It then falls to the Commission, where it proposes to make a finding of an abuse of a dominant position, to show that the arguments and evidence relied on by the undertaking cannot prevail and, accordingly, that the justification put forward cannot be accepted.[62]

This ruling indicates that the burden of proof under the Article 102 process should be similar to that under Article 101. Competition authorities have to prove the existence of a dominant position and the anti-competitive effects of allegedly abusive conduct, which hinders competition in the relevant market. Then the undertaking concerned will be expected to counter-argue objective justification. Finally, the competition authorities have to weigh and balance pro-competitive benefits and anti-competitive effects. Interestingly, this approach resembles the three-stage analysis applied in the United States (US) when evaluating the legality of unilateral conduct under Section 2 of Sherman Act (the equivalent of Article 102 TFEU) as articulated in *United States v Microsoft*[63] and recently confirmed by the head of the antitrust division of the US Department of Justice,[64]. Under the US approach, the competition authorities (or the plaintiff) must first 'demonstrate that the monopolist's conduct indeed has the requisite anticompetitive effect' that 'must harm the competitive *process* and thereby harm consumers'. Second, the defendant (the monopolist) may rebut this prima facie accusation by providing a 'pro-competitive justification', which is not a mere pretext, to prove that 'its conduct is indeed a form of competition on the merits' which, for instance, leads to greater efficiency or enhances consumer appeal. This will shift the burden back to the plaintiff to rebut the justification. Finally, if the defendant's pro-competitive justification is not rebutted, 'the plaintiff must demonstrate that the anticompetitive harm of the conduct outweighs the pro-competitive benefit'.[65] Returning to the Article 102 process mentioned above, it should be underlined that this process, and in particular the final balancing stage, has also been expressly recognized by the CJEU in *British Airways v Commission* – a loyalty rebates related case – where the CJEU held:

[62] *Microsoft Corporation v Commission* (n 43), *para* 688.

[63] *United States v Microsoft* 253 F.3d 34 (DC Cir 2001); *Standard Oil Co v United States* 221 US 1, 31 (1911): There, United States Supreme Court held that 'when [Section 2 of the Sherman Act] is thus harmonized with and made, as it was intended to be, the complement of [Section 1], it becomes obvious that the criteria to be resorted to in any given case for the purpose of ascertaining whether violations of [Section 2] have been committed is the rule of reason guided by the established law'. See also M Popofsky, 'Defining Exclusionary Conduct: Section 2, the Rule of Reason, and the Unifying Principles Underlying Antitrust Rules' (2006) 73 *Antitrust Law Journal* p 435; M Popofsky, 'Section 2, Safe Harbours, and the Rule of Reason' (2008) 15 *George Mason Law Rev* p 1265.

[64] C Varney, *Vigorous Antitrust Enforcement in This Challenging Era*, Remarks as prepared for the Center for American Progress, 11 May 2009, Available at www.usdoj.gov/atr/public/speeches/245711.pdf (last visited 2 July 2009).

[65] *United States v Microsoft* (n 63), at 58–59.

> It has to be determined whether the exclusionary effect… which is disadvantageous for competition, may be counterbalanced, or outweighed, by advantages in terms of efficiency which also benefit the consumer. If the exclusionary effect of [the conduct] bears no relation to advantages for the market and consumers, or if it goes beyond what is necessary in order to attain those advantages, [the conduct] must be regarded as an abuse.[66]

It follows from the above that the CJEU and the General Court tend to apply a balanced, effects-based analysis, or a rule of reason, to scrutinize unilateral anti-competitive practices conducted by dominant firms under Article 102 TFEU, rather than apply a per se (or quasi per se) condemnation. Moreover, it appears that the CJEU, while weighing and balancing anti-competitive effects and advantages (pro-competitive benefits) of conduct under Article 102 TFEU, examines cumulatively whether the conduct is (i) suitable (whether it benefits consumers and relates to the market and consumers), (ii) necessary to attain the pro-competitive benefits, and (iii) proportionate in terms of weighing and balancing exclusionary effects and efficiency. Simply put, a proportionality test may be applied in the process of evaluating abusive conduct under the rule of reason. However, prior to *Sot. Lelos kai Sia* it was still not clear how a refusal to supply, particularly in the pharmaceutical sector, would be evaluated under such a rule of reason.

3.2. Sot. Lelos kai Sia: The Rule of Reason Approach

Internal market integration, as provided for by Article 3(1)(g) EC, now replaced by Protocol No 27 to the TEU (the correlative anti-competitive practices of limiting production or markets being expressly listed in Articles 101(1)(b) and 102(b) TFEU), has been, and continues to be, an important goal of EU competition law.[67] Parallel trade has traditionally enjoyed the special protection of the Community courts and the Commission under both predecessor Articles 81 and 82 EC, now Articles 101 and 102 TFEU. The CJEU has ruled that a dominant undertaking, in general, abuses its dominance, and thus per se violates Article 102 TFEU if

[66] *British Airways* (n 46), para 86 (see also paras 68–69).

[67] The CJEU, *eg* in *British Airways* (n 46), para 106, held that 'Article 82 EC is aimed not only at practices which may cause prejudice to consumers directly, but also at those which are detrimental to them through their impact on an effective competition structure, such as is mentioned in Article 3(1)(g) EC'. According to the Treaty of Lisbon amending the Treaty on European Union and the EC Treaty, signed by the Heads of State or Government of the 27 member states in Lisbon on 13 Dec. 2007, [2007] OJ C306/1, the EC Treaty will be replaced by the Treaty on the Functioning of the European Union (TFEU), in which Article 3.1(g) EC is removed. However, the objective of establishing a single market on the basis of undistorted competition is still addressed in the Protocol [No 27] on the internal market and competition annexed to the TFEU. Put differently, the TFEU and the Protocol broadly reflect the *status quo*. Therefore, by interpreting Arts 101 and 102 of the TFEU, ie Arts 81 and 82 EC, in combination with the Protocol on the internal market and competition, one can say that there is no substantive change to EU competition law in the TFEU.

its conduct restricts parallel trade in the products it puts on the market.[68] In *Sot. Lelos kai Sia*, GSK, as noted above, was held to have a dominant position on the relevant market in the patented medicinal products in dispute. From November 2000 to February 2001, GSK refused to meet Greek wholesalers' orders with the undoubted aim and effect of limiting 'parallel exports by those wholesalers to the markets of other Member States in which the selling prices of the medicinal products in dispute are higher'.[69] Thus, the main substantive question referred for a preliminary ruling in this case was, like the one in *Syfait*, whether such a refusal was a per se violation of Article 102 TFEU.

On the basis of the refusal to supply case law rather than that relating to parallel trade restrictions as such, AG Jacobs in *Syfait* argued that a refusal to supply by a dominant undertaking with the intention of limiting parallel trade would not automatically and necessarily result in an abuse of dominance. He listed three reasons to support this argument: first, the obligation to supply of a dominant firm only exists 'on occasion' or in exceptional circumstances; secondly, such an obligation can be circumscribed by objective justification; and thirdly, a refusal to supply aimed at limiting parallel trade needs to be scrutinized on the basis of the specific economic and regulatory context of the specific case.[70] He also classified the intent to restrict parallel trade and partition the market into a primary, ultimate intent and an ancillary, indirect one which is 'an inevitable consequence' of legitimate conduct. In the light of this he concluded that the existence of an intent to limit parallel trade should not be the decisive factor leading automatically to a finding of abuse.[71] Instead, AG Jacobs would consider the allegedly abusive conduct of a dominant undertaking in the light of the factual and economic context of the conduct even when its intention was to limit parallel trade. This is similar to the interpretation of Article 101(1) TFEU by the General Court in *GSK v Commission* in 2006 – a dual pricing case – which related to the general sales conditions of a subsidiary of GSK in Spain which implemented both a low price system for medicinal products used in Spain and a high price system for exported products, all in order to prevent parallel trade. Here the General Court said:

> [T]he application of Article 81(1) EC... cannot depend solely on the fact that the agreement in question is intended to limit parallel trade in medicines or to partition the common market, which leads to the conclusion that it affects trade between

[68] Case C-26/75 *General Motors Continental NV v Commission* [1975] ECR 1367, para 12 (constituting an abuse of a dominant position if the conduct has 'the effect of curbing parallel imports by neutralising the more favourable level of prices which may apply in other sales areas in the Community'); Case C-226/84 *British Leyland Public Limited Company v Commission* [1986] ECR 3263, para 24 (constituting an abuse of a dominant position if the conduct can be construed as the manifestation of a deliberate intention... to create barriers to re-importations which come into competition with [the dominant undertaking's] approved distributors'). See also *Sot. Lelos kai Sia* (n 1), paras 37 and 65.

[69] *Sot. Lelos kai Sia* (n 1), para 36

[70] Opinion of AG Jacobs, paras 53 and 66–68, in *Syfait* (n 2).

[71] Ibid, para 71.

> Member States, but also requires an analysis designed to determine whether it has as its object or effect the prevention, restriction or distortion of competition on the relevant market, to the detriment of the final consumer.[72]

However, contrary to the view of AG Jacobs, and even the General Court's view under Article 81(1) EC mentioned above, the CJEU in *Sot Lelos kai Sia* based its judgment on Article 3(1)(g) EC with a view to protecting the single market thereby creating benefits and increasing product variety for consumers. The CJEU found:

> [T]here can be no escape from the prohibition laid down in Article 82 EC for the practices of an undertaking in a dominant position which are aimed at avoiding all parallel exports from a Member State to other Member States, practices which, by partitioning the national markets, neutralise the benefits of effective competition in terms of the supply and the prices that those exports would obtain for final consumers in the other Member States.[73]

The CJEU has thus maintained a strongly negative attitude to conduct which restricts parallel trade. This attitude is, to some extent, shared by AG Ruiz-Jarabo Colomer. Although recognizing the objectiveness of the concept of 'abuse' under Article 82 EC, AG Ruiz-Jarabo Colomer contended in his opinion that a refusal to supply with the intention of limiting parallel trade is contrary to the objectives, and a serious infringement of the EC Treaty, especially Article 3(1)(g).[74] Moreover, AG Trstenjak in her opinion in *GSK v Commission*, delivered in June 2009, followed the strict view of the CJEU in *Sot Lelos kai Sia* and rejected the General Court view mentioned above. In particular, she observed that limitation of parallel trade 'is to be regarded as a restriction of competition by object' despite the particular legal and economics characteristics of the pharmaceutical sector.[75]

However, neither the CJEU nor AG Ruiz-Jarabo Colomer stopped their consideration there. AG Ruiz-Jarabo Colomer observed that:

> Article 82 EC does not provide a basis for attributing conduct which is abusive per se to undertakings in a dominant position, even when the circumstances of the case show that there is intent and an anticompetitive effect caused by that conduct.[76]

[72] Case T-168/01 *GlaxoSmithKline Services Unlimited v Commission* [2006] ECR II-2969, para 119 (appeal dismissed in joined Cases C-501/06 P, C-513/06 P, C-515/06, C-519/06 Judgment of 6 October 2009 OJ C 282 of 21.11.2009, p 2; Opinion of AG Trstenjak delivered on 30 June 2009 (the AG argued that a dual pricing policy intended to restrict parallel trade has as its objects the restriction of competition (without the need of considering the detriment to final consumers), but supported the General Court view that such restriction should be examined under the rule of reason on the basis of a possible contribution to the promotion of technical progress or innovation).

[73] *Sot. Lelos kai Sia* (n 1), para 66.

[74] Opinion of AG Ruiz-Jarabo Colomer, paras 46–47 and 53–54, in *Sot. Lelos kai Sia* (n 1).

[75] Opinion of AG Trstenjak, para 155, in *GSK v Commission* (n 72).

[76] Ibid, para 123. Moreover, AG Mazák, in his opinion in *France Télécom* (n 44), contended that according to CJEU case law, just as in the US, a recoupment possibility is a requirement for predatory pricing under Art 82 EC. He argued that without the 'possibility of recouping losses, consumers and their interests should, in principle, not be harmed', thereby, 'the dominant undertaking is probably

He suggested applying the rule of reason, or an 'analysis of the merits', under Article 82 EC.[77] In particular he listed three grounds allowing a dominant undertaking to justify its allegedly abusive conduct, namely (i) market regulation that is out of the control of the dominant undertakings involved, (ii) the legitimate protection of their business interests, and (iii) proof of net positive economic effects.[78] The CJEU did not completely follow this opinion, but it explicitly recognized the first two grounds as objective justifications.[79] This is similar to the second step in the argument of AG Jacobs where he contended that even if a refusal to license by a dominant undertaking which aims at limiting parallel trade is prima facie an abuse, that undertaking would still have the possibility of providing an objective justification of its conduct in order to escape condemnation. Since AG Jacobs proposed to scrutinize allegedly abusive conduct on the basis of the factual and economic context as the first step, he only listed three grounds justifying a refusal to supply in the second step, namely the regulation of price and distribution in the pharmaceutical sector, the economics of innovation, and no benefits for ultimate consumers from parallel trade.[80] The last ground was not accepted by the CJEU because the Court continues to favour the view that parallel trade benefits ultimate consumers in terms of both product prices and product variety, but his first two grounds are similar to the first two grounds of AG Ruiz-Jarabo Colomer as well as to two features commonly scrutinized by the CJEU, namely the sectoral market regulation and the protection of legitimate business interests.

Regarding sectoral market regulation, AG Jacobs argued that the non-harmonized regulation of price and distribution in the European pharmaceutical sector, rather than the commercial policies of pharmaceutical manufacturers, leads to price differentials in the EU market which then encourages parallel trade.[81] Such regulation also imposes public service obligations on pharmaceutical manufacturers to ensure sufficient supply within each national territory. Consequently, he contended that a refusal to supply by a dominant pharmaceutical manufacturer which does not violate the sectoral regulation would be ineffective to prevent parallel trade.[82] By contrast, the CJEU and AG Ruiz-Jarabo Colomer focused on competition possibilities for the business community with respect to the sectoral market regulation. Although both of them recognized the impact of the regulation in question on pharmaceutical

engaged in normal competition' (paras 69–76). However, the CJEU, in line with its case law, rejected that argument (*France Télécom* (n 44), para 37).

[77] Ibid, para 72.

[78] Ibid paras 79 and 123(2).

[79] *Sot. Lelos kai Sia* (n 1), paras 67–69.

[80] Opinion of AG Jacobs, para 76 (in detail, see respectively paras 77–88, 89–95, and 96–99), in *Syfait* (n 2).

[81] Regarding pharmaceutical price regulation, see OECD, *Pharmaceutical Pricing Policies in a Global Market* (Paris, OECD Publishing, 2008), pp 97–101. Available at http://www.oecd.org/document/36/0,3343,en_2649_33929_41000996_1_1_1_37407,00.html (last visited 2 July 2009).

[82] Opinion of AG Jacobs, paras 84–88, in *Syfait* (n 2).

prices, they concluded that such regulation still provided pharmaceutical companies with a degree of discretion concerning prices. Those companies may, therefore, violate competition law if their acts fall within that degree of discretion.[83] This means that, at least in the EU, *ex post* competition rules will apply to anti-competitive practices despite the existence of *ex ante* sector-specific regulation, unless the regulation provides a dominant undertaking with no margin of freedom with respect to the practices in question.[84]

As to the protection of legitimate business interests, the two Advocates General and the CJEU agreed that a dominant undertaking can reasonably and proportionately protect its own commercial interests. However, their approaches to evaluating the reasonableness and proportionality of the refusal to supply in question are not similar. AG Jacobs focused on the incentives of innovation and the economics of innovative pharmaceutical industry while AG Ruiz-Jarabo Colomer went further by considering not only research and development (R&D) issues in the industry but also the net positive economic effects of the refusal. But in the end, he too opined that there was no causal link between any negative impact on R&D incentives and parallel trade, and that the refusal did not generate any net positive economic benefits. However, the CJEU did not go further into, or clearly identify its position on these issues. The Court just ruled that a refusal to supply an order is only reasonable and proportionate and thus falls outside the scope of Article 82 EC, if the order is out of the ordinary in the light its size in the relation to the requirements of the local market and the business relations of the parties concerned.[85] Consequently, there is no violation of Article 82 if a dominant firm refuses to supply (i) a new customer, or (ii) an existing customer with quantities ordered in excess of those ordinarily purchased by that customer, taking into account the requirement of the local market.

Although both their analyses of the facts of GSK's refusal to supply and their conclusions differed, the CJEU and the two AG followed the same red thread under the rule of reason approach: a refusal to supply by a dominant undertaking, even one which aims at limiting parallel trade, needs to be scrutinized under a more flexible approach than a per se or quasi per se rule. This shows that the goal of maintaining and protecting the integrated single market cannot prevail over other goals of EU competition policy. Protection of competition and consumer welfare is clearly the highest priority even where it

[83] *Sot. Lelos kai Sia* (n 1), paras 61–63; Opinion of AG Ruiz-Jarabo Colomer, paras 90–93, in *Sot. Lelos kai Sia* (n 1). See also Opinion of AG Trstenjak, para 166, in *GSK v Commission* (n 72).

[84] This was recognized by the General Court in Case T-271/03 *Deutsche Telekom AG v Commission* [2008] ECR-II 477, paras 88–89 (appeal (pending) in Case C-280/08) where the court ruled that the German telecommunications regulation in question did not eliminate any possibility of competitive activity by Deutsche Telekom, but allowed Deutsche Telekom sufficient scope to fix its charges at a level which would enable it to end or reduce margin squeezing; thus the Deutsche Telekom conduct violated Art 82 EC.

[85] *Sot. Lelos kai Sia* (n 1), para 77.

may tend to limit market integration.[86] However, the preliminary ruling of the CJEU in *Sot Lelos kai Sia* left certain issues open for the application of the rule of reason in practice, particularly in the pharmaceutical sector.

3.3. Issues Left Open in Sot Lelos kai Sia from the Rule of Reason Perspective

First of all, the CJEU did not provide any guidance on the distinction between ordinary and extraordinary orders from customers who have had prior business relations with a dominant undertaking. The fact of this case showed that there were three alternatives which could be taken into account, namely quantities equivalent to national consumption plus 18 per cent as proposed by GSK, those required for prescription medicines plus 25 per cent as stipulated by the Greek pharmaceutical authority, or average quantity of previous orders plus 20 per cent as suggested by some wholesalers in the course of the dispute.[87] However, the CJEU merely required national courts to link the 'ordinary' character of an existing customer's order in terms of local market requirements. It is far from easy for national courts to determine whether or not an order is ordinary unless the factual and economic contexts of a specific case are considered. Furthermore, even if the size of an order falls to be evaluated in the context of local market requirements, national courts need to consider the ability of the dominant undertaking to meet the order. Consequently, every case of refusal to supply needs to be determined on its merits.

Second, the CJEU did not distinguish between inter-brand and intra-brand competition and focused on the latter. The CJEU held that:

> [W]here a medicine is protected by a patent which confers a temporary monopoly on its holder, the price competition which may exist between a producer and its distributors, or between parallel traders and national distributors, is, until the expiry of that patent, the *only form of competition which can be envisaged*.[88]

It is generally accepted that IPRs are rights to exclude third parties from exploiting the intellectual property without the right holders' consent; thus IPRs are negative rights. They provide the right holders with a temporary legal monopoly, rather than with an economic monopoly which confers market power on the right holder.[89] Competition by outright imitation is, therefore, excluded by IPRs; but competition by substitution, or inter-brand competition, remains possible and permissible. Competition authorities should consider both intra-

[86] See also Opinion of AG Trstenjak, para 161, in *GSK v Commission* (n 72).

[87] *Sot. Lelos kai Sia* (n 1), d, paras 14, 17, and 72.

[88] Ibid para 64 (emphasis added).

[89] See eg, Case 24/67 *Parke, Davis and Co v Probel, Reese, Beintema-Interpharm and Centrafarm*, [1968] ECR 55, p 72; Case 40/70, *Sirena Srl v Eda Srl and others,* [1971] ECR 69, para 5 and 16; *Magill* (n 56), para 46. In the U.S., see *Illinois Tool Works Inc v Independent Ink, Inc,* 547 US 28, 45–46 (2006).

and inter-brand competition when scrutinizing anti-competitive practices relating to supply-distribution relationship. Moreover, anti-competitive conduct affecting intra-brand competition may be permissible if inter-brand competition is available and increased.[90] In *Sot Lelos kai Sia*, the above CJEU observation is only correct within the restricted context of GSK's patented products or intra-brand competition, but would not necessarily hold if inter-brand competition is duly taken into account. As a result, objective justification, or the rule of reason, is not in fact applied if it is limited to intra-brand competition. Due to this shortcoming, the CJEU did not go on to examine the 'causal link' between parallel trade and any negative impact on R&D within the pharmaceutical industry,[91] although the General Court has considered and even recognized such a link in *GSK v Commission*; AG Trstenjak also recently supported it.[92]

Finally, comparing the *Sot Lelos kai Sia* ruling with the related Article 101 TFEU dual pricing case in *GSK v Commission*, one may find that the issue of destination-based pricing in the pharmaceutical industry under Article 102 TFEU remains controversial. A refusal to supply and a dual pricing system, both of which aim at restricting parallel trade, are two sides of the same coin. As noted above, the dual pricing system in *GSK v Commission* was supported by both the General Court and AG Trstenjak under the Article 81 EC rule of reason. It seems likely that the CJEU will support the General Court when it reviews the case. However, purely within the context of Article 82 EC scrutiny, due to the limited scope of the *Sot Lelos kai Sia* ruling, it is difficult to predict the legality of a dominant undertaking's charging low prices for domestic use of its products and high prices for export, in contrast to an outright refusal to supply. In any case, one must apply the rule of reason when examining the legality of such conduct.

4. TOWARDS A FULL FLEDGED RULE OF REASON FOR A REFUSAL TO SUPPLY

Sot Lelos kai Sia is a good example of judicial analysis moving from the per se (or quasi per se) rule to the rule of reason based on the factual and economic contexts of the specific case in the Article 102TFEU context. This has been followed by

[90] See eg *Continental T V, Inc v GTE Sylvania Inc*, 433 US 36, 57–59 (1977); *Leegin Creative Leather Products, Inc v PSKS, Inc*, 551 US 877 (2007) (the US Supreme Court holding that both price and non-prices vertical restraints should be analysed under the rule of reason); and Case C-279/06 *CEPSA Estaciones de Servicio SA v LV Tobar e Hijos SL* [2008] ECR I-6681, para 72; Case C-260/07 *Pedro IV Servicios v Total* [2009] ECR I-2437, paras 81–83 (The CJEU implicitly ruled that price-fixing in the supply-distribution needs to be evaluated under the rule of reason).

[91] *Sot. Lelos kai Sia* (n 1), para 70.

[92] *GSK v Commission* (n 72), paras 263 and 308 (the General Court found that the causal link raised by GSK seems to be 'relevent, reliable and credible', then concluded that the Commission had failed to treat seriously GSK's claims); Opinion of AG Trstenjak, paras 211, 242–44, and 262, in *GSK v Commission* (n 72).

CJEU rulings after *Sot Lelos kai Sia*. In *Kanal 5*,[93] the CJEU had to deal with the issue of whether a copyright management organisation, which enjoyed a de facto monopoly on the market for copyrighted music for television broadcasts in Sweden, violated Article 82 EC by not only charging Swedish commercial television broadcasting companies on the basis of a percentage of their revenue and the amount of music broadcast but also applying different royalty rates to commercial and public channels. As to revenue-based royalties, the Court ruled that such conduct may constitute an abuse of imposing unfair purchase prices under Article 82(a) unless two conditions are satisfied: (i) the amount of the royalties 'corresponds partly to the revenue' of the commercial channel and is 'proportionate' to the amount of the copyrighted musical works which are actually or likely broadcast, and (ii) there is not any less anti-competitive method of calculation of remuneration.[94] When these two conditions are considered, the nature of the IPRs is necessarily taken into account in order to create 'an appropriate balance' between the financial interests of the holders and the users of IPRs.[95] The CJEU seems implicitly to recognize a link between IPRs, or *ex ante* incentives to innovate, and the price of using IPRs, which was not mentioned in *Sot Lelos kai Sia*. As to the discrimination issue, the Court held that the mere proof of different conditions for similar transactions is insufficient to condemn conduct under Article 82(c). The existence of competitive disadvantage must be proved, eg by showing at least that the undertaking's customers are competitors on the same relevant market. Even if this is shown, price discrimination may be objectively justified by analysing the downstream market.[96]

In *France Télécom*,[97] a predatory pricing case in the telecommunications sector, the CJEU ruled, following its case law, predatory pricing only violates Article 82 EC if two requirements are proved, namely below cost pricing and the dominant undertaking's intent to eliminate its competitors.[98] However, the Court also indicated the positive side of a recoupment analysis. It found that the possibility of recouping may help assist competition authorities in rejecting attempts to justify below-cost pricing raised by defendants; and the showing of a recoupment possibility can help prove that the dominant undertaking in question had indeed a plan or intent to eliminate its rivals.[99]

All of those reflect a trend whereby the EU is moving to a more flexible approach when anti-competitive conduct is scrutinized under Article 102 TFEU. It is supported by the Article 82 EC Guidance, which states that a dominant

[93] *Kanal 5* (n 44).

[94] Ibid, paras 40–41.

[95] Ibid, paras 30–31.

[96] Ibid, paras 45–47.

[97] *France Télécom* (n 44).

[98] Case C-62/86 *AKZO Chemie BV v Commission* [1991] ECR I-3359, paras 70–71; Case C-333/94 Tetra Pak International SA *v Commission* [1996] ECR I-5951, paras 41 and 44; *France Télécom* (n 44), para 110.

[99] *France Télécom* (n 44), para 111. See also A Emch and GK Leonard, 'Predatory Pricing after linkLine and Wanadoo' (2009) 5 *Global Competition Policy* pp 1, 5.

undertaking may justify its anti-competitive conduct 'on the ground of efficiencies that are sufficient to guarantee that no net harm to consumers is likely to arise'.[100] In particular, the Commission accepts such justification only if the dominant undertaking can demonstrate that the following four conditions apply cumulatively, with a sufficient degree of probability, and on the basis of verifiable evidence: (i) efficiencies are likely as a result of the conduct, (ii) the efficiencies outweigh any likely negative effects on competition and consumer welfare in the affected markets, (iii) the indispensability of the conduct to the realisation of the efficiencies – there must be no less anti-competitive alternatives to the conduct that are capable of producing the same efficiencies, and (iv) the conduct in question does not eliminate effective competition, by removing all or most existing sources of actual or potential competition.[101] The second condition, ie positive net efficiencies, which is read in line with the general principle of 'no net harm to consumers', results in allowing consumers a fair share of the net efficiencies. The four conditions articulated by the Commission are thus similar to the four requirements under Article 101(3) TFEU, namely efficiency gains, a fair share for consumers, indispensability, and no elimination of competition. The Commission seems thus to apply a full-fledged rule of reason, or a balanced analysis, by looking at the likely pro-competitive and anti-competitive aspects of a dominant undertaking's conduct and determining whether the net effect of the conduct on balance harms competition and consumers or not.[102]

With respect to a refusal to supply under Article 102 TFEU, it appears that the Commission will apply a two-step analysis. First of all, the anti-competitive effects of such a refusal on competition and consumers are examined. In particular, three aspects are scrutinized by the Commission, namely (i) the objective necessity of the product/service as an input for a downstream business, supply of which is refused, (ii) the elimination of effective competition on the downstream market caused by the refusal, and (iii) the harm to consumers caused by the refusal.[103] If anti-competitive effects are found, the Commission will consider efficiency claims made by the dominant undertaking and then balance and weigh the anti-competitive effects and likely efficiencies. In this second step, the Commission will take into account the incentives for and reward of investment and innovation in the input business.[104] This two-step analysis is similar to that under Article 101 TFEU. However, a literal interpretation of Article 102 TFEU cannot support a two-step analysis. That is why AG Jacobs contended that such a two-step analysis under Article 102 TFEU is 'somewhat artificial'.[105] In *Sot. Lelos kai Sia*, the CJEU seemed, indeed, to suggest a single

[100] Art 82 Guidance (n 3), para 30 (and, para 31) (emphasis added). See also European Commission, *Directorate General Competition Discussion Paper on the Application of Article 82 of the Treaty to Exclusionary Abuses*, 2005, para 60.

[101] Ibid, para 30.

[102] This approach is similar to the U.S. one. See Varney (n 64), p 13.

[103] Art 82 Guidance (n 3), para 81.

[104] Ibid, paras 89–90.

[105] Opinion of AG Jacobs, para 72, in *Syfait* (n 2).

step analysis as to whether refusal conduct such as GSK's constitutes an abuse on the basis of the ordinary nature of the orders in question.[106]

One could argue that a three-stage process, similar to that under Section 2 of the Sherman Act, should be supported. Initially, competition authorities would have to prove both anti-competitive effects and consumer harm as a result of the refusal. Then, the dominant undertaking may justify its refusal by raising efficiencies. Finally, the competition authorities will balance the anti-competitive effects and the efficiencies. In other words, we argue that a full-fledged rule of reason regarding a refusal to supply under Article 102 TFEU should be followed in the EU.

5. CONCLUSION

In the light of the growing complexity of competition cases and the significance of innovation efficiency, the per se rule or categorical approach under Article 102 TFEU no longer accurately reflects the effects of allegedly abusive conduct of a dominant undertaking on a relevant market. Inflexible reliance on the categories of abusive conduct listed in Article 102 TFEU unnecessarily complicates competition litigation, creates inaccurate results and more type I errors (false positive), and thereby reduces incentives for businesses, especially competition in innovation itself. [107] The abandonment of the per se or quasi per se approach and a move to the rule of reason, with greater reliance on empirical evidence, factual contexts, and economic analyses results in better application of Article 102 TFEU. However, this change in approach may also lead to uncertainty. It appears that no sound competition policy can be developed on a case-by-case basis.[108] Competition authorities and courts should provide guidance to the business community in sectors which are regarded as prone to anti-competitive practices and subject to parallel trade, as is the case with the pharmaceutical sector.[109]

It is clear from *Sot. Lelos kai Sia* that although the pharmaceutical industry in the EU is a strictly regulated sector, it still allows for a margin of discretion. Competition within that margin should be governed and protected by EU competition law. The degree of price and distribution control in the sector cannot preclude the competition rules from applying. While any conduct limiting parallel trade in this sector may be regarded as a restriction of competition which harms

[106] See also Kingston (n 59), p 697.

[107] For a similar view from the perspective of U antitrust law, See MA Lemley and CR Leslie, 'Categorical Analysis in Antitrust Jurisprudence', 93 *Iowa L Rev* 1207, 1270 (May 2008).

[108] Varney (n 64), p 17.

[109] In that respect, See European Commission, Pharmaceutical Sector Inquiry – Preliminary Report, 28 November 2008, available at http://ec.europa.eu/competition/sectors/pharmaceuticals/inquiry/index.html (accessed 2 July 2009). Now Technical Annex to Executive Summary of Pharmaceutical Sector Report, available at http://ec.europa.eu/competition/sectors/pharmaceuticals/inquiry.

market integration under the standardized assessment of competition law, such conduct is no longer automatically prohibited by Article 102 (or 101) TFEU. A dominant undertaking which has refused to supply its medicinal products, especially patented ones, has a reasonable chance of justifying its conduct by the demonstration of likely efficiencies resulting from the refusal. Competition authorities, after demonstrating the anti-competitive effects of such refusal and giving the dominant undertaking the opportunity to show efficiencies, will have to balance and weigh those effects and efficiencies. In doing so it seems they must thus apply a proportionality principle, including suitability, necessity (of the refusal), and balancing (of harms and efficiencies). In this process, the importance of competition on innovation and the particular features of the pharmaceutical sector should be respected and taken into account.

Last but not least, it should be emphasized that the *Sot. Lelos kai Sia* ruling still leaves some uncertainty both on how to define an ordinary order and on the effects of inter-brand competition and competition on innovation in the pharmaceutical sector. Such uncertainty is inter alia indicated by the fact that both the pharmaceutical industry and the parallel traders claimed victory after the ruling.[110] Naturally, this will result in further litigation, not only at the EU but also at national levels, through which the rule of reason relating to refusal to supply in the EU pharmaceutical sector may perhaps be elaborated on. We hope the view of the Commission as expressed in the Article 82 Guidance will be officially recognized by the EU and national courts.

[110] S Mulrenan, *Pharma Companies Rejoice at GSK Judgment* (2008) Managing IP, 22 September, available at www.managingip.com/Article.aspx?ArticleID=2015538 (last visited 2 July 2009).

The Swedish Marketing Act (2008:486)

In accordance with a decision[1] by the Riksdag (Parliament), the following is enacted.[2]

Introductory provision

Section 1

The purpose of this Act is to promote the interests of consumers and business in connection with the marketing of products and to prevent marketing that is unfair to consumers and traders.

Provisions concerning marketing can be found in

– the Aviation Act (1957:297),

– the Consumer Credit Act (1992:830),

– the Package Tours Act (1992:1672)

– the Tobacco Act (1993:581),

– the Alcohol Act (1994:1738),

– the Deposit Guarantee Act (1995:1571)

– the Radio and Television Act (1996:844),

– the Act on the Obligation to Give Notice of Certain Financial Operations (1996:1006),

[1] Government Bill 2007/08:115, Report 2007/08:CU21, Riksdag Communication 2007/08:222. Issued 5 June 2008.

[2] Cf Directive 2006/114/EC of the European Parliament and the Council of 12 December 2006 concerning misleading and comparative advertising (OJ L 376, 27.12.2006, p 21, Celex 32006L0114), Council Directive 89/552/EEC of 3 October 1989 on the coordination of certain provisions laid down by Law, Regulation or Administrative Action in Member States concerning the pursuit of television broadcasting activities (OJ L 298, 17.10.1989, p 23, Celex 389L0552), Directive 97/7/EC of the European Parliament and the Council of 20 May 1997 on the protection of consumers in respect of distance contracts (OJ L 144, 4.6.1997, p 19, Celex 31997L0007), Directive 1999/44/EC of the European Parliament and Council of 25 May 1999 on certain aspects of the sale of consumer goods and associated guarantees (OJ L 171, 7.7.1999, p 12, Celex 31999L0044). Directive 2000/31/EC of the European Parliament and Council of 8 June 2000 on certain legal aspects of information society services, in particular electronic commerce, in the internal market (OJ L 178, 17.7.2000, p 1, Celex 32000L0031), Directive 2002/58/EC of the European Parliament and Council of 12 July 2002 concerning the processing of personal data and the protection of privacy in the electronic communications sector (OJ L 201, 31.7.2002, p 37, Celex 32002L0058), Directive 2002/65/EC of the European Parliament and Council of 23 September 2002 concerning the distance marketing of consumer financial services and amending Council Directive 90/619/EEC and Directives 97/7/EC and 98/27/EC (OJ L 271, 9.10.2002, p 16, Celex 32002L0065) and the Directive 2005/29/EC of the European Parliament and Council of 11 May 2005 concerning unfair business-to-consumer commercial practices in the internal market and amending Council Directive 84/450/EEC and Directives 97/7/EC, 98/27/EC and 2002/65/EC of the European Parliament and the Council and Regulation (EC) No 2006/2004 of the European Parliament and the Council (OJ L 149, 11.6.2005, p 22, Celex 32005L0029).

– the Marketing of Crystal Glass Act (1996:1118),
– the Act on Consumer Protection in Timeshare Contracts (1997:218),
– the Act on Cross-Border Payments within the European Economic Area (1999:268),
– the Investor Compensation Act (1999:158)
– the Act on Electronic Commerce and other Information Society Services (2002:562),
– the Deposits Business Act (2004:299),
– the Price Information Act (2004:347),
– the Distance and Doorstep Selling Act (2005:59),
– the Insurance Contracts Act (2005:104),
– the Insurance Mediation Act (2005:405), and
– the Franchise Disclosure Act (2006:484)

Scope of the Act

Section 2

The Act applies when traders market or seek to acquire products as part of their business activity.

The Act also applies to television broadcasts by satellite that are governed by the Radio and Television Act (1996:844).

The Act also applies when the Consumer Ombudsman fulfils his obligations as competent authority under Regulation (EC) No 2006/2004 of the European Parliament and of the Council of 27 October 2004 on cooperation between national authorities responsible for the enforcement of consumer protection laws.[3]

Definitions

Section 3

For the purposes of this Act the following terms have the meaning set out below

transaction decision: a decision made by a consumer or a trader concerning whether, how and under what conditions a product is to be bought, if all or part of the purchase sum is to be paid, if the product is to be retained or transferred, or if a contractual right in connection with the product is to be exercised, regardless of whether the consumer or trader decides to make a transaction or refrain from making a transaction,

electronic mail: an addressed or otherwise individualised electronic message in the form of text, voice, sound or image, sent via a public communications network and which can be stored on the network or in the recipient's terminal equipment until the recipient retrieves it,

good marketing practice: generally accepted business practices or other established norms aimed at protecting consumers and traders in the marketing of products,

consumer: a natural person who makes a transaction mainly for purposes that fall outside business activity,

marketing: advertising and other measures in the course of business activities which are intended to promote the sale of and access to products including a trader's actions, omissions or other measures or behaviour before, during or after sale or delivery of products to consumers or traders,

[3] OJ L 364, 9.12.2004, p 1 (Celex 32004R2006).

trader: a natural or legal person who makes a transaction for purposes connected with that person's own business activity,

products: goods, services, real property, employment opportunities and other commodities.

Unfair marketing

Annex to the Directive

Section 4

Annex I to Directive 2005/29/EC of the European Parliament and of the Council of 11 May 2005 concerning unfair business-to-consumer commercial practices in the internal market and amending Council Directive 84/450/EEC, Directives 97/7/EC, 98/27/EC and 2002/65/EC of the European Parliament and of the Council and Regulation (EC) No 2006/2004 of the European Parliament and of the Council[4] shall have the force of law in Sweden. The Government has published the relevant annex in the Swedish Code of Statutes.

In an examination of a matter in accordance with any of the provisions of Annex I to the Directive this Act shall be applicable.

The provisions of points 1–31 of Annex I to the Directive shall be applicable even if the marketing in question is directed towards traders.

The provisions of point 14 of Annex I to the Directive shall be applied to measures that have been taken in breach of this point unless the measure is covered by the Lotteries Act (1994:100).

Good marketing practice

Section 5

Marketing shall be consistent with good marketing practice.

Section 6

Marketing that contravenes good marketing practice under Section 5 is to be regarded as unfair if it appreciably affects or probably affects the recipient's ability to make a well-founded transaction decision.

Aggressive marketing

Section 7

A trader may not use aggressive marketing.

Marketing is to be regarded as aggressive if it involves harassment, coercion, physical violence, threats or other aggressive ways of bringing pressure to bear.

Aggressive marketing is to be regarded as unfair if it appreciably affects or probably affects the recipient's ability to make a well-founded transaction decision.

Aggressive marketing as specified in points 24–31 of Annex I to Directive 2005/29/EC are always to be regarded as unfair.

[4] OJ L 149, 11.6.2005, p 22 (Celex 32005L0029).

Misleading marketing

Section 8

Marketing that is misleading under any of the provisions of Sections 9, 10 or 12-17 is to be regarded as unfair if it affects or probably affects the recipient's ability to make a well-founded transaction decision.

Misleading marketing as specified in points 1-23 of Annex I to Directive 2005/29/EC are always to be regarded as unfair.

Identification of advertising

Section 9

All marketing shall be formulated and presented in such a way that it is clear that it is a matter of marketing.

The party responsible for the marketing shall also be clearly indicated. However, this does not apply to representations whose sole purpose is to attract attention ahead of follow-up representations.

Prohibition of misleading marketing

Section 10

In the course of marketing a trader may not make any incorrect statement or other representation that is misleading with respect to the trader's own or another person's business activity.

The first paragraph applies in particular to representations which concern 1. the product's existence, nature, quantity, quality and other distinguishing characteristics, 2. the product's origin, uses and risks such as impact on health or environment, 3. customer service, processing of complaints and method and date of manufacture or supply, 4. the product's price, basis for calculating the price, special price advantages and payment terms, 5. the qualifications, position on the market, commitments, trademarks, trade names, distinctive symbols or other rights of the trader or of another trader, 6. awards or distinctions awarded to the trader, 7. terms of delivery for the product, 8. service needs, spare parts, exchange or repairs, 9. the trader's commitment to comply with codes of conduct, and 10. the consumer's rights under law or other regulation.

Further, a trader may not omit material information when marketing his own or another person's business activity. Misleading omission also refers to cases where the material information is provided in an unclear, incomprehensible, ambiguous or other inappropriate manner.

Limitations in the means of communication etc.

Section 11

When assessing whether a representation is misleading under Section 10, third paragraph, the limitations in time and space of the means of communication used may be taken into account, as well as the measures taken by the trader to provide the information in some other way.

Invitations to purchase

Section 12

Marketing is misleading if in a representation the trader offers consumers a specific product with a stated price without clear presentation of the following material information:

1. the product's distinguishing characteristics to the extent appropriate to the media and product,
2. price and unit price stated as stipulated in Sections 7-10 of the Price Information Act (2004:347),
3. the identity and geographical address of the trader,
4. terms and conditions of payment, delivery, performance and processing of complaints if these deviate from normal practice in the industry or for the product in question,
5. information concerning the right of withdrawal or the right to cancel a purchase which must be supplied to the consumer by law.

Marketing is also misleading if the trader in a representation offers consumers several specific products at a common price, without the offer containing material information under points 1-5 of the first paragraph.

Misleading packaging dimensions

Section 13

A trader may not in the course of marketing, use packaging which, through its dimensions or other aspects of its outer appearance is misleading as to the product's quantity, size or form.

Misleading copies

Section 14

A trader may not, in the course of marketing, use copies that are misleading in that they can easily be confused with another trader's known and distinctive products. This does not, however, apply to copies the design of which is primarily intended to render the product functional.

Bankruptcy sales

Section 15

A trader, in the course of marketing, may only use the expression "bankruptcy", by itself or in conjunction with another expression, where the products are offered for sale by the estate in liquidation/bankruptcy or on its behalf.

Clearance sales

Section 16

A trader, in the course of marketing products, may only use the expressions "slutförsäljning" (final sale), "utförsäljning" (clearance sale) or another expression with the equivalent implication if

1. it relates to a final sale of the trader's entire stock or a clearly defined part of that stock,

2. the sale takes place during a limited period, and
3. the prices are significantly lower than the trader's normal prices for equivalent products.

Discount sales

Section 17

A trader, in the course of marketing products, may only use the expression "realisation" (discount sale) or another expression with the equivalent implication if
1. the products offered for sale form part of the trader's ordinary range,
2. the sale takes place during a limited period, and
3. the prices are significantly lower than the trader's normal prices for equivalent products.

Comparative advertising

Section 18

A trader may, in its advertising, directly or indirectly refer to another trader or such trader's products provided that the comparison
1. is not misleading,
2. refers to products which fulfil the same needs or are intended for the same purpose,
3. objectively refers to material, relevant, verifiable, and distinguishing characteristics of the products,
4. does not give rise to confusion between the trader and another trader or between their products, trademarks, business names, or other distinctive marks,
5. does not discredit or disparage another trader's business, circumstances, products, trademarks, business name or other distinctive marks,
6. in respect of goods bearing a designation of origin, at all times pertains to goods of the same designation,
7. does not take unfair advantage of the reputation associated with another trader's trademark, business name, or other distinctive marks or the designation of origin of the goods, and
8. does not present a product as an imitation or copy of a product with a protected trademark or business name.

Unsolicited advertising

Section 19

A trader may, in the course of marketing to a natural person, use electronic mail, a telefax or automatic calling device or any other similar automatic system for individual communication that is not operated by an individual, only if the natural person has consented to this in advance.

Where a trader has obtained details of a natural person's electronic address for electronic mail in the context of a sale of a product to that person, the consent requirement stipulated in the first paragraph shall not apply, provided that,
1. the natural person has not objected to the use of the electronic address for the purpose of marketing via electronic mail,
2. the marketing relates to the trader's own similar products and

3. the natural person is clearly and explicitly given the opportunity to object, simply and without charge, to the use of such details for marketing purposes, when they are collected and in conjunction with each subsequent marketing communication.

Section 20

In marketing via electronic mail the communication shall at all times contain a valid address to which the recipient can send a request that the marketing cease. This also applies to marketing to a legal person.

Section 21

A trader may use methods for individual distance communication other than those referred to in Section 19, unless the natural person has clearly objected to the use of such methods.

Warranty information

Section 22

A trader who, in the course of marketing, offers to accept liability for a product or a part of a product or for some feature of a product for a specified period by means of a warranty or similar commitment shall, at the time of sale, provide the buyer with clear information concerning the content of the commitment and such information as is necessary for the buyer to bring a claim under it. The buyer shall also be informed that his legal rights are not affected by the commitment.

The commitment and information shall be provided in a document or some other readable and permanent form that is accessible to the buyer.

Prohibitions and orders

Prohibition of certain marketing

Section 23

A trader whose marketing is unfair may be prohibited from continuing with that or other similar practices.

A prohibition under the first paragraph may also be issued against 1. an employee of the trader, 2. another person acting on behalf of the trader, and 3. any person who has otherwise materially contributed to the marketing in question.

Order to provide information

Section 24

A trader who, in the course of marketing, neglects to provide material information may be ordered to provide such information.

Such an order may also be issued against 1. an employee of the trader, and 2. another person acting on behalf of the trader.

An order under the first paragraph may include an obligation to provide information 1. in advertisements or other representations that the trader uses in the course of marketing, 2. through labelling of the goods or in some other form at the point of sale, or 3. in a certain form to consumers who so request.

Order to provide technical aids

Section 25

A service provider under the Act on Electronic Commerce and other Information Society Services (2002:562) who, in contravention of Section 10 of that Act, fails to provide such technical aids as are referred to there may be ordered to provide such aids.

Conditional financial penalty

Section 26

A prohibition under Section 23 or an order under Section 24 or 25 shall be subject to a conditional financial penalty, unless there are particular grounds rendering this unnecessary.

Interim orders

Section 27

The court may order that a prohibition under Section 23 or an order under Section 24 or 25 shall apply until further notice if

1. the applicant demonstrates probable cause for his claim, and
2. it can be reasonably assumed that the defendant, by taking or by omitting to take a specific action, can reduce the effectiveness of a prohibition or order.

The provisions of Chapter 15, Section 5, second to fourth paragraphs and Sections 6 and 8 of the Code of Judicial Procedure apply to orders under the first paragraph. The decision may be implemented with immediate effect.

Orders and injunctions

Section 28

In cases of minor importance, the Consumer Ombudsman may issue orders and injunctions concerning

1. prohibitions as referred to in Section 23 (injunctions),
2. orders as referred to in Section 24 (information orders), or
3. orders as referred to in Section 25.

The order or injunction shall be subject to a conditional financial penalty.

In order for it to be valid, the trader must accept the order or injunction immediately or within a certain period. If the order has been accepted it applies as a final and non-appealable judgment.

Acceptance after the stipulated period is not valid.

Market disruption charge

Grounds for imposing a charge

Section 29

A trader may be ordered to pay a special charge (market disruption charge) if the trader, or a person acting on behalf of the trader, intentionally or negligently contravenes

- Section 7,
- Section 8 and any of the provisions of Sections 9, 10, 12–17,

– Section 18,

– Section 20 or

– any of the provisions of Annex I to Directive 2005/29/EC.

The same applies if a trader intentionally or negligently contravenes any of the provisions of

– Section 14, first paragraph, point 2 or 3 or Section 14 a, first paragraph, point 2 or 3 of the Tobacco Act (1993:581),

– Chapter 4, Section 10 of the Alcohol Act (1994:1738),

– Chapter 7, Section 3, 4 or 10, first or third paragraph of the Radio and Television Act (1996:844),

– Section 11 of the Deposit Guarantee Act (1995:1571) or Section 8 of the Deposits Business Act (2004:299) as regards an offer that is not directed solely to persons other than consumers.

The provisions of the first and second paragraphs also apply to a trader who intentionally or negligently contributes materially to the infringement.

The charge accrues to the State.

Section 30

A market disruption charge may not be imposed on a person for infringement of a prohibition or failure to comply with an order issued subject to a conditional financial penalty under this Act.

Amount of the charge

Section 31

The market disruption charge shall be fixed at no less than five thousand kronor and no more than five million kronor.

The charge may not exceed ten per cent of the trader's annual turnover.

The annual turnover shall refer to the turnover for the immediately preceding financial year.

If the infringement occurred during the trader's first year of business or if information concerning the annual turnover is otherwise not available or is incomplete, the amount of annual turnover may be estimated.

If an action is brought against more than one trader, the charge shall be separately determined for each of them.

Section 32

In determining the market disruption charge, particular attention shall be given to the seriousness and duration of the infringement.

In minor cases, no charge shall be imposed. The charge may be waived if there are exceptional grounds for doing so.

Payment of the charge

Section 33

The market disruption charge shall be paid to the Legal, Financial and Administrative Services Agency within thirty days of the judgment becoming final and non-appealable, or such later date as specified in the judgment.

If the charge has not been paid within the period stipulated in the first paragraph, the Legal, Financial and Administrative Services Agency shall submit the unpaid charge for collection. The Act on the Collection of Debts to the State (1993:891) contains provisions on collection.

Statutory limitation

Section 34

A market disruption charge may only be imposed if the application to institute proceedings has been served on the party to whom the claim is addressed within five years of cessation of the infringement.

Section 35

A market disruption charge shall lapse if the judgment has not been executed within five years of the date on which it became final and non-appealable.

Attachment

Section 36

In order to secure a claim relating to a market disruption charge the court may order attachment. In that case the provisions of Chapter 15 of the Code of Judicial Procedure concerning attachment to secure a claim shall apply.

Damages

Section 37

A person who intentionally or negligently violates a prohibition or an order issued under Section 23, 24 or 25, or Section 7, Section 8 or any of the provisions of Sections 9, 10, 12–17, or any of the provisions of Sections 18–22 or any of the points in Annex I to Directive 2005/29/EC, shall compensate any consumer or other trader for any damage arising from this violation.

When determining compensation to a trader, account may be taken of circumstances other than of an economic nature.

Section 38

Entitlement to damages is forfeited if proceedings are not instituted within five years from the time the damage arose.

Erasure

Erasure etc. of misleading representations

Section 39

In the event of an infringement of a prohibition subject to a conditional financial penalty under Section 23 or of the provisions of Sections 9, 10, 12–17 or of Section 18 or of any of points 1–23 in Annex I to Directive 2005/29/EC, the court may, where reasonable, order that any misleading representation on goods, packaging, printed matter, business documents or similar shall be erased or altered so that it is no longer misleading. If this objective cannot be achieved by other means the court may order that the property be destroyed.

Security measures

Section 40

If the applicant demonstrates probable cause for the granting of an application under Section 39 and it can be reasonably assumed that the defendant, by taking or by omitting to take a specific action, will reduce the effectiveness of an order for erasure, the court may order appropriate measures to apply until further notice. The provisions of Chapter 15, Section 3, second paragraph, Section 5, second to fourth paragraphs and Sections 6 and 8 of the Code of Judicial Procedure apply to such measures. The order may be implemented with immediate effect.

If an application is presented under Section 39 in proceedings for the imposition of a conditional financial penalty pursuant to this Act, instead of the provisions of the first paragraph, the property may be seized. In that case the provisions of Chapter 27 of the Code of Judicial Procedure concerning seizure in criminal cases shall be applied. The order may be implemented with immediate effect.

Section 41

Orders concerning erasure of misleading representations under Section 39 and orders concerning security measures under Section 40 shall be made on the application of a party to the court where proceedings concerning the application for a prohibition under Section 23, a market disruption charge under Section 29 or damages under Section 37 are pending.

Orders to erase representations due to infringement of a prohibition subject to conditional financial penalty under Sections 23 and 26 may be made on the application of a party to the court where proceedings concerning the imposition of the conditional financial penalty are pending.

Obligation to provide information etc.

Section 42

At the request of the Consumer Ombudsman: 1. any party so requested shall give a statement and provide necessary information in proceedings concerning the application of this Act, 2. a trader shall provide such documents, samples of goods and suchlike which may be of significance for the investigation of a matter where a prohibition or order under Section 23, 24 or 25 can be assumed to be at issue.

Section 43

A person who is subject to a prohibition or order under Section 23, 24 or 25 shall be obliged, at the request of the Consumer Ombudsman, to provide any information, documentation, samples of goods and suchlike as are necessary in order to verify compliance with the prohibition or order.

Section 44

Where necessary for supervision in a matter referred to in Section 42, point 2 or Section 43, the Consumer Ombudsman may request the trader to make available for inspection such premises or corresponding locations, with the exception of dwellings, where the business activities are conducted.

Section 45

In the event of non-compliance with a request under Section 42, 43 or 44, the Consumer Ombudsman may order the person concerned to fulfil his or her obligation, subject to a conditional financial penalty.

Section 46

If there are particular grounds, the Consumer Ombudsman may pay compensation for samples or suchlike referred to in Sections 42 and 43.

The Government or an agency appointed by the Government may issue regulations concerning the obligation of a trader to reimburse the Consumer Ombudsman for expenses incurred in taking and examining samples in cases referred to in Section 43.

Where and by whom proceedings may be instituted

Prohibitions and orders

Section 47

Proceedings in respect of a prohibition or order under Section 23, 24 or 25 shall be instituted at the Market Court. If the same applicant, or another applicant in consultation with that applicant, institutes concurrent proceedings concerning a market disruption charge under Section 29 or damages under Section 37 with reference to the marketing in question, proceedings concerning a prohibition or order shall, however, be instituted at Stockholm District Court.

Proceedings in respect of a prohibition or order may be instituted by 1. The Consumer Ombudsman, 2. a trader affected by the marketing in question, or 3. a group of consumers, traders or employees.

An interim order under Section 27 shall be ordered by the court where proceedings under the first paragraph are pending.

Market disruption charge

Section 48

Proceedings in respect of a market disruption charge under Section 29 shall be instituted at Stockholm District Court by the Consumer Ombudsman.

If the Consumer Ombudsman decides in a particular case not to commence proceedings for the imposition of a market disruption charge, an individual trader affected by the marketing in question or a group of traders may institute such proceedings.

An attachment order under Section 36 shall be issued by the court before which proceedings for a market disruption charge are pending. If proceedings have not yet been instituted, the provisions of the first paragraph concerning court of jurisdiction shall apply.

Imposition of conditional financial penalty

Section 49

Proceedings for imposition of a conditional financial penalty which have been ordered pursuant to this Act shall be instituted at a district court that is competent under Chapter 10 of the Swedish Code of Judicial Procedure. Such proceedings may always be instituted at Stockholm District Court.

Proceedings may be instituted by the person who requested the order subject to a conditional financial penalty and by the Consumer Ombudsman.

Damages

Section 50

Proceedings in respect of damages under Section 37 shall be instituted at Stockholm District Court. Such proceedings may also be instituted at a district court that is competent under Chapter 10 of the Swedish Code of Judicial Procedure.

Appeals

Section 51

Decisions of the Consumer Ombudsman under Sections 42–44 and concerning orders subject to a conditional financial penalty after such requests may be appealed to Stockholm District Court.

The same applies to decisions on compensation under Section 46 or under regulations issued pursuant to that Section.

Section 52

Judgments and decisions of a district court in cases and matters under this Act can be appealed to the Market Court. Judgments and decisions in cases concerning imposition of conditional financial penalties ordered pursuant to this act shall, however, be made to the court of appeal in accordance with the provisions of the Conditional Financial Penalties Act (1985:206).

Decisions in the course of proceedings on matters referred to in Section 27 and Section 40, first paragraph, may be appealed separately. Decisions in proceedings handled by the Market Court shall be deemed to concern measures under Chapter 15 of the Swedish Code of Judicial Procedure.

Legal force

Section 53

A judgment in which the issue of prohibition under Section 23 or order under Sections 24 and 25 has been adjudicated, shall constitute a bar to initiating new proceedings under Sections 23, 24 or 25 with reference to the marketing in question. Such a judgment does not, however, prevent the same issue being heard again as a result of a change in circumstances.

Composition of the court etc.

Section 54

At the main hearing of a case under this Act Stockholm District Court shall be composed of four members, two of whom shall be legally trained judges and two financial experts. One of the legally trained judges shall be president of the court.

If, after the main hearing has started, one of the members of the court is prevented from attending, the court is nevertheless competent.

Unless otherwise provided in Section 55, the district court shall be composed of one legally qualified judge

1. at a main hearing in cases referred to in Chapter 1, Section 3 a, second and third paragraphs of the Swedish Code of Judicial Procedure,

2. at determination of cases without a main hearing, and

3. at proceedings that do not take place at a main hearing.

In cases referred to in the third paragraph a financial expert may also be a member of the district court.

Section 55

When determining cases without a main hearing and when considering issues which are part of the proceedings, Stockholm District Court may be composed as stipulated in Section 54, first paragraph, if there are particular grounds with regard to the nature of the case or issue.

Section 56

In cases that only concern damages under Section 37 Stockholm District Court may be composed as follows from Chapter 1, Section 3 a, 3 c and 3 d of the Swedish Code of Judicial Procedure.

Section 57

At proceedings concerning matters referred to in Section 51, Stockholm District Court shall be composed of one legally qualified judge or one legally qualified judge and one financial expert. However, if there are particular grounds with regard to the nature of the matter, the district court may be composed as stipulated in Section 54, first paragraph.

Section 58

The Government shall appoint for a specified period persons to serve as financial experts under Section 54. Should circumstances arise while a financial expert is participating in the processing of a case or matter which entail the termination of his or her appointment, the appointment shall be regarded as continuing to be valid for the case or matter in progress.

A person who is to serve as a financial expert shall be a Swedish citizen and may not be a minor or an undischarged bankrupt or have an administrator appointed for them by a court under Chapter 11, Section 7 of the Children and Parents Code.

Procedural provisions

Proceedings heard at Stockholm District Court and the Market Court

Section 59

Unless otherwise provided in this Act, the provisions of the Swedish Code of Judicial Procedure concerning civil cases in which out-of-court settlement of the matter is not permitted shall be applied to cases of prohibitions or orders under Sections 23, 24 or 25 and cases concerning a market disruption charge under Section 29.

In cases concerning damages under Section 37, the provisions of the Swedish Code of Judicial Procedure concerning civil cases in which out-of-court settlement of the matter is permitted are applicable.

In matters referred to in Section 51 the Act on the Examination of Non-Contentious Matters (1996:242) is applicable, unless otherwise provided in this Act.

Section 60

When the Market Court hears cases and matters following an appeal under Section 52, the provisions of Chapters 49, 50 and 52 of the Swedish Code of Judicial Procedure and of Section 39, first paragraph of the Act on Non-Contentious Matters (1996:242) concerning the court of appeal shall instead apply to the Market Court. Leave to appeal is not required, however, for the Market Court to examine a decision of the district court.

Section 61

If proceedings are brought under this Act by a person other than the Consumer Ombudsman, the court shall notify the Consumer Ombudsman of the proceedings.

When proceedings are brought concerning a market disruption charge or damages the district court shall notify the Market Court of the proceedings.

Consolidation

Section 62

Proceedings for damages under Section 37 may only be consolidated in the district court with other proceedings under this Act.

Intervention

Section 63

In proceedings concerning prohibitions or orders under Sections 23, 24 or 25, the person entitled to take legal action under Section 47, second paragraph is entitled to participate in the proceedings as an intervenor under Chapter 14 of the Swedish Code of Judicial Procedure.

Litigation costs

Section 64

In proceedings under this Act, Chapter 18 of the Swedish Code of Judicial Procedure applies with respect to litigation costs. The provisions of Chapter 18, Section 16 of the Swedish Code of Judicial Procedure shall not, however, be applicable in proceedings concerning prohibitions or orders under Sections 23, 24 or 25. In such proceedings the court may determine that each of the parties shall bear its own litigation costs.

Non-attendance

Section 65

The provisions of the Swedish Code of Judicial Procedure concerning prosecutors shall apply to the Consumer Ombudsman as a party in cases and matters under this Act, with respect to orders addressed to parties and non-attendance of parties.

Other provisions

Section 66

The Government may, with reference to a foreign state, provide as follows.

As regards goods bearing an incorrect or misleading designation of origin, by which the goods, directly or indirectly, are indicated to have been produced or manufactured in the foreign state or in a region or place in the foreign state, measures may be adopted under Section 39 in cases other than those referred to there. However, this is not applicable if the designation in accordance with trade practice only serves to indicate the nature of the goods or if it is accompanied by a clear statement that the goods were not produced or manufactured in the state or place mentioned.

Proceedings concerning measures under the second paragraph shall be instituted in Stockholm District Court by the Consumer Ombudsman or, where the Consumer Ombudsman has decided not to institute proceedings, by any person who conducts business in goods of the same nature as the goods to which the proceedings relate.

1. This Act enters into force on 1 July 2008, at which time the Marketing Act (1995:450) shall cease to apply and the Act amending the Marketing Act (2005:706) shall be repealed.

2. The provisions of Sections 4–22 and 29–36 shall also be applicable to marketing started before the Act enters into force, unless the measure was permitted under older regulations.

3. Prohibitions and orders and injunctions and information orders issued under older regulations shall continue to apply.

4. The provisions concerning damages in Section 29 of the Marketing Act (1995:450) shall continue to be applicable as regards infringements occurring before the new Act enters into force.

5. The provisions of Section 49 shall also be applicable as regards imposition of conditional financial penalties ordered pursuant to the Marketing Act (1995:450).

Note: Annex 1 to the UCPD, Commercial Practices which are in all Circumstances Considered Unfair ("The Black list") has been promulgated *in extenso* as Swedish law in the form of a Government announcement. It is not reproduced here.

The Swedish Competition Act (2008:579)

Chapter 1 Introductory provision

Article 1

The purpose of this Act is to eliminate and counteract obstacles to effective competition in the field of production of and trade in goods, services and other products.

Article 2

This Act shall not apply to agreements between employers and employees relating to wages and other conditions of employment.

Article 3

The Council Regulation (EC) No 1/2003 of 16 December 2002 on the implementation of the rules on competition laid down in Articles 101 and 102 of the Treaty on the Functioning of the European Union (the Treaty) and the Council Regulation (EC) No 139/2004 of 20 January 2004 on the control of concentrations between undertakings contain provisions that are relevant to the implementation of this Act.

Article 4

The Government determines which courts and other authorities shall be competition authorities in accordance with the Council Regulation (EC) No 1/2003 of 16 December 2002 on the implementation of the rules on competition laid down in Articles 101 and 102 in the Treaty, if this is not stipulated in this Act.

Definitions

Article 5

For the purposes of this Act an undertaking shall be defined as a natural or legal person engaged in activities of an economic or commercial nature. To the extent that such activities involve the exercise of authority they shall not fall within the scope of this definition.

The term undertaking shall also include associations of undertakings.

Article 6

The provisions of the Act relating to agreements shall also apply to

1. decisions by an association of undertakings, and
2. concerted practices of undertakings.

Article 7

In this Act a primary agricultural association is defined as an economic association whose members are individual farmers or other undertakings engaged in agriculture, horticulture or forestry. If associations of such undertakings are members of an association, the latter is, however, only regarded as a primary agricultural association providing that such associations only contain local associations of undertakings operating activities of the kind specified.

The Act (2000:1025) on the meaning of the terms agricultural, horticultural and forestry produce as used in the Competition Act (2008:579) contains special provisions on what is meant by such produce under this Act.

Article 8

For the purposes of this Act a taxi undertaking is an undertaking providing or carrying out taxi services or comparable transport services.

A central booking service refers to a joint or independent function which receives orders and distributes transport assignments between taxi undertakings. The function can also perform related activities.

Article 9

According to this Act, a concentration shall be deemed to arise where

1. two or more previously independent undertakings merge, or

2. either one or more persons, already controlling at least one undertaking, or one or more

undertakings acquire whether by purchase of securities or assets, by contract or by any other means direct or indirect control of the whole or parts of one or more other undertakings.

The creation of a joint venture, which on a lasting basis fulfils all the functions of an autonomous economic entity, constitutes a concentration within the meaning of the first paragraph point 2.

Contents of the Act

Article 10

The Act contains provisions concerning

– anti-competitive co-operation between undertakings (Chapter 2),

– measures against anti-competitive co-operation between undertakings (Chapter 3),

– control of concentrations(Chapter 4),

– investigations of cases (Chapter 5),

– penalty of a fine (Chapter 6),

– appeals (Chapter 7), and

– court proceedings (Chapter 8).

Chapter 2 Prohibited restrictions of competition

Anti-competitive cooperation between undertakings

Article 1

Agreements between undertakings shall be prohibited if they have as their object or effect, the prevention, restriction or distortion of competition in the market to an appreciable extent, if not otherwise regulated in this act.

This shall apply, in particular, to agreements which:

1. directly or indirectly fix purchase or selling prices or any other trading conditions;

2. limit or control production, markets, technical development, or investment;

3. share markets or sources of supply;

4. apply dissimilar conditions to equivalent transactions with other trading parties, thereby placing them at a competitive disadvantage; or

5. make the conclusion of contracts subject to acceptance by the other parties of supplementary obligations, which by their nature or according to commercial usage have no connection with the subject of such contracts.

Exemptions from the prohibition on anti-competitive co-operation between undertakings

Article 2

The prohibition in Article 1 does not apply to agreements which

1. contributes to improving the production or distribution or to promoting technical or economic progress;

2. allows consumers a fair share of the resulting benefit;

3. only imposes on the undertakings concerned restrictions which are indispensable to the attainment of the objective referred to in paragraph 1, and

4. does not afford such undertakings the possibility of eliminating competition in respect of a substantial part of the utilities in question.

Article 3

Exemptions from the prohibition in Article 1 shall apply to categories of agreements laid down in

1. Act (2008:580) concerning block exemption on anti-competitive agreements on certain co-operation concerning taxi services,

2. Act (2008:581) concerning block exemption on vertical anti-competitive agreements,

3. Act (2008:582) concerning block exemptions on anti-competitive specialisation agreements

4. Act (2008:583) concerning block exemption on anti-competitive agreements concerning research and development.

5. Act (2008:584) concerning block exemption on vertical anti-competitive agreements in the motor vehicle sector

6. Act (2008:585) concerning block exemption on anti-competitive agreements in the insurance sector, and

7. Act (2008:586) concerning block exemption on anti-competitive technology transfer agreements.

If an individual agreement as a result of a block exemption according to the first paragraph is exempted from the prohibition in Article 1 but has effects which are incompatible with Article 2, the Swedish Competition Authority may determine that the agreement shall not be covered by the block exemption.

Article 4

The prohibition in Article 1 does not apply to those agreements within a primary agricultural association or its subsidiaries that concern co-operation between the members of the association on

1. the production, collection, processing, sale or related activities such as the use of jointly owned facilities, storing, preparation, distribution or marketing of agricultural, horticultural or forestry produce, or

2. the purchase of goods or services for such activity as is referred to in 1.

The first paragraph does not, however, apply to agreements which have as their object or effect

1.the prevention or impairment of free mobility of a member on the market

a) with respect to choosing a buyer or a supplier,

b) with respect to the possibility of leaving the association, or

c) in other respects of equivalent importance, or

2. that selling prices are directly or indirectly fixed for goods when the sale takes place directly between the member and a third party.

Article 5

The prohibition in Article 1 does not apply to a written agreement between taxi undertakings or between a central booking service and taxi undertakings if the agreement

1. concerns joint transport activities through co-operation by means of a central booking service or in other ways for the purpose of achieving efficiency gains or other such financial advantages,

2. is needed to satisfy the public interest in having access to taxi services, and

3. covers a maximum of 40 taxi vehicles.

The exemption under the first paragraph does not apply

1. to the extent that the co-operation concerns practices or conditions which involve or cover

a) the setting of joint prices,

b) the division of markets,

c) a period of notice for participating taxi undertakings which exceeds six months from the date when notice is given, or concerning an economic association, conditions that notice may not be given until six months at the earliest, or a longer period after entry, or

d) prohibition against participating taxi undertakings to compete after the expiry of the agreement with joint transport activity, and

2. to the extent that it is evident that the purpose of the joint transport activity or interest in access to taxi services in accordance with the first paragraph points 1 and 2 can be satisfied without the co-operation covering such practices or conditions as set out in 1.

Nullity

Article 6

Any agreements or provisions included in agreements that are prohibited under Article 1 shall be void.

Abuse of a dominant position

Article 7

Any abuse by one or more undertakings of a dominant position on the market shall be prohibited.

Such abuse may, in particular, consist in

1. directly or indirectly imposing unfair purchase or selling prices or other unfair trading conditions,

2. limiting production, markets or technical development to the prejudice of consumers,

3. applying dissimilar conditions to equivalent transactions with other trading parties, thereby placing them at a competitive disadvantage, or

4. making the conclusion of contracts subject to acceptance by the other parties of supplementary obligations, which by their nature or according to commercial usage have no connection with the subject of such contracts.

Chapter 3 Actions against restrictions on competition

Obligation

Article 1

The Swedish Competition Authority may require an undertaking to terminate an infringement of any of the prohibitions laid down in Chapter 2 Article 1 or 7 or Article 101 or 102 in the Treaty.

An obligation pursuant to first paragraph shall take effect immediately, unless other provision is made.

Article 2

If the Swedish Competition Authority decides in a particular case not to impose such an obligation pursuant to Article 1, the Market Court may do so at the request of an undertaking that is affected by the infringement.

Such a right to legal action, however, does not exist if the decision of the Swedish Competition Authority is based on Article 13 of the Council Regulation (EC) No 1/2003.

Article 3

If particular grounds exist, an obligation pursuant to Article 1 may be imposed for the period until a final decision is taken on the matter. The Market Court may only impose such an obligation following commencement of legal proceedings.

Commitments

Article 4

If the question has been raised as to whether an undertaking infringes any of the prohibitions laid down in Chapter 2 Article 1 or 7 or in Article 101 or 102 in the Treaty, a commitment offered by the undertaking may result in a decision by the Swedish Competition Authority stating that there are no longer grounds for action. Decisions made by the Authority may cover a specified period. As long as the decision applies, the Authority in the circumstances concerning the commitment, may not issue any obligation pursuant to Article 1 or 3.

The Swedish Competition Authority may revoke its decision under the first paragraph where

1. there has been a change in any of the facts which were material to the making of the decision,

2. the parties commit a breach of any obligation attached to the decision, or

3. the decision is based on incomplete, incorrect or misleading information which the parties have submitted.

Administrative fines

Article 5

The Stockholm City Court may, at the request of the Swedish Competition Authority order an undertaking to pay an administrative fine where the undertaking, or a person acting on behalf of the undertaking, intentionally or negligently has infringed the prohibitions in Chapter 2 Article 1 or 7 or Article 101 or 102 in the Treaty.

The proceeds of the fine shall go to the State.

Before the Swedish Competition Authority institutes proceedings against an undertaking regarding an administrative fine, the undertaking shall be given an opportunity to express its views on the draft summons application of the Authority.

Article 6

The administrative fine may not exceed ten per cent of the annual turnover of the undertaking in the preceding business year.

If an action relating to the fine is brought against several undertakings, the fine shall be determined individually for each undertaking.

Article 7

An administrative fine may not be imposed

1. in respect of measures taken in compliance with a decision pursuant to Article 1, 2 or a prohabition persuant to Article 27 or 30 issued under penalty of a fine in accordance with the provisions of this Act,

2. for measures which have been taken during the period when a decision on acceptance of the commitment pursuant to Article 4 first paragraph applies, if the measures are compatible with the decision, or

3. in minor cases.

Pursuant to first paragraph point 2 an administrative fine may be imposed, if the decision has been revoked pursuant to Article 4 second paragraph point 3.

Article 8

The administrative fine shall be set according to the sanction value of the infringement.

When assessing the sanction value, account must be taken of the gravity of the infringement and its duration.

When assessing the gravity of the infringement, particular account must be taken of the following:

1. the nature of the infringement,

2. the size and significance of the market, and

3. the infringement's actual or potential impact on competition in the market.

Article 9

As aggravating circumstances when considering the undertakings infringement particular account especially shall be taken of:

1. if an undertaking has persuaded another undertaking to join the infringement, or

2. if the undertaking has had a leading role in the infringement.

Article 10

As attenuating circumstances when considering the infringement of the undertaking special account shall be taken to whether the undertaking has participated in the infringement to a limited extent.

Article 11

When determining the amount of the administrative fine, besides the circumstances referable to the infringement itself, particular account shall be taken of the following:

1. whether the undertaking has previously infringed the prohibitions contained in Chapter 2, Article 1 or 7 or in Article 101 or 102 of the Treaty,

2. whether the undertaking has discontinued the infringement quickly after it has been pointed out by the Swedish Competition Authority, or

3. the financial status of the undertaking.

Leniency and reduction of administrative fine

Article 12

Leniency regarding an administrative fine may be granted for an undertaking which has infringed a prohibition contained in Chapter 2, Article 1 or in Article 101 of the Treaty, if the undertaking is the first to notify the infringement to the Swedish Competition Authority and if it is only owing to the information contained in the notification that the Authority has obtained sufficient material to take action against the infringement.

When the Swedish Competition Authority has already received sufficient material to take action against the infringement and no declaration in accordance with Article 15 has been made, leniency may be granted for the administrative fine regarding an undertaking that has infringed the said prohibition, provided

1. the undertaking is the first to provide such information that results in it being established that the infringement occurred, or

2. the undertaking in some other way has to a very significant extent facilitated the investigation of the infringement.

However, leniency may not be granted for the administrative fine regarding an undertaking that has compelled another undertaking to participate in the infringement.

Article 13

The fine may be set at a lower amount than would be the case when applying Articles 8-11 for an undertaking which has infringed the prohibition in Chapter 2 Article 1 or Article 101 in the Treaty, if the undertaking provides the Swedish Competition Authority such information that facilitates the investigation of the infringement to a significant extent.

When assessing the amount of the reduction, account must be taken of whether any other undertaking has already provided such information that has to a significant extent facilitated the investigation.

Article 14

In order to be granted leniency or reduction according to Article 12 or 13 the undertaking shall in addition to these provisions

1. provide all the information and evidence about the infringement the Swedish Competition Authority which the undertaking has or gets access to,

2. actively cooperate with the Swedish Competition Authority during the investigation of the infringement,

3. not destroy evidence or in another way hinder the future or the present investigation of the infringement, and

4. as soon as possible after an application or after it has provided the information stop its participation in the infringement.

Article 15

Upon application by an undertaking which notifies an infringement of a prohibition pursuant to Chapter 2 Article 1 or Article 101 in the Treaty, the Swedish Competition Authority shall state whether the conditions for granting immunity from the fine as provided for in Article 12 first paragraph, are fulfilled. Such a decision is binding on the Authority as well as the Stockholm City Court and the Market Court.

Fine order

Article 16

Instead of instituting proceedings regarding an administrative fine in accordance with Article 5, the Swedish Competition Authority may order an undertaking to pay such a fine (fine order).

Such an order may only be issued if the Swedish Competition Authority considers that the material circumstances regarding the infringement are clear.

Article 17

A fine order shall contain details of:

1. the undertaking to which the order refers,
2. the infringement and the circumstances that are necessary to characterise it,
3. the provisions applicable to the infringement, and
4. the administrative fine that the order imposes on the undertaking.

The undertaking shall be informed in the order that proceedings regarding an administrative fine may be instituted if the undertaking does not consent to the order within the time specified by the Swedish Competition Authority.

Article 18

If the undertaking consents to a fine order in writing within the time specified by the Swedish Competition Authority, proceedings may not be instituted under Article 5. A consent that is not given in this way is without effect.

Article 19

A fine order for which consent has been given shall upon appeal be set aside under the preconditions specified in Chapter 59, Section 6, first paragraph of the Code of Judicial Procedure. The provisions of the Code of Judicial Procedure regarding summary penalty order and the suspect, apply instead in this connection to fine order and undertaking respectively.

A party who wishes to appeal must do so in writing to Stockholm City Court within one year from consent being given for the order. In cases concerning appeal against a fine order, the Swedish Competition Authority is the respondent party.

If a fine order is set aside, the undertaking may not thereafter be imposed an obligation to pay a higher administrative fine for the same infringement.

Time limits

Article 20

The administrative fine may only be imposed if the summons application has been served on the party against whom the claim is directed within five years from when the infringement ceased. If the undertaking affected has received a decision within this period concerning an inspection according to Chapter 5, Article 3 or is given an opportunity to express its views on a draft summons application of the Swedish Competition Authority, this period shall instead be counted from the date on which that occurred. However, in such cases a fine may only be imposed if the party against whom the claim is directed has been served with the summons application within ten years from when the infringement ceased.

Provisional attachment

Article 21

In order to secure a claim for a fine, the Court may issue a provisional attachment order. The provisions of Chapter 15 of the Swedish Code of Judicial Procedure concerning provisional attachment in respect of debts shall in relevant parts be applicable. If a petition concerning a fine has not yet been submitted, legal proceedings on provisional attachment will be heard by the Stockholm City Court.

Payment of fines

Article 22

A fine shall be paid to the Swedish Competition Authority within thirty days of a judgment gaining legal force or the fine order was approved or a longer period as stated in the judgment or the fine order.

If the fine is not paid within the right period of time, the Swedish Competition Authority shall hand over the demand for collection. Provisions on collection are set out in the Act (1993:891) on the collection of debts to the state etc. Execution may take place according the provisions of the Enforcement Code.

Article 23

A fine that has been imposed shall lapse if the relevant judgment is not executed within five years gaining legal force or the fine order was approved.

Trading prohibition

Article 24

The Trading Prohibitions Act (1986:436) contains provisions on the issue of trading prohibitions for certain infringements of the prohibition contained in Chapter 2, Article 1 or in Article 101 of the Treaty.

Damages

Article 25

If an undertaking intentionally or negligently infringes any of the prohibitions contained in Chapter 2 Article 1 or 7, or in Article 101 or 102 in the Treaty, the undertaking shall compensate the damage that is caused thereby.

The right to such damages shall lapse if no action is brought within ten years from the date when the damage was caused.

Article 26

The Stockholm City Court shall always be competent to examine cases relating to damages pursuant to Article 25.

Anti-competitive sales activities by public entities

Article 27

A certain conduct by the State, a municipality or a county council within a sales activity covered by Chapter 1, Article 5, first paragraph, may be prohibited through an injunction,if such conduct

1. distorts, by object or effect, the conditions for effective competition in the market, or

2. impedes, by object or effect, the occurrence or the development of such competition.

An injunction may not be imposed in relation to conduct that can be justified by public interest considerations.

A certain sales activity by a municipality or a county council may also be prohibited in cases referred to in the first paragraph. However, such a sales activity may not be prohibited if it is compatible with law.

An injunction shall take effect immediately, unless decided otherwise.

Article 28

The provisions of Article 27 shall also be applicable to conduct or activities of another legal person if the State, a municipality or a country council directly or indirectly has a decisive influence over the legal person through ownership, financial participation, applicable rules or through any other means. The provisions concerning the State, a municipality or a county council shall then apply to the legal person.

Article 29

An injunction pursuant to Article 27 may also cover a practice or an operation that essentially corresponds with the practice or the operation that is prohibited.

Article 30

If there are particular reasons to do so, an interim injunction pursuant to Article 27 may be imposed. Such an injunction may only be imposed following commencement of legal proceedings.

Article 31

If the Court has rejected an application for an injunction pursuant to Article 27, the matter may be subject to retrial if there has been a change in any of the facts which were material to the outcome of the case.

An injunction pursuant to Article 27 may be subject to retrial, if there are particular reasons to abrogate or mitigate the prohibition.

Article 32

Cases concerning injunctions pursuant to Article 27 or retrial pursuant to Article 31, second paragraph, are tried by the Stockholm City Court on application by the Swedish Competition Authority. An application for retrial of an injunction may also be brought by the party against whom the injunction has been imposed.

If the Swedish Competition Authority in a particular case decides not to apply for an injunction pursuant to Article 27, an application for an injunction may be brought by an undertaking that is affected by the conduct or activity in question.

Chapter 4 Control of concentrations

Prohibition against concentrations

Article 1

A concentration shall be prohibited, if it significantly restrains occurrence or the development of effective competition within the country as a whole, or a substantial part thereof. During the examination of the concentration and the question whether it will be forbidden account shall specially be taken to whether it creates or strengthens a dominant position.

A prohibition may only be carried out if no significant national or security- or supply interest will be set aside.

To the extent that the creation of a joint venture, which constitutes a concentration in accordance with Chapter 1 Article 9 second paragraph, has the aim or effect of coordinating the competitive behavior of the undertakings which remain independent, in the examination of a prohibition against the concentration, the co-ordination shall be appraised in accordance with Chapter 2 Articles 1 and 2.

Article 2

If it is sufficient to eliminate the adverse effects of a concentration, a party to a concentration, instead of being subject to a prohibition pursuant to Article 1, may instead be required

1. to divest an undertaking, or a part of an undertaking, or
2. to take some other measure having a favorable effect on competition.

An obligation under the first paragraph may not be more extensive than is required to eliminate the harmful effects of a restriction on competition.

Article 3

In consequence of a decision to prohibit a concentration, a transaction which constitutes a part of a concentration or has as its aim to carry out a concentration shall be void. This does not, however, apply to such transactions constituting an acquisition which has taken place on a regulated market as referred to in1 Chapter, paragraph 5, point 20 in the Market Securities Act (2007:528), an equivalent market outside the area of the European Economic Agreement or multilateral trading facilities referred to in 1 Chapter, paragraph 5, point 12 in the Market Securities Act or by a bid at an executive auction. In such cases, the undertaking making the acquisition may be ordered to divest the assets acquired.

Article 4

If a question has arised whether there will be a prohibition pursuant to Article 1 or an obligation pursuant to Article 2, a commitment from a party to the concentration may lead the Swedish Competition Authority to leave the case without any further actions.

Article 5

A decision by the Swedish Competition Authority not to take any action with regard to a concentration shall also cover restrictions directly related and necessary to the implementation of the concentration that has been notified.

Notification of a concentration

Article 6

A concentration shall be notified to the Swedish Competition Authority if

1. the combined aggregate turnover in Sweden of all the undertakings concerned in the preceding financial year exceeds SEK 1 billion, and
2. at least two of the undertakings concerned had a turnover in Sweden the preceding financial year which exceeds SEK 200 million for each of the undertakings.

Article 7

If the turnover requirement according to Article 6 point 1 is fulfilled, but the turnover does not exceed what is laid down in Article 6 point 2, the Swedish Competition Authority may

1. require a party to a concentration to notify the concentration, where particular grounds exist for so doing, or

2. a party and other participants in a concentration voluntarily notify a concentration.

Article 8

If a concentration consists of several transactions between the same persons or undertakings, whereby parts of one or more undertakings are acquired, for the purpose of calculating the turnover the transactions which have taken place within a period of two years shall be treated as only one concentration.

Article 9

A concentration pursuant to Article 6, shall be notified by the party or parties acquiring control over an undertaking or a part thereof. If the concentration means that two or more undertakings consolidate, the notification shall be made by these undertakings.

Article 10

A notification of a concentration between undertakings may be made as soon as a party or some other participant can demonstrate that they intend to implement a concentration.

A notification of a concentration between undertakings shall be made before the concentration is implemented.

Special investigations of concentrations

Article 11

The Swedish Competition Authority shall within 25 working days from a complete notification of a concentration decide to carry out a special investigation of the concentration or leave it without any further actions.

If the Authority within the period in the first paragraph has received a commitment from a party to the concentration aiming to a decision where the Authority shall leave the concentration without any further actions, the period will be prolonged to 35 working days.

Article 12

During a period pursuant to Article 11 a party to a concentration or some other participant may not take any action to put the concentration into effect. This prohibition is not valid if the Authority, before the period has expired, has decided to leave the concentration without any further actions.

If there are certain reasons, the Authority may grant an exemption from the prohibition laid down in the first paragraph.

If it is necessary to secure the prohibition in the first paragraph, the Authority may decide about a prohibition or a obligation to the parties or other participant of a concentration.

Action on a concentration

Article 13

If the Authority, within the period of time pursuant to Article 11, has decided about a special investigation, the Authority may make a summons of application to the Stockholm City Court concerning a prohibition pursuant to Article 1 or an obligation pursuant to Article 2.

Such a summons of application shall be made within three months from a decision concerning a special investigation of the concentration. Before the Authority makes its summons of application it shall give the party of the concentration or other participants the opportunity to comment the application.

If the Authority has decided to leave a concentration without any actions, may a summons of application pursuant to first paragraph by brought to the Court only if the decisions of the Authority are based on false information from a party to the concentration or other participants.

Article 14

The Stockholm City Court may, at the request of the Swedish Competition Authority, extend the time limit pursuant to Article 13 second paragraph by not more than one month at a time, if the parties on a concentration give their consent. If another participant has notified the concentration according to Article 7 second point even his consent is necessary. If the concentration have taken place in the manner provided for in Article 3 second point, the consent of the acquiring party is sufficient.

If there are exceptional reasons, the lime limit may be prolonged without such consent as mentioned in the first paragraph.

Article 15

A prohibition or obligation pursuant to Article 1 or an obligation pursuant to Article 2 may not be imposed more than six months after an action has been brought before the Stockholm City Court.

The time limit in first paragraph may be extended, under the same conditions as mentioned in Article 14. A prohibition pursuant to Article 1 or an obligation pursuant to Article 2 may not be imposed more than two years after a concentration has occurred.

Article 16

If an appeal is made against the judgment of the Stockholm City Court, the Market Court shall make a ruling within three months of expiry of the period for appeal. The provisions in Article 15 second paragraph also apply to the Market Court's examination of the case.

Prohibition before final decision

Article 17

The Stockholm City Court may, before a prohibition or obligation finally has been settled and at the request of the Swedish Competition Authority, prohibits the parties and other participants in a concentration from taking any measure to put the concentration into effect. Such a decision demands that a prohibition is motivated by a public interest stronger than the inconvenience caused by such a measure.

Time limit for decisions on concentrations

Article 18

A motion about a prohibition pursuant to Article 17 may not be granted unless the party to whom the decision applies and the party who has made the notification in accordance with Article 7 second point have been given the opportunity of expressing their views. If the concentration has taken place in the manner stated in the second sentence of Article 3, only the party making the acquisition has to be given the opportunity of expressing its views.

If exceptional grounds exist, a prohibition pursuant to Article 17 may be imposed immediately and apply until otherwise decided, without hearing those mentioned in first paragraph.

An application pursuant to Article 17 shall be in written, where no action is pending.

Article 19

A prohibition pursuant to Article 17 which has been decided on where no action is pending, shall be withdrawn immediately, if the Swedish Competition Authority does not bring an action pursuant to Article 13. The same shall apply where the Authority decides not to take any action concerning the concentration.

Legal force and review

Article 20

If the Court has left an application of summons concerning prohibition or obligation pursuant to Article 1 or 2, the matter may be reviewed where one party or another participant of the concentration have given false information about the facts of significant matter for the outcome of the case. Such an application of summons shall take place within one year from the final judgment of the case.

Article 21

A prohibition pursuant to Article 1 or an obligation pursuant to Article 2 may be reviewed, where there are reasons to abrogate or mitigate the prohibition or the obligation because it is no longer necessary or appropriate.

An application of summons shall be brought to the Stockholm City Court by the Swedish Competition Authority or someone affected by the decision.

Chapter 5 The investigation of competition cases

Investigations initiated by the Swedish Competition Authority

Article 1

Where this is necessary for the performance of its duties under this Act, the Swedish Competition Authority may require

1. undertakings or other parties to supply information, documents or other material;

2. persons who are likely to be in a position to provide relevant information to appear at a hearing at a time and place decided by the Authority; or

3. a municipality or county council engaged in activities of an economic or commercial nature to account for the costs of and revenues from these activities.

An obligation pursuant to first paragraph shall take effect immediately, unless other provision is made.

Article 2

In connection with questionings in accordance with Article 1, first paragraph, item 2, statements made by the party being questioned shall be written down. The statement shall be read up or an opportunity given to the party questioned to examine the record in some other way.

The record shall be drawn up and examined before the questioning is concluded or, if the questioning is particularly extensive or covers complicated material circumstances, as soon as possible thereafter.

The party questioned shall be asked whether he or she has any objection regarding the content of the record. An objection that does not result in any amendment being made shall be noted. The record may not be changed after the examination.

Article 3

Upon application by the Swedish Competition Authority, the Stockholm City Court may decide that the Authority may carry out an inspection on the premises of an undertaking to establish whether it has infringed any of the prohibitions contained in Chapter 2 Article 1 or 7, or Article 101 or 102 in the Treaty, where

1. there is reason to believe that an infringement has been committed,

2. the undertaking does not comply with an obligation imposed pursuant to Article 1 first paragraph point 1, or there is a risk of evidence being withheld or tampered with, and

3. the importance of the action taken is sufficient to outweigh the interference or other inconvenience caused to the parties affected by it.

Article 4

A decision pursuant to Article 3 may also refer to an undertaking other than that to be investigated, if

1. the conditions in Article 3 first paragraph, points 1 and 3 are satisfied,

2. there is a strong indication that the undertaking referred to in the application is in possession of evidence, and

3. the said undertaking does not comply with an obligation imposed pursuant to Article 1 first paragraph point 1, or where there is otherwise a risk of evidence being withheld or tampered with.

Article 5

A decision pursuant to Article 3 may also concern homes and other premises of the board and employees in the undertaking which is subject to investigation, if

1. The conditions in Article 3 point 1 and 3 are satisfied,

2. There are indication that the party referred to in application is in possession of evidence,

3. The party referred to in application does not comply with an obligation imposed pursuant to Article 1 first paragraph point 1 or where there is otherwise a risk of evidence being withheld or tampered with, and

4. The investigation concerns an infringement which is serious.

Article 6

When carrying out an inspection the Swedish Competition Authority shall be empowered to,

1. examine the books and other business records,

2. take copies of or extracts from the books and business records,

3. ask for oral explanations on the spot; and
4. have access to any premises, land, means of transport and other areas.

Article 7

A decision about an inspection may be issued without the party referred to in the application being given the opportunity to be heard if it is thought that the inspection would otherwise be undermined.

Decisions pursuant to the first paragraph shall only be communicated to the Swedish Competition Authority. When an inspection is initiated, the Authority shall present a copy of the decision to the party on whose premises the inspection shall be carried out.

Article 8

A decision concerning an inspection shall specify

1. the subject matter and purpose of the inspection,
2. the date on which the inspection is to begin; and
3. the Swedish Competition Authority's powers under Article 6.

Decision pursuant to first paragraph shall take effect immediately, unless the Court decides otherwise.

Article 9

The party on whose premises the inspection is to be carried out shall have the right to summon a legal representative.

Pending the arrival of such a representative, the inspection shall not begin. However, this shall not apply, where

1. the inspection is unduly delayed as a result, or
2. the decision to conduct an inspection is taken pursuant to Article 7 first paragraph.

Article 10

The Swedish Competition Authority may request assistance from the Enforcement Service in carrying out the measures referred to in Article 6 points 1, 2 and 4.

The provisions of the Enforcement Code are applicable to such enforcement as laid down in Enforcement Code about execution on obligation other than an obligation to pay or eviction. The Enforcement Services shall not, however, inform the party being inspected prior to the commencement of such inspection.

Article 11

Action taken pursuant to Article 1 or 6 may not relate to written documents

1. the contents of which may be assumed to be such as to preclude the possibility of examining a member of the Swedish Bar Association or any of his associates as a witness about it; and

2. which are in his possession or in that of the person protected by his duty of professional secrecy.

If the Swedish Competition Authority is of the opinion that a certain document should be subject to the investigation under first paragraph, and the party subject to the action claims that the document is a privileged communication, the document shall immediately be sealed and delivered without delay to the Stockholm City Court by the Swedish Competition Authority.

The Stockholm City Court shall without delay determine whether the document shall be included in the inspection by the Swedish Competition Authority.

Article 12

At measures taken by the Swedish Competition Authority pursuant to Article 1 or Article 6 there is no obligation to disclose business secrets of a technical nature.

Article 13

Persons or undertakings that are subject to an obligation to supply information under this Act must not be unduly burdened.

Examination requested by the European Commission or an authority in another Member State

Article 14

The provisions in Article 1 and Articles 11-13 concerning obtaining information also apply when the Swedish Competition Authority takes action at the request of a competition authority of another Member State in the European Union.

Article 15

The provisions in Articles 3-13 about inspections also apply to an application which the Swedish Competition Authority makes at the request of a competition authority of another Member State in the European Union.

Article 16

The provisions in Article 6 and Articles 9—13 also apply when the Swedish Competition Authority at the request of the Commission of the European Community carries out an inspection as laid down in Article 22 (2) in the Council Regulation (EC) No 1/2003. However, the provision of Article 9 second paragraph, first sentence, does not apply if it may be feared that the relevance of the inspection would be impaired, if it was not commenced immediately.

The first paragraph also applies when the Swedish Competition Authority, at the request of the Commission, undertakes an inspection pursuant to Article 12 (1) of the Council Regulation (EC) No 139/2004.

Article 17

When the Commission of the European Communities has ordered an inspection pursuant to Article 20 (4) of the Council Regulation (EC) No 1/2003 or pursuant to Article 13 (4) of the Council Regulation (EC) No 139/2004, the Swedish Enforcement Authority may on application by the Swedish Competition Authority decide on enforcement assistance in order to enable such inspection to be implemented.

Article 10, second paragraph applies in connection with enforcement assistance in accordance with the first paragraph.

Article 18

Questions concerning prior authorization concerning Article 21 (3) in the Council Regulation (EC) No 1/2003 are examined by the Stockholm City Court at the request of the Swedish Competition Authority.

If a decision about prior authorization has been given pursuant to first paragraph, the provisions in Article 17 about assistance are applicable.

Legal assistance to an authority in another state

Article 19

The Swedish Competition Authority may issue an obligation pursuant to Article 1, if it is so requested by an authority in a state with which Sweden has entered into an agreement on the provision of legal assistance in competition cases. If such an obligation is made the provisions in Articles 11-13 apply.

Article 20

On application by an authority in a state with which Sweden has entered into an agreement on the provision of legal assistance in competition cases, the Stockholm City Court, on application by the Swedish Competition Authority, may decide that the Authority may carry out an inspection of an undertaking or of some other person to assist the other state in its investigation of whether its rules on competition have been infringed, if

1. the conditions in Article 5, paragraphs 1-3 are satisfied, and
2. the practice which is being investigated is of such a nature that under the application of this Act or the competition rules of the European Community, the practice would have constituted an infringement of Chapter 2 Article 1 or 7 or Article 81 or Article 82 in the EC Treaty, if any of these regulatory frameworks had been applied to the practice.

In cases pursuant to first paragraph, the provisions in Articles 6-13 apply.

Chapter 6 Fine

Penalty of a fine

Article 1

The following obligations or prohibitions may be imposed under penalty of a fine:

1. an obligation pursuant to Chapter 3 Article 1, 2 or 3,
2. an injunction pursuant to Chapter 3, Article 27 or 30,
3. an injunction pursuant to Chapter 4, Article 1,
4. an obligation pursuant to Chapter 4, Article 2 or 3
5. an injunction or obligation pursuant to Chapter 4, Article 12, third paragraph.
6. an injunction pursuant to Chapter 4, Article 17, and
7. an obligation pursuant to Chapter 5, Article 1.

A decision to conduct an inspection pursuant to Chapter 5 Article 3 or 20 may be imposed under penalty of a fine. The Swedish Competition Authority may also impose under penalty of fine a decision concerning the fulfillment of obligations pursuant to Chapter 4 Article 6 or 7 point 1.

The Swedish Competition Authority may make a decision to accept a commitment pursuant to Chapter 3 Article 4 first paragraph or Chapter 4 Article 4 subject to the penalty of a fine. Such a decision takes effect immediately, unless otherwise decided.

Imposition of fines

Article 2

Actions for the imposition of fines pursuant to the provisions of this Act shall be brought before a district court by the Swedish Competition Authority. In the case of fines imposed by the Market Court at the instance of an undertaking, an action for the award of fines may also be brought by that undertaking.

The Stockholm City Court shall always be competent to examine cases pursuant to first paragraph.

Chapter 7 Appeals

Article 1

Appeals may be made to the Market Court against decisions taken by the Swedish Competition Authority on the following matters

1. obligations which the Authority has issued pursuant to Chapter 2 Article 3 second paragraph,
2. obligations pursuant to Chapter 3 Article 1 first paragraph or Article 3,
3. decisions pursuant to Chapter 3 Article 4 second paragraph,
4. prohibitions or obligations pursuant to Chapter 4 Article 12 third paragraph,
5. obligations pursuant to Chapter 5 Article 1, and
6. revocation of an exemption pursuant to Article 29 (2) of the Council Regulation (EC) No 1/2003.

No appeals may be made against other decisions taken by the Swedish Competition Authority under the provisions of this Act.

Article 2

Appeals against judgments and decisions of the Stockholm City Court may be lodged with the Market Court. However, this only applies to judgments and decisions in cases concerning damages when such a case has been jointly processed with a case concerning administrative fine in accordance with Chapter 8, Article 7.

The first paragraph does not apply to cases where the action is brought for the judicial confirmation of the imposition of a default fine in accordance with Chapter 6, Article 2.

Appeals against decisions of the district court dealing with matters referred to in Chapter 3, Article 30 and Chapter 4, Article 17 may be made separately.

Chapter 8 Court procedures

Applicable regulation

Article 1

Without prejudice to the provisions of this Act, the provisions in Articles 2-4 shall be applicable.

In other cases than those mentioned in the first paragraph, the Act (1996:242) on Examination of Non-Contentious Matters is applicable.

Article 2

The provisions of the Code of Judicial Procedure concerning disputes where settlement out of court is not permitted shall apply to cases referred to in

– Chapter 3, Articles 2 and 5, 27 and 31 and Article 32, second paragraph,

– Chapter 3, Article 21 and Chapter 4, Article 17, even if proceedings have not been instituted, and

– Chapter 4, Articles 13 and 20 and Article 21, second paragraph.

Article 3

In cases concerning setting aside a fine order for which consent has been given in accordance with Chapter 3, Article 19, the following provisions apply.

Chapter 52, Sections 2, 3 and 5 to 12 of the Code of Judicial Procedure apply in connection with processing in Stockholm City Court. In this connection provisions referring to the Court of Appeal shall apply instead to the City Court.

Chapters 49 and 52 of the Code of Judicial Procedure apply regarding appeals against a decision by the City Court as a result of an appeal against a fine order. The provisions contained in the Code referring to the Court of Appeal shall apply instead to the Market Court.

The City Court and the Market Court may decide that a fine order may not be enforced until further notice.

Article 4

The provisions contained in the Code of Judicial Procedure regarding criminal cases apply to cases concerning judicial confirmation of the imposition of a default fine in accordance with Chapter 6, Article 2.

Article 5

In cases and matters pursuant to Chapter 7 Article 2, the provisions in the Swedish Code of Judicial Procedure relating to courts of appeal in Chapters 49, 50 and 52, as well as in Article 39 first paragraph in the Act (1996:242) on Examination of Non-Contentious Matters shall instead be applicable to the Market Court.

Joint processing

Article 6

Cases and matters under this Act may be joined when the case and examination is dealt with by the same court, if there are benefits for the examination. The proceeding shall take place according the provisions in Article 2.

The first paragraph does not apply to cases referred to in Chapter 6, Article 2. The same applies to cases concerning damages unless such a case is jointly processed with a case concerning administrative fine in accordance with Article 7.

When matters are joined in one proceeding in the Market Court of cases according to Chapter 3 Article 2 and matters under this Act, the rules of district courts laid down in the Code of Judicial Procedure shall apply. In other cases the rules for the Courts of appeal shall be applied.

Article 7

Stockholm City Court may decide, if appropriate, that a case concerning damages shall be jointly processed with a case concerning administrative fine. If the continued joint processing would entail significant inconvenience, the City Court may decide to separate the cases.

Constitution of the district court

Article 8

At main proceedings in cases referred to in Chapter 7 Article 2 second paragraph, except penalty of a fine, the district court shall consist of four members, two of which shall be legally qualified judges and two shall be experts in economics. One of the legally qualified judges shall be chairperson of the Court.

If, after the main proceedings have begun, one of the members is prevented from being present, the Court still constitutes a quorum.

At main proceedings in cases referred to in Chapter 1, Article 3 a second or third paragraphs of the Swedish Code of Judicial Procedure the district court shall consist of a legally qualified judge. In such cases, however, an expert in economics may also participate as a member of the Court.

Article 9

At decisions in cases without main proceedings and at examination of issues related to the proceedings, the district court shall consist of a legally qualified judge. In such cases, , an expert in economics may also participate as a member of the Court. However, if there are particular grounds concerning the nature of the case or the issue, the district court may have the constitution as referred to in Article 8 first paragraph.

Article 10

At examinations of cases referred to in Chapter 5 Article 3 third paragraph, 18 or 20 in its facts, the district court shall have the constitution referred to in Article 8 first paragraph. However at such examinations, the district court may instead consist of a legally qualified judge, or such a judge and an expert in economics if this is sufficient taking into account the nature of the case.

In other proceedings of cases the district court shall consist of a legally qualified judge or such a judge and an expert in economics.

Article 11

The Government appoints for a given period of time those who shall serve as experts in economics on Stockholm City Court.

If, while an expert in economics is participating in the examination of a case, circumstances should occur which entail the expiry of the appointment, the appointment shall irrespective of this be considered as having continuous validity during the current case.

That person who shall serve as expert in economics shall be Swedish citizen and may not be a minor or be in bankruptcy or have a trustee pursuant to Chapter 11 Article 7 of the Code on Parents, Guardians and Children.

The Swedish Competition Authority as a party

Article 12

For the purposes of matters covered by this Act the provisions of the Swedish Code of Judicial Procedure relating to prosecutors shall, with respect to orders concerning parties and the non-appearance of a party, apply to the Swedish Competition Authority.

Statement from other than a party

Article 13

A statement which has been submitted by the Commission of the European Community or the Swedish Competition Authority, thereby applying Article 15 of the Council Regulation (EC) No 1/2003, may be taken into account by the Court without the plea of a party. The parties shall be provided the opportunity to comment on the statement.

Hearing at the Court

Article 14

Chapter 36, Section 16, second paragraph of the Code of Judicial Procedure applies in connection with judicial questioning of a party or other person regarding what he or she has stated at the Swedish Competition Authority upon a questioning in accordance with Chapter 5, Article 1.

Costs of legal proceedings

Article 15

In cases and matters pursuant to this Act, the provisions in Chapter 31 the Swedish Code of Judicial Procedure relating to costs of legal proceeding, unless nothing else is stipulated in this Act.

In cases pursuant to Chapter 3 Article 2 and Article 32, second paragraph and in cases concerning damages Chapter 18 in the Swedish Code of Judicial Procedure is applicable.

If particular grounds exist, the Court may, in such a case as referred to in Chapter 3 Article 2 or Article 32, second paragraph decide that each one of the parties is liable for their own legal costs.

Article 16

In cases referred to in Chapter 3, Article 5, compensation for litigation costs is payable for reasonable expenses that have been incurred after a party has been given an opportunity to express its views on the draft summons application of the Swedish Competition Authority. In such cases compensation may be payable to the state for the expenses of the Swedish Competition Authority that have subsequently arisen owing to a party intentionally or by carelessness having occasioned unnecessary litigation.

Article 17

In cases as referred to in Chapter 4, Article 13, compensation for litigation costs are payable for reasonable expenses incurred after a party has been given an opportunity to express its views on the draft summons application of the Swedish Competition Authority. If such a case is dismissed on the grounds of the Swedish Competition Authority having withdrawn its action, the state is not liable for the litigation costs of the parties. This provision only applies when the withdrawal results from the parties to a concentration between undertakings having withdrawn their notification to the Swedish Competition Authority.

Article 18

If a case for damages has been jointly processed with a case concerning administrative fine, the party who brought the action for damages is only liable for the special costs that such a party has caused. A party who has requested an administrative fine is not liable for such costs.

Index

www.ingramcontent.com/pod-product-compliance
Lightning Source LLC
LaVergne TN
LVHW020413220926
848484LV00017B/2561/J
* 9 7 8 1 8 4 1 1 3 9 4 4 9 *